THE RISE OF GAY RIGHTS AND THE FALL OF THE BRITISH EMPIRE

This book argues that there is an important connection between ethical resistance to British imperialism and the ethical discovery of gay rights. By closely examining the roots of liberal resistance in Britain and resistance to patriarchy in the United States, this book shows that fighting the demands of patriarchal manhood and womanhood plays an important role in countering imperialism. Advocates of feminism and gay rights (in particular, the Bloomsbury Group in Britain) play an important public function in the criticism of imperialism because they resist the gender binary's role in rationalizing sexism and homophobia in both public and private life. The connection between the rise of gay rights and the fall of empire illuminates larger questions of the meaning of democracy and of universal human rights as shared human values that have appeared since World War II. The book also casts doubt on the thesis that arguments for gay rights must be extrinsic to democracy and that they must reflect Western, as opposed to "African" or "Asian," values. To the contrary, gay rights arise from within liberal democracy, and its critics polemically use such opposition to cover and rationalize their own failures of democracy.

David A. J. Richards is Edwin D. Webb Professor of Law at New York University School of Law, where he teaches constitutional law and criminal law. He also teaches a seminar, "Resisting Injustice," with NYU University Professor Carol Gilligan and the seminar "Retributivism in Criminal Law Theory and Practice" with psychiatrist James Gilligan. Richards is the author of seventeen books, including, most recently, *The Deepening Darkness: Patriarchal Resistance and Democracy's Future* (with Carol Gilligan, 2009) and *Fundamentalism in American Religion and Law: Obama's Challenge to Patriarchy's Threat to Democracy* (2010). Two of his books were named best academic books of their years. He was Shikes lecturer in civil liberties at the Harvard Law School in 1998 and has served as vice president of the American Society for Political and Legal Philosophy.

The Rise of Gay Rights and the Fall of the British Empire

LIBERAL RESISTANCE AND
THE BLOOMSBURY GROUP

DAVID A. J. RICHARDS
New York University School of Law

CAMBRIDGE
UNIVERSITY PRESS

CAMBRIDGE UNIVERSITY PRESS
Cambridge, New York, Melbourne, Madrid, Cape Town,
Singapore, São Paulo, Delhi, Mexico City

Cambridge University Press
32 Avenue of the Americas, New York NY 10013-2473, USA

Published in the United States of America by Cambridge University Press, New York

www.cambridge.org
Information on this title: www.cambridge.org/9781107659797

© David A. J. Richards 2013

This publication is in copyright. Subject to statutory exception
and to the provisions of relevant collective licensing agreements,
no reproduction of any part may take place without the written
permission of Cambridge University Press.

First published 2013
First paperback edition 2013

A catalogue record for this publication is available from the British Library

Library of Congress Cataloguing in Publication Data
Richards, David A. J.
The rise of gay rights and the fall of the British empire : liberal resistance and the Bloomsbury group / David A.J. Richards, New York University, School of Law.
  pages cm
Includes bibliographical references and index.
ISBN 978-1-107-03795-3 (hardback)
1. Gay rights. 2. Gay rights – Great Britain. 3. Patriarchy. 4. Democracy. I. Title.
HQ76.5.R5293   2013
323.3′264–dc23   2012049384

ISBN 978-1-107-03795-3 Hardback
ISBN 978-1-107-65979-7 Paperback

Cambridge University Press has no responsibility for the persistence or
accuracy of URLs for external or third-party internet websites referred to in
this publication, and does not guarantee that any content on such websites is,
or will remain, accurate or appropriate.

For Nicholas C. Bamforth

Where, after all, do universal human rights begin? In small places, close to home – so close and so small that they cannot be seen on any map of the world. Yet they *are* the world of the individual person: the neighborhood he lives in; the school or college he attends; the factory; farm or office where he works. Such are the places where every man, woman, and child seeks equal justice, equal opportunity, equal dignity without discrimination. Unless these rights have meaning there, they have little meaning anywhere. Without concerted citizen action to uphold them close to home, we shall look in vain for progress in the larger world.

Eleanor Roosevelt, 1958[1]

---

[1] Eleanor Roosevelt, "In Your Hands," available at http://www.udhr.org/history/inyour.htm.

Contents

Acknowledgments		*page* ix
	Introduction	1
1	Democracy and Patriarchy	11
2	Imperialism and Patriarchy	40
	Roman Patriarchy	43
	British Patriarchy	80
3	The Rise of Gay Rights	97
4	The Fall of Empire	140
	The Fall of Empire from the Rise of Gay Rights to the 1967 Decriminalization	144
	The Fall of Empire in the Era of Gay Rights in the United States and Britain	165
	American Resistance Movements	167
	Impact on Britain and Elsewhere	181
	Conservative Reaction in the United States	185
	Limited Impact on Britain and Elsewhere	203
5	Gay Rights in Former British Colonies: Legacy of Empire?	208
	Canada	210
	South Africa	213
	India	222

6   Gay Rights as Universal Human Rights   231

Bibliography   245
Index   267

Acknowledgments

Work on this book arose from collaborative work with two remarkable friends, Carol Gilligan and Nicholas C. Bamforth, which took the form of two separate books written with each of them, *The Deepening Darkness: Patriarchy, Resistance, and Democracy's Future* (Cambridge: Cambridge University Press, 2009, with Carol Gilligan) and *Patriarchal Religion, Sexuality, and Gender: A Critique of New Natural Law* (Cambridge: Cambridge University Press, 2008; with Nicholas C. Bamforth). The perspectives we developed in these books led me to write *Fundamentalism in American Religion and Law: Obama's Challenge to Patriarchy's Threat to Democracy* (Cambridge: Cambridge University Press, 2010) as well as this book.

The immediate inspiration for this book arose from Nicholas Bamforth's taking his sabbatical leave from Oxford University in 2011–12 at New York University School of Law, as he did in the past when we collaborated on our first book together. I am grateful to the people that made possible Nicholas's year-long residence in New York, including Professor Richard Stewart, who sponsored his status during that year as a Hauser Global Fellow. Regular weekly lunch conversations with Nicholas – sharing with me his knowledge of British history and culture – were indispensable to my work on this book, and Nicholas gave me well-detailed critical comments on the manuscript that saved me from many mistakes and made this a better work than it would otherwise have been. I am much in debt to Nicholas for his remarkable critical intelligence and unstinting generosity to me during my work on this book. Nicholas is, for me, a model of the very best in academic life – independent liberal voice, demanding critical intelligence, collegial generosity, and humane sympathy.

I am also much in debt to Carol Gilligan, with whom I have cotaught a seminar now called "Resisting Injustice" for more than ten years at the New York University School of Law and with whom I coauthored *The Deepening Darkness*. Her astonishing intelligence and supportive generosity, as well as her profound insights into human developmental psychology, were indispensable inspirations to the writing of this book.

During April 2012, I visited at the invitation of my friend and former student Professor Luis Rodriguez the Facultad de Derecho, Universidad Autonoma de Madrid. There I delivered to the faculty parts of this book on two occasions, and I am grateful for their illuminating and helpful comments and support. I must warmly acknowledge, in particular, my very real thanks to Professor Rodriguez as well as Professors Silvina Alvarez, Juan Carlos Bayon, Elena Beltran, Jose Luis Colomer, Liborio Hierro, Francisco Javier Laporta, and Cristina Sanchez.

I am grateful as well to the New York University School of Law Filomen D'Agostino and Max E. Greenberg Faculty Research Fund, which supported research and writing both over summers and during a midsabbatical leave taken in the spring term of 2012. I must thank as well Dean Richard Revesz for providing support for the preparation of the index. Thanks are also due to my assistant, Lavinia Barbu, for her help and support, and to Liz Evans and Denise To, our law librarians, for their invaluable research assistance. I am grateful as well for conversations with Phillip Blumberg, from whom I learned much, and for the advice of my colleague, Sujit Choudhry, on issues of Indian constitutionalism, including sending me some of his own recent work.

John Berger, my editor at Cambridge University Press, enthusiastically urged on my work on the argument of this book, as soon as I told him about the idea of it, and I am grateful for his support throughout. I am grateful as well for the illuminating and supportive reviews of the manuscript by its three readers for Cambridge: Shannon Gilreath, Marc Spindelman, and Nicholas Owen.

Finally, all my work on this book was nourished by conversations with my life partner, Donald Levy, Professor of Philosophy Emeritus (Brooklyn College), whose love makes all things possible.

New York, New York, September 2012

Introduction

Arguments for gay rights play an increasingly important role in the legal understanding of basic constitutionally protected human rights in many nations. This development has in turn given rise to controversies over the use of comparative and international law in arguments about gay rights. Conservative jurists and reactionary politicians have responded to this practice with hostility. Particularly vocal criticisms include Justice Antonin Scalia's dissent in *Lawrence v. Texas* (2003)[1] or Zimbabwe's President Robert Mugabe's appeal to homophobia as based on distinctly African values.[2] On the other hand, critics from the left have suggested that such international comparisons may involve a "we-know-best" subversion of local conceptions of justice, perhaps amounting to a form of imperialism.[3]

My argument in this book is that there is an important connection between ethical resistance to imperialism and gay rights – indeed, that the rise of gay rights connects to and facilitates criticisms of imperialism arising from a democratic conception of human rights that, among other factors, leads to and prepares the way for the fall of empire, in particular, the British Empire. This thesis casts doubt on the claim that arguments for gay rights must be extrinsic to democracy and that they must reflect as well Western, as opposed to "African" or "Asian," values. Gay rights could hardly be dismissed as extrinsic to a nation that takes itself to be a constitutional democracy if it is one of the forms of resistance that makes democracy possible. Although there are many important differences between ancient Greek and modern homosexuality, as we later

---

[1] See *Lawrence v. Texas*, 539 U.S. 558, 586–605 (2003), especially at 598.
[2] See Wikipedia, LGBT rights in Zimbabwe; see also Stephen Chan, *Robert Mugabe: a Life of Power and Violence* (Ann Arbor: University of Michigan Press, 2003), pp. 123–4, 143.
[3] For such discussion, see Nicholas Bamforth, "An 'imperial' strategy: The use of comparative and international law in arguments about LGBT rights," in *Queer Theory: Law, Culture, Empire*, edited by Robert Leckey and Kim Brooks (New York: Routledge, 2010), pp. 157–72.

see (Chapter 6), it is surely worth noting that the first important democracy in human history, that of ancient Athens, memorialized its founding by bronzes in the agora of the gay lovers Harmodios and Aristogeiton, whose resistance unto death to the attempt of a tyrant to seduce one of them was regarded in popular tradition as having freed Athens from tyranny.[4] The Athenians certainly lacked our more egalitarian idea of gay rights (as a relationship between equals), but such resistance to tyranny, centering on the protection of the intimate relations of gay lovers, rests on normative features that prefigure the modern ethical idea of gay rights. We see in Athens how such normative features of gay rights arise within democracies, resting on its deepest values. Further, gay rights could hardly have been supposed to be an imperialistic imposition when, in fact, the condemnations of gay sex that still exist in ex-British colonies were, in fact, impositions of British imperialism,[5] and gay rights was one of the movements within Britain that seriously and fundamentally questioned its imperialism. The values of the gay rights movement are not imperialistic but rather are values that contest imperialism on the basis of universal human rights. Attacks on gay rights, as in America's conservative movement, rooted in patriarchal religion, and in Zimbabwe, Uganda, and Singapore thus, paradoxically, reflect the antidemocratic patriarchal imperialism they claim to repudiate.

The thesis of this book thus has serious consequences for various arguments about gay rights that are now current in many nations. I ask: Why has this thesis not been seen? What has it been so difficult to see?

My interest in this question arises from a long-standing professional interest, as a political theorist and constitutional lawyer, in giving the best arguments for the recognition of gay rights that I can, but it is also, for me, quite personal: how does one, as gay man and scholar, understand the place and weight of arguments for gay rights in two related cultures, British and American, that have nourished my education and my life? It is often a mark of the continuing power of deep, irrational prejudice, connecting such prejudice to trauma and dissociation, that it expresses itself in loss of voice and memory. For example, if anything should show the continuing power of anti-Semitism (including its irrational conception of the Jews as supremely powerful), it should be the Holocaust (the genocidal murder of six million European Jews); yet, Holocaust denial, in defiance of the facts, remains alive and altogether too powerful today.[6] I am concerned, as gay man and scholar, that homophobia (arising

---

[4] See K. J. Dover, *Greek Homosexuality* (London: Duckworth, 1979), at p. 41.
[5] On this point, see Michael Kirby, "Legal Discrimination against Homosexuals – A Blind Spot of the Commonwealth of Nations?" *European Human Rights Law Review* 1 (2009): 21–36.
[6] For an important recent study focusing on Britain, see Anthony Julius, *Trials of the Diaspora: A History of Anti-Semitism in England* (Oxford: Oxford University Press, 2010).

from a long tradition of unspeakabilty – perhaps the most radical silencing of ethical voice of any unjustly despised minority) is yet another, still powerful, irrational prejudice – so powerful that its effects cannot be seen. It shows its continuing power in the ways people in general, and even gays in particular, do not understand or grapple with the history of gay persecution, including the ways gays have themselves been drawn into complicity with comparable forms of denial by not being able to see what is before their eyes and implicit in their experience: gay rights arising from resistance to patriarchy and imperialism as a form of patriarchy. Such loss of memory and of voice are the marks of traumatic loss and disruption of loving relationship. It is only through the close study of the experience of gay love, as it has arisen against all the odds and because of resistance to the injustice of such loss, that we can understand and do justice to gay rights as the ethical discovery about our shared humanity that it is.

The gay novelist Alan Hollinghurst, in his recent novel *The Stranger's Child*,[7] powerfully shows the dimensions of such denial in the experience over several generations of a British family and others in relation to a gifted poet, Cecil Vance. Cecil writes during the period leading up to his death in World War I, analogous to the historical Rupert Brooke. Cecil, a gay man, had had a passionate affair with George Sawle, to whom several of his poems were written. Because of the curiosity and interference of George's sister, Daphne, Cecil at one point defensively pretends interest in Daphne and claims one of his most important poems was written to her. Daphne in turn later marries and divorces Cecil's brother. In part because of the repressive culture of denial she takes to be axiomatic, Daphne is able to invent a past for herself and put it into print. Yet, as she secretly acknowledges, she was drunk during most of the crucial incidents so cannot really recall them. This is even before her own inability meaningfully to notice the feelings and motives of others, let alone to take them into account, cut her off from real human relationships. Thus, although her life ends in material squalor and social isolation, she can live off her self-invented memories.

The life of her brother George is altogether more tragic, a tragedy tied to the power of the closet. George seeks love with Cecil. Half realizing Cecil is using him, he does not wish to acknowledge it but is then forced (or perhaps desperately chooses) to bury all his real feelings for the rest of his life, engaging in a lifeless marriage without passion and taking a dull job at a dreary provincial university. One of the novel's most fascinating points is the juxtaposition of Cecil's abandonment of George (presumably before the start of World War I)

[7] Alan Hollinghurst, *The Stranger's Child* (New York: Alfred A. Knopf, 2011).

in contrast to George's own fear of "discovery," as seen through an argument with his mother after she reads his letters from Cecil. A particularly poignant scene recalls a punt trip on the Cam during which Cecil is reading poetry to a boy with whom he is now having sex, while an anonymous and silent figure (in fact, the abandoned George) sits at the back of the punt making sure the champagne stays chilled. All of this seems to occur before Cecil's brief wartime fling with Daphne, so clearly Cecil has dumped George as a sex object by this stage. All of this leaves one wondering <u>how far the rest of George's life, as we hear of it in the novel, is an emotional shutting down in response to a youthful betrayal</u>.

From a British perspective, Hollinghurst has clearly set the Vance family up as "new money." Their Victorian pile was built only in the 1880s (i.e., thirty years before the start of the novel), and they received their title – a hereditary KBE, not a peerage, which is what a truly grand "old money" family would have – essentially for building up a large industrial enterprise, something new to the Victoria era. All of this slips from view because of the preeminence given to the architecture of their Victorian pile known as Corley, yet the architecture would only have the significance it had given the newness of the house. The novel thus reflects on the transience of what appears to be established or permanent in any time period; to those who lack the relevant financial or social advantages of what is essentially a nouveau riche family, such trappings come to seem the essence of age-old England. The fact that the family, and its wealth, largely disappear from the picture as the twentieth century progresses ironically underlines this point.

What the novel shows is not only the damage of denial experienced by the characters who knew and loved Cecil, but the role these characters (including their damaged memories) play in the novel's portrait of gay men's later search for some truthful understanding of these destructive forces in the historical understanding of nations like Great Britain and the United States. In the current book, I attempt to recover a truthful understanding of both these destructive forces and the emergence of resistance in Britain and the United States, considering as well the close connection between <u>rights-based feminism</u> and gay rights. In addition, I connect these forces not only to the explicit imperialism of the British Empire but to the more implicit imperialism of U.S. expansion, which includes not only its destruction of Amerindian peoples but also its persistent racism and ill advised, sometimes imperialistic, wars.

What is, I believe, of enormous interest in my account is the important role both feminism and gay rights play in the criticism of imperialism, which I link to their criticism of patriarchy. Because my argument turns on psychological claims rooted in the effects of patriarchy on imperialism, I offer first a general account of patriarchy and then show in some detail how the account illuminates features of two imperialisms I have studied closely, the Roman Empire and the British Empire. It is against this psychological and cultural background that I focus on what I call the rise of gay rights, which started in the United States but flourished, in particular, in a group of close friends in Britain who lived and wrote in a new, experimental way. The group in question, often called the Bloomsbury Group, has been the subject of many studies: the secrets of its members (including the important role gay love played in their lives) have now been told. Yet, it is quite remarkable, in my view, how little these studies take seriously what seems to me most ethically creative about their lives and works – namely, the ways they challenged the enforcement of the gender binary that holds patriarchy in place by breaking what I call in this text the patriarchally imposed Love Laws. This ethical creativity has two dimensions: first, an ethical discovery about the common grounds of feminism and gay rights in men and women who resist patriarchy; second, the ways in which this resistance also led them to resist political patriarchy – in particular, the imperialism of the British Empire.

My argument is an interpretive one, trying to make the best interpretive sense I can of the lives and work of these remarkable friends. What I believe I have shown is that, through their resistance to patriarchy in both their lives and work, they came to see, and live, and flourish in the three components of what later theorists would defend as the case for feminism and gay rights: (1) that loving, nonreproductive sexual relations (whether heterosexual or homosexual) are not evil but a great human good; (2) that such love gives rise to and is sustained by nonhierarchical relationships among equals, as friends and lovers; and (3) that such love and relationship resist the role patriarchy has heretofore uncritically played in both our personal and political lives. Acceptance of this argument did not only lead to decriminalization of gay and lesbian sex but to the decriminalization of contraceptive use and access to abortion services and related developments (including the liberalization of divorce laws). Such developments recognized a general and universal human right to intimate life that, like all human rights, must be extended to all persons as equal bearers of such rights. My focus here on gay rights is because the resistance that gave rise to gay rights so directly contested the patriarchally enforced gender binary of masculinity and femininity and thus exposed how problematic and indeed unjust the enforcement of the gender binary was both in intimate life generally and in our political lives. The traditional repression of homosexuality was quite extreme (including its unspeakability), effectively barring any sexual feeling and expression whatsoever for homosexuals. This denigration of one's identity, as gay or lesbian, is at the heart of what make homophobia so grave, so dehumanizing an injustice.⁸ So, when Lytton Strachey, for example, came to resist this repression (coming to regard gay sex as a human and ethical good), he found himself resisting the repressive demands of patriarchy, in particular, the gender binary that patriarchy enforces; this resistance to hegemonic conceptions of imperial masculinity and femininity was required to experience erotic love in a way not otherwise possible. It thus made possible the more cogent criticism of patriarchy generally in Strachey's published works as well as a deeper understanding of the general right of all persons to intimate life.

Strachey's close friend Virginia Woolf, both through her remarkably egalitarian marriage to Leonard Woolf and her lesbian relationship with Vita Sackville-West and as evidenced in her novels and essays, joined Strachey in resisting British patriarchal conceptions of femininity and masculinity in private and public life (including an understanding and criticism of British imperialism that she shared with Leonard). Leonard, a close friend of Strachey, wrote important books that were critical of British imperialism, calling for new forms of international organization as well as for resistance to German fascism. So gay rights plays the pivotal role in my argument that it does because it most clearly exemplifies the process of resistance to patriarchy that was broadly shared by all the friends and lovers I study, whether homosexual or heterosexual. I believe my argument makes the best sense of their lives and shows us how and why they came to the ethical discoveries they made. By ethical discoveries, I mean of the moral good of nonreproductive sexual love, its connections to egalitarian relationships in general, and its profound understanding, criticism, and repudiation of imperialism as an evil because it is antidemocratic and rights-denying.

I believe these features of the lives and works of the Bloomsbury Group have not been seen because resistance to patriarchy always elicits violently reactionary forces that denigrate and repress such reasonable criticism of patriarchal demands. Noel Annan, in his important study *Our Age*,⁹ exemplifies this problem by viewing the friends I study and others as "the cult of homosexuality."¹⁰ Annan certainly sees the impact of this group on the post–World War II liberalization of British values, but it does not do justice to their

---

⁸ On this point, see Janet E. Halley, "The Politics of the Closet: Towards Equal Protection for Gay, Lesbian, and Bisexual Identity," *U.C.L.A. Rev.* 36 (1988–9): 915; Cheshire Calhoun, "Denatruralizing and Desexualizing Lesbian and Gay Identity,"*Va. L. Rev.* 79 (1993): 1859; Cheshire Calhoun, "Sexuality Injustice," *Notre Dame J. of Law, Ethics, and Public Policy* 9 (1995): 241.
⁹ See Noel Annan, *Our Age: English Intellectuals between the World Wars – A Group Portrait* (New York: Random House, 1990).
¹⁰ Ibid., p. 98.

ethical discoveries, including their links to the criticism of patriarchy, to regard them as an insular, fanatical cult when, in fact, they were so open to new forms of antipatriarchal democratic and democratizing human experience, including the legitimate pleasures of nonreproductive sexual love. Everything can be discussed, it seems, but patriarchy – the elephant in the room. But, what precisely makes the group I study so ethically important is the role resistance to patriarchy played in both their lives and works, including their criticism of imperialism. Their astonishing criticism of both British patriarchy and imperialism were, of course, minority ethical and political views when they made them during a period, between World Wars I and II when the British Empire was apparently at its political height. But if we are to understand why the British Empire, in the wake of World War II, was to prove so fragile and how and why Britain would so rapidly disassemble its empire and become so different a nation playing so different a role internationally, we need to take seriously the conditions leading to the moral growth of a people. These include, among other things, the ethical discoveries of the group under study here, a once-minority ethical heritage that would under changed circumstances enjoy broader and deeper ethical and political democratic support.

It is certainly true that the three components of what I call the case for feminism and gay rights emerge into articulate public consciousness only much later, reflecting the impact of the American human rights movements in general and the gay rights movement in particular on British and European activism (a point I make in Chapter 4).[11] But it is an important part of that story, or should be, to connect it to earlier ethical discoveries (a connection even Noel Annan makes) and to bring to attention how and why it has been so easy to forget them or trivialize them, a work of forgetting that suggests the continuing power of patriarchal culture.

The focus of my argument on feminism and gay rights emerging in resistance to patriarchy enables one to explore not only the development and vindication of these arguments in Britain and the United States and Europe but also in several nations that are ex-colonies of Britain – Canada, South Africa, and India. My argument proceeds as follows.

Chapter 1 offers a general view of human ethics, rooted in what contemporary baby research, neuroscience, and evolutionary psychology (in particular, the pathbreaking work of Sarah Hrdy) tells us about our relationality. It offers a general view of how patriarchy arose as a way of structuring human life in high civilizations. I argue that patriarchy is in tension with democracy and that

---

[11] On this point, Jeffrey Weeks, *Coming Out: Homosexual Politics in Britain, from the Nineteenth Century to the Present* (London: Quartet Books, 1977), pp. 185–206.

resistance to patriarchal demands arises from breaking the Love Laws central to patriarchy.

Chapter 2 addresses the patriarchal conception of political authority that flourished in the imperial systems that have historically dominated human culture, a conception that Francis Fukuyama in his recent book does not fundamentally question.[12] Imperialism is marked by two defining features: first, it began to self-identify in terms of the rule of its emperor, or linguistic equivalent; second, "it began to issue orders to formerly autonomous states in the certainty that those orders would be obeyed."[13] Both features are marks of patriarchy, almost always supported by patriarchal religions. Imperialisms have sometimes had democratic features, as in the imperialism of the Athenian democracy[14] and the Roman Republic or the increasingly liberal democratic features of the government of Great Britain during the long growth of the British Empire.[15] I also examine, in some depth, the forms of personal and political psychology that sustained patriarchy in the development of both the Roman Empire and the British Empire, a comparison that British imperialists quite clearly made.

Chapter 3 addresses the emergence of resistance through what I call gay rights. Feminism has the ethical importance it does because, properly understood, it resists the gender binary, which has had the consequence of questioning and rejecting not only the conception of Athenian citizenship that Aristotle defended but patriarchal controls on women's free sexuality as well. Gay rights arose from such feminist resistance. What feminist analysis enables one to see is that patriarchy is not only unjust to women but, in some respects, more unjust to men. It is men, after all, who are largely the victims of violence by other men, and it is men – over our long human history of unjust wars motored by a patriarchal imperialism, which destroyed even democratic Athens – who have largely fought and died in these wars.

I closely examine the roots of liberal resistance in Britain and the United States. The role of such resistance even under the British Empire should not be understated because eventually, in the works of J. A. Hobson[16] and

---

[12] See Francis Fukuyama, *The Origins of Political Order: From Prehuman Times to the French Revolution* (New York: Farrar, Straus & Giroux, 2011).

[13] Kimberly Kagan, ed., The Imperial Moment (Cambridge, Mass.: Harvard University Press, 2010), at p. 173.

[14] See Kimberly Kagan, *The Imperial Moment*, Loren J. Samons II, "Athens: A Democratic Empire," pp. 12–31.

[15] See Kimberly Kagan, *The Imperial Moment*; Nicholas Canny, "Great Britain," pp. 60–77.

[16] See J. A. Hobson, *Imperialism: A Study* (New York: Cosmo Classics, 2005; originally published, 1905).

Leonard Woolf,[17] it would object to imperialism itself. These strands of liberal resistance may have played some significant role not only in Britain's resistance to German fascism during World War II but also in its call for protection of human rights in the European Convention as its empire unwound.[18]

If resisting the demands of patriarchal manhood plays an important role in resisting imperialism, it is not surprising that advocates of feminism and gay rights play an increasingly important role because they resist in their nature the role the gender binary plays in rationalizing sexism and homophobia. The development of the Bloomsbury Group is central to understanding British resistance, starting with the celebration of gay sexual love by, among others, Lytton Strachey and John Maynard Keynes in the discussion group called the Apostles at Cambridge University. This revolutionary way of thinking was legitimated, in their view, by what they saw as a breakthrough in ethics found in the moral philosophy of G. E. Moore, their teacher and fellow Apostle. This philosophy informed and shaped the rights-based feminism of Virginia Woolf as these young men moved their discussions to the living rooms of the two remarkable sisters of Thoby Stephens, a friend from Cambridge, Vanessa and Virginia.

Virginia, very much at the insistence of her friend Lytton Strachey, married Leonard Woolf, also a member of the Apostles, who was just returning from imperial service after seven years in Ceylon, which had led to his skepticism about the British Empire and a novel based on his experiences there. In marrying Leonard, a Jew, Virginia broke the Love Laws, marrying a man whose love she acknowledged (even to her lesbian lover, Vita Sackville-West) as indispensable to her life and creativity.

In addition to Edward Carpenter, several other important British writers and gay men play a role in such resistance – notably, E. M. Forster, J. R. Ackerley, and Christopher Isherwood. All of these men, including Carpenter, spend significant amounts of time in India. There is little doubt that the interest in India is in part rooted in the search for an alternative belief system to the hegemonic Christian homophobia they experienced in Britain – for Isherwood, Hinduism (for the later American gay poet Allen Ginsberg, Buddhism); for Carpenter, his own original synthesis of Indian influences. Both Forster and Ackerley wrote novels based on their experiences in India, and, in the case of Forster, the novel A *Passage to India* is an important exposure of the sexual hypocrisy Forster came to see as underlying British imperialism in India,

---

[17] Leonard Woolf, *Imperialism and Civilization* (London: The Hogarth Press, 1928).
[18] See, on this point, A.W. Brian Simpson, Human Rights and the End of Empire: Britain and the Genesis of the European Convention (Oxford: Oxford University Press, 2004).

including sexual desire across the ethnic boundaries defined by the patriarchal Love Laws that separated the English imperialists, men and women, from any possibility of real connection.

Chapter 4 turns to the implications of my argument for understanding the development of gay rights and its emergence into public consciousness, both in Great Britain and the United States.

Chapter 5 argues that the appeal of the continuing use of comparative and international human rights arguments for gay rights, which I endorse, draws on the normative basis for feminism and gay rights that my earlier historical argument justifies and supports. I show how and why these arguments arose and were vindicated in three former British colonies – Canada, South Africa, and India. In each case, I show that British imperial practice never encouraged democracy in its colonies. Arguments for gay rights, rather, arose in the context of an indigenous national leadership that shaped its conception of nationality in terms of written constitutions in which respect for human rights played a prominent role. There thus is no connection between imperialism and gay rights. On the contrary, both feminism and gay rights developed as internal criticisms of then-dominant imperial assumptions and practices; indeed, in Britain, both forms of activism played a not-insignificant role in exposing the contradictions between British imperialism and its growth as a rights-respecting democracy. I argue that the cumulative effect of World War I, the unjust terms of the peace settlement (sharply criticized by one of the gay men in my earlier narrative of resistance, John Maynard Keynes), and finally World War II was to make clear the bankruptcy of imperialism, leading to regimes in Britain and Europe – both domestic and international – much more securely based on respect for universal human rights. The attempt, therefore, to assimilate gay rights, let alone feminism, into imperialism is, against this historical background, quite unjustified, indeed absurd. To the extent that nations in Africa or Asia continue to endorse homophobic laws and practices, they draw anachronistically on precisely the precedents that patriarchal British imperialism taught them.[19] They do not question imperialism or patriarchy but enforce practices hostile both to democracy and human rights.

Concluding the book is Chapter 6, which explores how my argument clarifies the normative basis for gay rights as universal human rights.

---

[19] On this point, see Michael Kirby, "Legal Discrimination against Homosexuals."

1

Democracy and Patriarchy

John Locke, the father of liberal constitutionalism, begins the great argument of the *Second Treatise* only after he has refuted Filmer's patriarchal defense of absolute monarchy in the *First Treatise*. It is a tribute to the power and influence of Locke's argument for liberal democracy in the *Second Treatise* that almost no one, except a few feminists, even read let alone remember the *First Treatise*. But the few feminists, such as Carole Pateman,[1] who have taken the *First Treatise* seriously are, I have come to think, on to something. It may be that Locke never grappled with the degree to which even he did not take seriously the ongoing tension between democracy and patriarchy, even in his own argument. In Nathaniel Hawthorne's great novel, *The Scarlet Letter*,[2] Hawthorne certainly thought so, and in a recent book in part inspired by Hawthorne, *The Deepening Darkness*,[3] Carol Gilligan and I have tried to clarify how and why the tension between democracy and patriarchy remains so unexamined in American politics, to sometimes catastrophic effect. My aim here, consistent with this larger argument, is to offer a historically informed account of the tension between democracy and patriarchy, including both its underlying personal and political psychology and how it may be and has been resisted.

Moral philosophers differ in their sense of the basis for ethics, some pointing to reason, others to emotion. There is reason to doubt that any basis for ethics can be valid that so rigidly enforces the gender binary (reason as male versus emotion as female) and is so false to the interdependent role of reason and

---

[1] See Carole Pateman, *The Sexual Contract* (Cambridge, UK: Polity Press, 1988).
[2] Nathaniel Hawthorne, *The Scarlet Letters* (New York: Penguin, 1983; originally published, 1850).
[3] Carol Gilligan and David A.J. Richards, *The Deepening Darkness: Patriarchy, Resistance, and Democracy's Future* (Cambridge, UK: Cambridge University Press, 2009).

emotion in our ethical lives. I offer human relationality as an alternative, more reasonable basis for the role ethics plays in human life. By human relationality, I mean our empathic capacity to read the human world, to enter into and interpret and give weight to the emotions and thoughts of humans, our own point of view as well as others. I believe its naturalistic basis can be seen in three remarkably convergent findings of the contemporary human sciences: neurobiology, the research on babies, and the evolutionary origins of mutual understanding.

What Carol Gilligan and I found heartening and deeply validating was the extent to which the view of human nature and the human condition that we have come to in the course of our research has been supported and elucidated by research in neurobiology, as well as the infant research and evolutionary anthropology. We had, it appears, been telling a false story about ourselves. Antonio Damasio, a neurobiologist, discovered from his studies of brain injury that the splitting of reason from emotion is a manifestation not of development but of trauma and leads to significant loss of the ability to make decisions. His exploration of consciousness revealed that our nervous systems are hardwired to connect mind and body, emotion and thought. More precisely, we register our experience from moment to moment in our bodies and our emotions, picking up the feeling or the music of what happens, which then plays in our minds, our thoughts. When injury or trauma splits mind from body and thought from emotion, we become lost in disassociation and lose our way in navigating the human world.[4]

What the infant research has shown is that when infants are studied in relationship to their caretakers (usually their mothers), they are relationally attuned to their caretakers because their caretakers are attuned to them, and so infants relationally attune themselves to others as a way of seeking or confirming others' caretaking interests in them.[5] As Alison Gopnik recently observed:

---

[4] See Antonio R. Damasio, *Descartes' Error: Emotion, Reason, and the Human Brain* (New York: Avon Books, 1994); Antonio R. Damasio, *The Feeling of What Happens: Body and Emotion in the Making of Consciousness* (New York: Harcourt Brace & Company, 1999); Antonio R. Damasio, *Looking for Spinoza: Joy, Sorrow, and the Feeling Brain* (Orlando, FL: Harcourt, 2003).

[5] See L. Murray and C. Trevarthen, "Emotional Regulation of Interaction between Two-Month-Olds and Their Mothers," in *Social Perception in Infants*, edited by T.M. Fields and N.A. Fox (Norwood, NJ: Ablex, 1985); L. Murray and C. Trevarthen, "The Infant's Role in Mother-Infant Communication," *Journal of Child Language* 13 (1986): 15–29; Edward Z. Tronick, "Emotions and Emotional Communication in Infants," *American Psychologist* 44, no. 2 (1989): 112–19; E. Z. Tronick and M. K. Weinberg, "Depressed Mothers and Infants: Failure to Form Dyadic States of Consciousness," in *Postpartum Depression and Child Development*, edited by L. Murray and P. J. Cooper (New York: Guilford Press, 1997); E. Z. Tronick and A. Gianino,

We used to think that babies and young children were irrational, egocentric, and amoral. Their thinking and experience were concrete, immediate, and limited. In fact, psychologists and neuroscientists have discovered that babies not only learn more, but imagine more, care more, and experience more than we would ever have thoughts possible. In some ways, young children are actually smarter, more imaginative, more caring, and even more conscious than adults are.[6]

Such relationality takes the form, early on, of empathy and shared intentionality, and even forms of moral life, altruism, distinguishing good acts from bad, and demands of justice (that a good act should meet with a positive response and a bad act with a negative one).[7]

Sarah Hrdy has powerfully integrated the infant research with convergent data from anthropology, paleontology, and animal research to make a convincing case that a crucially important aspect of our evolution as a species was the flexible forms of caretaking we developed (*alloparenting*).[8] In contrast to our closest genetic family, the great apes and chimpanzees, human alloparents (including grandmothers, siblings, husbands, brothers, sons, etc.) crucially assisted in caring for, nurturing, and feeding highly vulnerable and fragile human babies during the Pleistocene when we began our distinctive evolutionary trajectory to larger brains. Hrdy argues that the development of shared parenting led to the kinds of intimate relationality of babies to caretakers, which was necessary, indeed imperative, to enable babies to read and respond appropriately to the reliability of caretakers – caretakers who were necessary for their survival. At an early age, practically from birth, human babies scan faces, make eye contact, and engage the attention of others. They show the rudiments of a finely tuned empathy, an ability to read others' intentions, a desire for connection with others, and attentiveness to others' responses and curiosity about their emotions. Hrdy takes the view that this relationality

---

"Interactive Mismatch and Repair Challenges in the Coping Infant," *Zero to Three*, 6:1–6; Beatrice Beebe and Frank Lachmann, *Infant Research and Adult Treatment: Co-Constructing Interactions* (Hillsdale, NJ: The Analytic Press, 2002); Daniel N. Stern, *The Interpersonal World of the Infant* (New York: Basic Books, 1998).

[6] Alison Gopnik, *The Philosophical Baby: What Children's Minds Tell Us about Truth, Love, and the Meaning of Life* (New York: Farrar, Straus & Giroux, 2009), p. 4.

[7] See Alison Gopnik, *The Philosophical Baby*, pp. 202–33; Michael Tomasello, *Why We Cooperate* (Cambridge, MA: MIT Press, 2009); Paul Bloom, "The Moral Life of Babies: Can Infants and Toddlers Really Tell Right from Wrong?" *The New York Times Magazine*, May 9, 2010, pp. 44–9, 56, 62–3, 65; David Brooks, "The Moral Naturalists," *The New York Times*, July 23, 2010, A23.

[8] See Sarah Blaffer Hrdy, *Mothers and Others: The Evolutionary Origins of Mutual Understanding* (Cambridge, MA: Belknap Press of Harvard University Press, 2009).

developed long before our cortical enlargement – indeed, made it possible – so that we may say that such relationality is fundamental to everything else in our species' development. This might explain the role of music in our lives as an emotional language we could share communally long before we were capable of intellectual language.[9] What Hrdy makes clear is that throughout most of our history as a species, we were hunter-gatherers. During this period when the human population was quite small and vulnerable to extinction, relationships between men and women were both egalitarian and flexible. And as Bowles and Gintis have recently argued, cooperation within groups, not always related by kinship, may have been crucial to our survival both in peace and even in war over limited resources.[10] Such flexible arrangements may have included what we find today in some contemporary hunter-gatherers – men acting as alloparents while women crucially play economic roles in gathering nuts and fruits. Our evolutionary selection for alloparenting explains why in the human species women live much longer after menopause than females in other species. Such human grandmothers play an evolutionarily crucial role not only in shared parenting (helping and indeed training their daughters in the demands of birth and parenting) but in the food gathering of tubers, which only someone quite experienced would know how to gather. Because during this period there was little access to meat and fruits, such knowledge of gathering tubers may have been key to the survival of our species, particularly in light of the demands our larger brains placed on high calorie intake.

Contrary to the impression fostered by some of the dioramas one sees in natural history museums as well as by conservative politicians, it is not the nuclear family or exclusive maternal care but the capacity for mutual understanding and alloparenting or communal childrearing that are coded in our genes. The so-called traditional family, the nuclear or patriarchal family, is neither traditional nor original in an evolutionary sense. Quite the contrary. As Hrdy observes: "[P]atriarchal ideologies that focused on both the chastity of women and the perpetuation of male lineages undercut the long-standing priority of putting children's well-being first."[11] Putting children's well-being first requires not the traditional patriarchal family, but the care for the infant of at least three alloparents, gender unspecified. Hrdy argues that much of

[9] For an argument along these lines, see Steven Mithen, *The Singing Neanderthals: The Origins of Music, Language, Mind, and Body* (London: Weidenfeld & Nicolson, 2005). On the similarities between music and language, see Aniruddh D. Patel, *Music, Language, and the Brain* (Oxford: Oxford University Press, 2008).

[10] On this point, see Samuel Bowles and Herbert Gintis, *A Cooperative Species: Human Reciprocity and Its Evolution* (Princeton: Princeton University Press, 2011).

[11] See Sarah Hrdy, *Mothers and Others*, p. 287.

contemporary sexist and homophobic family politics about the conventional mother/father family is the reading back of contemporary patriarchy into a history that, in fact, shows just the opposite – namely, the importance of flexible shared parenting (alloparenting) to our species survival.[12]   10,000 - 1900 BC

For Hrdy, patriarchy enters the human picture in the Neolithic when we become agrarian and urban. Because patriarchy did not prevail during the long period of human history when we were hunter-gatherers, Wendy Wood and Alice Eagly have powerfully argued, consistent with Hrdy's argument, that it is not an empirically reasonable reading of the evolutionary record that our species was hardwired for patriarchy.[13] What marks our species is its intelligent flexibility in changing its survival strategies as circumstances changed. From this perspective, what explains the relatively late development of patriarchy is what Wood and Eagly call a biosocial model of "the interactive relations between the physical attributes of men and women and the social contexts in which they live."[14] Under the new pattern of settled life and agriculture, in which men's upper-body strength became important in plowing, human population exploded, and there was now competitive pressure on scarce resources governed by property rights. Men were then pulled into closer patriarchal relationships with other men for purposes of politics and war with the associated consequences for the role of women.[15] As Wood and Eagly put it:

> [S]ex-differentiated social arrangements emerge because women's childbearing and nursing of infants enable them to efficiently care for very young children and cause conflict with roles requiring extended absence from home and uninterrupted activity. Similarly, men's greater speed and upper-body strength facilitate their efficient performance of tasks that require intensive bursts of energy. Thus, the cross-cultural pattern of each sex's activities should reflect women's reproductive roles and men's size and strength.[16]

In these circumstances, patriarchy arises in high civilizations as a cultural practice that enforces a gender binary that may have made no comparable human sense previously (a matter to which we return shortly) and that we increasingly resist today.

---

[12] See on these points Sarah Hrdy, *Mothers and Others*, pp. 239–43, 264–5.
[13] See Wendy Wood and Alice H. Eagly, "A Cross-Cultural Analysis of the Behavior of Women and Men: Implications for the Origins of Sex Differences," *Psychological Bulletin* 128, no. 5 (2002): 699–727.
[14] Wood and Eagly, op. cit., p. 701.
[15] See, on these points, Sarah Hrdy, *Mothers and Others*, pp. 204–8, 239–43, 261–5, 287–90.
[16] See Wood and Eagly, op. cit., p. 704.

Both the infant research and Hrdy's evolutionary argument place relationality at the center of a distinctively human psychology. Human babies are so relationally sensitive, and their caretakers so sensitive to them, because the caring relationship plays the pivotally important role it does in the care a remarkably exposed and fragile and vulnerable human baby requires to survive and flourish. Moreover, our human species could not have evolved and survived in the way it has if relationality had not been at the heart of human psychology, available to men as well as to women, flexibly sharing caretaking as circumstances required.

It is such relationality of both babies and their caretakers that is the naturalistic basis of the psychology I call the "ethics of care": the sensitivity both of babies to those who will care for them and of the caretakers who give such care enables the relationships of love, trust, and sociability that then make possible and sustain the complex personal and social intelligence of a fully human life lived in community, and in time, one that flexibly adjusts to changing circumstances, including ecological changes.[17] The ethics of care arises from the natural facts of the fragility and long relational dependencies of human young and the continuing role of caring relationships throughout human life.[18] It is because our lives so depend on relationships that an ethics of care takes as its central tenet that we are responsible for one another, as equal members of a common moral community, and that we must extend to others the same care as we require for ourselves. The ethics of care is thus in its nature a democratic ethics and one that rejects the gender binary because it fails to do justice to relationality as a human developmental competence. Such an ethics also calls for respect for the values of equal liberty on which constitutional democracy rests. Prominent among these values of equal liberty is finding and speaking in one's free voice, as the expression of one's own reasonable convictions and the relationships to which they give rise. It is these values that make possible and sustain real relationships between equals, and thus support democracy.

We are by nature *homo empathicus* rather than *homo lupus*. Cooperation is wired into our nervous systems, and our brains light up more brightly when we opt for cooperative rather than competitive strategies – the same area of the brain is lit up by chocolate. Findings in neurobiology and evolutionary anthropology converge with findings in developmental psychology to shift the paradigm by changing the question. Even under the most unfavorable

---

[17] On this point, see Rick Potts, *Humanity's Descent: The Consequences of Ecological Instability* (New York: Avon Books, 1996).

[18] On this point, see Melvin Konner, *The Evolution of Childhood: Relationships, Emotion, Mind* (Cambridge, MA: Belknap Press of Harvard University Press, 2010).

circumstances, humans display capacities to resist injustice, as in the Christmas truce of 1914 when British and German soldiers stopped fighting in World War I and the soldiers exchanged small gifts,[19] or as with the women who took astonishing risks under the Nazis – Magda Trocmé, the pastor's wife in Le Chambon-sur-Lignon who responded when Jews knocked at her door by saying "Come in"; and Antonina Zabinska, the zookeeper's wife in occupied Warsaw, who hid Jews in the zoo in the center of the city. What they said, when asked how they came to do this, is that they were human.[20] Naturalistic observations of resistance in young girls as well as young women making the abortion decision display the role of antipatriarchal voice in such resistance. And Niobe Way's revelatory study of adolescent boys shows the human depth of loving relationships between and among boys – a humanity shared by women and men but difficult to see because the patriarchal gender binary remains still so powerful in our ostensibly democratic culture.[21] Why is it so difficult to see what is before our eyes: our common humanity? Rather than asking how we gain the capacity to care, how we develop a capacity for mutual understanding, how we learn to take the point of view of the other or to overcome the pursuit of self-interest, I am prompted to ask: how do we lose the capacity to care? What inhibits our ability to empathize with others and read their intentions? What stunts our desire to cooperate with others, and, more painfully, how do we lose the capacity to love? It is the absence of care or the failure to care that calls for explanation.

If Sarah Hrdy is right, relationality and democracy held sway during much of human prehistory.[22] Patriarchy, however, is inconsistent with democracy because it accords hierarchical authority to priest-fathers over women and other men and boys, rationalizing its authority on the basis of the repression of the moral voices of well over half the human species. In contrast, democracy calls for equal care and respect for all persons, including equal human rights to free conscience and voice. Accordingly, patriarchy, which is inconsistent with democracy, only could have achieved the power it did by attacking the relationality of the ethics of care and of democracy. Carol Gilligan and

---

[19] See discussion of this episode in Carol Gilligan, *Joining the Resistance* (Cambridge, UK: Polity Press, 2011), p. 165.
[20] See Carol Gilligan, *Joining the Resistance*, p. 164.
[21] Niobe Way, *Deep Secrets: Boys' Friendships and the Crisis of Connection* (Cambridge, MA: Harvard University Press, 2011).
[22] On the egalitarianism of hunter-gatherer societies, which was human life for most of our history, see Christopher Boehm, *Hierarchy in the Forest: The Evolution of Egalitarian Behavior* (Cambridge, MA: Harvard University Press, 2011). See also Christopher Boehm, *Moral Origins: The Evolution of Virtue, Altruism, and Shame* (New York: Basic Books, 2012).

I argue that what makes this psychologically possible for our otherwise relational human natures is the ways in which patriarchy requires traumatic breaks in relationship in the initiation of both boys, quite early on, and girls, later on, into patriarchy. It is the experience of such traumatic loss that replaces real relationship with identification with the gender stereotypes and gender binary required by patriarchy. The psychological power of trauma is shown in both loss of voice and memory, rendering problematic our relational human natures, in effect, enacting and reenacting in our lives a false story of ourselves. The traumatic violence that patriarchy inflicts in turn gives rise to propensities to repressive violence directed at any challenge to the patriarchal gender binary. Because these challenges (in the form of resistance to injustice) arise from an ethical voice rooted in our relationality, patriarchy expresses itself in attitudes that rationalize the repression of this voice and thus our relationality. The aim of the argument in this book is to clarify how patriarchy has historically done this, focusing, in particular, on the patriarchal legacy of Western Christianity and the role it has played in rationalizing anti-Semitism. I use anti-Semitism as an illuminating model for a range of irrational prejudices (including not only extreme religious intolerance, but racism, sexism, and homophobia) that are, I argue, supported and rationalized by patriarchy. This study includes the role of patriarchy in the twentieth-century totalitarianisms that almost brought civilization, as we know it, to an end.

We cannot be sure that at least some forms of patriarchal arrangements may not have existed before the Neolithic, and certainly there were forms of violence within and between human communities.[23] Bernard Chapais has thus argued that distinctively human society arose from pair-bonding, including the role that the exogamous marriage of a woman outside her family of origin may have played in supporting larger cooperative kinship networks.[24] The support of larger patterns of human sociability of such arrangements made women, in Lévi-Strauss's words, the "most precious possession,"[25] prefiguring the idea of women as property that developed under patriarchy. Gerda Lerner, in her important treatment of the rise of patriarchy in the high civilizations of the Neolithic, finds no convincing evidence for an earlier period of more

---

[23] See Lawrence H. Keeley, *War before Civilization: The Myth of the Peaceful Savage* (New York: Oxford University Press, 1996). See also Azar Gat, *War in Human Civilization* (Oxford: Oxford University Press, 2006), pp. 1–145; Steven Pinker, *The Better Angels of Our Nature: Why Violence Has Declined* (New York: Viking, 2011), pp. 2–4, 36–56.

[24] See Bernard Chapais, *Primevel Kinship: How Pair-Bonding Gave Birth to Human Society* (Cambridge, MA: Harvard University Press, 2008).

[25] Cited in Bernard Chapais, *Primeval Kinship*, at p. 248.

Democracy and Patriarchy

matriarchal forms of culture.[26] Consistent with Wood and Eagly, Lerner offers a complex and nuanced account of why patriarchy became so dominant in the high agricultural, sedentary civilizations of the Neolithic, one that regards the objectified exchange of women as reproducers as the first form of private property, an institution common in those civilizations.[27]

Patriarchy in these high civilizations takes the form of according autocratic hierarchical authority to a priest-father, rationalizing his hierarchical authority over all others, men and boys and women and girls.[28] Patriarchal religion is thus at its heart defining religious, ethical, and political authority in terms of hierarchy and the divisions that the gender binary requires. Such authority resides in an autocratic priest-father who alone has access to ultimate religious and ethical truth. Both the imperial authority of the Roman and Chinese emperors rested on their roles as the hierarchically supreme apex of patriarchal religions, an authority that also rationalized leadership in war and conquest, including the extraordinary levels of conflict in early China and the endless wars under the Roman Republic and Empire.[29] The linkage of religious and political authority reached an extreme in the long history of ancient Egypt – the pharaoh himself being god continually reincarnated.[30]

Such forms of patriarchal religion enforced the gender binary, calling for traumatic breaks in real relationships in sons to mothers and men to women, the loss in relationship replaced by identification with gender stereotypes, including the idealization of good women and men and the devaluation of bad women and men. Such loss expressed itself as well in codes of honor, so that any threat, real or imagined, including an insult to one's honor as a man elicited violence, explaining the close connection between patriarchy and the rationalization of male violence elicited by insult to a patriarchally defined

---

[26] See Gerda Lerner, *The Creation of Patriarchy* (New York: Oxford University Press, 1986), pp. 15–35.

[27] See Gerda Lerner, *The Creation of Patriarchy*, pp. 36–53. For a more recent study along similar lines, see Kent Flannery and Joyce Marcus, *The Creation of Inequality: How Our Prehistoric Ancestors Set the Stage for Monarchy, Slavery, and Empire* (Cambridge, MA: Harvard University Press, 2012).

[28] For a recent important study, see Kent Flannery and Joyce Marcus, *The Creation of Inequality: How Our Prehistoric Ancestors Set the Stage for Monarchy, Slavery, and Empire* (Cambridge, MA: Harvard University Press, 2012).

[29] On these points, see Walter Scheidel, ed., *Rome and China: Comparative Perspectives on Ancient World Empires* (Oxford: Oxford University Press, 2009); Fritz-Heiner Mutsschler and Achim Mittag, *Conceiving the Empire: China and Rome Compared* (Oxford: Oxford University Press, 2008); Kimberly Kagan, *The Imperial Moment* (Cambridge, MA: Harvard University Press, 2010).

[30] Toby Wilkinson, *The Rise and Fall of Ancient Egypt* (New York: Random House, 2010).

image of manhood, including the willingness to die in imperialistic wars. One important aspect of such male honor was patriarchal control over women, often in loveless arranged marriages to advance patriarchal ends, and close controls over women's sexuality in service of such ends. Lerner argues that under patriarchy the "oppression of women antedates slavery and makes it possible" because the enslavement of men built on an experience of the subordination of women. "Women's sexuality and reproductive potential became a commodity to be exchanged or acquired for the service of the family,"[31] and slavery, including the enslavement of women as well as men, built on this model.[32] Patriarchal control over women's sexuality was ferociously enforced: under Babylonian law, both the wife and the adulterer must be put to death,[33] and the Assyrian penalties for a self-induced abortion were its severest punishments, "[i]mpalement and refusal of burial."[34] Patriarchal ideology even erased the role of women in procreation, which was regarded as essentially a male act, a view the Greek playwright, Aeschylus, would have Apollo espouse in the last play of his great trilogy, the *Oresteia*, discussed later in the chapter.[35] The play shows the ideological power of the assumptions that Aristotle, otherwise a careful observer, would argue was not mere mythology but a scientific truth.[36]

What the cultural creation of patriarchy shows us, as Lerner makes quite clear, is how myth, religion, science, and politics – all features of high patriarchal cultures – unite in an ideological attack on what must have been obvious even at its creation: the facts of human relationality. At the center of patriarchal demands is control of women's sexuality, including an aggressive war on women's free sexuality, as an expression of their own convictions and the relationships to which they give rise (including whether and when to have children).[37] But the same control thus patriarchally exercised over women extends to men as well, because the repudiation or denial of relationality within the family forges a hierarchical absolutism[38] that then makes psychologically possible the acceptance of absolutism in religion and in politics,

---

[31] Gerda Lerner, *The Creation of Patriarchy*, p. 77.
[32] Gerda Lerner, *The Creation of Patriarchy*, pp. 99–100.
[33] Ibid., pp. 113–15, 170.
[34] Ibid., p. 120.
[35] Ibid., pp. 184–8, 204–5.
[36] Ibid., pp. 205–11.
[37] For a brilliant interpretation of the Adan and Eve narrative in Genesis along these lines, see Ibid., pp. 196–7.
[38] Ibid., p. 140.

including absolute rule by priest-kings[39] under male creator gods (Babylonia and Assyria).[40]

A cultural war on something so deep and longstanding in our distinctively human natures as our relationality leaves its marks or traces in the revelatory works of great artists of these periods, who register the great psychological burdens that the ostensible benefits of high civilizations require and who show us the underlying psychology of trauma that supports patriarchy. Great artists are uniquely sensitive to the issues of voice that interest me, including the cultural and psychological forces that can lead men into patriarchal manhood: accepting its desolating losses as in the nature of things and adopting a way of life that rationalizes a violence that knows no reasonable limits. And such artists are also attuned to the voices of resistance. There are two great works of art from this period that show this: *Gilgamesh* from ancient autocratic Babylonia, and the *Oresteia* from the dawning of democracy in Athens.

The oldest literature that has come down to us, *Gilgamesh*, reveals the psychological burdens patriarchy inflicts on its heroic men. *Gilgamesh* shows us a powerful, terrifying ruler, whose exercise of power included sexual violence against women: "[N]or the wife of the noble; neither the mother's daughter/ nor the warrior's bride was safe."[41] To secure "the wise shepherd, protector of the people,"[42] the gods create an equal for Gilgamesh, "the double,/the stormy-hearted other, Enkidu," a wild, feral creature.[43] Gilgamesh sends a temple prostitute to have sex with Enkidu, who is longing for a companion, but Enkidu can only find the intimate relationship he seeks with his equal, Gilgamesh. Gilgamesh and Enkidu wrestle, after which they "embraced,/ and kissed, and took each other by the hand."[44] When told by his mother that Enkidu would not forsake him, Gilgamesh "listened, and wept, and felt his weakness./ Then Enkidu and Gilgamesh embraced."[45] Thus, Gilgamesh becomes the good ruler the gods want him to be.

What strikes one about this astonishing and most ancient of narratives is its identification of an intimate relationship between equals as the core of what releases men from their violence and makes possible a strength in resisting

---

[39] Ibid., pp. 123–40.
[40] Ibid., p. 153.
[41] David Ferry, *Gilgamesh: A New Rendering in English Verse* (New York: Farrar, Straus & Giroux, 1993), p. 4.
[42] Ibid., p. 4.
[43] Ibid., p. 5.
[44] Ibid., p. 15.
[45] Ibid., p. 16.

and overcoming enemies not otherwise possible: "[T]he strong companion, powerful as a star,/ the meteorite of the heavens, a gift of the gods ... [t]wo people/ companions,/ they can prevail together against the terror."[46] Such men have sex with women. However, heterosexual sex, whether with a prostitute (Enkidu) or with a goddess (Gilgamesh rejects the goddess Ishtar's sexual overtures later on), does not ultimately satisfy human needs for a real and loving connection, person with person, because under patriarchy, such sex is either degraded (the prostitute) or idealized (the goddess). Sexual intimacy with a woman could only satisfy this human need if women were free and the equals of men, a thought the ancient epic does not entertain. The intensely homoerotic relationship of Enkidu and Gilgamesh can meet this need because they are, as men, free and equal. They become human, released from wildness and from uncontrollable propensities to violence, through an intimate relationship that enables them to listen, to weep, and to feel not only their strength but also their weakness – an insight that can readily be extended in the present context to all persons, independent of gender or sexual orientation.

Oresteia was written and staged at the dawn of the Athenian democracy by an Athenian patriot, Aeschylus, who had fought at the battle of Marathon in 490 B.C.E. when the Athenian democracy defeated the Persian monarchy. The Greek invention of democracy took the form of revolutionary discoveries of forms of democratic political life and human capacities to sustain the forms of dialogue central to democratic politics, including the emergence of a secular and independent Greek intelligentsia not embedded in traditional religious hierarchies.[47] However, the Athenian democracy was, by contemporary standards, quite limited: it was limited to men, and only men ethnically connected to current citizens (Aristotle, not born to Athenians, could not be a citizen); and both slavery and the subjection of women were accepted practices. Within these limits, Athens developed and practiced a highly participatory democracy, uniting ordinary working men with wealthy elites in a common democratic life, including free speech and debate in the assembly, law courts, and theatre.[48] The resistance that led to Athenian democracy apparently included the protection of intimate relationships from tyrannical

---

[46] Ibid., pp. 10, 26.
[47] On this point, see Christian Meier, *The Greek Discovery of Politics*, translated by David McLintock (Cambridge, MA: Harvard University Press, 1990), pp. 41, 127. See also Christian Meier, *A Culture of Freedom: Ancient Greece and the Origins of Europe*, translated by Jefferson Chase (Oxford: Oxford University Press, 2012); Christian Meier, *Athens: A Portrait of the City in Its Golden Age*, translated by Robert and Rita Kimber (New York: Metropolitan Books, 1993).
[48] See, for important recent studies, Josiah Ober, *Democracy and Knowledge: Innovation and Learning in Classical Athens* (Princeton: Princeton University Press, 2008); *Political Dissent in Democratic Athens: Intellectual Critics of Popular Rule* (Princeton: Princeton University Press,

intervention: as I earlier observed, Harmodios and Aristogeiton killed Hipparkhos, the brother of the tyrant Hippias, in 514 B.C.E. and were regarded in popular tradition as having freed Athens from tyranny; a commemorative bronze statue of them stood in the Athenian agora (a marble copy may be found in the National Museum of Naples). Both Harmodios and Aristogeiton perished in consequence of their act; Harmodios was the homosexual lover of Aristogeiton, and Hipparkho's unsuccessful attempt to seduce him was the start of the quarrel that had the spectacular outcome of leading to the Athenian democracy.[49]

Although Athens was a democracy and may have arisen in resistance to tyrannies over intimate relationship, it remained highly patriarchal in its treatment of women. What is of interest in the *Oresteia* is how a great artist explores the tensions between democracy and patriarchy. This story of Orestes is a play about justice, about civil justice replacing blood vengeance as the foundation for Athenian democracy and the birth of civilization. It witnesses the origin of the trial as a democratic means of resolving disputes. Yet, underneath this civic story, a family story roils. The plot follows the working out of tensions between family and state, between loyalty to blood relatives and civic obligations, between the emotions carried by the Furies and reason personified by Apollo and Athena. Casting the deciding vote at his trial, Athena acquits Orestes for the crime of killing his mother. Following his acquittal, the Furies lose their power and are persuaded by Athena to enter the city of Athens as the Eumenides, the good spirits.

Typically read as dramatizing the founding of the democratic state, the *Oresteia* can also be read as a dramatic rendering of the foundations of patriarchy. The title suggests that we are witnessing the initiation of Orestes into what is clearly a patriarchal social order. Athena symbolizes the power that women can wield in patriarchy: she is solely of the father, a girl completely separated from women, a daughter born out of the head of Zeus.

This ancient tragedy offers a startlingly apt psychological analysis of the origins of patriarchy. Called the *Oresteia*, it focuses our attention on Orestes and his relationship to his father, Agamemnon.[50] Yet, the trilogy follows the development of a civilization that both records and turns its back on a traumatic loss. The chorus members' insistent questions – How can we respond to what we know? What can we say? – become our questions. We see Orestes forgiven

---

1998); *Mass and Elite in Democratic Athens: Rhetoric, Ideology, and the Power of the People* (Princeton: Princeton University Press, 1989).
[49] See K. J. Dover, *Greek Homosexuality* (London: Duckworth, 1978), p. 41.
[50] See David R. Slavitt, ed. and trans., *Aeschylus I: The Oresteia* (Philadelphia: University of Pennsylvania Press, 1998).

for killing his mother, Clytemnestra; we hear him spoken of as the good son, loyal to his father, obeying the gods; we hear the grief and anger of the Furies – the women who insist on remembering Iphigenia, the daughter sacrificed by Agamemnon, and who pursue Orestes for killing his mother – spoken of as an impediment to justice; we see the Furies becoming the good women, the kindly spirits as the price of their admission to the city.

A history of trauma haunts Aeschylus's trilogy and explains the dissociation that we witness: the separation of both men and women from women, the division of reason from emotion, the sharp line between public and private. Dissociation is a response to trauma: it is a brilliant but costly way of surviving the experience of being overwhelmed. <u>The surviving self dissociates itself from the overwhelmed self by not knowing, not feeling, acting as if what happened never happened or does not matter. The trauma becomes walled off so that one comes not to know what one knows.</u>

We noticed in the course of the trilogy that the return of Orestes eclipses the killing of Iphigenia, just as his acquittal for murder justifies the repudiation of Clytemnestra. Electra explicitly denies that she is like her mother and transfers her love for both her mother and her sister, Iphigenia, to her brother. The stories we know are retold with new beginnings. The official story now starts with Clytemnestra's murder of Agamemnon; the history of Athenian democracy begins with an act of public treason rather than with the now-unspoken story of family horror and child sacrifice. Thus, the traumatic origins of patriarchy disappear from its public record, and the dissociations between reason and emotion, public and private, men and women come to seem as natural as the separation between day and night, light and darkness.

The trauma at the root of patriarchy involves the loss of women: in the stories of Atreus and Meneleus, a man's loss of a woman to another man. Like patriarchy itself, the trauma is gendered. In both stories, children are sacrificed by a man who has found himself helpless in the face of loss and powerless to eradicate shame. The response is horrendous violence, which becomes the proving ground for masculinity and honor.

The tension between the two stories – the psychological drama of trauma and its aftermath and the political drama of establishing civic order – is exquisitely held in a counterpoint of speech and silence. Not knowing gives way to knowing; remembering is followed by forgetting. What can we know, what can we see, what can we say, how shall we respond? These questions became central to our concerns. What do we know about gender, what can we know, what do we see and hear, what do we feel and think, what histories do each of us carry – personally, in our families, our sexualities, our cultures? What visions of gender do we hold, and how do we incorporate our experiences and beliefs about gender into our cultures, our civilization, our cities, our legal system?

Both these works, *Gilgamesh* and the *Oresteia*, reveal the devastating psychological impact of patriarchal values and institutions on human relationality and also suggest the roots in relationship of resistance. Ancient Babylonia was patriarchal at all social and political levels, yet its one surviving humane artistic masterpiece, *Gilgamesh*, shows us the price its patriarchal heroes pay – namely, uncontrollable propensities to violence and sexual relationships to women in which loving relationships with real women on terms of equality are literally not unthinkable. Only a loving relationship between two men as equals releases men from their violence into some measure of humanity, which suggests what form resistance to patriarchy must take.

In contrast, Athens combined democracy with patriarchal institutions and values, and it is not surprising that its democratic freedoms would make possible a deeper and more revealing artistic exploration of the tensions in the psyches of democratic citizens caught between the conflicting demands of democracy and patriarchy. Women with real voices (often angry, indignant voices) are thus much more central in Aeschylus's dramatic narrative, and traumatic loss (marked by loss of voice and memory) is revealed as the mechanism that makes possible the psychology Aeschylus believes democratic citizenship requires. What gripped us about the *Oresteia* is that we saw revealed there the developmental psychology Carol Gilligan had studied in the work on contemporary girls and young women and contrasted with the different development of young boys. At a developmentally immature age, boys endure traumatic loss in loss of relationship, whereas girls and young women remain relationally quite close to their mothers and others and face patriarchal demands that disrupt relationships at a much later age when they are developmentally more mature. The traumatic breaks in real relationships to women, which Aeschylus may have regarded as the necessary price to pay for democratic citizenship, expressed itself in an identification with patriarchal ideals, which not only suppress relationship and any voice that might challenge them but also express themselves in propensities to violence against any real or imagined threat to their hierarchical authority. The Athenian democracy, for all its collective deliberative brilliance on so many important issues,[51] became an increasingly aggressive, imperialistic state and destroyed itself by overreaching in an unjust and unnecessary war with Syracuse in Sicily, an ally of Sparta.[52]

---

[51] On this point, see Josiah Ober, *Democracy and Knowledge*.
[52] See Thucydides, *History of the Peloponnesian War*, translated by Rex Warner (Harmondsworth, England: Penguin, 1986).

The Roman Republic was never as democratic as Athens, resting on hierarchical relationships that were highly patriarchal[53] with the important difference that Roman elite women were educated, had money, and sometimes exercised considerable political power, albeit usually behind the scenes. The little democracy the republic allowed was effectively buried by Augustus when he established the autocratic rule of the Roman emperor over an empire that had largely been won during the four hundred years of relentless, aggressive, imperialistic militarism of the Roman Republic. Augustus rationalized the burial of the republic in terms of an appeal to Roman patriarchy, including protecting the patriarchal family against the Roman women, including his own daughter, Julia, who notoriously challenged and defied the patriarchal restrictions imposed on her desires for loving sexual relationships. Carol Gilligan and I argued in *The Deepening Darkness* that two great Roman artists, Vergil at the time of Augustus and Apuleius later, exhibit remarkable sensitivity to the burdens Roman patriarchy imposed on both men and women, including resistance to these demands by Roman women.

Vergil, writing for Augustus at the end of the civil wars that end the Roman Republic and establish the Roman Empire, shows us how Roman patriarchal religion requires Aeneas to break his loving relationship with a woman certainly his equal, Queen Dido of Carthage, leading to a loveless marriage to serve the ends of founding Rome and propensities to violence in war of a once humane man turned into a savage.[54] Vergil writes his great poem for Augustus at the time Augustus becomes the first Roman emperor.

In contrast, Apuleius writes his great novel, *The Golden Ass*, during second-century Roman Empire, a period of comparative peace "during which," as Gibbon wrote, "the condition of the human race was most happy and prosperous."[55] In contrast to the centuries of imperial misrule and recurrent civil wars over the imperial succession both before and after the second century, the period in question was marked by much more responsible government and a general peace. Apuleius's novel, although written in Latin, was based on an earlier Greek novel, only expanded to include two remarkable sections, the myth of Cupid and Psyche and the appearance of the Egyptian goddess Isis. These myths reveal the psychology of Roman women's resistance to patriarchal demands in relationships to Roman men. Such resistance flourished

---

[53] On this point, see Christian Meier, *A Culture of Freedom*, p. 14.
[54] For fuller discussion and support of all these points, see Carol Gilligan and David Richards, *The Deepening Darkness*, at pp. 53–81.
[55] Cited in Gilligan and Richards, *The Deepening Darkness*, p. 82.

during this period when Romans were released from the continual demands that war and civil war had earlier and would later impose on their psyches.

The great interest in the Cupid and Psyche narrative is its exquisite psychological exploration of the place of both dissociation and objectification in sustaining the gender stereotypes patriarchy enforces (the taboo on seeing and knowing the person one loves) and how resistance arises from breaking the taboo. Beautiful Psyche is worshipped as the new Venus, but such idealization cuts her off from any real relationships, and she is depressed, alone, and suicidal. But Psyche breaks the patriarchal taboo on seeing and knowing her lover, seeing him in light of her experience as the tender, loving, desirable boy he is. Breaking through her dissociation, Psyche falls in love with love, and her resistance to patriarchal demands inspires Cupid's resistance as well, as he helps her through the ordeals Venus imposes on her, finally leading to their marriage.

The interest in the concluding chapter of the novel, when the goddess Isis appears to and converts the narrator/Apuleius, is that it shows how resistance to patriarchy may be supported by one of the few antipatriarchal religions seen in the historical record – the religion of Isis, centering on the worship of a woman goddess. The cult of Isis plays the role it does in the conversion of the narrator/Apuleius because among religions in the second-century Roman Empire, it was a religion that uniquely spoke to women's experience as sexual lovers, mothers, and moral agents – having an authority of voice outside and under the radar of patriarchy, including a role in the rituals of the religion as priestesses. Isis was the sister and lover of Osiris, who was killed and dismembered by his brother Seth (symbolized by the ass), his body parts then spread across Egypt. Isis lovingly gathers the fragments of her lover (except his penis, which is lost) and brings him back to life and wholeness through her powers of sexual love. Her own powers replace the lost member, as she literally resurrects her husband through the sexual erection she, mystically, makes possible.

The hymns to Isis that have come down to us reflect the syncretism of the period: Isis appears under other names, as Demeter/Ceres, Aphrodite, Venus, and so on. Although her worship called for sexual abstinence for certain periods, she is, in contrast to Diana and Cybele, clearly a sexual goddess whose powers are shown in sexual relationships and call for the equality of women and men: "thou didst make the power of women equal to that of men."[56] We know that the condition of women in Egypt was markedly freer and more equal than

---

[56] Ross Shepard Kraemer, ed., *Women's Religions in the Greco-Roman World: A Sourcebook* (New York: Oxford University Press, 2004), at p. 456.

it was in ancient Greece and even Rome. And, of course, women ruled in Egypt, notably in the Ptolemaic period, a fact that shocked Romans (as in their shock at Cleopatra of Egypt, the lover of Antony). The Isis religion, in the form that enjoyed appeal within the Roman Empire (Osiris being replaced by Serapis), dated from the early Ptolemies, combining, syncretically, Greek and Egyptian elements. Its roots, however, lie in an Egyptian experience of women's lives that obviously had broader appeal, as the appeal of the Isis religion to Greeks and Romans shows,[57] not to mention the responses of Caesar and Antony to Cleopatra or of Aeneas to the Carthaginean Dido, who was similar in many ways.

There have, of course, been few religions that were not patriarchal, which means that the study of the Isis religion may be particularly helpful in understanding the distinctive contribution of antipatriarchal religions. In fact, *The Golden Ass* is one of our best sources on the Isis religion and is always treated as such in serious discussions of the terms and conditions of this religion.[58] Book 11, for example, offers a detailed narrative of its central rituals. But *The Golden Ass* also affords a deeper insight into how and why the Isis religion had the appeal it did for a highly civilized Roman man and artist like Apuleius, enabling him to come to the remarkable insights we have discussed in the story of Cupid and Psyche.

What distinctively marks the Isis religion is the authority it gives to women's intimate sexual experience as lovers, which must include under patriarchy the sense of the patriarchal men to whom they are attracted as psychologically

[57] On these points, see Sarah B. Pomeroy, *Goddesses, Whores, Wives, and Slaves: Women in Classical Antiquity* (New York: Schocken Books, 1995); Sarah B. Pomeroy, *Women in Hellenistic Egypt: From Alexander to Cleopatra* (Detroit, MI: Wayne State University Press, 1990); Roger S. Bagnall, *Egypt in Late Antiquity* (Princeton, NJ: Princeton University Press, 1993); Ross Shepard Kraemer, *Her Share of the Blessings: Women's Religions Among Pagans, Jews, and Christians in the Greco-Roman World* (New York: Oxford University Press, 1992); John Ferguson, *The Religions of the Roman Empire* (Ithaca, NY: Cornell University Press, 1970); Walter Burkert, *Ancient Mystery Cults* (Cambridge, MA: Harvard University Press, 1987); Robert Turcan, *The Cults of the Roman Empire* (Malden, MA: Blackwell, 2005); Mary Beard, John North, and Simon Price, *Religions of Rome*, Vol. 1-A. *History* (Cambridge: Cambridge University Press, 2004). For specialized studies of the Isis religion itself, see R. E. Witt, *Isis in the Ancient World* (Baltimore: The Johns Hopkins University Press, 1971); Sharon Kelly Heyob, *The Cult of Isis among Women in the Graeco-Roman World* (Ann Arbor, MI: UMI Dissertation Services, 2003); John B. Stambaugh, *Sarapis under the Early Ptolemies* (Leiden, the Netherlands: E.J. Brill, 1972); Petra Pakkanen, *Interpreting Early Hellenistic Religion* (Athens: E. Souvatzidakis, 1996); Malcolm Drew Donalson, *The Cult of Isis in the Roman Empire* (Lewiston, NY: The Edwin Mellen Press, 2003); Friedrich Solmsen, *Isis among the Greeks and Romans* (Cambridge, MA: Harvard University Press, 1979).
[58] See, for example, Mary Beard et al., *Religions of Rome*, Vol. 2-A. *Sourcebook* (Cambridge: Cambridge University Press, 2005), at pp. 298–300.

fragmented by the dissociation from loving relationship imposed on them. The Dido-Aeneas episode in the *Aeneid* starkly reveals this psychology. What differentiates Psyche from Dido is her resistance to dissociation in herself and the way her own resistance brings her lover to such resistance as well. When Cupid abruptly leaves her, Psyche is as despairing and suicidal as Dido was when Aeneas abandoned her. But Apuleius shows as well the psychological strengths in young women that enable them, more easily than young men, to resist the tragic terms that patriarchy remorselessly imposes on their love and, by holding onto and pressing their love through trials and tests, to elicit even from such men a resistance not otherwise psychologically possible.

It is as a response to and rejection of the conversion narrative in *The Golden Ass* that we interpret the importance of Augustine's alternative narrative of conversion in *Confessions* for later Christianity and the Western culture it shaped. Augustine, who certainly knew *The Golden Ass* intimately, read into the Christian tradition, which had many antipatriarchal features, the older Roman patriarchal psychology of the *Aeneid*. Augustine himself literally reenacts traumatically (life imitating art) Aeneas's rejection of the woman he loved to follow the patriarchal demands of his mother for a suitable arranged Roman marriage. Augustine, however, goes beyond even his mother's Christian piety when, in converting to Christianity, he finds his ideal lover in a relationship to a patriarchal God that precludes any sexual life whatsoever, a traumatic denial of sexual relationship that expresses itself in identification with the gender stereotypes that enforce patriarchy. It is through Augustine that this patriarchal psychology is read into Catholic Christianity, the patriarchal structures of which (e.g., an all-male, celibate priesthood) are more Roman than Christian.

In *The Deepening Darkness*, Carol Gilligan and I trace the force of objectifying gender stereotypes in the crucial role that Augustine's interpretation of the Adam and Eve narrative plays in his conception of a human nature flawed by original sin.[59] His support for the use of Roman imperial power to repress heresy is rationalized in terms of the flaw in human nature that requires authoritarian coercive power to keep it from making the mistakes, including mistakes in belief, that it cannot avoid on its own.

It is the crucial role of unjust gender stereotypes, in Augustine's thought, that explains the sense of insulted manhood he displays at any dissent from Catholic religious orthodoxy as well as his willingness to use and rationalize violence in repressing such dissent. Such propensities to violence are of a piece with his expression of rage at pagan rituals of goddess-mothers and his role as well in the repressive violence of Christian anti-Semitism, rationalizing the

---

[59] See Gilligan and Richards, *The Deepening Darkness*, pp. 102–18.

imposition of a servile political status on Jews because, as he put it, "The Jew is the slave of the Christians."[60] Key to this psychology is the repressive violence directed at sexual voice and experience itself, which is seen as demonic. What makes the study of this psychology in Augustine riveting is that it displays clearly <u>how and why the repression of sexual voice has been so important in both the construction and transmission of various forms of structural injustice. It rationalizes violence in terms of gender stereotypes that themselves rest on the repression of sexual voice.</u>

By carrying patriarchy into his own sexuality, Augustine rationalizes what becomes an influential cultural pattern of religious intolerance that represses any sexual voice that does not conform to patriarchal authority. By repressing his own sexual experience, he renders himself psychologically armored against the reasonable claims of a free voice that would contest his views and for this reason rationalizes repressive violence against such ways of life. This psychological dynamic also explains why the free sexuality of women became so demonized under the Catholic Roman emperors. The movement over time to severer penalties for adultery culminated in the provisions of Constantius and Constans in 339, which not only called for severe enforcement of the law against adultery but also decreed that adulterers be punished "as though they were manifest parricides."[61]

Within the framework of our argument, Augustine's marking of the Jews as "carnal Israel" is not incidental to their persecution. I would go further and argue that the Jews provided a remarkable example, within limits, of a resistance grounded in the protection of intimate personal life, including sexual love and relationship. In Judaism before the diaspora, the temple priesthood was not celibate. Celibacy was only advocated by sects, like that of Qumran, opposed to dominant Jewish belief and practice. After the diaspora, temple rituals and the associated priesthood play no role in rabbinical Judaism; Jewish belief and practice increasingly centers in the home and in synagogues where the Hebrew Bible is studied under rabbis, meaning teachers, chosen by believers. Like other Jewish men, rabbis marry and have family lives. Sexual love and family relationships are at the center of Jewish belief and practice, including religious commandments for husbands to give pleasure in sex to their wives on

---

[60] Quoted in David A. J. Richards, *Women, Gays, and the Constitution: The Grounds for Feminism and Gay Rights in Culture and Law* (Chicago: University of Chicago Press, 1998), at p. 403.

[61] See David Cohen, "The Augustan Law on Adultery: The Social and Cultural Context," in David I. Kertzer and Richard P. Saller, *The Family in Italy from Antiquity to the Present* (New Haven, CT: Yale University Press, 1991), pp. 109–26, at p. 125.

the sabbath.[62] The philosopher Martin Buber thus philosophically explicates the Jewish sense of God in terms of a relational and loving care and sensitivity of one human, made in God's image, to another, very much on the model of caring egalitarian relationships within a family.[63]

Because Jewish resistance took the form it did (defending both the sexual body and an antiheroic conception of manhood), Augustinian Christianity, centered in the repression of sexual voice, turned on the Jews with repressive force. The entire role of grace in Augustine's thought, interpreting Paul, arises from the doctrine of original sin that Augustine finds in the Adam and Eve narrative, rejecting sexuality because it blocks access to God. The Pauline attack on the role of law in Judaism, which subjects sexual love to ethical constraints and reasoning underlying the law, arises from what Jews found so unreasonable, the rejection of sexuality because it blocked access to God.[64] The Jews accept no such doctrine of original sin because God is known through, among other human blessings, the good of sexual love. The role of law is to address our rational autonomy, offering reasonable constraints within which we should pursue this good. From the Jewish point of view, it is the Christian repudiation of sexuality, which is so unreasonable and so difficult to comply with, that explains the role of grace in Pauline/Augustinian Christianity: only the love of God makes such asceticism possible. Augustine's search in *The Confessions* for a more perfect lover (which he finds in an incorporeal God) makes sense against this background.

When the Jews rejected this conception of God as unreasonable, their view stood as a stinging rebuke to Augustinian Christianity, and Augustine took the sharpest objection. He made his point in terms of "carnal Israel," explaining that "the Jews... prove themselves to be indisputably carnal."[65] Yet, his ire more repressively targeted heretical Christians (the Donatists, the Pelagians); in contrast to Chrysostom and Ambrose, Augustine called for an end to violent assaults against synagogues, Jewish property, and Jewish persons, which he

---

[62] On these and related points, see Daniel Boyarin, *Carnal Israel: Reading Sex in Talmudic Culture* (Berkeley: University of California Press, 1993).

[63] On this point, see Gilligan and Richards, *The Deepening Darkness*, pp. 122–3.

[64] On Paul's life and thought, see Samuel Sandmel, *The Genius of Paul: A Study in History* (Philadelphia: Fortress Press, 1979); Daniel Boyarin, *A Radical Jew: Paul and the Politics of Identity* (Berkeley: University of California Press, 1994); Alan F. Segal, *Paul the Convert: The Apostolate and Apostasy of Saul the Pharisee* (New Haven, CT: Yale University Press, 1990); Jacob Taubes, *The Political Theology of Paul*, translated by Dana Hollander (Stanford, CA: Stanford University Press, 2004).

[65] Cited in Daniel Boyarin, *Carnal Israel: Reading Sex in Talmudic Culture* (Berkeley: University of California Press, 1993), at p. 1.

did not when it came to pagans or Christian heretics. But he wanted the Jews to survive only on terms of subordination, which would make of their obduracy an example to all others.[66] He thus called for a legally enforced moral slavery of the Jews, a degradation of whole classes of persons to a servile status (including limits imposed on access to influential occupations, intercourse with Christians, living quarters, and the like), justified, as it expressly was, by Augustine in the quite explicit terms of a legitimate slavery: "The Jew is the slave of the Christian."[67]

This cultural background of enforced moral slavery – supported, as it was, by orthodox Christianity (both Catholic and Protestant) – can explain the development of even more lethal forms of anti-Semitism in the modern period. Augustinian intolerance was, as we have seen, highly patriarchal and thus gendered. The repression of sexual voice in himself made Augustine extraordinarily sensitive, as a patriarchal man, to any questioning of the terms of his repression. And no group raised such questions more forcefully than the Jews – thus, "carnal Israel." Augustine, however, operated within an ethical system that imposed Christian limits on the persecution of the Jews.

In the modern period, a leader like Hitler, who accepted no such limits, was inspired by Friedrich Nietzsche's hatred of Christianity (much deeper than any animus against the Jews),[68] and expounded a crackpot racist science, nevertheless popularized an aggressive form of political anti-Semitism that drew its appeal from the highly patriarchal form of European anti-Semitism inherited from Augustine. For an anti-Semite like Hitler, Jewish resistance in matters of sexuality and gender became the target of his genocidal rage, a rage elicited by the humiliation of German manhood at Versailles and directed at the traditional scapegoat for such reverses, the Jews, whose resistance was what made them so wounding to German manhood.[69]

---

[66] On this point, see James Carroll, *Constantine's Sword: The Church and the Jews: A History* (Boston: Houghton Mifflin Company, 2001), at pp. 208–19.

[67] Cited in Gavin I. Langmuir, *History, Religion, and Antisemitism* (Berkeley and Los Angeles: University of California Press, 1990), p. 294.

[68] On the hatred underlying asceticism, especially Christian asceticism, see Friedrich Nietzsche, *On the Genealogy of Morals*, translated by Douglas Smith (Oxford: Oxford University Press, 1996), pp. 77–136. Nietzsche criticizes the Jews largely because they prepare the way for Christianity. See ibid., pp. 35–6. To the extent the Jews are less ascetic than Christians, they are, for Nietzsche, in fact less objectionable than Christians.

[69] On the powerful role of patriarchal conceptions of gender in Hitler's fascism, see Claudia Koonz, *Mothers in the Fatherland: Women, the Family, and Nazi Politics* (New York: St. Martin's Press, 1987); Claudia Koonz, *The Nazi Conscience* (Cambridge, MA: Belknap Press at Harvard University Press, 2003).

What made political anti-Semitism so powerful in Germany and Austria was the highly gendered form that Hitler clearly drew on (including the romantic nationalism, rooted in anti-Semitic stereotypes, in Richard Wagner's operas that so inspired him).[70] It was also an anti-Semitism that Hitler, of course, strategically fomented – one that, through the experience of traumatic loss and German defeat in World War I, made possible a psychology that created an enemy within, a scapegoat, whose fault was resistance and history of resistance to dominant arrangements. It was the sense of humiliated patriarchal manhood that expressed itself in the violence, and glorification of violence, in Hitler's fascism, both at home and abroad, with Hitler himself taking the role of an autocratic Roman emperor, possessing ultimate patriarchal authority over politics and religion. Hitler modeled his politics on the political religion of fascism that Mussolini had earlier invented in Italy. This brand of fascism self-consciously arose on the basis of Mussolini's successful attempt to revive Roman patriarchal psychology and political religion in terms appropriate to the traumatic experience of defeated soldiers in World War I. Ancient Roman patriarchal psychology is thus very much in play in these modern developments.

The modernist political techniques of state-imposed terror that Hannah Arendt identifies and describes in *The Origins of Totalitarianism*[71] arose in Nazi Germany and Stalinist Russia, both states that ostensibly rested on secular ideologies deeply hostile to conventional religions – not only Judaism but Christianity as well. These secular ideologies were certainly supposed by their advocates to be scientific (not religious), but the science was the pseudo-science of Hitler's racism or of what Stalin supposed the iron laws of history required. These ostensibly scientific demands rationalized the total repression of the ethical constraints and sensitivities that had held earlier forms of Christian anti-Semitism under at least some measure of control (exemplified by Augustine himself). Without any such controls, totalitarianism expanded earlier modes of state repressiveness to embrace the forms of state-enforced terror that, as Arendt argues, were aimed at crushing the faculties of the

---

[70] See Leon Poliakov, *The Aryan Myth: A History of Racist and Nationalist Ideas in Europe*, translated by Edmund Howard (London: Sussex University Press, 1971), pp. 380–457. For good general studies of Wagner and Wagnerism (including their political uses by Hitler), see L. J. Rather, *Reading Wagner: A Study in the History of Ideas* (Baton Rouge: Louisiana State University Press, 1990); David C. Large and William Weber, eds., *Wagnerism in European Culture and Politics* (Ithaca, NY: Cornell University Press, 1984).
[71] See Hannah Arendt, *The Origins of Totalitarianism* (New York: Harcourt Brace Jovanovich, 1978).

human mind, making psychologically possible a form of extraordinary romantic, abject devotion to the patriarchal leader, no matter how wrong or vicious his aims. In *Where Do We Fall When We Fall in Love?* Elisabeth Young-Bruehl has observed that the mechanism of such crushing of our humane faculties centered on totalitarianism's attempt to substitute the state's "antinatural technologization" for the intimate relationality of family life.[72] Heinrich Himmler thus spoke of the heroism required to execute the Holocaust, and his adjutant addressed recent recruits: "[Y]ou are disciplined, but stand together hard as Krupp steel. Don't be soft, be merciless, and clear out everything that is not German and could hinder us in the world of construction."[73]

The power and appeal of patriarchy are nowhere better exemplified than in the modern period, for it is a modernist form of patriarchy that shapes Nietzsche's influential attack not only on feminism and liberal values of equality and human rights but also on Judaism and Christianity[74] – all in the name of a kind of ethical perfectionism that takes as ultimate such values of human excellence as courage and artistic creativity that, on his view, few people possess.[75] Nietzsche's appeal to a Superman reveals the fundamentalist roots of this conception, calling on such ostensibly perfectionist grounds for a return to a Greek form of radical patriarchy, hierarchically ruled by the patriarch who displays this human excellence, all else being in service of him.[76] What is striking to me is that Nietzsche should have been taken so seriously, striking a chord of patriarchal rage at modern values of liberal equality and thus revealing how powerful and resonant patriarchy was, particularly in nations with undeveloped and insecure liberal democratic constitutional institutions, institutions that raised reasonable doubts about patriarchal culture and values. It was the power and appeal of patriarchy, I suggest, that led Nietzsche's nihilistic attack on liberal equality to be taken so seriously, including by Mussolini and then Hitler.[77]

---

[72] Elisabeth Young-Bruehl, *Where Do We Fall When We Fall in Love?* (New York: Other Press, 2003), p. 36.
[73] For Himmler on heroism, see Ian Kershaw, *Hitler: 1936–1945: Nemesis* (New York: W.W. Norton, 2000), at pp. 604–5; for Himmler's adjutant, see ibid., pp. 242–3.
[74] See Friedrich Nietzsche, *The Birth of Tragedy and On the Genealogy of Morals*, translated by Francis Golffing (New York: Doubleday & Company, 1956), at pp. 134–5.
[75] On Nietzsche's ethical perfectionism and its normative consequences, see David A. J. Richards, *A Theory of Reasons for Action* (Oxford: Clarendon Press, 1971), pp. 116–17.
[76] On the personal psychological roots of Nietzsche's rage in repressed homosexuality, see Joachim Kohler, *Zarathustra's Secret: The Interior Life of Friedrich Nietzsche*, translated by Ronald Taylor (New Haven, CT: Yale University Press, 2002).
[77] On Hitler's reading of Nietzsche and, at one point, giving Mussolini a complete copy of his works, see Ian Kershaw, *Hitler: 1889–1936: Hubris* (New York: W.W. Norton, 1998), p. 240;

Democracy and Patriarchy

Benito Mussolini forged in Italy a politically successful fascist ideology and practice on which Hitler was later to model his own form of German fascism. As a political movement, Mussolini's movement was, in contrast to liberalism or Marxism (both of which it opposed as enemies), remarkably empty of any coherent political theory;[78] what marked fascism was, rather, its "legitimation of violence against a demonized internal enemy."[79] Because the appeal of fascism was never its ideas, its force lay in political psychology, which reflects the Roman patriarchal psychology that I study at length in this book. My point is not merely the cosmetic one that fascism first arose and flourished in modern Italy on the ruins of the Roman Empire but that the roots of the political psychology of fascism lay in the traumatic experience of soldiers in World War I (in which both Mussolini and Hitler served), a psychology that Mussolini self-consciously came to understand and mobilize in terms of support for the violence, against internal and external enemies, modeled on the violence of ancient Rome. A few weeks after Mussolini first took power, his triumph was marked by a new national symbol – not "the fasces of the Risorgimento" but "the Roman version, presumably to cleanse its emblem of a past that included a symbol of liberty, the Phrygian cap."[80]

Mussolini found in the traumatic war experience of the Italian soldiers the basis for a political psychology he was to rationalize, mobilize, and extend into what Emilio Gentile has properly called the modern political religion of fascism, a religion very much modeled on Roman patriarchal religion.[81] It included mass parades and rituals centering on honoring dead war heroes or heroes of the fascist revolution (the audience identifying themselves with the dead hero by responding collectively, when his name was called, "present"),[82] a heroic idealization covering desolating loss in the familiar pattern of Roman patriarchal political psychology. Roman funeral rituals, in which family members wore masks of deceased heroes, come to mind. Mussolini's political

---

Ian Kershaw, *Hitler: 1936–1945: Nemesis* (New York: W.W. Norton, 2000), p. 597. See also Joachim Kohler, *Zarathustra's Secret*, p. xix.

[78] On this point, see Robert O. Paxton, *The Anatomy of Fascism* (New York: Vintage Books, 2004), pp. 3–23.

[79] See ibid., at p. 84. Mussolini himself defined fascism not positively but solely in terms of its enemies. On this point, see Benito Mussolini, "The Political and Social Doctrine of Fascism," in Benito Mussolini, *My Autobiography with "The Political and Social Doctrine of Fascism,"* translated by Jane Soames (Mineola, NY: Dover Publications, 2006), at pp. 227–40.

[80] Emilio Gentile, *The Sacralization of Politics in Fascist Italy*, translated by Keith Botsford (Cambridge, MA; Harvard University Press, 1996), p. 44.

[81] See, in general, Emilio Gentile, *The Sacralization of Politics in Fascist Italy*. For a good general study, see Michael Burleigh, *Sacred Causes: The Clash of Religion and Politics, from the Great War to the War on Terror* (New York: HarperCollins, 2007).

[82] See Gentile, *The Sacralization of Politics in Fascist Italy*, at p. 27.

religion, like that of Augustus, also included massive building programs that were self-consciously to connect modern Rome with its Roman past,[83] as well as new forms of historic representation and education: Augustan Rome culminating in Mussolini, the modern imperial autocrat, the patriarchal Caesar.[84] In fact, Mussolini thought of his improvisatory politics more as that of Julius Caesar than Augustus,[85] but he publicly identified himself not only with Augustus but with "a Constantine or a Justinian,"[86] a secular and religious autocrat.

The success of Mussolini shows us the power of Roman patriarchal psychology in the modern world. It flourishes specifically when the experience of traumatic modern warfare is rationalized and supported in terms of a humiliated patriarchal manhood. What makes Mussolini's success so important is that it shows the continuing malign power of Roman patriarchal psychology, quite self-consciously invoked and supported by the forms of political religion Mussolini innovated, appealing always to the example of Rome.[87]

If anything, Hitler's experience as a soldier in World War I was more traumatic than Mussolini's,[88] and his fascism was correspondingly more fanatical, more lethal, and probably more sincere. Like Mussolini's, Hitler's politics appealed to the traumatized war experience of defeated German soldiers that expressed itself in the political violence, for example, of the Freikorps against what they took to be the left-wing enemies of Germany.[89] Of course, anti-Semitism was much more at the center of Hitler's sense of the enemy than it was for Mussolini. Hitler drew on Nietzsche, as had Mussolini. Nietzsche, however, hated the form of political anti-Semitism developing in Germany and elsewhere and all forms of irrationalism and nationalism.[90] Nonetheless, his highly patriarchal views were all too easily interpreted by Hitler not only

---

[83] See Borden W. Painter, Jr., *Mussolini's Rome: Rebuilding the Eternal City* (New York; Palgrave Macmillan, 2005).
[84] Claudio Fogu, *The Historic Imaginary: Politics of History in Fascist Italy* (Toronto: University of Toronto Press, 2003).
[85] See Jan Nelis, "Constructing Fascist Identity: Benito Mussolini and the Myth of *Romanita*," *Classical World* 100, no. 4 (2007): 391–415, at pp. 405–7.
[86] See R. J. B. Bosworth, *Mussolini* (London: Hodder Arnold, 2002), at p. 243.
[87] See Jan Nelis, "Constructing Fascist Identity: Benito Mussolini and the Myth of *Romanita*," *Classical World* 100, no. 4 (2007): 391–415; Romke Visser, "Fascist Doctrine and the Cult of the Romanita," *Journal of Contemporary History* 27 (1992): 5–22.
[88] See Ian Kershaw, *Hitler: 1889–1936: Hubris* (New York: W.W. Norton, 1998), at pp. 101–5. On Mussolini, see Bosworth, *Mussolini*, pp. 114–20.
[89] See Klaus Theweleit, *Male Fantasies*, 2 Vols. (Mineapolis: University of Minnesota Press, 1987).
[90] For a defense of Nietzsche along these lines, see Walter Kaufman, *Nietzsche*, 4th ed. (Princeton, NJ: Princeton University Press, 1974).

as debunking liberal values of equal human rights but also as legitimating the untrammeled expression of a political anti-Semitism that manipulatively rationalized a pseudo-science of race in support of its genocidal aims. What I see so starkly in the modern period is how powerful patriarchy really is: not only distorting politics and religion (as we saw in our studies of Rome and Augustinian Christianity) but also undermining science and ethics itself. Like religion and politics, ethics and science can be corrupted by patriarchy.

The great historical lesson of the totalitarianisms of the twentieth century, which almost brought civilization as we know it to cataclysmic destruction, is the terrifying price we pay when our technology is so much in advance of our ethics and politics. We know that the political violence of fascism was motivated by an aggressively political anti-Semitism and that it fed on and cultivated a sense of manhood based on codes of honor at least as old as the *Iliad*. Unjust gender stereotypes were central to a Nazi manhood hardened to the genocidal murder of six million Jews.[91] And the bloodly totalitarianism of Stalin's communism (including the starvation of at least five million peasants)[92] was crucially actuated by an indoctrination into an ideal of the soldier constantly on duty[93] that, as with Hitler's fascism, bizarrely justified state-imposed mass killing as self-defense.[94] It is no accident that there are close links in totalitarian political method between fascism and Soviet communism, based, as they are, on conceptions of a hardened manhood committed to violence against any dissent to or doubt about the terms of state-enforced structural injustice.[95] In light of modern technologies of violence, both forms of totalitarianism achieved appalling levels of genocidal murder and mayhem.

Anti-Semitism is seminal to my analysis because its historical development so clearly exemplifies the pivotal role of patriarchy both in giving rise to and sustaining such an irrationalist prejudice. Not only is it the historically most ancient and enduring of such prejudices, its structure also gives us a model for how patriarchy uses such prejudices in rationalizing its unjust demands. Recall that it is the traumatic loss imposed on intimate life by patriarchy that leads, through the repression of personal sexual voice, to identification

---

[91] For a general study of this gender issue in German fascism, see Claudia Koonz, *The Naxi Conscience*; see also Claudia Koonz, *Mothers in the Fatherland*.
[92] See Robert Conquest, *Stalin: Breaker of Nations* (New York: Penguin, 1991), at pp. 163–5.
[93] See Walter Laqueur, *The Dream That Failed: Reflections on the Soviet Union* (New York: Oxford University Press, 1994), p. 13.
[94] On all these and other points in this paragraph, see Francois Furet, *The Passing of an Illusion: The Idea of Communism in the Twentieth Century*, translated by Deborah Furet (Chicago: University of Chicago Press, 1999).
[95] On these points, Arthur Koestler, *Darkness at Noon*, translated by Daphne Hardy (New York: Bantam Books, 1968; first published, 1941), at pp. 124–9, 134–7, 153, 182–5, 189–90, 205.

with the patriarchally imagined voice of the father, dividing love from desire through an idealization of women one loves as asexual and a denigration of the sexual women one desires. For these reasons, patriarchy imposes two demands on men and women: a sharp and quite rigid gender binary that places men and women in their approved roles and a gender hierarchy that places men over women. Augustine thus patriarchally forges a conception of Christian manhood (idealized sexually ascetic men, denigrated sexual women) that places the Jews, who challenge this conception of gender and sexuality, in a hierarchically subordinate status (as women) to Christians (as men). What patriarchy found in thus forging anti-Semitism was that it could create differences where none exist and accord them fundamental religious and political importance in rationalizing its authority.

If patriarchy could do this with the Jews, it could, of course, do this to any group that it wants to place into a position of moral slavery to serve its ideological ends. The Jews were subjected to such moral slavery by dominant Christian institutions because they were deprived of the range of basic rights accorded Christians and thus made subject to Christians on the basis of dehumanizing stereotypes that, because of the abridgement of basic rights, they were never permitted to resist or rebut. It is on this model that patriarchy created and sustained the subordinate status of people of color, women, and homosexuals on the basis of irrationalist prejudices that, like anti-Semitism, crucially denigrate the group in terms of a rigid gender binary that rationalizes hierarchy (the dominant group of men over the subordinate sexualized group, whether people of color, women, or homosexuals). What I call the Love Laws of patriarchy, establishing who can be loved, how, and how much, then enforce this hierarchy.

This analysis thus explains a striking common feature of all these forms of irrational, dehumanizing prejudice in terms of what the novelist Arundhati Roy has called

the Love Laws.... The laws that lay down who should be loved, and how.

And how much.[96]

The Love Laws at the heart of patriarchy have a tragic impact on our lives and loves. They enforce the demands of patriarchy that separate and divide us from one another and from our common humanity. The form of the Love Laws is historically familiar: prohibitions on sexual relations, including marriage, between Jews and non-Jews, between people of color and not of color (antimiscegenation laws), between married women and men not their

---

[96] Arundhati Roy, *The God of Small Things* (New York: HarperPerennial, 1998), at p. 33.

husbands (Augustus's ferocious anti-adultery legislation) or on nonprocreative sex between married couples (laws criminalizing heterosexual sodomy, use of contraceptives, or access to abortion), between gay men or between lesbians, between the touchable and the untouchable.

The Love Laws arise from the disruption of loving sexual relationships, indeed, from their repudiation as unmanly by the light of patriarchal manhood. Such disruption is pivotally important to patriarchal psychology because it is the traumatic breaking of such relationships that leads to loss of voice and memory, aligning one's own voice with the patriarchal voice that required such disruption, as a condition of manhood. It is identification with such an idealized patriarchal voice that leads to the narcissistic idealisms that underlie prejudices like anti-Semitism, racism, sexism, and homophobia and that rationalize atrocity. My analysis is consistent with Elisabeth Young-Bruehl's psychoanalytically informed interpretation of the ways in which such prejudices are best understood as social mechanisms of defense that exemplify features of hysterical, obsessional, and narcissistic disorders, rooted in repression that expresses itself in forms of violence.[97] What my account adds to Young-Bruehl's *The Anatomy of Prejudices* is a historically informed understanding of the pivotal role of patriarchy with respect to sustaining both the repression of voice underlying prejudice and its expression in violence.

If we can kill as powerful and connecting a human emotion as sexual love, we can, as patriarchy requires, kill all sympathy and its expression, humane ethical imagination and relationality, forging the enemies and scapegoats required by patriarchy and visiting on them illimitable atrocity as what manhood and honor both permit and indeed require. All forms of such prejudice make war on loving connection across the barriers such prejudices artificially impose precisely because such loving connection exposes the lies that such prejudices enforce. What supports the stability of the practices underwritten by patriarchy is the repression of a free and loving sexual voice and the relationships to which such a voice would otherwise lead. The Love Laws direct patriarchal violence against this very real threat to its authority.

---

[97] See Elisabeth Young-Bruehl, *The Anatomy of Prejudices* (Cambridge, MA: Harvard University Press, 1996). See also Young-Bruehl, *Where Do We Fall When We Fall in Love?*

2

Imperialism and Patriarchy

A patriarchal conception of political authority flourished in the imperial systems that have historically dominated human culture, a fact noted by Francis Fukuyama in his recent book.[1] Imperialism is marked by two defining features: first, it began to self-identify in terms of the rule of its emperor, or the linguistic equivalent of such a ruler; second, "it began to issue orders to formerly autonomous states in the certainty that those orders would be obeyed."[2]

Various forms of Western imperialism, which arose self-consciously in the wake of the decline and fall of the Roman Empire, drew both vocabulary (*kaiser* in German and *czar* in Russian mean "caesar") and a sense of their legitimate place in history from Rome, often measuring their achievements and their sense of looming threats from the study of Roman expansion and decline. It is thus no accident that generations of British imperialists, including Winston Churchill, closely read and studied Gibbon's multivolume *The Decline and Fall of the Roman Empire*.[3] Western imperialisms also shared a common Augustinian patriarchal Christianity, albeit sometimes violently at odds over their quite different Catholic (Roman and Orthodox) and Protestant interpretations of the relationship of their Christianity to the legitimation of political authority. Perhaps the most extreme form of such imperialism was the theocratic Orthodox Catholic absolutism of the Russian czar over both church and state, at war not only with the competing imperialisms of the Ottoman Turks but of Protestant Britain.[4]

---

[1] See Francis Fukuyama, *The Origins of Political Order: From Prehuman Times to the French Revolution* (New York: Farrar, Straus & Giroux, 2011).
[2] Kimberly Kagan, ed., *The Imperial Moment* (Cambridge, MA: Harvard University Press, 2010), at p. 173.
[3] Edward Gibbon, *The Decline and Fall of the Roman Empire*, Volumes I–III (New York: Modern Library, n.d.).
[4] See Orlando Figes, *The Crimean War: A History* (New York: Metropolitan Books, 2010).

European imperialisms competed aggressively not only over European interests but over imperialist claims over non-European peoples as well. The patriarchal structure of British imperialism in India, a culture also rooted in patriarchy, actually strengthened divisions among Indians – both interreligious divisions (Islam vs. Hinduism within India; the division of Pakistan and India, for which the British bear considerable responsibility[5]) and intrareligious divisions (the caste system within Hinduism). The resulting strength of patriarchy in Indian culture today remains very much in tension with its robust democracy and clarifies ongoing problems of continuing violence between Muslims and Hindus (both within India and between Pakistan and India) and among castes. Such problems cannot be responsibly addressed until the inconsistency of patriarchy and democracy is responsibly addressed.

A comparable connection between Western and Asian patriarchy, mutually compromised by one another, explains how Japan turned to aggressive militarism, very much modeled on fascist Germany and Italy. At the time of the modernizing opening of Japan to the world under the Meiji Restoration, Japanese authorities came to believe that patriarchy explained Western progress and imperialism. Accordingly, they spread the indigenous patriarchal samurai warrior culture throughout Japanese society and made the emperor into a patriarchal priest-god, a worship that would motivate the aggressive fascism that united the Japanese with Germany and Italy in World War II.[6] Japan's postwar democratic constitution forbids aggressive war, but no constitution can bar the return of repression if the underlying problem of patriarchy in public and private life is not taken seriously. A particularly close but one-sided and closed dependence of sons on mothers, which may be the case in contemporary Japan,[7] does not, in my view, give rise to resistance if the women in question continue to accept their role in patriarchy and do not challenge the gender binary that enforces this role. Their sons, never experiencing a mother's resisting voice, remain, like Roman men,[8] traumatically divided from any real relationship based on free and equal voice.

Patriarchy in China has, if anything, a longer and more culturally powerful history than in Japan, supporting over many dynasties and several millennia an

---

[5] For a balanced exploration of this question, see Yasmin Khan, *The Great Partition: The Making of India and Pakistan* (New Haven, CT: Yale University Press, 2007).

[6] See, in general, Ian Buruma, *The Wages of Guilt: Memories of War in Germany and Japan* (New York: Meridian, 1995); see also Ian Buruma, *Behind the Mask: On Sexual Demons, Sacred Mothers, Transvestites, Gangsters, and Other Japanese Cultural Heroes* (New York: New American Library, 1984), at pp. 200–1.

[7] See Takeo Doi, *The Anatomy of Dependence*, translated by John Bester (Tokyo: Kodansha International, 1973).

[8] On this point, see Gilligan and Richards, *The Deepening Darkness*.

imperial system that is centered on the emperor as a patriarchal high priest – an imperial system more durable and certainly less democratic than that of Rome.[9] Patriarchy reads ethics through the prism of the gender binary and thus mandates the hierarchies and divisions that sustain patriarchy, as we can see in the ways imperialist rulers, such as in Qing China, used parallel ethnic divisions and hierarchies to support its rule.[10] It is a remarkable feature of the life and politics of Mao Zedong that he not only wrote sensitively early in his life about the plight of Chinese women under patriarchy (based on love for his feminist wife who was murdered by his enemies) but had laws passed that forbade arranged marriages.[11] Nonetheless, the totalitarian control he came to exercise in Communist China with its disastrously inhumane consequences for the Chinese people shows the continuing power of patriarchal models in a China that had formally repudiated its imperial past. Ongoing Chinese political authoritarianism, with its deep hatred of free speech and what it would expose, for example, about the political murders of nonviolent democratic resisters in Tiananmen Square, remains very much in thrall to Chinese patriarchy. Patriarchy rules China from its imperial grave.

We need to remember that none of the monstrous rulers of the twentieth century (Hitler, Mussolini, Stalin, Mao, Pol Pot) were religious but rather were men deeply committed to allegedly secular, but crackpot, "scientific" ideologies. What unites them is the role patriarchy played in forming their sense of themselves as hierarchical priest-rulers who violently repress any reasonable voice critical of their authority and indeed wage war on human relationality, rationalizing genocidal murder.

Notably, imperialisms have sometimes had democratic features, as in the imperialisms of the Athenian democracy[12] and the Roman Republic[13] or the increasingly liberal democratic features of the government of Great Britain during the long growth of the British Empire.[14] I focus here particularly on

---

[9] On this comparison, see Walter Scheidel, ed., *Rome and China: Comparatives Perspectives on Ancient World Empires* (Oxford: Oxford University Press, 2009); Fritz-Heiner Mutschler and Achim Mittag, eds., *Conceiving the Empire: China and Rome Compared* (Oxford: Oxford University Press, 2008).

[10] On this point, see Jane Burbank and Frederick Cooper, *Empires in World History: Power and the Politics of Difference* (Princeton, NJ: Princeton University Press, 2010), at pp. 208–9.

[11] See Jonathan Spence, *The Search for Modern China*, 2nd ed. (New York: W. W. Norton, 1999), at pp. 294, 391; Jonathan Spence, *Mao Zedong* (New York: Penguin, 2006), at pp. 27, 33, 38, 44, 48–9, 61.

[12] See Kimberly Kagan, *The Imperial Moment*; Loren J. Samons II, "Athens: A Democratic Empire," pp. 12–31.

[13] See Kimberly Kagan, *The Imperial Moment*; Arthur M. Eckstein, "Rome in the Middle Republic," pp. 32–9.

[14] See Kimberly Kagan, *The Imperial Moment*; Nicholas Canny, "Great Britain," pp. 60–77.

the forms of personal and political psychology that sustained patriarchy in the development of both the Roman Empire and the British Empire, a comparison that British imperialists quite clearly made.[15] For example, when Lord Palmerston was called to explain his decision to blockade Greece in his speech in the Houses of Parliament on June 25, 1850, he cited the Roman principle of "Civis Romanus sum," applying it to the British case: every British subject in the world should be protected by the British Empire, just as a Roman citizen had been under the Roman Empire.[16] This principle was evidently well known to British citizens because the male protagonist of George Orwell's novel *Burmese Days* cites it in defense of what he takes (falsely, as it turns out) to be the privileged status of British citizens, like himself, when abroad.[17] If there is a tension between democracy and patriarchy, that tension is visible in the politics and art of Athens, Rome, and Britain, particularly in resistance movements – the feminist movements in Britain and the United States, both of which grew out of the shared aims and mutual influences of their respective abolitionist movements, and, more inchoately, the gay rights movements initiated in Britain by Edward Carpenter, inspired, importantly, by the poetry and prose of the great American poet Walt Whitman.[18] I begin with Roman patriarchy and then compare it with British patriarchy.

ROMAN PATRIARCHY

There are two important strands in the historical literature on ancient Rome. First is the literature on the public political and military life of Rome,[19] which

---

[15] On this point, see Philip Magnus, *Kitchener: Portrait of an Imperialist* (New York: E. P. Dutton, 1968), pp. 24–5; Robert I. Rotberg, *The Founder: Cecil Rhodes and the Pursuit of Power* (New York: Oxford University Press, 1988), pp. 5, 8, 94, 519.

[16] See Wikipedia, "Civis Romanus sum."

[17] See George Orwell, *Burmese Days* (Orlando, FL: Harvest Books, 1962; originally published 1936), at p. 49.

[18] For an excellent treatment, see Sheila Rowbotham, *Edward Carpenter: A Life of Liberty and Love* (London: Verso, 2008). See also David A. J. Richards, *Women, Gays, and the Constitution*.

[19] For an illuminating overview and summary of this literature, see F. W. Walbank, A. E. Astin, M. W. Frederiksen, R. M. Ogilvie, *The Cambridge Ancient History*, 2nd ed., Vol. VII. *The Rise of Rome to 220 B.C.E.* (Cambridge: Cambridge University Press, 1989); A. E. Astin, F. W. Walbank, M. W. Frederiksen, R. M. Ogilvie, *The Cambridge Ancient History*, 2nd ed., Vol. VIII. *Rome and the Mediterranean to 133 B.C.E.* (Cambridge: Cambridge University Press, 1989); J. A. Crook, Andrew Lintott, Elizabeth Rawson, *The Cambridge Ancient History*, 2nd ed., Vol. IX. *The Last Age of the Roman Republic, 146–43 B.C.E.* (Cambridge: Cambridge University Press, 1994); Alan K. Bowman, Edward Champlin, Andrew Lintott, *The Cambridge Ancient History*, 2nd ed., Vol. X. *The Augustan Empire, 43 B.C.E.–A.D. 69* (Cambridge: Cambridge University Press, 1996); Alan K. Bowman, Peter Garnsey, Dominic Rathbone, *The Cambridge*

started as a small city-state under the rule of elected kings. Upon their expulsion, it turned into a form of aristocratic republic that aggressively expanded over the next four centuries to rule the entire Mediterranean basin and much more. Its success led to civil wars that discredited republican government, making possible the transition under Augustus to what Roman republicans traditionally despised: the rule of kings – to wit, autocratic imperial rule that was to endure for yet another four hundred years. Its decline was given a still classical statement in Gibbon's masterpiece, *The Decline and Fall of the Roman Empire*.[20] The second important strand in the literature is the more recent work on the Roman family.[21] These two literatures, with a few notable exceptions,[22] exist largely in isolation from one another: that on public life was written mainly by men, that on family life mainly by women. I find a link between these two literatures in the concept central to our inquiry – patriarchy.

Patriarchy is an anthropological term denoting families or societies ruled by fathers. It sets up a hierarchy – a rule of priests – in which the priest, the *hieros*, is a father, *pater*. As an order of living, it elevates some men over others

---

Ancient History, Vol. XI. *The High Empire*, A.D. 70–192 (Cambridge: Cambridge University Press, 2000); Alan K. Bowman, Peter Garnsey, Averil Cameron, *The Cambridge Ancient History*, 2nd ed., Vol. XII. *The Crisis of Empire*, A.D. 193–337 (Cambridge: Cambridge University Press, 2005); Averil Cameron, Peter Garnsey, *The Cambridge Ancient History*, Vol. XIII. *The Late Empire*, A.D. 337–425 (Cambridge: Cambridge University Press, 1998).

[20] See Edward Gibbon, *The Decline and Fall of the Roman Empire*, Vols. I–IIII (New York: The Modern Library, n.d.; originally published in six volumes between 1776 and 1788).

[21] See, for example, Judith P. Hallett, *Fathers and Daughters in Roman Society: Women and the Elite Family* (Princeton, NJ: Princeton University Press, 1984); Susan Treggiari, *Roman Marriage* (Oxford: Clarendon Press, 1991); Richard P. Saller, *Patriarchy, Property and Death in the Roman Family* (Cambridge: Cambridge University Press, 1994); Suzanne Dixon, *The Roman Mother* (Norman: Oklahoma University Press, 1988); Suzanne Dixon, *The Roman Family* (Baltimore: The Johns Hopkins University Press, 1992); Beryl Rawson, ed., *Marriage, Divorce, and Children in Ancient Rome* (Oxford: Clarendon Press, 2004); Suzanne Dixon, *Reading Roman Women* (London: Duckworth, 2001); Jane F. Gardner, *Women in Roman Law and Society* (Bloomington: Indiana University Press, 1995); Sarah B. Pomeroy, *Goddesses, Whores, Wives, and Slaves: Women in Classical Antiquity* (New York: Schocken Books, 1995); Eva Cantarella, *Pandora's Daughters: The Role and Status of Women in Greek and Roman Antiquity*, translated by Maureen B. Fant (Baltimore: The Johns Hopkins University Press, 1987); Rebecca Langlands, *Sexual Morality in Ancient Rome* (Cambridge: Cambridge University Press, 2006); Richard A. Bauman, *Women and Politics in Ancient Rome* (London: Routledge, 1992); John K. Evans, *War, Women and Children in Ancient Rome* (London: Routledge, 1991); Miles McDonnell, *Roman Manliness: Virtues and the Roman Republic* (Cambridge: Cambridge University Press, 2006).

[22] See Judith P. Hallett, *Fathers and Daughters in Roman Society*; John K. Evans, *War, Women, and Children in Ancient Rome*.

and all men over women; within the family, it separates fathers from sons (the men from the boys) and places both women and children under a father's authority.[23]

The Roman conception of authority was highly patriarchal in both the public and private domains, and at the core of both, as my interpretation of patriarchy suggests, lay Roman religion. Roman politics, personal life, and religion were tightly integrated, a fact that has led astute students of ancient Rome, from Polybius[24] to Niccolo Machiavelli,[25] to think of Roman religion as easily manipulable by its leading politicians to serve their ends, including their aggressive imperialistic adventures. Except for the Vestal Virgins, the various orders of Roman priests, including the augurs required to signify that the gods were propitious to some proposed undertaking, were occupied by leading politicians (Julius Caesar, for example, was elected *pontifex maximus*).[26] Although the various priesthoods under the republic look to our eyes highly decentralized, the interpretation of all religious questions was in the hands of the Senate, as final arbiter, and the Senate was also the main body that conducted foreign policy, including Rome's wars.[27] The senators, called the Fathers, thus exercised a patriarchal authority over the meaning of Roman religion.[28]

The transition from an elected monarchy to a republic in fifth-century B.C.E. Rome led to the apparent increase in positions of political leadership (for both patrician and plebeian males) because under Rome's republican form of government, political responsibilities were much more broadly shared than under the monarchy. It was the duty of all male citizens who satisfied property requirements to leave their farms and serve in Rome's armies.[29] Correspondingly, it is under the republic that we see the beginning of Rome's expansion

---

[23] Carol Gilligan, *The Birth of Pleasure* (New York: Alfred A. Knopf, 2002), pp. 4–5.
[24] See Polybius, *The Rise of the Roman Empire*, translated by Ian Scott-Kilvert (London: Penguin, 1979), at p. 349.
[25] See Niccolo Machiavelli, *The Discourses*, in *The Prince and Discourses* Max Lerner ed. (New York: The Modern Library, 1950), pp. 101–540, at pp. 145–58.
[26] See Christian Meier, *Caesar: A Biography*, translated by David McLintock (New York: Basic Books, 1982), at pp. 160–2, 164, 169. See also Adrian Goldsworthy, *Caesar: Life of a Colossus* (New Haven, CT: Yale University Press, 2006).
[27] On this point, see Andrew Lintott, *The Constitution of the Roman Republic* (Oxford: Oxford University Press, 2004), pp. 65–88.
[28] On this point, see Mary Beard, "Priesthood in the Roman Republic," in Mary Beard and John North, eds., *Pagan Priests: Religion and Power in the Ancient World* (Ithaca, NY: Cornell University Press, 1990), at pp. 19–48.
[29] See R. E. A. Palmer, *The Archaic Community of the Romans* (Cambridge: Cambridge University Press, 1970), pp. 220 ff.

of military operations.[30] What is historically remarkable is the extraordinary belligerence:

> The Roman's state bellicosity is indicated not only by the frequency with which it went to war, but also by the high proportion of its citizen manpower that was regularly committed to military service.... These figures [of military service]... represent a very high level of military involvement as Roman citizens, which as far as we know cannot be matched by any other pre-industrial state.[31]

The Roman view was that Rome fought only just wars,[32] but on close examination, there is good reason to believe that their wars often cannot be justified,[33] resting rather on a militaristic ethos that led the leaders and people of the Roman Republic to regard imperialistic conquest as their mission. The Roman style of war, exemplified by two of its greatest generals, Julius Caesar and Pompey, was always highly aggressive,[34] and <u>political power under the republic was tied to military leadership and success.</u> Cicero, an orator, lawyer, and writer but not a military leader, remained largely on the periphery of political power during the civil war and ultimately was murdered when it served the interests of Antony and Octavian.[35] Violence became a way of life for Romans, directed not only against the state's enemies but increasingly against one another.[36]

Roman patriarchy legitimated this militaristic ethos, imposing its hierarchical religious demands not only in public life but in private life as well. In the Roman home, fathers were the priests, with authority over domestic rituals and lives. The remarkable powers of the Roman father, the *patria potestas*, gave him

> unlimited authority over all his legitimate children, irrespective of whether or not they were married, and of their offspring as long as he lived. Thus,

---

[30] On this point, see R. M. Ogilvie, *A Commentary on Livy Books 1–5* (Oxford: Oxford at the Clarendon Press, 1965), at pp. 234, 283–9, 302, 307–9, 314–21, 353–66, 390–411, 521–5, 567–74, 584–9, 597–606, 620–32.

[31] F. W. Walbank et al., *The Cambridge Ancient History*, Vol. VII. *The Rise of Rome to 220 B.C.E.*, at p. 383.

[32] Ibid., p. 384.

[33] For a powerful questioning of the Roman view, shared by some historians, see William V. Harris, *War and Imperialism in Republic Rome 327–70 B.C.E.* (Oxford: Clarendon Press, 1985).

[34] On this point, see Adrian Goldsworthy, *Caesar: Life of a Colossus* (New Haven, CT: Yale University Press, 2006), circa and at p. 303.

[35] See, in general, Anthony Everitt, *Cicero: The Life and Times of Rome's Greatest Politician* (New York: Random House, 2003). On Cicero's limited role in Roman politics, see Anthony Everitt, *Augustus: The Life of Rome's First Emperor* (New York: Random House, 2006), p. 67.

[36] See Andrew Lintott, *Violence in Republican Rome* (Oxford: Oxford University Press, 1999).

for example, the *pater familias* has the right to expose his child, to scourge him, to sell him, to pawn him, to imprison him, and, *in extremis*, even to kill him.[37]

Exercising such patriarchal authority in their families, Roman fathers were in turn subject to the patriarchal authority exercised by the Fathers in the Senate.

These interacting and reinforcing patterns of patriarchy both rest on and explain evidence of an underlying personal and political psychology in both the men and women who sustained the belligerent militarism of the Roman Republic and Empire. I am struck, in this connection, by the way Josephus, a close and respectful observer of the Roman army in action (during the imperial period), describes Roman men:

> [T]heir nation does not wait for the outbreak of war to give men their first lesson in arms; they do not sit with folded hands in peace time only to put them in motion in the hour of need. On the contrary, as though they had been born with weapons in their hand, they never have a truce from training, never wait for emergencies to arise. Moreover, their peace manoeuvres are not less strenuous then veritable warfare; each soldier daily throws all his energy into his drill, as though he were in action. Hence that perfect ease with which they sustain the shock of battle: no confusion breaks their customary formation, no panic paralyzes, no fatigue exhausts them; and as their opponents cannot match these qualities, victory is the invariable and certain consequence. Indeed, it would not be wrong to describe their manoeuvres as bloodless combats and their combats as sanguinary manoeuvres.[38]

According to Josephus, Roman men are so steeped in militarism that they appear "as though ... born with weapons in their hand."

Of course, no baby is born this way. Quite the opposite; human babies are remarkable for their relationality, their desire for and responsiveness to human connection. Because Josephus's Romans are neither relational nor emotionally sensitive, these human capacities have been blunted or stamped out of them. My question, then, is how could Roman patriarchal culture structure both private and public life to render this outcome seemingly natural or inevitable?

I turn in this regard to the contemporary literature on trauma and its effects on human neurophysiology and psychology.[39] The now well-documented

---

[37] Emiel Eyben, "Fathers and Sons," in Beryl Rawson, ed., *Marriage, Divorce, and Children in Ancient Rome*, pp. 114–43, at p. 115. Eyben notes that these powers were significantly limited by the time of the Roman Empire.

[38] Josephus, *The Jewish Wars Books III–IV*, translated by H. St. J. Thackeray (Cambridge, MA: Harvard University Press, 1997), p. 27.

[39] See, for example, Bessel van der Kolk, Alexander C. McFarlane, and Lars Weisaeth, eds., *Traumatic Stress: The Effects of Overwhelming Experience on Mind, Body, and Society* (New

consequence of trauma is a loss of voice and of memory – in particular, loss of the voice of intimate relationship. This loss or suppression of voice, however, is often masked by an identification with the voice of the person who imposed the trauma and an internalization of the demands that this more powerful person imposes on one's life. The crucial mechanism here is dissociation: the psychological process through which the surviving self separates itself from the self that was overwhelmed. A voice that speaks from experience is silenced in favor of a voice that carries more authority, leading to a replacement of one's personal sense of emotional presence and truth with what Sandor Ferenczi, a Hungarian psychoanalyst, describes as an "identification with the aggressor,"[40] the taking on as one's own the voice and demands of the oppressor. This process, leading to what Ferenczi observed as false compliance, is in itself largely unconscious, due in part to the loss of memory that follows the traumatic rupture of relationships.[41]

Josephus's observations suggest a personal and political psychology in which such traumatic breaks in intimate relationships are both normal and normative, justified by the demands of patriarchy: in effect, an institutionalized trauma that supports and sustains the required militaristic ethos. In the case of Roman patriarchy, these demands took the form of a highly gendered code of honor, coupled with institutionalized practices of shaming. The honor of a Roman citizen rested on his being willing and able, with the complicity of women, to engage in both Roman politics and its expression in continual imperialistic wars. This involved not only military service with its risks of injury and loss of life but also a willingness to disrupt personal relationships.

A family living under the rule of the Roman *patria potestas* experienced a form of oppression at the center of intimate life, including control over inheritance and genealogy as well as the use of force to hold people in line.[42] Even if many Roman fathers declined to exercise these powers oppressively, the legitimation of such power, as a model for what legitimate power is,

---

York: Guilford Press, 1996); Judith Herman, *Trauma and Recovery* (New York: Basic Books, 1997).

[40] See J. Laplanche and J.-B. Pontalis, *The Language of Psycho-Analysis*, translated by Donald Nicholson-Smith (New York: W.W. Norton, 1973), at pp. 208–9.

[41] Sandor Ferenczi, "The Confusion of Tongues between Adult and Child," English translation in *International Journal of Psychoanalysis* (1949), 30, 225, German original in *Internationale Zeitschrift fur Psychoanalyse*. (1933) 19, 5. Paper read at the Twelfth International Psycho-Analytical Congress, Wiesbaden, September, 1932.

[42] For a good general treatment, see Susan Treggiari, *Roman Marriage: Iusti Coniuges from the Time of Cicero to the Time of Ulpian* (Oxford: Oxford University Press, 2002). See also Richard P. Saller, *Patriarchy, Property and Death in the Roman Family* (Cambridge: Cambridge University Press, 1994).

makes the traumatic disruption of any intimate relationship, including that between fathers and sons, acceptable. Polybius, a Greek whose hometown had been damaged by Romans, noted in mixed horror and admiration that "there have been instances of [Roman] men in office who have put their own sons to death, contrary to every law or custom, because they valued the interest of their country more dearly than their natural ties to their own flesh and blood."[43] In place of intimate relationship, the son identifies with the honor of his father, and of his father before him – honor descending through a line of fathers.

The mechanism of such honor codes is again beautifully illustrated by Polybius, who portrays the ritual he describes as very much at the heart of the psychology of Roman imperialism:

> Whenever one of their celebrated men dies, in the course of the funeral procession his body is carried with every kind of honour into the Forum to the so-called Rostra.... The whole mass of the people stand round to watch, and his son, if he has left one of adult age who can be present, or if not some other relative, then mounts the Rostra and delivers an address which recounts the virtues and successes achieved by the dead man during his lifetime. By these means the whole populace... are so deeply engaged that the loss seems not to be confined to the mourners but to be a public one which affects the whole people. Then after the burial of the body... they place the image of the dead m an in the most conspicuous position in the house.... This image consists of a mask, which is fashioned with extraordinary fidelity both in the modeling and its complexion to represents the features of the dead man.... And when any distinguished member of the family dies, the masks are taken to the funeral, and are there worn by men who are considered to bear the closest resemblance to the original....
>
> They all ride in chariots... and when they arrive at the Rostra they all seat themselves in a row upon chairs of ivory. It would be hard to imagine a more impressive scene for a young man who aspires to win fame and practice virtue....
>
> [T]he most important consequence of the ceremony is that it inspires young men to endure the extremes of suffering for the common good in the hope of winning the glory that awaits upon the brave.[44]

Such rituals enacted the patriarchal relationship of fathers to sons, leading sons to identify with a sense of family honor stretching into the past. Because fathers were often absent from family life (either through absence in war, death in war, or, given the significant age differences from their wives, through natural

---

[43] Polybius, *The Rise of the Roman Empire*, at p. 348.
[44] Polybius, *The Rise of the Roman Empire*, at pp. 346–7.

death), Roman matrons, as wives and mothers, became crucial players in the patriarchal system.

Women, in the terms of this gender ideology, did not exist as persons with a mind and sexuality of their own, for the terms of Roman arranged marriage respected neither. Such powers of fathers, or even of brothers over their sisters (Augustus married his beloved sister, Octavia, to Antony), were, under the republic, important means to social solidarity. This was particularly true among otherwise highly competitive men of the Roman Republic, struggling for leadership and honor in politics and war. By enlisting the power of fathers or brothers, such men often sought to elevate their status and political appeal through marriage to a higher-status woman, as Octavian did through his marriage to Livia.[45] Thus are new alliances formed. Pompey and Julius Caesar managed, for example, to cooperate politically as long as Pompey was married to Caesar's sister; when she died and Pompey refused Caesar's request that a comparable marriage be arranged,[46] the cooperation collapsed, and civil war followed.

This function of arranged marriage under Roman patriarchy led to the particular weight that Romans traditionally placed on the chastity and fidelity of women, for only such limitations on women's sexuality could ensure their husbands that the women's children were theirs. An honor code of this sort invests men's sense of honor in a control over women's sexuality that disrupts any relationships women might otherwise form or want to form. Indeed, such control is a perquisite of male honor in such a patriarchal system, and any attack on it constitutes an insult that elicits and justifies violence. The link between traumatic disruption of intimate relationships and violence is thus reinforced.

Marriages in Rome were arranged by fathers, crucially to advance dynastic ends. Consequently, the relationships of Roman wives to their husbands could be emotionally shallow.[47] For example, Augustus married his daughter, Julia, successively, to Marcellus, Agrippa, and Tiberius, the last of whom she apparently deeply disliked. And at the order of Augustus, Tiberius divorced a beloved wife to marry Julia.[48] The political career of Augustus himself (then called Octavian) evidently took off only when he married Livia, whose father

---

[45] See, in general, Judith P. Hallett, *Fathers and Daughters in Roman Society*.
[46] On this point, see Adrian Goldsworthy, *Caesar: Life of a Colossus* (New Haven, CT: Yale University Press, 2006), at p. 294.
[47] On this point, see Judith P. Hallett, *Fathers and Daughters in Roman Society*, at pp. 69, 211–48, 235 ff.
[48] Suetonius, *The Twelve Caesars*, translated by Robert Gravves (London: Penguin, 1979), at pp. 112–13.

and then husband had both fought against Octavian and Antony at Philippi. Livia's father, upon defeat by Octavian and Antony, had committed suicide. Nonetheless, with the support of her husband (by whom she was then pregnant), she divorced him to marry Octavian.

Although Augustus apparently loved Livia and their marriage had unusually egalitarian features (including consultations with his highly intelligent, astute wife on all matters public and private), Livia came to marry Augustus very much in the context of Roman patriarchal marriage. Not only was she, a higher-status woman, chosen at least in part by Augustus to advance his status and career, she also married him under the shadow of traumatic loss (her father's suicide) and, given the military and political failures of her husband, to preserve her own life and his, as well as the life of her son by her first husband, Tiberius. Livia's living out the idealized conception of a good Roman wife makes sense against this background; her profound influence on her husband is, consistent with Roman patriarchy, never a public matter, always staying within the strict bounds of propriety.[49] With Livia, his mother, very much in his corner, Tiberius was to succeed Augustus as emperor even though he was not Augustus's child.

Livia's strategic moves following traumatic loss exemplify the psychology of Roman patriarchal womanhood.[50] The power of fathers and even husbands to inflict such losses on both men and women gives rise to an armored psychology that is consistent with the gender roles required of them, including the violence triggered by any violations of women's chastity. These patriarchal values are discernible in Livy's history of Rome, in which he gives us two notable examples of such violence. Both associate the founding or refounding of republican government with revulsion against violence spurred by threats to the chastity of wives or daughters.

First is the expulsion of the last king of Rome, Tarquinius Superbus, explained by Livy in terms of the lust of his son, Sextus Tarquinius, for Lucretia, the beautiful wife of a friend, Collatinus. Sextus entered the bedroom of Lucretia armed with his sword and threatening her life, but "the fear of death could not bend her will." Failing that, Sextus put the threat as one to

---

[49] For fuller discussion, see Anthony A. Barrett, *Livia: First Lady of Imperial Rome* (New Haven, CT: Yale University Press, 2002); Susan E. Wood, *Imperial Women: A Study in Public Images 40 B.C.E.–A.D. 69* (Leiden, The Netherlands: Brill, n.d.).

[50] Herod's wife, Mariamne (as told in Josephus), is a good contrast. Herod killed her brother and grandfather but loves her, so he gives her too much license. She insults and betrays him, leading to her own execution – a patriarchal horror story. See Josephus, *The Jewish War Books I–II*, translated by H. St. J. Thackeray (Cambridge, MA: Harvard University Press, 1997), at pp. 205–11.

her posthumous honor: he would kill her and then her slave and lay the naked body of the slave next to hers, a situation that, when discovered, would lead to the general belief "that you have been caught in adultery with a servant" (meaning a slave).[51] Lucretia yielded on these terms, but when she explained to her father and husband what had happened, they insisted she was morally innocent. Livy narrates her reply:

> "What is due to *him*," Lucretia said, "is for you to decide. As for me, I am innocent of fault, but I will take my punishment. Never shall Lucretia provide a precedent for unchaste women to escape what they deserve." With these words she drew a knife from under her robe, drove it into her heart, and fell forward, dead.[52]

It was the righteous indignation of Lucius Junius Brutus, son of the king's sister Tarquinia, at this outrage that led to the violent expulsion from Rome of its last king and his family and the establishment of the republic around 509 B.C.E.

In what Livy calls "the second crime in Rome," the dictatorial powers of the *decemvirs* were ended in 449 B.C.E.: "Its origin was lust, and in its consequences it was no less dreadful than the rape and suicide of Lucretia which led to the expulsion of the Tarquins."[53] Appius, one of the *decemvirs*, lusted after a beautiful girl, Verginia, the daughter of Verginius, a centurion then serving in the Roman army. Verginius had already betrothed his daughter to an ex-tribune, Icilius. To achieve his ends, Appius ordered a dependent of his own to claim against all comers in court that Verginia was his slave and thus available for sexual relations, as slaves were in Rome. The claim and the trial, although completely fraudulent, were sustained by Appius even against the protests of Verginius and Icilius. To protect the reputation of his daughter from the sexual relations that seemed imminent, Verginius killed her, an act that aroused Romans to violently overthrow the *decemvirs* and reestablish the republic.[54]

What interests me about both cases is the violent response to the alleged unchastity of wives or daughters – not only against the men who threaten rape but also the suicide or murder of women (Lucretia and Verginia). In each narrative, the insult to the honor of husbands or brothers elicits violence against both perpetrators and victims. Lucretia, as Livy portrays her, is what

---

[51] Livy, *The Early History of Rome*, translated by Aubrey De Selincourt (London: Penguin, 2002), at p. 101.
[52] Ibid., p. 102.
[53] Ibid., p. 246.
[54] Ibid., pp. 246–66.

patriarchy requires her to be: dissociated through trauma from her experience and identifying with her patriarchal role.[55]

Within these structures of Roman patriarchy lay the relationship of mothers to their sons. Such relationships were rigidly controlled by the duty of mothers to educate their sons into assuming their patriarchal roles. At least two of Rome's most remarkable leaders (Julius Caesar and Octavian, later Augustus) were unusually close to their mothers, with both mothers actively involved in advancing their son's careers.[56] Tacitus, writing in the late first or early second century C.E., discussed the mother's role in raising children in a passage that presented Caesar's mother, Aurelia, as an ideal:

> In the good old days, every man's son, born in wedlock, was brought up not in the chamber of some hireling nurse, but in his mother's lap, and at her knee. And that mother could have no higher praise than that she managed the house and gave herself to her children. . . . In the presence of such a one no base word could be uttered without grave offence, and no wrong deed done. Religiously and with the utmost diligence she regulated not only the serious tasks of her youthful charges, but the recreations also and their games. It was in this spirit, we are told, that Cornelia, the mother of the Gracchi, directed their upbringing, Aurelia that of Caesar, Atia of Augustus: thus it was that these mothers trained their princely children.[57]

Yet, Roman mothers of the elite often had little to do with babies, who were cared for by nurses, often slaves, endearingly addressed by their young charges as "tatae."[58] Indeed, sometimes a Roman mother like Agrippina the Younger, mother of Nero, through the vagaries of Roman politics, was absent entirely from her son's life in some of his earliest years.[59] At later stages, however, as Tacitus observes, the patriarchal system enlisted Roman matrons, often in collaboration with their brothers, into playing important roles in the inculcation in their sons of the required sense of patriarchally defined responsibilities,

---

[55] On the long history of the role of Lucretia in patriarchal fantasy (including Renaissance story that she kills herself because of shame because she enjoyed the rape), see Ian Donaldson, *The Rapes of Lucretia: A Myth and its Transformations* (Oxford: Clarendon Press, 1982).

[56] On Julius Caesar's relationship to this mother, see Adrian Goldsworthy, *Caesar*, at pp. 33, 35, 36, 49–50, 52, 59, 87, 100, 125–6, 146, 148, 293–4; on Octavian's relationship, see Anthony Everitt, *Augustus: The Life of Rome's First Emperor* (New York: Random House, 2006), at pp. 32, 45.

[57] Tacitus, A *Dialogue on Oratory*, in Tacitus, *Agricola, Germania, Dialogus*, translated by W. Peterson (Cambridge, MA: Harvard University Press, 1970), pp. 231–47, at p. 307.

[58] See, Suzanne Dixon, *The Roman Mother*, at pp. 146–9.

[59] Agrippina was exiled by Caligula, her brother, to the Pontian isles, during which time Nero was brought up by his aunt Domitia. See Anthony A. Barrett, *Agrippina: Sex, Power and Politics in the Early Empire* (New Haven, CT: Yale University Press, 1996), pp. 69–70.

roles characterized by "disciplinarian skills rather than indulgence or overprotectiveness, even towards small children."[60]

The model here was Coriolanus's mother (Venturia, in Livy's history); she persuaded her son, who had been unjustly exiled from Rome, not to fight against the city of his birth, thus saving Rome at his expense.[61] The consequence was an anger directed toward mothers, so that even when a woman like Livia played a supportive and evidently important role in her husband's political life and success, she was, as mother to Tiberius, "that feminine bully, his mother."[62] Livia, ambitious for her son to become emperor, supported Augustus's order that Tiberius divorce his wife to marry Julia (Augustus's daughter), a separation that was traumatic for Tiberius. Against this backdrop, we can make sense of Tiberius's rather rigid identification with Roman gender ideology, in terms of which he would later criticize his mother whenever she exercised political responsibilities inconsistent with his view of the proper role and station of women.[63] Similarly, and more drastically, Nero, who would never have become emperor without his mother's strenuous efforts on his behalf, when challenged by his imperious mother to disrupt both his intimate sexual liaisons and his artistic interests, turned to homicidal violence against her.[64]

A number of historians have observed the pivotal role of honor in Roman politics and culture. A kind of emulative competition by men and women in terms of the honor code was as important to Roman personal and political psychology as the more material consequences of their imperial wars, including the wealth that poured into Rome as booty and tribute from their wars and the huge numbers of slaves thus secured who played a key role in Roman economy and culture (defeated enemies were often enslaved).[65] Roman public and private life both rested on and supported the gender ideology that the Roman honor code sustained – one in which almost any insult to

---

[60] Suzanne Dixon, *The Roman Mother*, at p. 145.
[61] Livy, *The Early History of Rome*, at pp. 156–7.
[62] Tacitus, *The Annals of Imperial Rome*, translated by Michael Grant (London: Penguin, 1998), p. 34.
[63] On this point, see Tacitus, *The Annals of Imperial Rome*, at p. 41.
[64] See, in general, Anthony A. Barrett, *Agrippina*; Edward Champlin, *Nero* (Cambridge: MA: Belknap Press of Harvard University Press, 2003).
[65] On the forms and extent of Roman violence, see Keith Hopkins, *Conquerors and Slaves* (Cambridge: Cambridge University Press, 1978); Keith Hopkins, *Death and Renewal* (Cambridge: Cambridge University Press, 1983). On the competitive codes of Roman honor, see J. E. Lendon, *Empire of Honour* (Oxford: Oxford University Press, 2005); Carlin A. Barton, *Rome Honor: The Fire in the Bones* (Berkeley: University of California Press, 2001). See also Carlin A. Barton, *The Sorrows of the Ancient Romans: The Gladiator and the Monster* (Princeton, NJ: Princeton University Press, 1993).

manhood elicited violence.[66] As traumatic loss in intimate relationships deadens the psyche's inborn responsiveness and suppresses personal voice, it gives rise to the armored terms of gender identity that the honor code enforces. Indeed, the stability of patriarchy requires the suppression of any voice in women or men that might, on reasonable grounds, contest its terms, a suppression that itself relies on the power of gender by deeming the resisting voice in men unmanly or effeminate and in women unwomanly.

Until the late republican period, the Roman patriarchal system had organized and mobilized these psychological propensities to violence into forms of politics and war that maintained a remarkable level of national solidarity. There were, of course, deep internal constitutional conflicts between patricians and plebeians, and Rome sometimes experienced devastating defeats, for example, early in its history by the Gauls (who sacked Rome)[67] and at the hands of Hannibal in 216 B.C.E. at Cannae in the Second Punic War, a war nonetheless ultimately won by Rome.[68] But the presence of powerful enemies secured a remarkable solidarity among Roman citizens, directing outward the violence motivated by insult. It was only when Rome decisively defeated its most powerful antagonists (in particular, Carthage in the Third Punic War) that Roman violence turned internecine in the civil wars, which started with something Roman politics had not seen before: the murder by patricians of the Gracchi brothers, tribunes of the people, with whom patricians deeply disagreed. As Montesquieu trenchantly observed, "There had to be dissensions in Rome, for warriors, who were so proud, so audacious, so terrible abroad could not be very moderate at home."[69] Thus, when secure at home without powerful enemies, "Their fierce humor remained; the citizens were treated as they themselves had treated conquered enemies, and were governed according to the same plan."[70] Montesquieu notes the power over Romans of the extreme form of patriarchy that governed both their public and private lives, so that under the republic, its laws "are observed not through fear, nor through reason, but through passion."[71] Once this passion for patriarchal order and status could no longer be satisfied by a common enemy, it turned into conflict

---

[66] For a contemporary exploration of this psychology of violent manhood, see James Gilligan, *Violence: Reflections on a National Epidemic* (New York: Vintage Books, 1996).
[67] See Livy, *The Early History of Rome*, at pp. 365–435.
[68] See Livy, *The War with Hannibal*, translated by Aubrey De Selincourt (London: Penguin, 1965), pp. 144–9.
[69] Montesquieu, *Considerations on the Causes of the Greatness of the Romans and Their Decline*, translated by David Lowenthal (Indianapolis, IN: Hackett Publishing Company, 1965), p. 93.
[70] Ibid., p. 136.
[71] Ibid., p. 45.

among Romans themselves, for example, the conflict between Julius Caesar and Pompey.

One of the marks of how unusual a personality Julius Caesar had as a Roman man was his resistance to the dictator Sulla's demand that he divorce his wife (Caesar was nearly executed over this matter), when, in contrast, Pompey supinely obeyed Sulla's similar command.[72] Of course, Caesar was as aggressively successful a military leader as Pompey, willing, like Pompey, to inflict appalling costs on Rome's enemies.[73] But Caesar's remarkable gifts as a Roman leader, including the devotion of his troops to him – "a love affair"[74] – and his vaunted clemency to his political enemies, show that resistance to patriarchal demands was sometimes possible even for Roman men.[75] Yet, Caesar's assassination suggests how dangerous such resistance could be.

When Julius Caesar comes to explain his reasons for taking up arms against Pompey, he pinpoints the problem in Pompey's "desire that no one should match his own status"[76] and gives his reasons for undertaking civil war in terms of an unjust threat to his dignity. Caesar, describing himself (as he usually does in his writings)[77] in the third person, observes that "his standing had always been his first consideration, more important than his life."[78]

There is inherently a tension between democracy and patriarchy. Democracy defines legitimate politics in terms of the equal voice of those subject to political power. Patriarchy, imposing the hierarchal rule of fathers, denies the equal voice of those subject to its rule (lesser men and women and children). In their treatment of women in ancient Athens, the patriarchal structures of ancient Greece were certainly as bad – indeed, worse – than those of Rome.[79] But the Athenian democracy protected the right of free speech in the democratic assembly, which allowed for questioning of its institutions. It also encouraged forms of philosophy and theater that exposed its mistakes and the tragic costs of its policies, including those inflicted on women. The Athenian democracy, with rights of free speech and participation much broader

---

[72] On this point, see Adrian Goldsworthy, *Caesar*, pp. 57–9, 91.
[73] See ibid., pp. 303, 355.
[74] Anthony Everitt, *Augustus: The Life of Rome's First Emperor* (New York: Random House, 2006), p. 35.
[75] For Caesar's political resistance to the Senate's execution of Catiline, see Adrian Goldsworthy, *Caesar*, p. 135.
[76] Julius Caesar, *The Civil War*, translated by John Carter (Oxford: Oxford University Press, 1998), at p. 5.
[77] See, for example, Julius Caesar, *The Conquest of Gaul*, translated by S. A. Handford (London: Penguin, 1982), in which Caesar always speaks of himself in the third person.
[78] Julius Caesar, *The Civil War*, at p. 8.
[79] For illuminating comparisons, see Sarah B. Pomeroy, *Goddesses, Whores, Wives, and Slaves*.

than those of Rome, lived nonetheless in very real tension with its patriarchal treatment of women.

In contrast, Roman entertainment both expressed and reinforced the prevailing militaristic ethos, taking the form of gladiatorial contests, a custom that apparently replaced human sacrifice as an offering to the dead.[80] This ethos also explains the contempt of Romans for the critical power of a theater like that of the Athenian democracy[81] or for any philosophy that would fundamentally question their institutions and practices (the Greek skeptical philosopher Carneades, who questioned Romans' beliefs in their just wars, was for this reason promptly exiled).[82] The Roman prejudice against philosophy[83] was only overcome when it was adapted to serve their practices, as in the case of Roman stoicism.[84] Roman elites studied the philosophy they found congenial (including epicureanism as well as stoicism); most spoke Greek, and some wrote in Greek (e.g., Marcus Aurelius).[85] Roman prejudices against the theater in general and actors in particular ran so deep that horror at Nero's love of acting publicly in plays may have been as much responsible for his downfall as his other excesses (even the judicious Tacitus refers to Nero's acting as "the national disgrace").[86]

In contrast to Athens, under the republic, the Roman democratic assemblies, which both made laws and elected the leading officials of the state, were open to all male citizens, but the agenda was set by officials, and no right of free speech inhered in the citizenry. Only in the aristocratic Senate was there anything like free and open debate, and even there the terms were set by officials and dominant politicians.[87] The terms of the Roman honor code were thus effectively sacrosanct, enforcing a highly gendered sense of identity that, if insulted, expressed itself in violence.

The Roman Republic was, therefore, much less democratic than Athens and even more compromised by the extreme form of patriarchy that governed

---

[80] Andrew Lintott, *Violence in Republican Rome*, p. 40. See also Keith Hopkins, *Death and Renewal* (Cambridge: Cambridge University Press, 1983), at pp. 1–30.
[81] See Catharine Edwards, *The Politics of Immorality in Ancient Rome* (Cambridge: Cambridge University Press, 2002), pp. 118–19.
[82] See Donald Earl, *The Moral and Political Tradition of Rome* (Ithaca, NY: Cornell University Press, 1967), pp. 40–1. See Tim Whitmarsh, *Greek Literature and the Roman Empire: The Politics of Imitation* (Oxford: Oxford University Press, 2001), p. 10.
[83] On the Roman prejudice against philosophy, see Ibid., p. 91.
[84] See Donald Earl, ibid., p. 61.
[85] See, in general, Tim Whitmarsh, *Greek Literature and the Roman Empire*.
[86] Tacitus, *The Annals of Ancient Rome*, translated by Michael Grant (London: Penguin, 1996), at p. 383.
[87] See, on these points, Andrew Lintott, *The Constitution of the Roman Republic*, at pp. 191–213.

both its public and private life. Nonetheless, it certainly had democratic features, including not only the democratic assemblies but the tribunes of the people, who could veto the actions of the Senate and interpose their authority to stop hostile state action against a plebeian. In addition, over its long constitutional history, the republic eventually opened even membership of the Senate to nonpatricians and Roman citizenship well beyond the ethnic limitations of democratic Athens.[88] Its patriarchy, however, ran so deep in the Roman psyche that <u>if democracy or patriarchy had to go, it was clear which option Romans would embrace</u>. Thus, in the wake of the civil wars and under the leadership of Augustus, Romans sacrificed their republic and embraced an autocratic monarchy much like their earlier kingship and more congenial to their patriarchal religion.

The period of the civil wars becomes a kind of laboratory for us in showing how republican institutions could function in the circumstances of Rome's remarkable imperialistic success, a success those institutions had undoubtedly made possible. What this experiment reveals are not only the competitive struggles for honor among such highly individualistic, talented politicians and military leaders as a Marius and a Sulla, Pompey and Caesar, Octavian and Antony but also a generation of Roman elite women who, in relationship to these driven, competitive men, bridle against the traditional, patriarchal view of women's roles. The civil wars destabilized both the republic and Roman patriarchy, as the lives of women in this period clearly show. When Augustus establishes the imperial system, he effectively buries the republic and seeks to reestablish, on sounder institutional grounds, the patriarchy he believes is more central to Roman identity than its long-standing republican institutions. The forms of resistance of Roman women to this reveal both the power of resistance and the rage patriarchal fathers unleashed on their defiant daughters.[89]

One can see the challenge to the patriarchal order both in political women – Hortensia, Fulvia, Sempronia, and later in Agrippina the Elder, and Agrippina the Younger – and in the freer sexual lives of these new Roman women, including Augustus's daughter and granddaughter, whose erotic lives became the subject of Roman poets like Catullus, Propertius, Tibullus, Ovid, and

---

[88] See, in general, Lintott, *The Constitution*; on the increasing openness of Roman citizenship as a distinctive mark of Roman politics and identity, see Emma Dench, *Romulus' Asylum: Roman Identities from the Age of Alexander to the Age of Hadrian* (Oxford: Oxford University Press, 2005).

[89] On the new woman, see Elaine Fantham, Helene Peet Foley, Natalie Boymel Kampen, Sarah B. Pomeroy, and H. Alan Shapiro, *Women in the Classical World* (New York: Oxford University Press, 1994), pp. 280–93.

even one woman poet, Sulpicia.[90] I begin with the political actions of women before turning to the expression of sexuality and its repression.

Hortensia and Fulvia became political actors during the last period of the civil wars when Octavian and Antony join with Lepidus in the triumvirate to defeat the assassins of Caesar. They then wage war on one another, leading to Octavian's triumph at Actium and the deaths by suicide of both Antony and Cleopatra. Hortensia, the daughter of Quintus Hortensius Hortalus, a great orator who rivaled Cicero in the courts, appears once in the historical record of Appian as she leads a group of wealthy Roman women who challenge a tax the triumvirs imposed on their property, first by protesting to the triumvirs' womenfolk. Both Octavian's sister Octavia and Antony's mother Julia received them with sympathy, but Antony's then-wife Fulvia brusquely rebuffed them. In response, Hortensia led these women to make a public demonstration, forcing their way to the triumvirate's tribunal in their forum.

Speaking for these women (many of whose husbands and fathers had been proscribed by the triumvirs, legitimating their murders and seizure of their property), Hortensia made a powerful appeal in the following terms:

> Do you allege that we, like our menfolk, have wronged you? If so, proscribe us too, as you proscribed them. But if we women have voted none of you an enemy of the state, nor torn down your houses, nor destroyed your army or put another in the field against you, nor prevented you enjoying command or honours, why do we share the punishment when we have not collaborated in the crime? Why should we pay tax, when we have no share in magistracies, or honours, or military commands, or in public affairs at all, where your conflicts have brought us to this terrible state?[91]

The triumvirs, disturbed by this unseemly display, instructed their attendants to clear the women, but the response of the Roman crowd was so hostile that the attendants were stopped and the matter postponed to the next day. At that

---

[90] See, in general, Paul Veyne, *Roman Erotic Elegy: Love, Poetry, and the West*, translated by David Pellauer (Chicago: University of Chicago Press, 1988); Maria Wyke, *The Roman Mistress* (Oxford: Oxford University Press, 2002). Regarding Sulpicia, see John Heath-Stubbs, trans., *The Poems of Sulpicia* (London: Hearing Eye, 2000); Stephen Hinds, "The Poetess and the Reader: Further Steps towards Sulpicia," *Hermathena* 143 (1987): 29–46; Mathile Skoe, "Sublime Poetry or Feminine Fiddling? Gender and Reception: Sulpicia through the Eyes of Two 19th Century Scholars," Nordic Symposium on Women's Lives in Antiquity, in *Aspects of Women in Antiquity: Proceedings of the First Nordic Symposium on Women's Lives in Antiquity, Goteborg 12–15 June 1997*, edited by L. L. Loven and A. Strömberg (Jonsered, Sweden: P. Astroms Forlag, 1998), pp. 169–82; Alison Keith, "*Tandem Venit Amor*: A Roman Woman Speaks of Love," in *Roman Sexualities*, edited by Judith P. Hallett and Marilyn B. Skinner (Princeton, NJ: Princeton University Press, 1997), pp. 295–310.

[91] Appian, *The Civil Wars*, translated by John Carter (London: Penguin, 1996), at p. 225.

time, the triumvirs narrowed the group of women to whom the tax would apply and included as well those men whose property was of a certain amount.[92]

Fulvia had her most famous involvement in public affairs in a relatively brief period, from 44 B.C.E., after Caesar's murder, to 40, when she died. This was a period when Octavian and Antony were at odds. Octavian was ready to take revenge on the murderers of Caesar, whom, after adoption by Caesar, Octavian called his father; Antony, however, was not ready – or not yet. After Antony's defeat by forces of the Roman Senate at Mutina in 43, Fulvia – with Antony's mother and others – acted aggressively as her husband's political agent in Rome. She visited the houses of senators to make sure that her husband was not declared, as Cicero had urged, a public enemy. Later, with both Antony and Octavian absent from Rome, Fulvia exercised more power over the Senate than Antony's brother, who was one of the consuls, the supreme Roman political status, for that year.[93] Subsequently, when Octavian returned to Rome, Antony was in the East beginning his affair with Cleopatra. Fulvia, in alliance with Antony's brother, decided to resist Octavian by force in ways unprecedented for Roman women: girding on a sword, leading assaults, holding councils of war with senators and knights.[94] Both her military efforts and those of Antony's brother failed.[95] Octavian's bloodthirstiness in this period included his brutal role in the proscriptions and his cruelties at Philippi,[96] where his own military performance was undistinguished and, by Roman standards, cowardly. All this stands in sharp contrast to Julius Caesar and his famous clemency for his former enemies, a clemency that did not stop them from murdering him, which Octavian never forgot. Fulvia escaped to Athens, where she later died, freeing Antony to make a new alliance with Octavian by marrying his sister Octavia.

The question of women as sexual actors was, however, even more incendiary. One sees in these women something experienced earlier in Roman history during the Bacchanalian scandals of the second century B.C.E. – namely, forms of resistance to Roman patriarchy that support my suggestion that such resistance is rooted in the psyche. The Romans had established a patriarchal religion that legitimated its gender ideology; for this reason, the Senate, as final arbiter of religion, was at times hostile to non-Roman Eastern religions under the republic, especially when those religions were interpreted as threatening the gendered honor code at the core of Roman patriarchy. (At other times,

---

[92] See also Richard A. Bauman, *Women and Politics in Ancient Rome*, at pp. 81–3.
[93] See ibid., pp. 86–7.
[94] Ibid., p. 88.
[95] Ibid.
[96] On this point, see Suetonius, *The Twelve Caesars*, at pp. 50–1.

Romans, although ideologically hostile to the East, were syncretic in their religious tastes, including the Far Eastern religions of Magna Mater/Cybele/Isis, etc.)[97]

In the second century B.C.E., the Greek cult of Bacchus, with its nocturnal rites in which women and men might pursue their interests in sexual relations, religiously legitimated free sexual associations of both sexes on terms of female leadership that flouted the control on women's sexuality imposed by Roman patriarchy. The response was one of hysteria and panic at the alleged Baccahanalian conspiracy.[98] When in 186 B.C.E. the Senate forbade such rites, Livy recorded a long speech to the Roman people in justification of the Senate's action. What threatened the Senate and its patriarchal religion was the impact of such free associations on the propensity to violence of Roman men by overriding their crucial role in protecting women's chastity as the rationale for such violence:

> What kind of gatherings do you suppose these to be, gatherings, in the first place, held at night, and, secondly, gatherings where men and women meet promiscuously? If you knew at what age male persons are initiated you would feel pity for them – yes, and shame. Citizens of Rome, do you feel that young men, initiated by this oath of allegiance, should be made soldiers? That arms should be entrusted to men called up from this obscene shrine? These men are steeped in their own debauchery and the debauchery of others; will they take the sword to right to the end in defence of the chastity of your wives and your children?[99]

Without the patriarchally imposed duty to defend the chastity of their women, the consul argues, how can Romans be the violent men that Roman patriarchy requires?

Writing about the conspiracy of Catiline during the period of the civil wars, Sallust identifies, among Cataline's adherents,

> a number of women who in their earlier days have lived extravagantly on money that they obtained by prostituting themselves, and then, when advancing age reduced their incomes without changing their luxurious tastes, had run headlong into debt. These women he thought, would do good service by

---

[97] For a good general treatment, see Mary Beard, John North, and Simon Price, *Religions of Rome*, Vol. 1. *A History*; Vol. 2. *Religions of Rome. A Sourcebook* (Cambridge: Cambridge University Press, 1998).

[98] On the Roman response, see Harriet I. Flower, *The Cambridge Companion to the Roman Republic* (Cambridge: Cambridge University Press, 2004), at pp. 148–9, 207.

[99] Livy, *Rome and the Mediterranean*, translated by Henry Bettenson (London: Penguin, 1976), at p. 410.

acting as agitators among the city slaves and organizing acts of incendiarism; their husbands, too, could be either induced to join his cause, or murdered.[100]

Only one such woman is named: Sempronia, the mother of Decimus Brutus, one of the assassins of Caesar. She was, Sallust tells us,

> favoured... not only with birth and beauty, but with a good husband and children. Well educated in Greek and Latin literature, she had greater skill in lyre-playing and dancing than there is any need for a respectable woman to acquire, besides many other accomplishments such as minister to dissipation. There was nothing that she set a smaller value on than seemliness and chastity, and she was as careless of her reputation as she was of money. Her passions were so ardent that she more often made advances to men than they did to her.[101]

Sallust may be coloring his history in the terms of patriarchy, recirculating stereotypes of female transgression. Nonetheless, what speaks through his narrative is an elite woman's resistance to precisely those patriarchal controls on her sexuality, a resistance that Roman patriarchy must and did condemn.

To put this matter in context, we need to see Octavian in perspective. In securing political power against enormous odds, he was coldly ruthless, not only perpetrating sadistic cruelties to enemies at Philippi but very possibly the human sacrifice of one hundred enemies at Perusia. Once the alliance of Octavian and Antony defeated Caesar's murderers at Philippi, Octavian's only real competitor for power was Antony – clearly, the much better soldier and thus, in the traditional Roman patriarchal scheme of things, the better man. Although Octavian was capable of great personal courage, his military record was poor, marred by incapacitating illness, for example, at Philippi and elsewhere. However, Octavian was much more calculating than Antony, often betraying his promises to him.[102] He wisely secured the indispensable support and help of two lifetime friends, Agrippa, a brilliant general and administrator, and Maecenas, an excellent diplomat and lover of the arts, who would gather around himself, and thus later around Augustus, poets of the stature of Propertius, Horace, and Vergil.

Octavian always held before his eyes the example of Julius Caesar: a man of military and political genius, courageous, an individualist, improvisatory, famously quick in his responses, one of Rome's best writers and orators, a passionate lover of women in and outside marriage including Cleopatra,

---

[100] Sallust, *The Conspiracy of Catiline*, in *The Jugurthine War/The Conspiracy of Catiline*, translated by S. A. Handford (London: Penguin, 1963), pp. 175–233, at p. 192.

[101] Ibid., at p. 193.

[102] See Anthony Everitt, *Augustus: The Life of Rome's First Emperor* (New York: Random House, 2006).

Queen of Egypt – perhaps the only woman among his sexual partners who was his equal[103] – and a lover of men. Octavian, in contrast, "constantly quoted such Greek proverbs as 'More haste, less speed,' and 'Give me a safe commander, not a rash one.'"[104] As I earlier observed, there was every reason to think that at the time of Julius Caesar's murder, Antony (the older, more courageous and able military man as well as experienced politician) would have the decisive competitive edge over Octavian, if a competition to the death between them should prove necessary. Consequently, Octavian may have hoped that such a competition would not be necessary. Antony had served under Caesar in his wars, was allied with him politically, and was not involved in his murder, an event which apparently shocked him as much as it did Octavian. Indeed, it was Antony's speech at Caesar's funeral that may have decisively turned the tide of the army and the people against the small group of senators (the Liberators, as they called themselves) who had killed Caesar.[105]

At first, Antony apparently found it difficult to take the nineteen-year-old Octavian seriously, and Octavian sought alliances with senators such as Cicero who were sympathetic to the Liberators, against Antony. But the alliances did not last long; under the triumvirate, Octavian allied himself with Antony and thus agreed to the savage murders of the proscriptions, including Cicero. Cicero's head and hands, used in his oratory, were cut off and prominently displayed on the Speakers' Platform in the Forum, and "it is said that Fulvia took the head in her hands, spat on it and then set it on her knees, opened its mouth, pulled out the tongue and pierced it with hairpins."[106]

Octavian's willingness to work with Antony was cemented by the marriage of Antony to Octavia, who, as Antony's wife, made notable efforts to maintain the alliance when it came under strain because of Antony's affair with Cleopatra. If Antony had been a more conventional Roman patriarchal man, all might have gone well. Certainly, Octavian was, as earlier suggested, a highly corporate leader and could have found a way to work with Antony. But Antony had something that Augustus would never achieve: the common touch, which was part of

> the man's popularity. His troops worshipped him not just for his swagger and profanity, but for the delight he took in public carousing and his pleasure in eating with his men. Many found even his sexual appetites attractive, tempered as they were by a fondness for helping others in their love affairs and a willingness to laugh with others at his own. Again, his lavish generosity

---

[103] See Adrian Goldsworthy, *Caesar*, p. 445.
[104] Suetonius, *The Twelve Caesars*, at p. 58.
[105] On this point, see Ronald Syme, *The Roman Revolution* (Oxford: Oxford University Press, 1985), at pp. 98–9.
[106] Anthony Everitt, *Cicero: The Life and Times of Rome's Greatest Politician* (New York: Random House Trade Paperbacks, 2003), at p. 319.

won him fervent supporters on his road to power. Another man with such traits might be called a braggart, a libertine, and a spendthrift. Antony was forgiven much because he was well-liked.[107]

In *The Second Philippic*, written in the short-lived period of his alliance with Octavian, Cicero had savagely attacked Antony for many of his excesses in eating and drinking and in sex, including his youthful homosexual affair with Curio, the second husband of Antony's then-wife Fulvia, about which Cicero obsessionally rants.[108] These were appetitive excesses that Romans were prepared to forgive. But there was another aspect of Antony's personality that more deeply disturbed patriarchal Romans: showing affection in public to his wife, "a mockery of Roman decorum and decency."[109] It was bad enough to show such affection for a Roman wife (Fulvia), but what Roman patriarchal men, including some of the soldiers who most loved Antony and had followed him for years, evidently could not stomach was his passionately demonstrative sexual love for a foreign woman, Cleopatra VII of Egypt.

Absolute ruler of a wealthy and ancient nation, Cleopatra was highly intelligent, politically ambitious, multilingual, and well educated, someone whom Antony took seriously not only as a sex partner, intimate friend, and fun-loving roisterer but, increasingly, as a political and even military leader. Antony never gave Cleopatra all she wanted or demanded; he rejected, for example, her desire to annex the lands ruled by Herod.[110] But this remarkable woman clearly opened the hearts and minds of two leading Roman men (Caesar and Antony) in ways no Roman woman had. With Caesar, for example,

> [i]t may be that the twenty-two-year-old queen was the first and only person, since the death of his daughter Julia, who had understood Caesar, that she not only amused him and allowed him to conquer her, but knew how to pierce the shell of isolation that increasingly surrounded this man of fifty-two, to tempt him out of it and release him from it – with such insight and affection, such subtlety and grace, that he could perhaps even learn from her and allow himself, in some measure, to be conquered by her, as by no other.[111]

Cleopatra ruled in Egypt both as absolute monarch and as a god (the new Isis) in the tradition of pharaonic rule. She neither understood nor sympathized

---

[107] Edward Champlin, *Nero* (Cambridge, MA: Belknap Press of Harvard University Press, 2003), at p. 172.
[108] Cicero, *Philippics*, translated by Walter C. A. Ker (Cambridge, MA: Harvard University Press, 2001), at pp. 109, 141, 149. On Curio, see Anthony Everitt, *Cicero*, at pp. 119–20; on Curio's marriage to Fulvia, see Richard A. Bauman, *Women and Politics in Ancient Rome*, p. 84.
[109] Ronald Syme, *The Roman Revolution*, p. 150. On this point, see Cicero, *Philippics*, at p. 141.
[110] See Hans Volkmann, *Cleopatra: A Study in Politics and Propaganda*, translated by T. J. Cadoux (London: Elek Books, 1958), at pp. 125–6.
[111] Christian Meier, *Caesar*, at p. 409.

with republican rule, and her influence on Caesar (and later Antony) may have spurred the increasingly monarchical quality of their ambitions. Caesar had brought Cleopatra to Rome with her young son by him. Claiming descent from Venus, Caesar set up in the Temple of Venus Genetrix, the mother of Aeneas, a golden statue of Cleopatra opposite that of the goddess. Cleopatra was in Rome at the time of Caesar's murder; thinking of herself as the new Isis, she may have experienced this event as the traumatic murder of Osiris. From this perspective, her passion for Antony may have had a deeply personal, religious significance: in sexually loving him, she brought back to life, as Isis did for Osiris (and all pharaohs over time), the man she loved.

Cleopatra's love for Antony had, if anything, a more profound impact on him both as a man and a military and political leader in ways that scandalized even the Romans who loved him, let alone his enemies, notably Octavian, who came to seek a way to defeat him decisively.[112] Perhaps the closest historical text to the events in question is Plutarch's *Antony* (the central influence on Shakespeare's play), where he describes Antony's love thus:

> Antony showed to all the world that he was no longer motivated by the thoughts and motives of a commander or a man, or indeed by his own judgment at all, but what was once said as a jest, that the soul of a lover lives in some one else's body, he proved to be a serious truth.[113]

The turning point for Octavian was Antony's divorce of Octavia, which not only broke the bonds that had united Octavian and Antony but, from the perspective of Octavian's highly patriarchal conception of honor, also dishonored him as Octavia's brother, an insult to honor that would elicit and legitimate violence. With the indispensable assistance in war of Agrippa and in diplomacy of Maecenas, Octavian had defeated Pompey's son, who had threatened Rome's food supply; Antony, in contrast, had had to abandon his war on the Parthians.

The decisive act, however, was Antony's marriage to Cleopatra in circumstances that included public ceremonies of their reigning as corulers of the Eastern Empire with Alexandria as their capital. A bitter propaganda war followed between Octavian and Antony in which the highly gendered terms of Roman patriarchy were prominently invoked on both sides.[114] Octavian could draw on not only the patriarchally defined invective of Cicero's *Second Philippic* but also Roman patriarchy's common sense that a woman ruler in

---

[112] For a more skeptical view, see Anthony Everitt, *Augustus*, at pp. 147–8, 156–7.
[113] Plutarch, *Antony*, in Plutarch, *The Lives of Noble Grecians and Romans*, translated by John Dryden (New York: Modern Library, n.d.), pp. 1105–53, at p. 1142.
[114] See Hans Volkmann, *Cleopatra*, pp. 155–62; Josiah Osgood, *Caesar's Legacy: Civil War and the Emergence of the Roman Empire* (Cambridge: Cambridge University Press, 2006), at pp. 344–7.

the domain of politics and war was unnatural and that a Roman political and military leader sharing rule with her was unnatural as well. When Rome declares war, it will do so on Cleopatra, the foreigner queen, not on Antony, the beloved and generous general who had, from the Roman point of view, lost his patriarchal mind to a woman. In this propaganda war, Antony never stood a chance, particularly once he refused the plea of his advisers that Cleopatra not be present at the final military confrontation with the forces of Octavian and Agrippa at Actium.

It is at this point that some of Antony's closest friends defected to Octavian, taking with them confidential information about Antony's will that Octavian would ruthlessly make public, including the provision, against all law and custom, that Cleopatra was to be his heir and that Antony and Cleopatra were both to be buried in Alexandria, not Rome. It is doubtful that there was ever much of a battle at Actium, and what took place there was abortive for Antony when he left in the midst of the sea battle to follow Cleopatra's ship back to Egypt. The soldiers who had loved Antony found all this incomprehensible. They defected to Octavian, leaving Antony and Cleopatra to commit suicide and be buried in Alexandria in a common tomb.[115]

Octavian won the conflict with Antony because, on balance, he was the more astute political and military leader of Roman men. Octavian identified himself with Apollo, Antony with Bacchus and Hercules. Octavian loved a Roman woman, Livia, who helped advance his political ambitions, but always within the closeted terms that patriarchal women traditionally observed; Antony loved a foreign women and queen, publicly sharing both political and military power with her in ways that scandalized Roman patriarchal values. Octavian identified his life and his rule, as Augustus, with traditional Roman patriarchal religion. Antony, in contrast, gravitated to the religions of Greece and Egypt, including the religion of Isis, which Augustus and Tiberius would forbid in Rome.[116] These differences clarify Octavian's victory and Antony's defeat.

Whether, as men in their relationships to the women they loved, they lived as differently as the propaganda war between them might suggest is another question. A letter we have from Antony to Octavian, before their decisive break, suggests an underlying common way of life:

> What has come over you? Do you object to my sleeping with Cleopatra? But we are married; and it is not even as though this were anything new – the

---

[115] For an illuminating history of these events, see Robert Alan Gurval, *Actium and Augustus: The Politics and Emotions of Civil War* (Ann Arbor: The University of Michigan Press, 1995); Josiah Osgood, *Caesar's Legacy*; Ronald Syme, *The Roman Revolution*.
[116] See Mary Beard et al., *Religions of Rome*, Vol. I-A. History, pp. 230–31.

affair started nine years ago. And what about you? Are you faithful to Livia Drusilla? My congratulations if, when this letter arrives, you have not been in bed with Tertullia, or Terentilla, or Rufilla, or Salvia Titisenia – or all of them. Does it really matter so much where, or with whom, you perform the sexual act?[117]

What came between them was their different relationships to Roman patriarchy: Octavian identifying himself with its traditional values and way of life, Antony coming through passionate sexual love to a stance of resistance.

After the defeat of Antony, Octavian, now Augustus, undertook to intensify the hold of patriarchy on Roman public and private life, as if patriarchy, not republican self-government, was essential to Roman political and military successes. This included the revival of ancient Roman religious rituals and a massive building program that would give them an architectural expression.[118] His wife Livia's restoration of a temple of Fortuna Muliebris revived the cult connected to the legend surrounding Coriolanus, established early in the fifth century B.C.E., which honored the patriarchal role exemplified by Coriolanus's mother in saving Rome at the expense of her son.[119] Augustus's program of restoration included legislation sponsored by him that sought to return Roman family life to its traditional forms, in particular, putting the patriarchal lid back on the men and women who had enjoyed greater sexual liberties in the late republic.

In contrast to Caesar's rule, Augustus's was a corporate undertaking that retained the forms of the republic but consolidated ultimate power in himself and his ruling circle (including, crucially, Agrippa, Maecenas, and, behind the scenes, Livia). He established an imperial autocracy and bequeathed it to his successors, who would render it even more autocratic and absolutist because it was much less intelligently corporate than Augustus's rule. This shift in political power achieved covertly what Caesar could not achieve overtly – the end of the republic – thus stripping the Roman Senate and people of the powers of self-government that they had enjoyed under the long history of republican government. To understand the depth of this conflict, we need to be clear that Octavian's success, as Augustus, turned at crucial points not only on the way he rather conspicuously lived his life as a patriarchal Roman man but also on the way, early in his political career, he aggressively used the gender ideology of Roman patriarchy against his enemies – in particular, Antony.

---

[117] Suetonius, *The Twelve Caesars*, at p. 86.
[118] On these points, see Paul Zanker, *The Power of Images in the Age of Augustus*, translated by Alan Shapiro (Ann Arbor: The University of Michigan Press, 1990); Karl Galinsky, *Augustan Culture* (Princeton, NJ: Princeton University Press, 1996).
[119] Anthony A. Barrett, *Livia*, at p. 205.

At the heart of this reactionary legislative program was the *Lex Julia de adulteriis coercendis*, which punished the nonmarital sexual relations of adultery and criminal fornication (any sexual relations of or with a virgin or a widow), adultery incontestably being the main offense condemned. Through this legislation, Augustus drastically curtailed the range of possible sexual partners for Roman men outside marriage, at least insofar as this range was defined at law. Exempt women included prostitutes, procuresses, slaves, convicted adulteresses, and foreigners not wed to Roman citizens. Other laws included the *Lex Julia et Papia*, which imposed restrictions on marriage (members of the senatorial order, for example, could not marry freedmen or freedwomen) and limited the rules of succession (for example, the unmarried could not inherit under a will). Further measures related to public life gave precedence to men with children in political life and prohibited unmarried from attending public spectacles and entertainments. None of these measures was popular because they limited the freedoms that Roman men and women had traditionally assumed. They were, however, required, Augustus argued, for the revival of Roman virtue, by which he meant patriarchal virtue.[120]

Before the passage of the *Lex Julia de adulteriis coercendis*, the repression of sexual misbehavior had been a private matter. If the husband caught an adulterous pair in the act, he might kill both parties on the spot. Other cases dealt with punishment by the father of the offending woman. Under the *Lex Julia*, such acts were punished for the first time by a trial in a standing criminal court, the *quaestio perpetua de adulteries*. Criminal penalties were ordained for the adulterous female spouse and her lover. These included exile to separate islands for both parties, as well as confiscation of one-half of the lover's property and one-third of the adulteress's, as well as one-half of her dowry. A woman convicted under the Augustan adultery statute was forbidden to remarry.[121] The movement over time to severer penalties culminated in the provisions of Constantius and Constans in 339, which called for severe enforcement of the law against adultery and also decreed that adulterers be punished "as though they were manifest parricides," by being sown up in a leather sack with a dog, a cock, a viper, and a monkey, and cast into a river or the sea.[122]

The *Lex Julia de adulteriis coercendis*, like most criminal statutes, allowed anyone to launch an accusation. Yet, unlike other criminal statutes, this statute

---

[120] See Thomas A. J. McGinn, *Prostitution, Sexuality, and the Law in Ancient Rome* (New York: Oxford University Press, 1998), at pp. 70–104.

[121] Ibid., pp. 140–215.

[122] See David Cohen, "The Augustan Law on Adultery: The Social and Cultural Context," in David I. Kertzer and Richard P. Saller, *The Family in Italy from Antiquity to the Present* (New Haven, CT: Yale University Press, 1991), pp. 109–26, at p. 125.

created a special right of accusation of the husband and father of the woman accused of adultery. The right of the father was as accessory to that of the husband, in the sense that it turned on the act of the latter (divorce) to be legitimized and stipulated that where both raised an accusation, the husband was to be preferred.

Another feature of the law was the *ius occidendi*. This granted the husband and father the right to kill the guilty party or parties on the spot. Here, the respective positions of husband and father were the reverse of the *ius accusandi*: the father was given pride of place. He might kill both daughter and lover (presumably, as an expression of legitimate patriarchal rage), but under no circumstances might the husband kill his wife.

The *Lex Julia* lowered the status of the wife found guilty of adultery to that of a prostitute and correspondingly defined the actions of a complaisant husband as *leocinium*, an accessory as fully liable as the principals. At the same time, it exempted true prostitutes and procuresses from its sanctions. They were able to practice their professions without fear of prosecution for adultery, fornication, or *lenocinium*. In short, the law created certain defined statuses for women, statuses that reflected a traditional complex of patriarchal values in establishing a firm connection between social rank and acceptable sexual behavior – good married women had sex only with their husbands, whereas bad married women had sex extramaritally and in doing so were the equivalent of prostitutes.

Roman men and women were not enthusiastic about this legislation, and two striking examples of Roman women's resistance to it have come down to us. In the first, some Roman women sought to evade the punishment meted out to a woman under the *Lex Julia*, as well as an outright ban placed on the practice of prostitution by women of the equestrian and senatorial orders. For example, Vistilia, of upper-class lineage, attempted to escape prosecution for adultery by claiming the exempt status of a prostitute. The Senate passed judgment on Vistilia, exiling her to an island, and decided that henceforth no women whose grandfather, father, or husband had been a Roman *eques* would be permitted to prostitute herself, thus closing the loophole in the adultery law that Vistilia had tried to exploit.[123]

The second and more striking example was of resistance within the imperial family itself, first by Julia the Elder, daughter of Augustus, and later by Julia the Younger, Julia's daughter. Julia was Augustus's only surviving child, the daughter of his marriage to Scribonia, whom he divorced to marry Livia. Consistent with the role played by patriarchal values in his public and private

---

[123] See Thomas A. J. McGinn, *Prostitution, Sexuality, and the Law in Ancient Rome*, at pp. 216–19.

life, Augustus carefully supervised the education of his daughter and granddaughters, making sure it

> included even spinning and weaving; they were forbidden to say or do anything, either publicly or in private, that could not decently figure in the imperial day-book. He took severe measures to prevent them forming friendships without his consent, and once wrote to Lucius Vinicius, a young man of good family and conduct: "You were very ill-mannered to visit my daughter at Baiae."[124]

Like other patriarchal Roman men, Augustus arranged marriages for Julia that were designed to advance his dynastic purposes. She was married first to Marcellus, the son of his sister Octavia, and then, after Marcellus's untimely death, to Agrippa, who had been so important in Augustus's rise to power and success. With Agrippa she had five children: Agrippina the Elder, Gaius, Lucius, Julia the Younger, and Agrippa Postumus, two of whom, Gaius and Lucius, were groomed by Augustus to succeed him (although both, to Augustus's grief, died as young men). After Agrippa's death, Augustus married Julia to Livia's son Tiberius, another possible successor to the principate, who, in fact, did succeed Augustus. Neither Julia nor Tiberius wanted the marriage: Julia was "defiant and unfriendly to her new husband,"[125] and Tiberius had been forced to divorce a woman he loved, Vipsania, who had already borne him one son and was pregnant with another. Suetonius tells us:

> Tiberius continued to regret the divorce so heartily that when, one day, he accidentally caught sight of Vipsania and followed her with tears in his eyes and intense unhappiness written on his face, precautions were taken against his ever seeing her again.[126]

Julia had evidently been having affairs with various men for years (as Augustus had with various women,[127] including the wife of his friend, Maecenas),[128] even during her marriage to Agrippa. When asked about how, in light of this, she had always managed to have children that resembled Agrippa, she replied: "Passengers are never allowed on board until the hold is full."[129] Augustus

---

[124] Suetonius, *The Twelve Caesars*, at p. 82.
[125] Tacitus, *The Annals of Imperial Rome*, p. 63.
[126] Suetonius, *The Twelve Caesars*, at pp. 112–13.
[127] Ibid., at p. 85.
[128] See Pat Southern, *Augustus* (London: Routledge, 2001), at p. 154. See also Anthony Everitt, *Augustus: The Life of Rome's First Emperor* (New York: Random House, 2006).
[129] Macrobius, *Saturnalia*, translated by Percival Vaughan Davies (New York: Columbia University Press, 1969), at p. 177.

had, of course, earlier passed the *Lex Julia*, which subjected such adulteries to criminal prosecution.

The crisis year for Julia and her father over this matter came, strikingly, in precisely the year 2 B.C.E., when Augustus, in light of his achievements, accepted the title *Pater Patriae*, Father of the Fatherland.[130] Augustus had by this time deeply invested his sense of self not only in traditional Roman patriarchal values but also in an attempt to legitimate his rule and end republican self-government by reviving ancient patriarchal religious practices, the neglect of which he believed and wanted others to believe had been responsible for the civil wars. The *Lex Julia* was clearly a cornerstone of what he regarded as his life's work – work Romans now rather sycophantically applauded. Julia's adulteries at this point took a conspicuously public form, including "revels and drinking parties by night in the Forum and even upon the Rostra"[131] (the platforms from which speakers spoke). Seneca gives us the fullest description:

> The deified Augustus relegated his own daughter, who was so promiscuous as to be beyond reproach of promiscuity, and made public the scandals of the imperial household: to wit, the lovers were admitted in droves, that the city was traversed with nightly revels, that the very Forum and speakers' platform, from which her father had proposed his legislation on adultery, received her vote as a venue for fornication, that there was a daily gathering about the statue of Marsyas, when, having turned from an adulteress into a prostitute, she sought the right to every sexual indulgence under a lover who was an utter stranger to her.[132]

Seneca, with typical rhetorical overkill, calls Julia a prostitute, as the *Lex Julia* would require. But both the publicity and the place of her sexual revels suggest public protest, specifically of her father's legislation. The statue of Marsyas may have been a place where prostitutes gathered, but Marsyas was also, symbolically, a satyr who challenged Apollo, the god with whom Augustus most closely identified. There is another point that Seneca strikingly underscores elsewhere, that the sex was freighted with a larger meaning both for Julia and her lovers, and the meaning clearly invokes, almost ritually, the love of Cleopatra and Antony (one of Julia's most prominent lovers was Iullus Antonius, the son of Octavia and Antony): "[A]ll the noble youths [were] bound

---

[130] See Beth Severy, *Augustus and the Family at the Birth of the Roman Empire* (London: Routledge, 2003), at pp. 158–61.

[131] Cassius Dio, *The Roman History: The Reign of Augustus*, translated by Ian Scott-Kilvert (London: Penguin, 1987), p. 199.

[132] Quoted in Thomas A. J. McGinn, *Prostitution, Sexuality, and the Law in Ancient Rome*, at pp. 168–9.

to her by adultery as though by an oath kept alarming his [Augustus's] feeble old age, as did Iullus and a second formidable woman linked to an Antony."[133]

Roman historians such as Velleius Paterculus tend to sexualize Julia, "setting up her own caprice as a law unto itself."[134] Seneca does so as well, but the sexual bond between Julia and her lovers, "adultery as though by an oath," suggests to me that there may have been a moral, even religious, point to the public form her actions took, a self-conscious enactment precisely of a Bacchanalian rite of the sort the Senate under the republic had (as we earlier saw) forbidden, and Bacchus had been, of course, the god with whom Antony most closely identified. It seems reasonable to think that we may have here a public religious rite that, by its timing, place, and the identity of its participants (the daughter of Augustus and the son of Antony) protested Augustus's legislation against adultery in an act of public resistance, defiantly invoking the memory of the lovers, Cleopatra and Antony, along with an alternative religious tradition, that of Bacchus or the cult of Isis, in which the sexuality of free women like Cleopatra was celebrated and valued. Julia would certainly have known of her father's many adulteries and, by identifying herself as an adulteress in this way, would also be raising the age-old question of the hypocrisy of the double standard, except that she was willing to admit in public to what Roman men like Augustus did in private.

Augustus's anger was extreme: "[H]e was filled with rage,"[135] and his actions were brutal:

> He wrote a letter about her case to the Senate, staying at home while a quaestor read it to them. He even considered her execution; at any rate, hearing that one Phoebe, a freedwoman in Julia's confidence, had hanged herself, he cried: "I should have preferred to be Phoebe's father!" Julia was forbidden to drink wine or enjoy any other luxury during her exile; and denied all male company, whether free or servile, except by Augustus' special permission and after he had been given full particulars of the applicant's age, height, complexion, and of any distinguishing marks on his body – such as moles or scars. He kept Julia for five years on a prison island before moving her to the mainland, where she received somewhat milder treatment.[136]

Most of Julia's lovers were exiled, but Iullus Antonius (brought up in the imperial household with Julia, himself a noted poet, married to one of the

---

[133] Seneca, *On the Shortness of Life*, translated by C. D. N. Costa (London: Penguin, 1997), at p. 7.
[134] Velleius Paterculus, *Res Gestae Divi Augusti* (Cambridge, MA: Harvard University Press, 2002), at p. 259.
[135] Cassius Dio, *The Roman History: The Reign of Augustus*, at p. 199.
[136] Suetonius, *The Twelve Caesar*, at pp. 82–3.

daughters of Octavia, and having served in various posts of distinction under the Augustan regime, including a priesthood, and as praetor, consul, and governor of a province) was compelled to commit suicide.[137] When it came to the son of Antony, Augustus's rage became homicidal.

Even to contemporaries who otherwise rarely challenged him, Augustus's actions (and the underlying rage) seemed disproportionate:

> [N]othing would persuade him to forgive his daughter; and when the Roman people interceded several times on her behalf, earnestly pleading for her recall, he stormed at a popular assembly: "If you ever bring up this matter again, may the gods curse you with daughters and wives like mine!"[138]

Seneca tells us that Augustus himself came to regret what he had done:

> Afterwards, when by lapse of time shame took the place of anger in his mind, he lamented that he had not kept silence about matters which he had not learned until it was disgraceful to speak of them, and often used to exclaim, "None of these things would have happened to me, if either Agrippa or Maecenas had lived."[139]

The later historian Tacitus makes clear how intemperately Augustus viewed what Julia had done and that his autocratic treatment of her did not conform either to Roman custom or to the due process required by his own legislation: "[H]e used the solemn names of sacrilege and treason for the common offence of misconduct between the sexes. This was inconsistent with traditional tolerance and even with his own legislation."[140]

It was Augustus's own frenzied interpretation of his daughter's resistance (as "sacrilege and treason") that may have led to Pliny's interpretation of it in terms of "her plots against her father's life,"[141] an interpretation considered baseless.[142] What I believe the record clearly shows is a daughter's increasingly public, conscientious resistance to her father's legislation targeting women's sexuality.

We know that Julia was the only child of Augustus, trained, as we have seen, in Augustus's own highly gendered conception of women's roles and one who,

---

[137] Velleius Paterculus, *Rest Gestae Divi Augusti*, at p. 259.
[138] Suetonius, *The Twleve Caesars*, at p. 83.
[139] Lucius Annaeus Seneca, *On Benefits* (North Sydney, Australia: Objective Systems Pty Ltd., 2006), at p. 415.
[140] Tacitus, *The Annals of Imperial Rome*, at p. 131.
[141] Pliny the Elder, *Natural History: A Selection*, translated by John F. Healy (London: Penguin, 2004), at p. 98.
[142] On this point, see Arthur Ferrill, "Augustus and His Daughter: A Modern Myth," in Carl Deroux, ed., *Studies in Latin Literature and Roman History II* (Bruxelles: Latomus, 1980), pp. 332–46.

for much of her life, did her duty as those roles demanded: her marriages were arranged by Augustus to advance his dynastic ends, and at least two of the children produced in those marriages were clearly intended by Augustus to succeed him – and would have, had circumstances permitted. Macrobius preserves more intimate details of Julia's relationship to her father ("she habitually misused the kindness of her own good fortune and her father's indulgence"),[143] including three incidents of her good-humored, witty responses to Augustus's attempts to hold her in line.[144] First, there was Augustus's shock at her wearing an immodest dress, but he kept silent, and upon seeing her in a more modest dress, praised her as wearing something "more becoming in the daughter of Augustus," to which Julia replied: "Yes, for today I am dressed to meet my father's eyes; yesterday it was for my husband's."[145] Second, at a display of gladiators, Augustus critically noted that the suite of his wife Livia contained older men of distinction, whereas Julia was surrounded by "young people of the fast set." Her father sent his daughter a letter of advice, "bidding her mark the difference between the behavior of the two chief ladies of Rome," to which she replied, "These friends of mine will be old men too, when I am old."[146] Third, when a friend urged Julia to conform more closely with Augustus's simple tastes she replied, "He forgets that he is Caesar, but I remember that I am Caesar's daughter."[147]

Macrobius also preserves deeper divergences both of ethics and temperament between Julia and her father. Julia's views of sexuality may have been those of the Roman daughter who, to someone asking in surprise why it was that among the lower animals the female sought to mate with the male only when she wished to conceive, replied, "Because they *are* the lower animals."[148] In addition, Macrobius writes of "her high spirits," noting that she

> had a love of letters and a considerable store of learning – not hard to come by in her home – and to those qualities were added a gentle humanity and a kindly disposition, all of which won for her a high regard; although those who were aware of her faults were astonished at the contradiction which her qualities implied.[149]

---

[143] Macrobius, *The Saturnalia*, p. 176.
[144] On Julia's wit, see Amy Richlin, "Julia's Jokes, Galla Placidia, and the Roman Use of Women as Political Icons," in Barbara Garlick, Suzanne Dixon, and Pauline Allen, *Stereotypes of Women in Power: Historical Perspectives and Revisionist Views* (New York: Greenwood Press, 1992), at pp. 65–91.
[145] Ibid., p. 177.
[146] Ibid., p. 177.
[147] Ibid., p. 177.
[148] Ibid., p. 177.
[149] Ibid., p. 176.

I am struck by the Roman patriarchal sense of a contradiction between Julia's free sexuality and her intelligence and goodness, "a gentle humanity and a kindly disposition," similar to what we observed earlier in Salust's description of Sempronia. In my view, there is no such contradiction. To the contrary, it is precisely the kind of free sexuality one finds in Julia and Sempronia that clarifies the psychological basis of their resistance to Roman patriarchal claims, in Julia's case, to her father's own legislation and the underlying hypocrisy she believed it reflected.

The wider significance of such resistance is suggested by the republican Roman historian Tacitus, who, in contrast to Lucan and Seneca, does not even attempt to justify the imperial autocracy[150] but anatomizes its moral and political enormities. Strikingly, he prefaces his own unusually powerful attack on Augustus's legislation dealing with the family, including the *Lex Julia* and other statutes, with the history of the treatment of Julia by her father. For Tacitus, Julia was critically questioning legislation that attacked essential freedoms of Roman republican liberty, making possible the supine and sycophantic citizenry that would accept "peace and the Principate."[151] Tacitus was in no sense what we would today call a feminist, but I am struck by the feminist edge in the way such an acute critic of the imperial system makes Augustus's legislation central to his criticism. As Tacitus saw it, Augustus's aim was to end the political equality central to the rule of law of the Roman Republic, noting that "when men ceased to be equal, egotism replaced fellow-feeling and decency succumbed to violence. The result was despotism."[152] Augustus's legislation was to quash the equal liberties of intimate sexual life so that men, losing any sense of a dignity rooted in personal freedom, would accept the loss of the republic. For this purpose,

> restraints [of essential liberties] were stricter. There were spies, encouraged by inducements from the Papian-Poppaean law, under which failure to earn the advantages of parenthood meant loss of property to the State as universal parent. The spreading encroachments of these informers grievously affected all citizens, whether in Rome, Italy, or elsewhere, and caused widespread ruin and universal panic.[153]

Tacitus describes the impact of such legislation on Roman male citizens, whose political competences required a psychological basis, both personally

---

[150] For such defenses, see Matthew B. Roller, *Constructing Autocracy: Aristocrats and Emperiors in Juliu-Claudian Rome* (Princeton, NJ: Princeton University Press, 2001).
[151] Tacitus, *The Annals of Imperial Rome*, at p. 133.
[152] Ibid., p. 132.
[153] Ibid., p. 133.

and politically, in "freedom and wholeheartedness,"[154] the right to make decisions regarding intimate matters of sexual love rooted in an appropriate respect for the essential freedoms of mind and body. What Augustus's legislation aimed to achieve was a legal and political war on precisely such freedoms, a traumatic disruption of intimate life that would give rise to a dissociation from one's mind and body and foster the acceptance of political autocracy – what Tacitus called the tyranny of imperial rule.[155]

Tacitus makes his critical point in terms of the impact of such legislation on Roman male citizens, but the very fact of Julia's resistance, as I understand it, shows that the same psychological process would apply to women as well. That Julia drew to her so many important Roman men supports my sense that we are dealing here with a significant historical example, perhaps one of the first such examples, of men joining with women to protect and sustain one of the freedoms at the heart of a democratic republic.

Thus understood, Augustus's rage makes sense as he faces, as an older man a daughter's resistance, which must have struck him to the heart as the return of the repressed, his old enemies Antony and Cleopatra, on whose defeat his own success depended. As Augustus breaks relationship with the daughter he clearly had loved, or thought he had loved, we glimpse the loneliness of a patriarchal man who had carried Roman patriarchy to its logical conclusion, ending the democratic republic Rome had historically enjoyed and under which it had prospered. In the midst of such division between Augustus and his daughter, we note that one person who reenters history at this point is Scribonia, the mother of Julia, with whom Julia had not lived for most of her life: "[H]er mother Scribonia accompanied her [Julia] and remained with her as a voluntary companion of her exile."[156]

That Julia's resistance reflects something psychologically deep in Roman women of her period and background is shown by its recurrence in her daughter, Julia the Younger, in 8 C.E. A new public scandal gripped Rome: Julia, it was alleged, had slipped into the adulterous ways of her mother. She was therefore relegated to a barren island where she would remain for twenty years.[157] This time, however, Augustus's anger extended not only to his granddaughter but to one of Rome's greatest poets, Ovid. Ovid was not actively complicit

---

[154] Leo Ferrero Raditsa, "Augustus' Legislation Concerning Marriage, Procreation, Love Affairs, and Adultery," in *Aufstieg und Niedergang Der Romischen Welt* (Berlin: Walter De Gruyter, 1980), pp. 278–339, at p. 329.
[155] On the role of disassociation as the basis for political tyranny, see ibid., pp. 329, 335.
[156] Velleius Paterculus, op. cit., at p. 259.
[157] See Tacitus, *The Annals of Imperial Rome*, at pp. 192–3; Ronald Syme, *The Roman Revolution*, p. 432.

with the scandal, yet Augustus was vindictive toward an erotic poet who had not served the state but, rather, had addressed himself to celebrating the erotic lives of Roman men and women. He used the occasion of Julia's disgrace "to make a demonstration – perhaps to find a scapegoat whose very harmlessness would divert attention from the real offences of Julia."[158] Ovid was exiled to Tomi, a Greek city on the coast of the Black Sea, where he would spend the rest of his life.

I am struck by the vindictiveness of Augustus's rage at the sexual voices and lives of his daughter and granddaughter and at a great Roman poet who took such voices seriously. Augustus had made a choice between democracy and patriarchy, clearly opting for patriarchy, a reactionary form of which he used to justify not only his victory over Antony but also his success in becoming Rome's first absolute ruler since the expulsion of the Tarquins.

At the end of his life, Augustus made two remarks, one directed at his public, the other for Livia alone: to his friends, "Have I played my part in the farce of life creditably enough?"[159]; to Livia, "Goodbye, Livia: never forget our marriage."[160] Augustus, self-consciously as actor, was <u>the man who not only acted as though traditional Roman institutions still existed but also claimed to have restored many such institutions.</u> Something had gone terribly wrong, leading to the civil wars, and Augustus's task had been to restore Roman institutions so that this internecine bloodshed would never occur again. In fact, Augustus ended what had made Rome the leading imperial power of the world, its republican government. In the acid terms of Tacitus, "there was nothing left of the fine old Roman character. Political equality was a thing of the past; all eyes watched for imperial commands.... [A]t Rome, consuls, senate, knights, precipitately became servile."[161]

Augustus was able to succeed in this charade, persuading others as well as himself, because he had come to value patriarchy as the supreme value of Roman life, eliminating its tension with republican institutions and values. Thus his appeal, at the moment of his death, surely as sincere as anything Augustus had said or done, to his highly patriarchal marriage as the one value never to be forgotten. Livia had played the role of good Roman wife as no woman of her generation did or could, which explains the honors Augustus heaped on her both during his life and after his death.[162] His daughter Julia,

---

[158] Ronald Syme, *The Roman Revolution*, at p. 468.
[159] Suetonius, *The Twelve Caesars*, p. 104.
[160] Ibid., p. 105.
[161] Tacitus, *Annals of Imperial Rome*, at pp. 33, 35.
[162] See, in general, Anthony A. Barrett, *Livia: First Lady of Imperial Rome* (New Haven, CT: Yale University Press, 2002).

however, came to resist such roles, and her conflict with her father became catastrophic for them both.

Augustus drew his power and appeal from the internecine violence of the civil wars, which he claimed to have ended. But the problem of Roman violence, rooted in the honor codes of patriarchy, did not end with Augustus. If anything, the violence, in an absolutist state form, had fewer limitations than had existed even in the worst days of the republic. No one studied more acutely how and why Augustus's concentration of power in the emperors corrupted them than did Tacitus, who shows how a good man and leader like Tiberius, once he acquiesced in the destruction of his personal happiness by divorcing the woman he loved, had "been transformed and deranged by absolute power."[163] If this could happen to Tiberius, it could happen to lesser men, and it often did, as the subsequent history of the Roman emperors clearly shows (think of Caligula, Nero, and Domitian in the first century alone). It is also under Augustus that the Roman army was put on an increasingly well-paid professional footing, no longer bound, as it had been under the republic, to the regular military service of citizens, and clearly owning allegiance to the emperor alone, who paid them. Roman soldiers thus increasingly lived in isolation from the rest of Roman culture, subject to Augustus's command, for example, that they not marry, an unthinkable requirement under the republic.[164] Over time, it was Roman armies rather than Roman citizens that determined who should rule in Rome, and the wars among these armies under the empire became as bad as, if not worse than, the civil wars. So Augustus, who thought he was solving the problem of Roman violence, had in fact exacerbated it. And the power of Roman elite women, if anything, increased.

Both Agrippina the Elder and her daughter Agrippina the Younger (wife of the Emperor Claudius and mother of Nero) were Roman political women very much on the model of Fulvia. As I have indicated, Roman elite women had always played important, indeed crucial, roles in Rome's patriarchal system, but behind the scenes. Livia, Augustus's wife, was in this mode; her husband took her advice seriously and often followed it, as shown by Augustus's remarkable practice of always writing down his speeches for Livia before he made them.[165] Her political shrewdness is attested by no less than Caligula, who referred to his great-grandmother as "Ulysses in petticoats."[166] Agrippina, mother and daughter, exercised their political power openly. Agrippina

---

[163] Tacitus, *The Annals of Imperial Rome*, at p. 225.
[164] See, on these points, Lawrence Keppie, *The Making of the Roman Army From Republic to Empire* (Norman: University of Oklahoma Press, 1984), at pp. 147–55.
[165] See Suetonius, *The Twelve Caesars*, at p. 94.
[166] Ibid., at p. 162.

the Elder joined her husband Germanicus when he led Roman troops in Germany. When after the death of Augustus the troops mutinied and refused to obey Germanicus, Agrippina, then pregnant and with her young son Caligula, shamed Roman troops into obedience to her husband. She later stepped in to rescue her husband from his mistakes, assuming the role of a commander by helping soldiers and, at a crucial point, blocking the demolition of a bridge over the Rhine by terrified Roman soldiers, thus saving her husband's armies across the river in Germany.[167] Tiberius, the new emperor, was enraged by the public role Agrippina took and, after the death of Germanicus, exiled her – this woman who so furiously resisted the soldiers that she lost an eye. Tiberius was later responsible for her death, as well as the deaths of her sons Nero and Drusus.

Agrippina the Younger displayed the same qualities as her mother both as the wife of Emperor Claudius and the mother of Nero, who, largely because of her efforts (which may have included the poisoning of Claudius), succeeded Claudius. Her assistance to her husband may have been as significant as Livia's to Augustus, but when her son became emperor, her insistence on playing a more public role in politics may have been one of the reasons he turned on her with homicidal rage.[168] Men like Tiberius and Nero were threatened in their honor by women like Agrippina, mother and daughter, and, as with patriarchal men everywhere, an insult to honor elicits violence.

In sum, the root of the problem, in my analysis, lay in Augustus's uncritical acceptance of Roman patriarchy, which, if anything, took a more rigid and absolutist form under his rule. Roman religion had always been highly patriarchal and political, but previously it was subject to final political control by a collegial body, the republican Senate. Under Augustus, the emperor as *pontifex maximus* centralized such control in himself, self-consciously reviving ancient rituals played out on the stage of a massive building program of new temples and the like and imposing on Romans of his generation the more rigid forms of patriarchy that his laws on the family both reflected and enforced. It was this patriarchal legacy that the Christian Church was to absorb uncritically when, under Constantine and his successors, it became the established church of the Roman Empire.

This study thus begins with the powerful role patriarchy played in Augustus's success. Its legacy was the patriarchal construction of manhood that he enlisted to rationalize what he achieved, including the legislative force he brought

---

[167] See, on these points, Anthony A. Barrett, *Agrippina: Sex, Power, and Politics in the Early Empire* (New Haven: Yale University Press, 1996), at pp. 26–7.
[168] For an illuminating study, see Anthony A. Barrett, *Agrippina*.

to bear on restricting women's sexuality. The loss of republican freedoms coincided with a loss of sexual freedom – a coincidence I continue to explore in this text and seek to explain. I earlier suggested that the study of Vergil's *Aeneid* clarifies the personal and political psychology that sustained the appeal of Augustus. I then turned to two conversion narratives that bear directly on our question: Apuleius's *Metamorphoses*, which plots a way out of patriarchy, much in the spirit of the resisting Roman women we have studied in this chapter, and Augustine's *Confessions*, which shows how a patriarchal construction of Roman manhood framed Christianity's understanding of its role and mission. It is of particular interest, in light of my observations thus far, that the conversion narrative of the *Metamorphoses* involves the achievement of equality in an intimate and healing sexual relationship between a man and a woman, Cupid and Psyche, leading to the birth of their daughter named Pleasure and reflected as well in the religion of Isis. In contrast, Augustine's *Confessions* tracks a conversion from sexuality to celibacy and from an intimate, loving relationship with a woman to misogyny and intolerance, including Christian anti-Semitism.

BRITISH PATRIARCHY

Several of the most striking features of Roman patriarchy have no analogue in British political experience. The most striking of these differences is the connection of Roman imperialism to the Roman Republic, based, quite early on, on ending the rule of kings, and a conception of republican rule crucially linked to universal military service by Roman citizens under the leadership of an aristocratic and highly competitive elite of military leaders, exemplified, as we have seen, by the connected military and political powers of Pompey and Julius Caesar. It is only relatively late in Roman history that the remarkable military successes of the Roman republican armies in defeating all external enemies led to the psychologically explosive vacuum of external enemies that expressed itself in the internecine civil wars and the end of the republic in the autocratic conception of imperial rule that followed for the next four centuries. What made this vacuum so psychologically incendiary was the extraordinary power of the patriarchal personal and political psychology over the Roman psyche: any challenge to one's patriarchally defined sense of honor elicited violence. Without a common enemy on whom this psychology could fasten, Rome's competitive aristocratic leaders turned on one another. After this period, the Roman Empire proper was ruled by emperors, several of whom were not skilled military leaders on the old republican model. Roman armies, in turn, were increasingly manned not by Roman citizens but by non-Romans paid by and owing allegiance to the emperor. These armies increasingly controlled the choice of emperor.

British citizenship was never defined, as its Roman counterpart was, by military service; most British men and citizens did not serve in the military and were not asked to exercise the political functions that the Roman Republic demanded of its citizens. "Since the triumph of Prussia's army of conscripts and reservists over the Austrians in 1866 and the French in 1870, all leading European states (Britain, sea-girt and guarded by the world's largest navy, was the exception) had accepted the necessity of submitting their young men to military training in early manhood and of requiring them, once trained, to remain at the state's disposition, as reservists, into late maturity."[169] Mandatory conscription was instituted in Britain only during World War I. Until that time, military service was one option among others for British men, including many of its leading politicians, who never served in the military. Britain certainly had its great military leaders, some of whom exercised political power (Wellington, for example), but the connections between military service and political power were never as close as they were under the Roman Republic: the British, during the growth of its empire, were preoccupied by economic matters, including the changes wrought in human life by the first industrial revolution in human history. British armies always included foreign mercenaries and increasingly depended on military service by people whom it colonially ruled (the sepoys in India).[170]

Many of the British elite who served in the colonies were not soldiers but civil servants who were also highly educated, independent scholars, and, in India in particular, undertook the close study of the complex history of Indian culture. One of them, Sir William Jones, in his remarkable address to the Asiatic Society in 1786, revealed the close affinity among Sanskrit, Greek, and Latin, and hence the ancient connection between India and Europe.[171] Others discovered what the dominant Hindu culture had buried, namely, the teachings on meditation and ethics of the historical Buddha and the important role Buddhism, with its ethical criticism of the caste system, had once played in Indian culture.[172] It was these discoveries that led to the growing interest in

---

[169] John Keegan, *The First World War* (New York: Alfred A. Knopf, 1999), p. 20.

[170] On this point, see David Killingray, "Imperial Defence," in *The Oxford History of the British Empire*, Vol. V. *Historiography*, edited by Robin W. Winks (Oxford: Oxford University Press, 1999), pp. 342–53, at pp. 349–50.

[171] See Michael J. Franklin, *Orientalist Jones: Sir William, Jones, Poet, Lawyer, and Linguist, 1746–1794* (Oxford: Oxford University Press, 2011); David Arnold, "Indo-European," *The Times Literary Supplement*, March 9, 2012, No. 5684, p. 9.

[172] On this point, see Charles Allen, *The Buddha and the Sahibs* (London: John Murray, 2003).

Indian thought in both Germany and Britain, an interest that surprised and impressed Gandhi during his stay in London as a law student, leading him to take more seriously his own Indian religious and philosophical culture.[173]

Moreover, except for the period of the interregnum after the English Civil War, Britain was governed by a hereditary monarch with war powers, whose constitutional powers over time were increasingly limited by both House of Commons and the House of Lords. Whereas the Roman Republic collapsed under the pressure of its success into the autocratic Roman Empire, the period of the greatest growth of the British Empire, in which monarchical power played a not unimportant role (Queen Victoria is thus named Empress of India), was one of increasing democratization and liberalization in British politics: the franchise is gradually expanded to include all men and, in 1928, women as well, and the political powers of the commons expanded at the expense of the powers of both the monarch and the lords.

Yet another significant difference between Rome and Britain is the matter of religion and the relationship of religion to politics. For most of its history, Rome was officially pagan, in which a form of civil religion was closely aligned with, indeed led by, the men of the Senate whose military prowess brought them to the political leadership of Rome (Julius Caesar as *pontifex maximus*). Only fairly late in the history of the Roman Empire does Christianity become the established church of the Roman Empire and the emperor combines an autocratic authority over both religion and politics, making possible a politically supported persecution not only of nonorthodox forms of Christianity (the Donatists), but the coercive repression of the pagan practices that had dominated Roman culture for so long; only the Jews were allowed some measure of toleration, but they were nonetheless sharply confined to certain places and occupations and forbidden to marry Christians.

While the teaching of Jesus of Nazareth in the Gospels has many notably antipatriarchal features,[174] the institutionalization of Christianity as the established church of an already highly patriarchal Roman culture interpretively reframed Christianity in highly patriarchal terms. Augustine of Hippo, the central figure in the justification of this development, illustrates how the underlying psychology of traumatic loss and identification, central to Roman patriarchy, explains as well how orthodox Christianity became so highly patriarchal. Augustine had been ordered by and obeyed his patriarchal mother, Monika, to break his relationship to the woman he sexually loved to engage in the marriage his mother had arranged for him to advance the family's

---

[173] On this point, see David A.J. Richards, *Disarming Manhood: The Roots of Ethical Resistance* (Athens, Ohio: Swallow Press, 2005), at pp. 92–7.
[174] On this point, see Gilligan and Richards, *The Deepening Darkness*, pp. 122–9.

purposes. This traumatic loss of real relationship explains how and why Augustine competitively beats his mother at her own patriarchal game, interpreting his own highly sensual experience of God, as the perfect or ideal lover, as requiring celibacy. Like Aeneas in *The Aeneid* who leaves Dido, the woman he loved as an equal, to fulfill his arranged destiny to found Rome and marry a woman he does not love, Augustine establishes the patriarchal model of the Catholic priesthood as celibate, requiring the sacrifice of human sexual love, as the requirement for the heroic patriarchal authority of an all-male hierarchical priesthood, deforming the teachings of Jesus as patriarchy requires. The psychological impact of traumatic loss in intimate life made possible Augustine's identification with the patriarchal terms of his interpretation of the Christian God and also explains the psychology of repressive violence that rationalized the theory of persecution of Christians who deviated from orthodoxy as well as of Pagans and the servile status he imposed on Jews as "the slave of Christians." The patriarchal character of Augustinian Christianity is shown both by its endorsement of patriarchal controls on human sexual love and of the repressive violence directed at any challenge to patriarchal authority.[175]

This form of Augustinian Christianity was long dominant in the nations and peoples that arose in the wake of the Roman Empire, rationalizing forms of monarchical hierarchical political absolutism, including forms of imperialism, that were legitimated by and enforced Augustinian hierarchical patriarchy in religion. Papal authority thus justified and delimited the imperial claims of Spain and Portugal in the New World including their duties, as Catholic monarchs, to repress false and institute true religion.[176]

Britain broke with the Catholic view of papal authority during the reign of Henry VIII, replacing the authority of the pope over Christianity with that of the monarch. Although these British arrangements were in fact closer to the authority the Roman emperors had over Christianity, the underlying Christianity remained largely Augustinian, including its theory of persecution (here, justifying Anglican Protestant repression of Catholics and even non-Anglican Protestants – Congregationalists and Quakers, for example). Its patriarchal character is shown by the religious as well as political authority accorded

---

[175] For fuller discussion of all these points, see Gilligan and Richards, *The Deepening Darkness*, pp. 102–18.
[176] For further discussion, see Anthony Pagden, "The Struggle for Legitimacy and the Image of Empire in the Atlantic to c. 1700," in Nicholas Canny, *The Oxford History of the British Empire*, Vol. 1. *The Origins of Empire: British Overseas Enterprise to the Close of the Seventeenth Century* (Oxford: Oxford University Press, 2001), pp. 34–54; Anthony Pagden, *Lords of all the World: Ideologies of Empire in Spain, Britain, and France c1500–c1800* (New Haven, CT: Yale University Press, 1998).

the British monarch, including its imperialistic claims over Catholic Ireland (which was to be a running sore of British oppression for centuries)[177] and in the Americas.[178]

However, Britain experienced in its English Civil War the first modern challenge to absolute monarchy based on a radical Protestant challenge to the antidemocratic terms of Augustinian Christianity. Although monarchical power was reestablished after the interregnum, it did so in a context of ongoing challenges to the terms of Stuart absolutism, culminating in the Glorious Revolution in which the House of Commons became increasingly powerful as a limit on the powers of the monarch.[179] The central political theorist of the new form of constitutionalism, justifying a right to revolution against monarchical absolutism (for example, the Glorious Revolution and even the English Civil War), was John Locke. Locke was also a central figure in one of the two important forms of resistance to Augustinian intolerance that developed, one from within Christianity, the other from Judaism. Both expressed themselves in the argument for toleration, one of the foundations of constitutional democracy.

Historically, the most influential forms of resistance to Augustinian intolerance came from within Christianity – in particular, the argument for toleration stated in variant forms in the late seventeenth century by Pierre Bayle and John Locke[180] that laid the foundations of modern democratic constitutionalism. The context and motivations of the argument were those of radical Protestant intellectual and moral conscience, reflecting on the political principles requisite to protect its enterprise against the oppressions of established churches, both Catholic and Protestant. Often, such arguments appealed directly to the spirit of the Gospels, questioning the highly patriarchal interpretive traditions (including Augustinian orthodoxy) that had corrupted their meaning.[181]

---

[177] Jane H. Ohlmeyer, "'Civilizinge of those rude parties': Colonization within Britain and Ireland, 1580s–1630s," in Nicholas Canny, ed., *The Oxford History of the British Empire*, Vol. I, pp. 124–47.

[178] John Shy, "The American Colonies in War and Revolution, 1748–1783," in P. J. Marshall, *The Oxford History of the British Empire*, Vol. II. *The Eighteenth Century* (Oxford: Oxford University Press, 2001), pp. 300–24.

[179] See Richard S. Benn, "The Glorious Revolution and America," in Nicholas Canny, ed., *The Oxford History of the British Empire*, Vol. I, pp. 445–66; Jack P. Greence, "Empire and Identity from the Glorious Revolution to the American Revolution," in P. J. Marshall, *The Oxford History of the British Empire*, Vol. II, pp. 208–30.

[180] For fuller examination of the argument in Locke and Bayle and its American elaboration, notably by Jefferson and Madison, see David A. J. Richards, *Toleration and the Constitution* (New York: Oxford University Press, 1986), at pp. 89–128.

[181] On this point, see Perez Zagorin, *How the Idea of Religious Toleration Came to the West* (Princeton, NJ: Princeton University Press, 2003).

Both Bayle and Locke call for a democratic equality in the interpretation of the Gospels, implicitly questioning the role a patriarchal priesthood had played in interpreting Christianity since Augustine. Moreover, both of their lives and works bespeak a resistance to the violence that Christian intolerance incites and its effects on intimate personal life. Bayle, for example, "suffered the worst blow of his life" when his brother, arrested for Bayle's publications in his stead, died in prison from appalling conditions because of his refusal, at the insistence of a Jesuit, to abjure his Protestantism.[182] And Locke's reading of the Adam and Eve narrative was less patriarchal than that of orthodox Christianity,[183] reflective perhaps of his own parents and their relationships to him.[184] Both Bayle and Locke were outsiders not only to Catholicism but to conventional patriarchal family life; neither married (Locke likely was homosexual in orientation).[185] Both advocated the principle of toleration as a way of questioning and delegitimating Augustine's rationale for the use of political power in religious persecution.[186]

Their enterprise of toleration arose from a moral ideal of the person and the need to protect that ideal from political threat. The ideal was respect for persons in virtue of their moral powers both rationally to assess and pursue ends and reasonably to adjust and constrain their pursuit of ends in light of the moral status of other persons as bearers of equal rights. The threat to this ideal came from the political idea and practice that the moral status of persons was not determined by the responsible expression of their own moral powers but, rather, by a hierarchical structure of society and nature in which they were embedded. That structure, classically associated with orders of being,[187] defined roles and statuses in which people were born, lived, and died and specified the responsibilities of living in light of those roles.

The political power exerted by this hierarchical conception was manifest not only in the ways people behaved but also in the ways it penetrated into

---

[182] Elisabeth Labrousse, *Bayle*, translated by Denys Potts (Oxford: Oxford University Press, 1983), p. 31.
[183] On this point, see Jeremy Waldron, *God, Locke, and Equality: Christian Foundations in Locke's Political Thought* (Cambridge: Cambridge University Press, 2002), pp. 21–43.
[184] On Locke's "very pious... and affectionate mother" and a relationship to a father with whom "he lived perfectly... as a friend," see H. R. Fox Bourne, *The Life of John Locke*, Vol. I (New York: Harper & Brothers, 1876), at p. 13.
[185] On this point, see Roger Woolhouse, *Locke: A Biography* (Cambridge: Cambridge University Press, 2007), at pp. 139, 148–9; on his relationships to women, see pp. 222–3.
[186] Both do not extend the principle of toleration to Catholics or atheists. For commentary and critique, see Richards, *Toleration and the Constitution*, pp. 95–8.
[187] See, in general, Arthur O. Lovejoy, *The Great Chain of Being* (Cambridge, MA.: Harvard University Press, 1964).

the human heart and mind, framing personal, moral, and social identity in its terms. The hierarchical structure – religious, economic, political – did not need to rely on massive coercion precisely because its crushing force on human personality had been rendered personally and socially invisible by a heart that felt and a mind that imaginatively entertained nothing that could render the structure itself an object of critical reflection.

In light of the moral pluralism made possible by the Reformation, liberal Protestant thinkers subjected the political power of the hierarchical conception to radical ethical criticism. Both Bayle and Locke argued as religious Christians, and their argument arose as an intramural debate among interpreters of the Christian tradition about freedom and ethics.[188] An authoritative Pauline strand of that tradition had given central weight to the value of Christian freedom. Like the Jewish tradition from which it developed, it had a powerful ethical core of concern for the requisites of moral personality; Augustine of Hippo thus had interpreted the nature of God on the model of moral personality, that is, the three parts of the soul – will, memory, and intelligence. Indeed, the argument for toleration arose from an internal criticism by Bayle of Augustine's argument for the persecution of the heretical Donatists; to wit, Augustine had misinterpreted central Christian values of freedom and ethics. The concern was that religious persecution had corrupted ethics and also, for this reason, the essence of Christianity's elevated and simple ethical core of a universal brotherhood of free people.

The argument for toleration was a judgment of and response to perceived abuses of political epistemology. The legitimation of religious persecution by both Catholics and Protestants (drawing authority from Augustine, among others) had rendered a politically entrenched view of religious and moral truth as the measure of permissible ethics and religion, including the epistemic standards of inquiry and debate. By the late seventeenth century when Locke and Bayle wrote, there was good reason to believe that this view, resting on the authority of the Bible and associated interpretive practices, had assumed contestable interpretations of a complex historical interaction between pagan, Jewish, and Christian cultures in the early Christian era.

The Renaissance rediscovery of pagan culture and learning reopened the question of how the Christian synthesis of pagan philosophical and Jewish ethical and religious culture was to be understood. Among other things, the development of critical historiography and techniques of textual interpretation had undeniable implications for reasonable Bible interpretation. The Protestant Reformation both assumed and further encouraged these new

---

[188] For the following discussion of their argument, see Richards, *Toleration*, pp. 25–7, 84–98, 105, 125–6.

modes of inquiry and encouraged as well the appeal to experiment and experience that were a matrix for the methodologies associated with the rise of modern science.[189] These new approaches to thought and inquiry had made possible the recognition that there was a gap between the politically entrenched conceptions of religious orthodoxy and the kinds of reasonable inquiries that the new approaches made available. The argument for toleration thus arose from a recognition of this disjunction between the reigning political epistemology and the new epistemic methodologies.

In light of the new modes of inquiry now available, prevailing conceptions of religious truth were often seen to rest not only on the degradation of reasonable standards of inquiry but on the self-fulfilling degradation of the capacity of persons reasonably to conduct such inquiries. To rectify these evils, the argument for toleration forbade, as a matter of principle, the enforcement by the state of any such conception of religious truth. The scope of legitimate political concern must rather rest on the pursuit of general ends such as life and basic rights and liberties, including the right to conscience. The pursuit of such goods was consistent with the full range of ends that free people might rationally and reasonably pursue.[190]

Yet another form of the argument for toleration was developed by Baruch Spinoza, in the Netherlands, somewhat earlier than the arguments of Locke and Bayle. For Spinoza, the argument was not grounded in a radical Protestant sense of Christian conscience but in a more secular conception of the inalienable right of philosophical reason, which would extend to all persons capable of such reason, whether theist or atheist.[191] Spinoza had been a learned member of the Jewish community of Amsterdam, but his interests in secular philosophy, inspired by the study of Descartes, led to his excommunication in part because his views on Bible interpretation led him to question traditional Jewish beliefs and rituals.[192]

Spinoza's development of the argument for toleration is remarkable not only for its more secular character and more expansive protection (even of atheists) but also because of its later role in Enlightenment thought and practice. Spinoza's position, subsequently interpreted as grounding a right of sexual freedom and even the rights of women,[193] has led Jonathan Israel to argue

---

[189] For a recent review of the question, see I. Bernard Cohen, ed., *Puritanism and the Rise of Modern Science: The Merton Thesis* (New Brunswick, NJ: Rutgers University Press, 1990).
[190] See Richards, *Toleration*, pp. 119–20.
[191] See Spinoza, *Theological-Political Treatise*, 2nd ed., translated by Samuel Shirley (Indianapolis, IN: Hackett Publishing Company, 2001), at pp. 103, 222–30.
[192] See Steven Nadler, *Spinoza: A Life* (Cambridge: Cambridge University Press, 1999).
[193] Spinoza's own views on women were conventionally sexist. See Benedict de Spinoza, *A Political Treatise*, in Benedict de Spinoza, *A Theological-Political Treatise and A Political*

that Spinoza initiated a more radical Enlightenment that was compromised and even covered over by the more moderate forms of Enlightenment thought sponsored by Locke and Bayle.[194] What strikes one today is the plausible psychological connection between Spinoza's much more contemporary understanding of the principle of toleration and his sense of the embodied self that arose from his Jewish background. He may have been a Jewish heretic,[195] but his distinctive philosophical doctrine, the unity of the mind and the body,[196] arose, I suggest, from a revulsion at the form of mind–body dualism that Descartes, a believing Catholic, had developed to support the consistency of the emerging science with traditional Catholic doctrines, including the immortality of the soul.[197] Although Spinoza was, in fact, a forbiddingly metaphysical thinker, many people today find his thought surprisingly modern and contemporary.[198]

Finally, Spinoza, like Locke and Bayle, never married,[199] and he became a more radical outsider to the religion of his birth than Locke and Bayle, both of whom remained believing Protestants. I wonder if Spinoza's more extreme outsider status to both the dominant patriarchal family life and religion of his time may not explain how and why he gave the argument for toleration a more muscular and expansive interpretation, questioning, as it did in his hands, the use of state coercion on sectarian religious grounds against the inalienable right of philosophical conscience.

It is one of the most important differences between Roman and British patriarchy that the Romans, to the extent they were interested in philosophy at all, appealed, developed, or drew on the Greek philosophical schools most congenial to patriarchal Roman imperialism. In contrast, Britain – precisely

---

Treatise, translated by R. H. M. Elwes (Mineola, NY: Dover Publications, 2004), pp. 281–387, at pp. 386–7.

[194] On all these points, see Jonathan I. Israel, *Radical Enlightenment: Philosophy and the Making of Modernity 1650–1750* (Oxford: Oxford University Press, 2001).

[195] For one view of his heresy, see Steven Nadler, *Spinoza's Heresy: Immortality and the Jewish Mind* (Oxford; Oxford University Press, 2001).

[196] See Benedict de Spinoza, *Ethics*, translated by Edwin Curley (London: Penguin, 1996).

[197] On the relationship between Descartes and Spinoza, see Edwin Curley, *Behind the Geometrical Method: A Reading of Spinoza's Ethics* (Princeton, NJ: Princeton University Press, 1988).

[198] See, for example, Antonio Damasio, *Looking for Spinoza: Joy, Sorrow, and the Feeling Brain* (Orlando, FL: Harcourt, 2003); Rebecca Goldstein, *Betraying Spinoza: The Renegade Jew Who Gave Us Modernity* (New York: Nextbook-Schocken, 2006).

[199] There is only one report of Spinoza's romantic involvement with a woman, probably apocryphal. See Steven Nadler, *Spinoza: A Life*, at pp. 108–9. One of his closest male friends, Simon Joosten de Vries, expresses in a letter to Spinoza "perceptibly physical yearning" for the presence of his friend that Spinoza deflects, which leads one biographer to speculate about homosexual feeling between the friends. See Margaret Gullan-Whur, *Within Reason: A Life of Spinoza* (New York: St. Martin's Press, 1998), pp. 141–3.

in the early stages of what is called the First British Empire[200] (the empire that ended with British loss of its most successful colonial experiment, the American colonies, in the American Revolution of 1776–81) – gave rise and increasingly appealed to the political liberalism of John Locke importantly based on the requirement that political communities could only be just if they respected inalienable human rights, including, prominently, the right to conscience central to the argument for toleration. Political liberalism, based on the right of each and every person to equal respect, including respect for basic human rights – was in its nature not only critical of monarchical absolutism, but, implicitly, of imperialism. Indeed, as we observed at the beginning of our argument, Locke developed the theoretical foundations of his political liberalism in *The Second Treatise of Government* on the basis of a criticism of Filmer's patriarchal theory of monarchical absolutism in *The First Treatise of Government*. To this extent, the criticism of patriarchy was, remarkably and for the first time in human history, self-consciously central to political philosophy. Nothing comparable occurred under the Roman Empire.

Lockean political liberalism was, however, philosophically and politically controversial even in Britain, although in fact both the democratization of the franchise and the liberalization of political power (removing, eventually, all religious disqualifications on political and educational opportunities) in Britain were in line with the demands, as the British came to understand those demands, during the most expansive period of the Second British Empire in the nineteenth and early twentieth centuries.[201] Locke himself supported imperialistic ventures in the Carolinas, including even slavery.[202] Thus, even Locke could not recognize the tension between patriarchy and liberal democracy. How should we understand this?

The study of Roman patriarchy and its underlying psychology gives us an answer, revealing the close connections between patriarchy in private and public Roman life that clarifies the psychology of patriarchy in Britain as well. Roman patriarchy legitimated a highly militaristic ethos, imposing its hierarchical religious demands in not only public but private life as well. In the Roman home, fathers were the priests, having authority over domestic rituals and lives. The remarkable powers of the Roman father, the *patria potestas*, gave him

---

[200] See P. J. Marshall, "The First British Empire," in Robin W. Winks, *The Oxford History of the British Empire, Vol. V. Historiography* (Oxford: Oxford University Press, 1999), pp. 43–53.
[201] On this point, see C. A. Bayly, "The Second British Empire," *id.*, pp. 54–72.
[202] On this point, see David A.J. Richards, *Conscience and the Constitution: History, Theory, and Law of the Reconstruction Amendments* (Princeton: Princeton University Press, 1993), pp. 73–4.

unlimited authority over all his legitimate children, irrespective of whether or not they were married, and of their offspring as long as he lived. Thus, for example, the *pater familias* has the right to expose his child, to scourge him, to sell him, to pawn him, to imprison him, and, *in extremis*, even to kill him.[203]

While exercising such patriarchal authority in their families, Roman fathers were in turn subject to the patriarchal authority exercised by the Fathers in the Senate. As we saw earlier, these interacting and reinforcing patterns of patriarchy both rest on and explain evidence of an underlying personal and political psychology in both the men and women who sustained the belligerent militarism of the Roman Republic and Empire. In our earlier discussion, I was struck, in this connection, by the way Josephus, a close and respectful observer of the Roman army in action (in the imperial period), describes Roman men, so steeped in patriarchy that they appear "as though ... born with weapons in their hand."[204]

Of course, no baby is born this way. Quite the opposite; human babies are remarkable for their relationality, their desire for and responsiveness to human connection. Josephus's Romans are neither relational nor emotionally sensitive, and thus these human capacities have been blunted or stamped out of them. My question, then, is how could Roman patriarchal culture structure both private and public life so as to render this outcome seemingly natural or inevitable?

I turned in this regard to the contemporary literature on trauma and its effects on human neurophysiology and psychology.[205] The now well-documented consequence of trauma is a loss of voice and of memory, in particular, loss of the voice of intimate relationship. This loss or suppression of voice, however, is often covered by an identification with the voice of the person who imposed the trauma and an internalization of the demands that this more powerful person imposes on one's life. The crucial mechanism here is dissociation: the psychological process through which the surviving self separates itself from the self that was overwhelmed. A voice that speaks from experience is silenced in favor of a voice that carries more authority, leading to a replacement of one's personal sense of emotional presence and truth with what Sandor

---

[203] Emiel Eyben, "Fathers and Sons," in Beryl Rawson, ed., *Marriage, Divorce, and Children in Ancient Rome*, pp. 114–43, at p. 115. Eyben notes that these powers were significantly limited by the time of the Empire.

[204] Josephus, *The Jewish Wars Books III-IV* H. St. J. Thackeray trans. (Cambridge: Harvard University Press, 1997), p. 27.

[205] See, for example, Bessel van der Kolk et al., *Traumatic Stress*. Judith Herman, *Trauma and Recovery*.

Ferenczi, the Hungarian psychoanalyst, describes as an "identification with the aggressor,"[206] the taking on as one's own the voice and demands of the oppressor. This process, leading to what Ferenczi observed as false compliance, is in itself largely unconscious, due in part to the loss of memory that follows the traumatic rupture of relationships.[207]

The key to understanding the psychological power of British patriarchy – even over its best liberal minds – is, I believe, the ways in which the patriarchal Augustinian orthodoxy on matters of gender and sexuality remained unquestioned and unquestionable, yet powerfully at the heart of private and public life under the Second British Empire. It is certainly true that the British did not share the Roman horror of a woman like Cleopatra ruling: women ruled in Britain, and one of them, Elizabeth I, was arguably one of their best monarchs. But Elizabeth self-consciously exercised her power on the patriarchal terms of Aeneas's traumatic self-sacrifice of her love life, a trauma heightened by the fate of her mother at the hands of her homicidally violent father. And Victoria, although she loved her consort, Albert, experienced his death as traumatic and spent the rest of her long life in mourning, increasingly allied not to her dead husband's liberalism but in support of British imperialism (see further discussion of both Victoria and Elizabeth I in Chapter 3). And women in Britain, particularly aristocratic women, exercised power under the radar of patriarchy, as had Roman women like Livia.

But the basic structure of personal and public life, for the men and women who served the Second British Empire, was rigidly defined by patriarchal norms. Kwasi Kwarteng, in his important book *The Ghosts of Empire*,[208] shows us the remarkably similar education of the small elite who administered the British Empire: as young boys, destined to serve the Empire at home and abroad, separated from their parents at young ages, entering into the rigors of highly hierarchical public school education in which flogging and sexual abuse were rampant, and education focused on classics or history.[209] The trauma of such separations led to identification with the patriarchal definition of manhood such schools imposed on British life, including the hierarchical

---

[206] See J. Laplanche and J.-B. Pontalis, *The Language of Psycho-Analysis*, translated by Donald Nicholson-Smith (New York: W.W. Norton, 1973), at pp. 208–9.

[207] Sandor Ferenczi, "The Confusion of Tongues between Adult and Child," English translation in *International Journal of Psychoanalysis* (1949), 30, 225, German original in *Internationale Zeitschriftt fur Psychoanalyse* (1933) 19, 5. Paper read at the Twelfth International Psycho-Analytical Congress, Wiesbaden, September, 1932.

[208] Kwasi Kwarteng, *Ghosts of Empire: Britain's Legacies in the Modern World* (New York: Public Affairs, 2011).

[209] Ibid., pp. 237–9.

authority older boys sometimes sadistically visited on younger boys. Athletic teamwork was much emphasized, preparing the small elite of British rulers for the kinds of collaborative work at home and abroad that imperial service would call for. University education at Oxford and Cambridge centered on classical languages, Greek and Latin, emphasizing the legitimacy and idealization of ancient patriarchal manhood as a model for life today.[210] Athletics remained important, as did social life generally: many did not complete university education.[211] Homosexuality, under such a rigidly defined system of gender segregation, was common but largely thought of in the highly patriarchal forms of homosexuality in the ancient Greek and Roman worlds, defined by its sexist contempt for the passive role in gay sex, and was associated, as in Rome, with slave boys and, in Greece, with boys and often slaves.[212] Homosexuality was also condemned as unspeakable by the Augustinian sexual morality that was enforced at large. Such patriarchally enforced silencing about the facts of human sexuality in all its variants locked both men and women into a rigidly defined patriarchal understanding of permissible sexuality immune to reasonable argument and experience. Patriarchy in this way both kills love and elicits repressive violence against any threat to its authority.

As under Roman patriarchy, relationships within marriage and between parents and children were often quite shallow. (Robert Graves observes how, at public school, a boy showed no grief at the death of his father, whom he hadn't seen for two years. He commented that such a boy "lives in a world completely dissociated from home life" with "a different moral system, even different voices," the consequence of parents who "lose all intimate touch with their children."[213]) Such training prepared men and women, as in Rome, for the long absences of husbands from wives, and of parents from children that imperial service abroad required. Indeed, as in the Roman armies, marriage in the British military was discouraged, and "married men were not selected for the SPS [civil service]"[214]; several of the leading imperialists – Kitchener in

---

[210] For an illuminating recent treatment, see Simon Goldhill, *Victorian Culture and Classical Antiquity: Art, Opera, Fiction, and the Proclamation of Modernity* (Princeton, NJ: Princeton University Press, 2011).

[211] In general, see David Gilmour, *The Ruling Caste: Imperial Lives in the Victorian Raj* (New York: Farrar, Straus & Giroux, 2005). See also Michael Rosenthal, *The Character Factory: Baden-Powell's Boy Scouts and the Imperatives of Empire* (New York: Pantheon, 1986).

[212] See Kenneth J. Dover, *Greek Homosexuality* (London: Duckworth, 1978); Craig A. Williams, *Roman Homosexuality*, 2nd ed. (New York: Oxford University Press, 2010).

[213] Robert Graves, *Good-Bye to All That* (New York: Anchor, 1998; originally published, 1929), p. 20.

[214] Kwarteng, *Ghosts of Empire*, p. 242.

the military[215] and Cecil Rhodes in South Africa[216] – clearly flourished outside marriage and better met the demands of British imperialism because they preferred men to women, relationships more consistent with the extraordinary demands they imposed on themselves as agents of British imperialism. The resulting emotional vacuum at the heart of personal life fueled a psychology of male honor that elicited surprising levels of aggressive violence, as in Kitchener and Rhodes, in response to any challenge to the patriarchal demands made by British imperialism.[217]

Patriarchal controls on women's sexuality were, if anything, more rigid, enforcing an unquestionable binary of idealized good women lacking sexual feeling and interests independent of patriarchal demands, and the degraded bad, sexual woman. It was Augustinian sexual morality that made and enforced this division, so that even as good a political liberal as William Gladstone, consumed by Augustinian shame over his own sexual feelings aroused by pornography, would seek, usually futilely, to persuade prostitutes to leave this life and flagellate himself in punishment for the most natural of human feelings.[218]

Virginia Woolf, who came from such a patriarchal family,[219] wrote perceptively of patriarchy's deadening intrapsychic effects on women's imagination and intelligence through its imposition on "good" women a self-sacrificing, and self-abnegating, idea: the "Angel in the House." Such service to the patriarchy killed a real human voice, the basis for creativity. In "Professions of Women," Woolf, considering the psychological blocs she had encountered as a creative woman, wrote of

> the Angel in the House, I will describe her as shortly as I can. She was intensely sympathetic. She was immensely charming. She was utterly unselfish. She excelled in the difficult arts of family life. She sacrificed herself daily ... in short she was so constituted that she never had a mind or a wish of her own, but preferred to sympathize always with the minds and wishes of others. Above all – I need not say it – she was pure. Her purity was supposed to be her chief beauty – her blushes, her great grace.... And when I came to

---

[215] On this point, see Philip Magnus, *Kitchener: Portrait of an Imperialist* (New York: E.P. Dutton, 1968), pp. 10, 127, 152, 235, 238, 245.

[216] On this point, see Robert I. Rotberg, *The Founder: Cecil Rhodes and the Pursuit of Power* (New York: Oxford University Press, 1988), at pp. 92, 404–8, 403–4, 680.

[217] On Kitchener's growing taste for violence, see Magnus, *Kitchener*, p. 227; on Rhodes's lack of guilt and shame, see Rotbert, *The Founder*, p. 685.

[218] See Roy Jenkins, *Gladstone* (New York: Random House Trade Paperbacks, 1997), pp. 100–15.

[219] On her controlling father, see Noel Annan, *Leslie Stephen: The Godless Victorian* (Chicago: University of Chicago Press, 1984).

write I encountered her with the very first words. The shadow of her wings fell on my page; I heard the rustling of her skirts in the room. Directly, that is to say, I took my pen in hand to review that novel by a famous man, she slipped behind me and whispered: "My dear, you are a young women. You are writing about a book that has been written by a man. Be sympathetic; be tender; flatter; deceive; use all the arts and wiles of our sex. Never let anybody guess that you have a mind of your own. Above all, be pure." And she made as if to guide my pen. I now record the one act for which I take some credit to myself, though the credit rightly belongs to some excellent ancestors of mine who left me a certain sum of money . . . so that it was not necessary for me to depend solely on charm for my living. I turned upon her and caught her by the throat. I did my best to kill her. My excuse, if I were to be had up on a court of law, would be that I acted in self-defense. Had I not killed her she would have killed me.[220]

Women and men – even the most liberal of them – were under this patriarchal system deformed in their understanding of the political liberalism many of them espoused. Patriarchy, as we have seen, draws its psychological power both from the trauma it inflicts in personal life and an intrapsychic identification with patriarchal ideals of gender that expresses itself in a belligerent repressive violence directed against any challenge to its authority. It is from this perspective unsurprising that political liberalism should have been more coherently realized in internal British democratic life than it was in its external relations in the Second British Empire, many of whose peoples were not only of non-Christian religions (notably, India) but people of color. It is quite true that Britain was, in the nineteenth century, a world leader in both the abolition of the slave trade and slavery itself in a way the United States was not[221]; but British politics dealt with slavery largely at a distance (in its colonies), not, as in America, slavery constitutionally entrenched at home, a much more difficult matter for democratic politics. Even in this period, British imperialist treatment of colonists who were British (New Zealand and Australia) or substantially British (Canada) was markedly different from those who were not.[222] The Roman Empire's broad assimilation of diverse ethnicities to Roman citizenship was not shared by the British.[223] Within Britain, previously

---

[220] Virginia Woolf, "Professions of Women," in Virginia Woolf, *Women and Writing* edited by Michele Barrett (Orlando, FL: Harvest Books, 1980), pp. 57–63, at p. 59.

[221] For an illuminating study, see Adam Hochschild, *Bury the Chains: Prophets and Rebels in the Fight to Free an Empire's Slaves* (Boston: Mariner, 2005).

[222] On this point, see Peter T. Marsh, *Joseph Chamberlain: Entrepreneur in Politics* (New Haven, CT: Yale University Press, 1994), at pp. 406–26.

[223] On this point, see Piers Brendon, *The Decline and Fall of the British Empire 1781–1997* (London: Vintage, 2008), at pp. 51, 149–50, 262, 360.

marginalized groups found and expressed their voices and had the impact on British politics that political liberalism required. British imperialism under the Second Empire largely affected people not in Britain, however. There was also a sharp disjunction between the increasingly democratic experience of life in Britain and the very different experience of the small elite who administered the Empire abroad, often accorded almost autocratic, hierarchical powers that would have been unthinkable in Britain.[224] The British abroad thus saw no problem in imposing on the colonies Britain's laws against homosexuality, but in fact Britons abroad enjoyed freedoms and privileges, including sexual freedoms, they would not have enjoyed in Britain.[225] It is this disjunction between life in Britain and in the colonies that explains the revelatory force of E. M. Forster's *A Passage to India* as he shows the British at home what life was like in the colonies, reflected in Mrs. Moore's shock at the change in her son when she visits him, a civil servant (a judge), in India: "Englishmen like posing as gods."[226] For this reason, imperialism, so experientially sharply divided from life in Britain, remained more congenial to the liberal imagination than it should have. There is no better example of this matter than John Stuart Mill.

Mill is one of the most fascinating examples of the tension between liberal democracy and imperialism during the Second British Empire. One of the greatest theorists of liberalism and feminism (author of *On Liberty* and *The Subjection of Women*), Mill at the same time earned his living, following his father, James Mill, as an official of the East India Company's imperial rule over India until the end of the Company's rule (over Mill's sharp objections) after the sanguinary Indian Mutiny of 1857.[227] Like his father, Mill never even visited India though he exercised an imperial rule over it. His justification for not extending the principle of liberty to India is put in these dismissive terms in *On Liberty*: "[W]e may leave out of consideration those backward states of society in which the race itself may be considered as in its nonage"[228]; he

---

[224] On this general point, see Kwarteng, *Ghosts of Empire*.

[225] On this point, see Ronald Hyam, *Empire and Sexuality: The British Experience* (Manchester: Manchester University Press, 1991); Robert Aldrich, *Colonialism and Homosexuality* (London: Routledge, 2003). See also Anne McClintock, *Imperial Leather: Race, Gender and Sexuality in the Colonial Contest* (New York: Routledge, 1995).

[226] See E. M. Forster, *A Passage to India* (San Diego, CA: Harvest Books, 1984; originally published, 1924), at p. 51.

[227] See Martin I. Moir, Douglas M. Peers, and Lynn Zastoupil, eds., *J. S. Mill's Encounter with India* (Toronto: University of Toronto Press, 1999); Lynn Zastoupil, *John Stuart Mill and India* (Stanford, CA: Stanford University Press, 1994); John Stuart Mill, *Writings on India* (Toronto: University of Toronto Press, 1990).

[228] John Stuart Mill, *On Liberty*, edited by Alburey Castell (New York: Appleton-Century-Crofts, 1947), p. 10.

then appealed to utilitarianism as the ultimate principle in ethics. The appeal of utilitarianism – consistent with a managerial, bureaucratic attitude – may make sense of Mill's insensitivity here as well as, more generally, of other English utilitarians in India.[229] But Mill's general argument in *On Liberty* is not consistent with utilitarianism,[230] so why utilitarianism here? Moreover, Mill's language about "backward" peoples suggests racism, but we know he was remarkable among intellectuals of his generation for denying that there was any race differences that could justify racism (and then denied gender differences, as a basis for sexism, as well).[231] If Mill's imperialism is as unjustified as it now appears to us to be, it may show the depth of the psychological hold of British patriarchal manhood, the psychology of "Anglo-Indian militarism,"[232] even over a man as liberal and feminist as Mill. Certainly, the tyrannies of his father in his childhood suggest trauma and identification (Mill, after all, takes up his father's role in the East India Company, becoming, as it were, his father).

Mill was by no means the only feminist to compromise liberal principles when British imperial supremacy was at threat. During World War I, Emmeline and Christabel Pankhurst, who had fought so violently for women's right to vote before the war, brought all suffragette activity to a halt, leading to the freedom of all imprisoned suffragettes, and supported the war uncritically and enthusiastically in opposition to the more principled feminist middle daughter of Christabel, Sylvia.[233]

If this is liberalism, its critics may be right.[234] We need an alternative approach. Resistance to British imperialism, on liberal grounds, would require another kind of resistance, one that crucially connected the injustice of British imperialisms to its continuing enforcement of patriarchal demands in the realms of sexuality and gender, what I call gay rights.

---

[229] See Eric Stokes, *The English Utilitarians in India* (Oxford: Oxford University Press, 1959).
[230] Consider Mill's view: "If all mankind minus one, were of one opinion, and only one person were of the contrary opinion, mankind would be no more justified in silencing that one person, than he, if he had the power, would be justified in silencing mankind." J. S. Mill, *On Liberty*, p. 16. Mill's view, under which the interest of one has greater weight than the interest of everyone else, is not what utilitarianism usually would be taken to demand.
[231] On these points, see Richard Reeves, *John Stuart Mill: Victorian Firebrand* (London: Atlantic Books, 2007), at pp. 219–21.
[232] Martin I. Moir et al., eds., *J. S. Mill's Encounter with India*, at p. 208
[233] On this point, see Adam Hochschild, *To End All Wars: A Story of Loyalty and Rebellion, 1914–1918* (Boston: Houghton Mifflin Harcourt, 2011), pp. 98–9.
[234] See Domenico Losurdo, *Liberalism: A Counter-History*, translated by Gregory Elliott (London: Verso, 2011).

3

The Rise of Gay Rights

We turn now to the close study of the resistance movement I call gay rights, several of whose British advocates (John Addington Symonds, Oscar Wilde, and Edward Carpenter) drew inspiration from the life and poetry of the American poet Walt Whitman, and two of whom (Wilde and Carpenter) visited, in what can only be called a quasi-religious pilgrimage, a man they regard as the prophet of gay rights. It is not at all surprising that both Wilde and Carpenter should have interpreted Whitman's great poetry collection *Leaves of Grass*, in particular, the "Calamus" poems, as calling for a new opening to homoerotic experience that was, for Whitman, connected to a more inclusive understanding of democracy. Indeed, I have no doubt this is the best interpretation of the poem, as I have argued at some length elsewhere.[1]

Oscar Wilde made a point of visiting Whitman when he lectured in the United States, telling a batch of reporters, "There is something so Greek and sane about his poetry."[2] Whitman evidently made no effort, as he would later do with Symonds (whom he never met), to conceal his homosexuality. Wilde later said, "The kiss of Walt Whitman is still on my lips."[3] Wilde, like Symonds, married and had children, but other than their common Hellenism (which Wilde, a brilliant undergraduate, had imbibed from Walter Pater at Oxford[4]), the similarity ends there. Symonds lived mainly abroad, did not publish his works on homosexuality to a general public in his lifetime, and, even then, the published works did so in a defensive and ambivalent way that certainly

---

[1] On this point, see David A. J. Richards, *Women, Gays, and the Constitution: The Grounds for Feminism and Gay Rights in Culture and Law* (Chicago: University of Chicago Press, 1998), pp. 297–310.
[2] Cited at ibid., p. 314.
[3] Cited at ibid., p. 314.
[4] See Linda Dowling, *Hellenism and Homosexuality in Victorian Oxford* (Ithaca, NY: Cornell University Press, 1994).

was not wholly honest to his convictions. Wilde forged a style of living and writing that explored homosexuality and ironic wit to question and probe the Victorian rigid boundaries of gender and class. Wilde's life would finally imitate his art, with a moving transparency and candor worthy of Whitman; in his 1895 speech at his first trial for consensual homosexual sex acts with rent boys, Wilde declared:

> The "Love that dare not speak its name" in this century is such a great affection of an elder for a younger man as there was between David and Jonathan, such as Plato made the very basis of his philosophy, and such as you may find in the sonnets of Michaelangelo and Shakespeare. It is that deep, spiritual affection that is as pure as it is perfect.... It is beautiful, it is fine, it is the noblest form of affection. There is nothing unnatural about it. It is intellectual, and it repeatedly exists between an older and a younger man, when the elder man has intellect, and younger man has all the joy, hope, and glamour of life before him. That it should be so the world does not understand. The world mocks it and sometimes puts one in the pillory for it.[5]

Wilde's model for homosexuality, both in his theory and practice, was decidedly ancient Greek, but after his second trial (the first jury was hung) his conviction and punishment (two years hard labor), were homophobically modernist. He would serve the full sentence, live abroad in exile thereafter, and die, a broken man, at age forty-six in 1900.[6]

Walt Whitman was as potent an influence on Edward Carpenter as he was on Symonds and Wilde, indeed more so, because Carpenter who attended Cambridge (not Oxford), did not bring to his relationship to Whitman or his understanding of gay relationships generally the distorting prism of the rather doctrinaire Hellenism through which Symonds and Wilde read Whitman. Carpenter's sexual tastes for workingmen (thus doubly breaking the Love Laws of class and of gender) were much like those of Whitman and led to his lifetime partnership of thirty years with George Merrill at their home, Millthorpe.[7] Carpenter made his pilgrimage to the United States to meet Whitman in 1877 (spending a week with Whitman at his home, and later meeting Emerson as well), and a second visit to meet Thoreau as well as Whitman in 1884. He wrote of Whitman as a prophet "annunciative of a

---

[5] Citation at Richards, *Women, Gays, and the Constitution*, p. 315.
[6] For fuller discussion and citations, see Richards, *Women, Gays, and the Constitution*, pp. 315–16.
[7] For an excellent recent biography, see Sheila Rowbotham, *Edward Carpenter: A Life of Liberty and Love* (London: Verso, 2008).

new order,"⁸ emphasizing the pluralistic religious and philosophical sources on which Whitman drew, many of them non-Christian (including Taoism, the Sufism of Persia, Hinduism, and Buddhism). In his numerous books, Carpenter developed and elaborated what he took to be Whitman's vision calling not only for respect for the dignity of gay/lesbian love, but explicitly connecting his argument to a rights-based feminism centering on issues of sexuality and gender, as part of a larger conception, following Whitman, of a new conception of democracy which, for Carpenter, included socialism⁹ and a criticism of the premises of British imperialism.¹⁰ E. M. Forster was a well-known author by the time he met Carpenter in 1913, when George Merrill, Carpenter's lover, broke through Forster's rather self-conscious reticence; "he touched my backside – gently and just above the buttocks,"¹¹ unleashing a flood of new feeling that Forster experienced as a release into a new world of possibilities. Forster wrote in his diary: "Forward rather than back, Edward Carpenter! Edward Carpenter! Edward Carpenter!"¹²

The connection of American and British gay rights was thus a close one, not unconnected to their roots in the American and British abolitionist movements, directed against American and British slavery, and to the feminist movement – the abolitionist feminism of the Grimke sisters, and others, that criticized both racism and sexism as resting on a common structural injustice,¹³ to be followed by American and British suffrage feminism, which were to secure the vote for women in the United States and Britain after World War I. However, although Whitman did have the effect on British gay rights that he clearly did have, he did not have any comparable effect in his homeland, the United States. Whitman himself, perhaps writing out of a sense of besieged loneliness if not isolation in the America of the Gilded Age, was to deny repeated queries by John Addington Symonds about the sexual component of Whitman's love between men and in an 1890 letter to Symonds called these "morbid inferences,"¹⁴ falsely claiming he had six children. Edward Carpenter, who had visited Whitman twice and was much closer in temperament, lifestyle, and philosophy to Whitman, complained understandably about Symonds's nescience in even eliciting, let alone publishing, such a letter

---

[8] Cited at Richards, *Women, Gays, and the Constitution*, p. 319.
[9] For a more detailed study of Carpenter's books, see Richards, *Women, Gays, and the Constitution*, pp. 317–27.
[10] On this point, see Rowbotham, *Edward Carpenter*, pp. 27, 303–4.
[11] Cited in Rowbotham, *Edward Carpenter*, p. 331.
[12] Cited in Rowbotham, *Edward Carpenter*, p. 331.
[13] For fuller discussion, see Richards, *Women, Gays, and the Constitution*.
[14] Cited in Richards, *Women, Gays, and the Constitution*, p. 304.

when the state of press censorship in the United States under the influence of the powerful purity movement was "ten times worse" than in Britain.[15] The American problem of censorship was to persist for some time, indeed until while after World War II, when the Supreme Court's liberalization of obscenity laws[16] was to make an open gay rights discourse possible in the United States; previously, such public advocacy was met with censorship and prison.[17]

I recognize that the label "gay rights" is an American invention dating from the 1969 Stonewall resistance in Greenwich Village, New York, which was later taken up in Britain and other countries. Paradoxically, rhetoric and reality were here at cross purposes: Britain by this time had decriminalized gay sex between consenting adults, but, as we shall see, not then on the ground of later American-style gay rights arguments. Decriminalization was only achieved in the United States in 2003 through the Supreme Court decision, *Lawrence v. Texas*.[18] My interest here is in not labels but the development of a movement of resistance that long antedated Stonewall and was more fully developed, as a resistance movement, in Britain than the United States, deeply connected to a sustaining network of friendships that expressed itself in a certain rights-based interpretation of feminism centering on issues of gender and sexuality, and to the British movement resisting imperialism. America may have given us the prophet of gay rights, but prophets are often left alone and even abandoned; having no resonance for their voices, they lose those voices and sometimes their minds, which is what may have happened to Whitman in the United States.

What makes British resistance so different is that it expressed itself in a network of good, close friendships, some of them erotic, some not, that shared common values, leaving but always coming back to one another. They stood with one another on the basis of those values, even when times were hard and the larger world hostile. What I am trying to capture by using the term "gay rights" somewhat inexactly is the essence of this movement (including its relationship to feminism and anti-imperialism) to make my point because the center of my narrative is the resisting moral experience of gay men and lesbians (among whom I include Virginia Woolf). Many of the figures I discuss (Lytton Strachey, John Maynard Keynes, Leonard and Virginia Woolf, Vanessa Bell, Duncan Grant, E. M. Forster) were members of the Bloomsbury Group and have been well studied in sometimes brilliant biographies

---

[15] On this point, see Richards, *Women, Gays, and the Constitution*, p. 304.
[16] See *Roth v. United States*, 354 U.S. 476 (1957).
[17] On this point, see Richards, *Women, Gays, and the Constitution*, pp. 327–37.
[18] 539 U.S. 558 (2003).

(for example, Michael Holroyd's biography of Lytton Strachey[19]). James Strachey, Lytton's brother and a psychoanalyst (who translated Freud's complete works for the Hogarth Press), had wanted Holroyd to write such a biography in part because he "believed that, had his brother lived longer, he would have turned what was implicit in his biographies into an explicit autobiographical campaign to achieve the same treatment under the law for homosexuality as for heterosexuality." (Virginia Woolf, however, doubted "James's prediction of the things, such things, his brother would have done".)[20] We cannot know who is right on this point, in particular because their views were formed in a period quite oppressive to any public discussion of homosexuality. But we know how they lived and what they wrote. What has, remarkably, not been studied in their lives and work (including, prominently, both Lytton Strachey and Virginia Woolf) is their role in resistance to patriarchy – in particular, breaking the Love Laws. This subject casts, I believe, a flood of light on their enduring ethical and political importance as a resistance movement, coming through new forms of love and friendship to expose the lies on which patriarchy rests, calling for a new form of political liberalism that included both protection of the right to intimate life and an attack on British imperialism. We should not overstate the homogeneity in their ethical views: Virginia Woolf was thus furious with E. M. Forster over his lack of feminist sensitivity at the failure of the London Library to admit women,[21] although both had earlier joined in public condemnation of the censorship of Radclyff Hall's explicitly lesbian novel, *The Well of Loneliness*.[22] (In contrast, the lesbian themes in Woolf's *Orlando* were "reviewed entirely in terms of its charm, its wit, and its idiosyncrasy."[23]) We must make the best interpretation we can of them from our point of view, emphasizing the strands in their lives and works (breaking the Love Laws, for example) that are most important. But we must start from the most truthful account of which we are capable that takes both their lives and their works seriously as the creative writers and artists they were.

What is original, and I believe illuminating, in my account is the prism of patriarchy and resistance to patriarchy through which I closely examine this resistance movement (Chapter 1). Resistance to patriarchy arises from finding in oneself a human voice that rejects the false relationships patriarchy demands and seeks to protect the relationality of human love and friendship

---

[19] Michael Holroyd, *Lytton Strachey: The New Biography* (New York: W.W. Norton, 1994).
[20] See ibid., p. XXIII.
[21] See Hermione Lee, *Virginia Woolf* (London: Vintage, 1997), at p. 663.
[22] See ibid., pp. 526–7.
[23] Hermione Lee, *Virginia Woolf*, p. 527.

in all its complexity. It is because patriarchy destroys love that resistance arises from love or the sense of love's possibilities in a full and complete life. Love and friendship are thus at the center of my resistance narrative. My account, rooted in an understanding of patriarchy, clarifies not only the role that the Love Laws play in supporting patriarchy but shows how, again and again in this resistance narrative, breaking the Love Laws is what makes possible the discoveries about human loving experience and moral experience more generally that characterize this resistance movement. It is by challenging the gender binary (enforced by the Love Laws) that they come to see that basic human rights cannot be limited to the masculine mind – conscience and speech – versus the feminine emotions and body but must include the right to intimate emotional and sexual life as well. This reflects a more democratic understanding of human rights precisely because it takes seriously the voices of the men and women, traditionally silenced by patriarchy, who now reasonably contest it.

To fix ideas, I have defined the Love Laws as the laws that lay down who should be loved, and how, and how much. These laws enforce the demands of patriarchy that separate and divide us from one another and from our common humanity. The form of the Love Laws is historically familiar: prohibitions on sexual relations, including marriage, between Jews and non-Jews, between people of color and not of color (antimiscegenation laws), between married women and men not their husbands (Augustus's ferocious antiadultery legislation) or on nonprocreative sex between married couples (laws criminalizing heterosexual sodomy, use of contraceptives, or access to abortion), between gay men or between lesbians, or between the touchable and the untouchable.

The resistance movement I call gay rights crucially arises through the breaking of the Love Laws, whether by Virginia Woolf marrying Leonard Woolf, a Jew; by celebrating the human good of gay sex, as Lytton Strachey and John Maynard Keynes came to understand and live it; by having gay sex with men of color while traveling abroad (E. M. Forster); or through the adulteries of Vanessa Bell with straight and gay men, with one of whom, Duncan Grant, she had a child. What was, I believe, at the center of its creativity as a resistance movement to patriarchal demands was what it came to mean to gay men and lesbians as well as the straight men, like Leonard Woolf, whom they loved, in particular, through their experiences of the human good and dignity of gay and lesbian sexual love and friendship and the larger fabric of friendship to which it led. Its larger moral creativity arose through its questioning of the traumatic loss patriarchy inflicted on intimate life and the psychological connections of that loss to a male violence elicited by any challenge to patriarchal demands. Through resistance centered in breaking the Love Laws, their human relationality and moral intelligence were less darkened by the collective stupidity that sustained patriarchy, enabling most of them to do something most Britons tragically could not: resist the injustice and catastrophic losses of World War I in which the competing European imperialisms destroyed one another. Several of them, notably Leonard Woolf and Goldsworthy Lowes Dickinson, would call for a League of Nations to avoid the repetition of such a catastrophe, and one of them, John Maynard Keynes, would see what the patriarchal rage of the victors in World War I refused to see – namely, that the humiliating and inhuman peace terms of the treaty with Germany would elicit from the defeated people a patriarchal violence that was even more catastrophic. And it was through his struggle for love as a gay man having sex with men of color that the novelist E. M. Forster would come to understand and write about the role the patriarchally imposed pedestal of good, asexual, white women versus the degraded status of bad, sexual women of color played in sustaining the injustice of British imperialism over people of color. Forster's ethical intelligence, questioning patriarchal demands, could embrace the humanity of people of color.

My story begins with a group of young men at Cambridge who were asked to join the Apostles, a surprisingly well-known although putatively secret, highly selective group that discussed papers regularly given by its members. In the past, the Apostles counted among its members leading Cambridge academics such as Henry Sidgwick; at the time we discuss here, G. E. Moore and Bertrand Russell were members (older members could also attend if they were in Cambridge). The young Cambridge students invited to the group include Lytton Strachey, John Maynard Keynes, E. M. Forster, Leonard Woolf, and Thoby Stephens, the brother of Virginia and Vanessa Stephens (later Virginia Woolf and Vanessa Bell).

Both Strachey and Keynes were sexually active gay men. They shared a sense of being physically unattractive[24] and were alive to the dangers of their sexual lives, as Oscar Wilde's conviction and disgrace were recent memories. "So long as no one has anything to do with the lower classes or people off the streets," Keynes wrote to Strachey on 20 June 1906, "and there is some discretion in letters to neutrals, there's not a scrap of risk – or hardly a scrap."[25] They were good friends until their friendship was dimmed, although never ended, by their competition for desirable lovers, most notably the painter, Duncan Grant, a cousin of Strachey, whom Strachey had introduced to Keynes. The

---

[24] Robert Skidelsky, *John Maynard Keynes: Hopes Betrayed 1883–1920* (New York: Viking, 1986), at p. 158.
[25] Quoted at ibid., p. 129.

sexual relationship of Grant and Keynes would last several years and include two months that "were probably the happiest in Maynard's life."[26] Having imbibed the sexist assumption that women were inferior to men, Keynes and Strachey had come to believe that homosexual relations to the intellectual and talented young men to whom they were attracted was a superior love, what they called the "Higher Sodomy."[27]

This interpretation of their homosexual loves was much deepened, in a way that would profoundly influence them and many others, by their encounter with G. E. Moore, fellow Apostle and the writer of *Principia Ethica*.[28] *Principia Ethica* is mainly known to contemporary moral philosophers for its questioning of any naturalistic analysis of ethical predicates such as "good" because it is always an open question whether the things identified by the analysis are good or whether analysis in fact defines the good.[29] Moore's argument is pointedly directed against the then dominant utilitarianism of Mill and Sidgwick, which depends on a naturalistic understanding of the good as pleasure, evil as pain. Moore argues that the good is an unanalyzable intuition and that we should replace the utilitarianism of pleasure over pain with a consequentialism of goods over evils, as we intuit them, subject to what he calls the principle of organic unity (namely, we must judge the overall value of something, which may be more or less than its component parts). The response of Strachey and Keynes to reading the book is remarkable. Strachey wrote to Moore that "your book has not only wrecked and shattered all writers on Ethics from Aristotle and Christ to Herbert Spencer and Mr. Bradley, it has . . . laid the true foundation of Ethics."[30] For Keynes, it was "the beginning of a new renaissance, the opening of a new heaven on earth."[31]

What Strachey and Keynes saw in the book may have been shaped not by its rather dry, intricate argument but what they had related to in Moore as a person and friend (a fellow Apostle). This unusually musical man (he was a good pianist of Beethoven sonatas) was rather good looking by British standards, possibly gay, and remarkably sympathetic to and understanding of gay men. Moore's sympathy extended evidently to thinking he was in love with another man, Alfred Ainsworth, with whom he lived for a period in Edinburgh, only

---

[26] Ibid., at p. 197.
[27] Ibid., p. 129.
[28] G. E. Moore, *Principia Ethica* (Mineola, NY: Dover, 2004; originally published, 1903). See, in general, Paul Levy, *Moore: G. E. Moore and the Cambridge Apostles* (Oxford: Oxford University Press, 1979).
[29] G. E. Moore, *Principia Ethica*, pp. 10–16.
[30] Quoted in Holroyd, *Lytton Strachey*, p. 89.
[31] Quoted in Holroyd, *Lytton Strachey*, p. 91.

to decide that both Ainsworth and he were not homosexual[32]; Moore would later marry happily and be known for his devotion to his children.[33]

If there was any part of Moore's argument on which Strachey and Keynes fastened their attention, it was his rather conclusory and brief discussion of the ideal in the last chapter. What are the ultimate goods? Moore responds:

> By far the most valuable things, which we know or can imagine, are certain states of consciousness, which may be roughly described as the pleasures of human intercourse and the enjoyment of beautiful objects.[34]

What Strachey, followed by Keynes, found here was "a scientific framework for his emotional impulses... giving a moral basis for the love that, since Oscar Wilde's imprisonment, dared not speak its name."[35]

One does not have to accept Moore's ideal utilitarianism or to be a gay man to see the good sense of an approach to ethics that centers on our relationality, our capacity to read other people's minds and feelings, and to enter into supportive, caring loves and friendships that give mutual expression to this capacity and take and give pleasure in its exercise. It is striking, in this connection, that when Keynes in his much later 1938 paper, "My Early Beliefs,"[36] reviews the role Moore played in the thought and lives of him and his friends, he emphasizes their attention paid to some parts of his ethical philosophy but ignoring of others: "We accepted Moore's religion, so to speak, and discarded his morals"[37] – what "was exciting, exhilarating, the beginning of a renaissance"[38] was its ethical vision: "The appropriate subjects of passionate contemplation and communion were a beloved person, beauty, and truth, and one's prime objects in life were love, the creation and enjoyment of aesthetic experience and the pursuit of knowledge. Of these love came a long way first."[39] Keynes, a great and influential economist, was the only member of this resistance group who served in the British government, a fact of public life and service that may have influenced his affair and 1924 marriage to the Russian dancer and actress Lydia Lopokova. Her artistic flamboyance and imagination seem akin to what had earlier sexually attracted Keynes to Duncan Grant, to whom Keynes continued to be financially generous, including at this

---

[32] On these points, see Levy, *Moore*, at p. 213.
[33] See ibid., pp. 290–2.
[34] Moore, *Principia Ethica*, p. 188.
[35] Holroyd, *Lytton Strachey*, p. 91.
[36] John Maynard Keynes, "My Early Beliefs," in *Two Memoirs* (New York: Augustus M. Kelley, 1949), pp. 78–103
[37] Ibid., p. 82.
[38] Ibid., p. 82.
[39] Ibid., p. 83.

death. As Keynes's most perceptive biographer observes: "Maynard and Lydia together were much more *socially* attractive than Maynard would have been on his own, or linked to a Bloomsbury blue-stocking."[40] Keynes never denies, however, what had moved him and others in Moore: "It is still my religion under the surface"[41]; he remained "an immoralist,"[42] by which he means, as he publicly wrote in 1925, that the conventional morality that was still the basis for the criminalization of contraception, abortion, and gay/lesbian sex was, in fact, not an ethical basis for laws.[43]

In his autobiography, Leonard Woolf, a straight man who was one of the Apostles, like Keynes, who was profoundly influenced by Moore, sharply questions Keynes's attempt to make of this influence a "religion." Rather, what it meant to him and his friends – straight or gay – was that his ideas and extraordinary integrity, depth, and personality

> suddenly removed from our eyes an obscuring accumulation of scales, cobwebs, and curtains, revealing for the first time to us, so it seemed, the nature of truth and reality, of good and evil and character and conduct, substituting for the religious and philosophical nightmares, delusions, hallucinations, in which Jehovah, Christ, and St. Paul, Plato, Kant, and Hegel had entangled us, the fresh air and pure light of plain common-sense.[44]

Common sense centrally included the moral good of sexual love and friendship, straight or gay.

One of Leonard Woolf's closest friends was Lytton Strachey, who, as Woolf observes, "always looked very queer and had a squeaky voice,"[45] mannerisms that tended "to excite animosity or ridicule at sight in the ordinary man, the Cambridge 'blood' or tough, for instance."[46] Woolf contrasts this flamboyant, gender-bending persona with his internal life as a friend: "To his intimate friends, though he could be momentarily infuriating, he was extraordinarily affectionate and lovable."[47] Strachey was not only one of Leonard's closest

---

[40] Robert Skidelsky, *John Maynard Keynes: The Economist as Savior 1920–1937* (New York: Allen Lane, 1992), p. 144.
[41] Keynes, "My Early Beliefs," p. 92.
[42] Ibid., p. 98.
[43] See John Maynard Keynes, "Am I a Liberal?" in *Essays in Persuasion* (Houndmills, England: Palgrave Macmillan, 2010), pp. 295–306, especially, p. 302.
[44] Leonard Woolf, *Sowing: An Autobiography of the Years 1880 to 1904* (San Diego, CA: Harcourt Brace Jovanovich, 1960), p. 147.
[45] Woolf, *Sowing*, p. 157.
[46] Ibid., p. 122.
[47] Ibid., p. 122.

friends but would become one of the closest male friends of his future wife, Virginia. Strachey, who came from an aristocratic background of distinguished officials of the British Empire (his father passed much of his active career in India), found his identity, as a gender-bending homosexual, in challenging and questioning dominant patriarchal conceptions of manhood and womanhood. In his Apostolic oratory at Cambridge, Strachey attacked imperialism.[48] Both his life and, as we shall see, his most important books questioned Victorian manhood and womanhood.

Probably, the most important development within this resistance movement after many of the Apostles left Cambridge was the continuation of many of its discussions in London, in particular because one of the Apostles, Thoby Stephens, introduced into these discussions his two remarkable sisters, Virginia and Vanessa. After the death of their father, Leslie Stephens, the four remaining children of Stephens and his second wife were the two boys, Adrian and Thoby, and the girls, Vanessa and Virginia, all of whom decided to live together in London in Bloomsbury. Vanessa attended art school and was bent on a vocation as a painter; Virginia, sharing her father's literary interests, would become a writer, starting with book reviews and working on the first of her novels. After the traumatic deaths of her mother and later her father, as well as a history of sexual abuse by her two Duckworth half-brothers, Virginia had already had several serious breakdowns. After Vanessa married Clive Bell and Thoby tragically died, Vanessa lived in a separate household in Bloomsbury with her husband, and Virginia lived with her brother Adrian, but there are frequent parties in both households attended by the siblings and their large group of friends.

We can see how these new forms of social relationship inspired several of them – notably, Duncan Grant, Virginia, and Adrian Stephens – to a comically resisting political performance directed at deflating imperialist pretensions, the Dreadnought Hoax of 1910. The conspirators, dressed in flamboyant costumes and mumbling an unintelligible language, pretended to be the emperor of Abyssinia and his suite. They were shown round one of the biggest and newest warships of His Majesty's Fleet (Virginia was dressed as "Prince Mendax," blacked up, with a moustache, flowing robes, and a turban, mumbling "Chuck-a-choi, chuck-a-choi"). The party refused refreshments, turned down a request for a twenty-one-gun salute, and returned to the shores. "The hoax combined all possible forms of subversion: ridicule of empire, infiltration of the nation's defenses, mockery of bureaucratic procedures, cross-dressing,

---

[48] Holroyd, *Lytton Strachey*, p. 80.

108   *The Rise of Gay Rights and the Fall of the British Empire*

and sexual ambiguity (Adrian and Duncan become lovers at about this time). Huge embarrassment was caused when the story came out,"[49] although the punishment was nominal (Duncan was abducted, refused to fight, and received two taps on his posterior).

These new forms of gender-integrated social life confronted the Apostles with highly intelligent, artistic women for the first time and clearly led to the breakdown of sexist assumptions that were the original basis of the "Higher Sodomy" as well as to the feminism most of them came to share. Vanessa and Virginia certainly knew that many of the Apostles were homosexual, but over time they formed intimate relationships with several of them. Vanessa had two children, Julian and Quentin, by Clive Bell, but the couple grew apart, Vanessa having an affair with the art historian and critic Christopher Fry and Clive with a succession of other women. The greatest love of Vanessa's life was a gay man, Duncan Grant, an artist with whom Vanessa was to work collaboratively and live for the rest of her life, although Duncan continued to have gay lovers. (As noted earlier, Grant had previously been the lover of both Lytton Strachey and Maynard Keynes.[50]) Vanessa persuaded Duncan to have a child with her, although Duncan told her he was unable to continue the sexual relationship thereafter[51]; this led to the birth of her third child, Angelica, who was not told the identity of her father for some time. Angelica eventually married one of Duncan's former lovers, to the understandable distress of her father. There is perhaps no more poignant and distressing example of the continuing and crippling power of patriarchal silencing over even such resisters than the disastrous deception of their own daughter, "treating me," as Angelica would later write, "as an object, and not as a human being."[52]

Lytton Strachey and Virginia Stephens became particularly close friends; both were remarkably witty and irreverent, brilliant, and well read, as well as innovative and successful writers. Leonard Woolf briefly met Virginia only before departing in 1904 for Ceylon, where he was a civil servant for a period of seven years. During this time, Lytton was his constant correspondent, and Virginia had several proposals of marriage but declined them all. The only

---

[49] Hermione Lee, *Virginia Woolf* (London: Vintage, 1997), p. 283.
[50] On their art, see Richard Shone, *The Art of Bloomsbury: Roger Fry, Vanessa Bell and Duncan Grant* (Princeton, NJ: Princeton University Press, 1999). On Duncan Grant, see Richard Shone, *The Art of Bloomsbury: Roger Fry, Vanessa Bell and Duncan Grant* (Princeton, NJ: Princeton University Press, 1999); Douglas Blair Turnbaugh, *Duncan Grant and the Bloomsbury Group* (Secaucus, NJ: Lyle Stuart, 1987).
[51] See Angelica Garnett, *Deceived with Kindness: A Bloomsbury Childhood* (London: Chatto & Windus, 1984), pp. 36, 164.
[52] Ibid., p. 136.

proposal she accepted, only later to withdraw, was from Lytton Strachey himself, showing how deep their intimacy and affinity, as well as respect and affection for one another as equals, had become. Strachey was relieved, but, already a close friend of Leonard Woolf and an intimate friend of Virginia's, decided that only Leonard, a robustly straight man, could be a good husband for her. Strachey began his matchmaking in letters to Leonard and continued it when Leonard returns on leave in 1911. Leonard had been a successful, meticulous civil servant, sometimes acting as a judge over disputes between natives, and clearly could have returned to Ceylon, looking to a distinguished career in the British civil service. Two events made that course impossible for him.

First, his experience as a servant of British imperialism had disillusioned him, as reflected in his novel *The Village in the Jungle*,[53] which may be compared with the comparable novel of another disillusioned servant of the British Empire, George Orwell's *Burmese Days*.[54] Woolf's concern, in contrast to Orwell, was not so much with the ways in which imperialism morally corrupts imperialists, both men and women, but the incommunicably different worlds in which even the most honest and impartial imperial judge lives in total ignorance of the people he judges, thus unable to see and deal with the ways in which corrupt natives use the system against honest natives. In Woolf's work, the tragedy of imperialism centered in the damage done to innocent natives, the unjustly imprisoned Silindu, who dies in prison, and the later despairing death of his abandoned wife, Punchi Menika. In Orwell's novel, the tragedy lies in the despair and suicide of its British imperialist protagonist, James Flory, abandoned by the British woman he thought he loved when she learns of his affair with a native Burmese woman. The second event that precluded Leonard's return to Ceylon was falling in love with and proposing marriage to Virginia Stephens.

Leonard came from a large Jewish family, and his sister, Bella, knowing of his loneliness, wrote him in 1909 urging him to marry. Knowing her brother, she told him he needed "a very special sort of girl . . . strong-minded and clever and [with] a sense of humor. . . . You must marry someone who can hold her own with you and yet be good-tempered." Women with brains stood to lose so much in marriage, wrote Bella, "in nine cases out of ten it is mere animalism – you *must* love with your *head* as much as with your heart or you're lost."[55]

---

[53] Leonard Woolf, *The Village in the Jungle* (London: Eland Publishing, 2005; first published, 1913).
[54] George Orwell, *Burmese Days* (Orlando, FL: Harvest Books, 1962; first published, 1934).
[55] Quoted in Victoria Glendinning, *Leonard Woolf: A Biography* (Berkeley, CA: Counterpoint, 2008), at p. 109.

Bella clearly knew her stoic, controlling brother well, sensing in him a need for someone who was his equal, including – above all, his intellectual and creative equal. At this time, Leonard was working on *The Village in the Jungle*, his first novel, which he discussed with Virginia. Likewise, she was struggling with her first novel (indeed, Leonard was to publish before Virginia). It was thus Virginia's powerful intelligence, creativity, and ambition, as well as her beauty, that drew Leonard so powerfully to her. It was, on his part, although he could not have known this when he married Virginia, to be a love in which "mere animalism" would come to play little part.

It took time for Virginia to accept Leonard's offer. In its favor were the strong support of her closest friends, her sister Vanessa and Lytton Strachey, as well as the fact that Leonard has been a close friend of her beloved, now dead brother, Thoby. In a remarkable letter to Leonard, Virginia discusses two impediments: first, "I feel angry sometimes at the strength of your desire. Possibly, your being a Jew comes in also at this point. You seem so foreign."[56] Second, "I feel no physical attraction to you."[57] The first point racializes Leonard's sexual desire for her, consistent with the anti-Semitism of the period, as foreign, even barbarian. In light of Virginia's self-consciousness about this point, her falling in love with and marrying Leonard shows that she came to see in him and feel something for him, as a person, that led her to break the Love Laws, of which she was well aware. It was the wisest decision she was ever to make, as a woman and an artist. Virginia's willingness to acknowledge her lack of sexual feeling for him was remarkably honest and might at least have reasonably warned Leonard that there would be sexual problems in this marriage.

It is doubtful, however, that Leonard, deeply in love, had any conception of Virginia's psychological frailties. Once married, they had sex, but Virginia's response was one of distress, not pleasure. What follows was something Leonard could not reasonably have anticipated: several years of psychological breakdowns, one nearly successful suicide attempt, and constant care not only by Leonard but by doctors and nurses as well. It is these breakdowns that led Leonard to decide, perhaps wrongly from Virginia's point of view, that they should not have children, which led to sex playing no role in their marriage for the rest of their lives. Virginia recovered from her breakdowns and, almost certainly because of Leonard's ongoing care and concerns, lived for the next twenty-five years with a sense of her growing creative powers and achievements as a writer and artist. Leonard became carefully alert to any sign of exhaustion in Virginia (usually after she finished one of her novels) and intervened; Nigel

---

[56] Lee, *Virginia Woolf*, p. 310.
[57] Ibid., p. 311.

Nicholson, the son of Virginia's lover, Vita Sackville-West, observed one of these episodes:

> Virginia, standing by the fireplace, was arguing, excitedly, when Leonard slowly rose from his chair and gently touched her on the shoulder. Without enquiry or protest, she followed him from the room, and they were absent for about a quarter of an hour. . . . In her excitement, Virginia might overstep the bounds of sanity, and Leonard, observing her closely, took her away to calm down. . . . The gesture with which he touched her on the shoulder was almost biblical in its tenderness, and her submission to him indicated a trust that she awarded to no other person.[58]

Leonard would write and publish in 1914 another novel, *The Wise Virgins*,[59] which was brazenly autobiographical, contrasting his own Jewish background with the world of his Cambridge friends and families. The antihero Harry, who is Leonard, is torn between an uneducated woman, Gwen, and the cultivated and socially superior sisters, Camilla and Katherine, who stand in for Virginia Stephen and Vanessa Bell. Harry marries Gwen. It was to be Leonard's last novel (subsequently, he would write nonfiction). For the rest of his life, he would be the first reader of his wife's novels and establish a rhythm and shared way of life, including their role as publishers of the Hogarth Press, which facilitate and make possible his wife's growing creative work. At some point, Leonard, steeped in G. E. Moore's ethics that love and the creation of beauty and truth were the ultimate ethical goods, realized that the woman he loved "is the only person whom I have known intimately who had the quality which one had to call genius,"[60] so that love and the creation of beauty and truth were, in their relationship, one. Although sex played little part in it, play, tenderness and the pleasure they took in one another remained until the end. It was a most unconventional marriage, certainly unconventional by the standards of Bloomsbury, but the love between them cannot be in doubt if we mean by love each coming to value and take pleasure in the individual person and voice of the beloved. Virginia would later come to the realization that her sexuality was lesbian and have a passionate and satisfying sexual affair for several years with Vita Sackville-West, herself a prolific writer and the wife of Harold Nicolson, a gay man. In the midst of their affair, Virginia would warn Vita "that Leonard was essential to her. In fact, their marriages were quite different. Virginia

---

[58] Nigel Nicolson, *Virginia Woolf* (London: Weidenfeld & Nicolson, 2000), at p. 80.
[59] Leonard Woolf, *The Wise Virgins* (New Haven, CT: Yale University Press, 2007; first published, 1914).
[60] Leonard Woolf, *Beginning Again: An Autobiography of the Years 1911–1918* (San Diego, CA: Harcourt Brace Jovanovich, 1964), p. 28.

and Leonard were much closer, professionally and politically, than Vita and Harold. They spent much more time together."[61] Leonard may only have come to a full understanding of his wife's lesbianism after her death,[62] but of her love for him there can be no doubt. Leonard was always the one to whom Virginia returned.

Perhaps, the best evidence of the quality of Virginia's feeling for her husband is the suicide note she wrote to her husband on the day of her death:

> Dearest,
> I want to tell you that you have given me complete happiness. No one could have done more than you have done. Please believe that. But, I know that I shall never get over this & I am wasting your life. It is this madness. Nothing anyone says can persuade me. You can work, & you will be much better without me. You see I cant write this even, which shows I am right. All I want to say is that until this disease came on we were perfectly happy. It was all due to you. No one could have been so good as you have been. From the very first day till now. Everyone knows that.
> V.[63]

A life, thus centered in the love of equals, explains, I believe, how and why, remarkably for Britons of this period, this group, which has already resisted the Love Laws, comes to resist the unjust violence and mayhem of World War I. It remains a historical puzzle how so unjust and stupid and catastrophically harmful a war took place at all, even more so how and why a nation like Britain should have become involved in such a war, conducted it so badly, and been so unable to stop the bloodshed when it careened out of all reasonable bounds. Why, in a democracy like Great Britain, was there so little resistance to entering such an unjust and monstrously costly war or to its conduct?[64] I believe both questions do not lend themselves fully to rational argument.[65] The underlying problem, rather, is a matter of political psychology – namely, that World War I was a war among competing European imperialisms: the empires of Russia, Austria-Hungary, Germany, France, and Great Britain. It was because the underlying patriarchal political psychology that supported imperialism was so dominant in these European countries, including in Great Britain, that the sense of insult to one's patriarchal imperial claims so easily elicited violence

---

[61] Lee, *Virginia Woolf*, p. 489.
[62] On this point, see Victoria Glendinning, *Leonard Woolf*, at p. 419.
[63] Hermione Lee, *Virginia Woolf*, pp. 759–60.
[64] On this point, see Adam Hochschild, *To End All Wars: A Story of Loyalty and Rebellion, 1914–1918* (Boston: Houghton Mifflin Harcourt, 2011).
[65] On the number of times intelligent statesmen could have stopped the impetus to war, see John Keegan, *The First World War* (New York: Alfred A. Knopf, 1999), pp. 48–70.

among politicians, even though most ordinary people did not want or expect war.[66]

It is against this background that we may study and understand why the resistance group we are examining, so remarkably for Britons of their period, both resisted World War I and would become important figures in the criticism of the terms on which World War I ended and of imperialism itself. The key, I believe, is that, having broken the patriarchally imposed Love Laws to center their lives in the love of equals, they were not constrained by the stereotypes and vulnerabilities to which patriarchy would otherwise have subjected them. It is the psychological mark of patriarchy that it confines the terms of argument and debate to those that support patriarchal demands, violently repressing any voice that challenges its authority, thus disabling people not only from consulting the full range of relevant arguments and voices but even from taking seriously their own experience or that of others. It is because patriarchy had less hold on the resistance group I am studying that they were more open not only to all relevant arguments and voices but to experience itself.

Lytton Strachey's gender-bending life and work brilliantly illustrate this point. Michael Holroyd's biography is as remarkable as it is because James Strachey, Lytton's younger brother and a psychoanalyst, gave Holroyd the kind of access, informed by James's deep love of his deceased brother, that enables us to see Lytton Strachey in all his flamboyant, highly intelligent, erotic, morally courageous complexity.[67] Strachey was always a sexually active gay man, and, although experiencing many disappointments in love, always searched for and wanted gay sexual love, having throughout his life a series of lovers for relatively short periods. Within the context of these loves, Strachey also had a remarkably loving relationship with a woman artist, Carrington, and the lover (Gerald Brenan) she eventually married, whom Strachey also apparently loved. Carrington had affairs with other men and with a woman but always came back to Strachey, from whom she received attention and support, including of her work as an artist. She also cared for Strachey, cooking for him and sharing a life together. When Strachey falls ill with a fatal cancer, Carrington is bereft, and Strachey, even as he knows he is dying, consoles her, telling her, he always wanted to marry her.[68] After Strachey's death, Carrington

---

[66] On this point, see Michael S. Neiberg, *Dance of the Furies Europe and the Outbreak of World War I* (Cambridge, MA: Belknap Press of Harvard University Press, 2011).

[67] See, in general, Holroyd, *Lytton Strachey*.

[68] See Holroyd, *Lytton Strachey*, p. 678. For a different interpretation of the Carrington-Strachey relationship, stressing what she takes to be its patriarchal features, see Julie Anne Taddeo, *Lytton Strachey and the Search for Modern Sexual Identity: The Last Eminent Victorian* (New York: Harrington Park Press, 2002), pp. 98–9. I am struck, in contract to Taddeo, by Strachey's

is suicidal, which Virginia Woolf, visiting with Leonard, clearly sees as a real probability (Carrington does kill herself). Virginia, who certainly understood depression and would herself commit suicide and herself loved Strachey, clearly sees in the love of Strachey and Carrrington the kind of tender, playful love of equals – however unconventional – she had experienced with Leonard, a love based not on sex but on loving the unique person and voice, including the creative voice, of the other.[69] Strachey clearly had loved deeply, and been loved in return.

Because he was grounded in this way, a man like Lytton Strachey, who had endured throughout his life the taunts directed against his antipatriarchal conception and style of manhood, was unmoved by the taunts directed at his ethical claim for conscientious objector status. Strachey was in a position reasonably to contest the terms of the patriarchal gender binary directed against him, that it was manly to fight but not manly to think for oneself and to resist demands to use violence that were unjustified. To understand the depth of Strachey's convictions on the matter, there was no chance, in light of his poor health, of his being called up after compulsory military service had been introduced in Britain (he was ultimately exempted on health grounds). However, he objected to conscription in principle, had worked for the No Conscription Fellowship, and, after the passing of the Military Service Bill, registered as a conscientious objector. On March 7, 1916, he appeared as a claimant for exemption before the Hampstead Advisory Committee and read the following statement:

> I have a conscientious objection to assisting, by any deliberate action of mine, in carrying on the war. The objection is not based upon religious belief, but upon moral considerations, at which I arrive after long and careful thought. I do not wish to assert the extremely general proposition that I should never, in any circumstances, be justified in taking part in any conceivable war; to dogmatize so absolutely upon a point so abstract would appear to me to be unreasonable. At the same time, my feeling that the whole system by which it is sought to settle international disputes by force is profoundly evil; and that, so far as I am concerned, I should be doing wrong to take any active part in it.

generous interest in and support of both Carrington's creative work as an artist and her various sexual relationships, which to me suggest genuine interest in Carrington as a person, something she never found in the same way from anyone else. Certainly, Strachey profited by Carrington's presence in his life, as a cook and housekeeper and much else, but the record to me bespeaks not one-sided patriarchal control, but reciprocity, equal respect, and real affection and tender concern on both sides.

[69] On Virginia's coming to appreciate Carrington and her relationship to Strachey (after initial jealousy), see Holroyd, *Lytton Strachey*, pp. 360–2.

These considerations have crystallized in my mind since the outbreak of war. Before that time, I was principally occupied with literary and speculative matters; but, with the war, the supreme importance of international questions was forced upon my attention. My opinions in general have been for many years strongly critical of the whole structure of society; and, after a study of the diplomatic situation, and of the literature, both controversial and philosophical, arising out of the war, they developed naturally with those which I now hold. My convictions as to my duty with regard to the war have not been formed either rashly or lightly; and I shall not act against those convictions, whatever the consequences may be.[70]

The committee rejected his claim. Strachey later attended, as a gesture of support, Bertrand Russell's trial for publishing an article advocating acceptance of a peace offer recently made by Germany. Russell was convicted and sentenced to six months' imprisonment in Brixton jail.[71]

As his statement makes clear, Strachey had come to believe that Britain's willingness to go to war and its conscription policy had made him "strongly critical of the whole structure of society," which in the essay "Militarism and Theology," published in 1918, he argues had made the most terrifying and bloodthirsty militarism perfectly acceptable to "the great mass of ordinary, solid, humdrum, respectable persons" who remain "the dominating force in human affairs."[72] The analogy explored by Strachey is the unreasonable certainty underlying intolerance in religion, which seems to me to make exactly the right point about the role Roman patriarchy had played in making the Christianity of the West in its own image, the Christianity to which most of the antagonists (the Ottoman Empire excepted) in World War I appealed. Strachey had found his vocation as an analyst of the role patriarchy had played in so shaping the conception of manhood and womanhood in Britain in ways that sustained the patriarchal political psychology that made such unjust violence acceptable. What Wyndham Lewis would parody in Strachey as "asserting his revolutionary pseudo-manhood"[73] was a profound investigation of what had made patriarchal manhood and womanhood so dominant and so dangerous in Britain, something a more conventional man like Lewis could not take seriously.

---

[70] Michael Holroyd, ed., *Lytton Strachey by Himself: A Self Portrait* (London: Heinemann, 1971), p. 136.
[71] Holroyd, *Lytton Strachey*, p. 411.
[72] Lytton Strachey, "Militarism and Theology," in Lytton Strachey, *Characters and Commentaries* (Westport, CT: Greenwood Press, 1961; originally published, 1933), pp. 223–7, at p. 223.
[73] Holroyd, *Lytton Strachey*, p. 362.

Another gay man, the poet Siegfried Sassoon, came to recognize the injustice of World War I later than Strachey and his friends. Sassoon had fought with notable bravery in the war, but he, like his fellow soldier, poet, and friend, Robert Graves, was shocked that the war, with its extraordinary level of casualties was allowed to continue, the government in the autumn of 1916 having been "offered peace terms on the basis of *status quo ante*," an offer rejected "by the 'Win-the-War' Coalition Government of Lloyd George."[74] Both Sassoon and Graves "could no longer see the War as one between trade-rivals; its continuance seemed merely a sacrifice of the idealistic younger generation to the stupidity and self-protective alarm of the elder."[75] Sassoon, unlike Graves, was moved to an act of public resistance, writing a letter to his commanding officer about why he could no longer serve:

> I am making this statement as an act of willful defiance of military authority, because I believe that the war is being deliberately prolonged by those who have the power to end it.
>
> I am a soldier, convinced that I am acting on behalf of soldiers. I believe that this war, upon which I entered as a war of defence and liberation, has now become a war of aggression and conquest. I believe that the purposes for which I and my fellow-soldiers entered upon the war should have so clearly stated as to have made it impossible to change them, and that, had this been done, the objects which actuated us would now be attainable by negotiation.
>
> I have seen and endured the sufferings of the troops, and I can no longer be a party to prolong these sufferings for ends which I believe to be evil and unjust.[76]

It was, at this point, that Graves, who agreed with Sassoon's views but was concerned for his future (such a public statement, even by a war hero, may have had dire consequences), intervened to get a medical board appointed to hear Sassoon's case and himself testified "[t]hough conscious of a betrayal of truth" that Sassoon was not sane and required medical care.[77] Sassoon was sent for care with Professor W. H. R. Rivers at Craiglockhart and eventually returned to the front to fight with his beloved men until the war ended.[78] Sassoon condemned what Graves had done, as Graves himself came to condemn himself: "a man of courage would not acquiesce as I [Graves] did."

---

[74] Robert Graves, *Good-Bye to All That*, p. 245.
[75] Ibid., p. 245.
[76] Quote in ibid., p. 260.
[77] Ibid., p. 263.
[78] See ibid., p. 264.

Graves could not remember his reply.[79] Inspired by what he had come to see as the tragedy of Britain's role in World War I, Strachey innovated a new kind of biography in *Eminent Victorians*,[80] published shortly after World War I and intended to expose the dark patriarchal underside of hitherto admired Victorian icons, Cardinal Manning, Florence Nightingale, Dr. Arnold, and General Gordon. Much the longest biography is the first, of Cardinal Manning, who, like Cardinal Newman, converted from Anglicanism to Catholicism, but, in contrast to Newman's flexible and humane intelligence, he was rigidly dogmatic. Strachey's contrast of Manning and Newman is "of the eagle and the dove,"[81] associating Manning's greater influence with a rather brutal, competitive masculinity in contrast to Newman's "half-effeminate diffidence."[82] Florence Nightingale's reputation as a self-sacrificing good woman is exploded; whatever her good works, "the qualities of pliancy and sympathy fell to the man; those of command and initiative to the woman."[83] Challenging Dr. Arnold's reputation as a reformer of public school education, he noted how he was, rather, treating "the boys of Rugby as Jehovah had treated the Chosen People: he would found a theocracy, and there should be Judges in Israel,"[84] reinforcing the punitive hierarchy of older boys over younger, making him "the founder of the worship of athletics and the worship of good form."[85] The cult of General Gordon, as a murdered hero of British imperialism, is debunked in terms of a religious fanatic wholly unqualified to deal with the complex political situation in which he found himself.

What makes Strachey's biography so remarkable is his focus on the role a rigidly unbending interpretation of patriarchal Christianity played not only in religion (Manning) but in rationalizing the rigors of British education in public schools (Dr. Arnold) and in the violent excesses of British militarism (General Gordon). Such a patriarchal culture could not even see clearly what had, in fact, made one of its "feminine" heroines, Florence Nightingale, so remarkable – namely, that her life and work defied the conventional gender binary because she was much more "masculine" than "feminine," and all the

---

[79] See ibid., p. 275. For fuller discussion of these events and Sassoon's later life, including his love affair with Stephen Tennant, his sudden marriage to a woman, and their estrangement, see Max Egremont, *Siegfried Sassoon: a Life* (New York: Farrar, Straus & Giroux, 2005).
[80] Lytton Strachey, *Eminent Victorians* (Lexington, KY: Forgotten Books' Classic Reprint Series, 2011) (originally published, 1918).
[81] Strachey, *Eminent Victorians*, at p. 74.
[82] Ibid., p. 66.
[83] Ibid., p. 148.
[84] Ibid., p. 183.
[85] Ibid., p. 207.

better because she defied the categories in which Victorian gender ideology tried falsely to fit her.

Strachey's two other long biographies deepen this analysis, focusing on two queens of Great Britain, Victoria and Elizabeth I. Strachey's focus in *Queen Victoria*[86] is, first, debunking the alleged intimacy of the marriage to Prince Albert, and, second, critically examining the role Victoria increasingly played, after Albert's death, as an icon of expansive British imperialism. On the first point, Strachey's suggestion, albeit rather euphemistically, is that Albert was homosexual,[87] and in fact experienced "no true companionship"[88] with Victoria, leading to her hierarchical worship of him as a kind of falsifying idolatry.[89] On the second point, Strachey interprets her desolate psyche after Albert's death as increasingly manipulated by Disraeli, when prime minister, to support more aggressive British imperialism, finding it "pleasant to be patriotic and pugnacious,"[90] and to resist and even frustrate, contrary to the limits on her power as a constitutional monarch, the more liberal foreign and domestic policies of Gladstone, when prime minister, whose sermons on her duty Victoria came to dislike. It was Disraeli who thus persuaded Victoria to become "Empress of India,"[91] a religious symbol of British imperialism, "a faith as well as a business."[92] Unlike her dead husband, Victoria had no understanding of scientific progress and was violently hostile to what she called "this mad, wicked folly of 'Woman's Rights.'"[93] Her long mourning of her husband until her own death "proclaimed Victoria's consecration to duty and the ideal of the dead."[94]

Strachey's portrait of Elizabeth I in *Elizabeth and Essex: A Tragic History*[95] analyzes her qualities as a monarch in sharp contrast to those of Victoria, bound to a demanding sense of duty as an idealized patriarchal woman on a pedestal always in hierarchical submission to a man (whether her husband or Disraeli's patriarchal imperialism). What made Elizabeth so remarkable as a British monarch who never marries is, on Strachey's analysis, that she

---

[86] Lytton Strachey, *Queen Victoria* (Fairfield, Iowa: 1st World Library, 2006) (originally published, 1921).
[87] On this point, see Strachey, *Queen Victoria*, pp. 90, 94–5.
[88] See ibid., p. 102; see also, p. 179.
[89] Ibid., p. 116,
[90] Ibid., p. 172.
[91] Ibid., pp. 226–7.
[92] Ibid., p. 259.
[93] Cited at Ibid., p. 256.
[94] Strachey, *Queen Victoria*, p. 253.
[95] Lytton Strachey, *Elizabeth and Essex: A Tragic History* (San Diego, CA: Harvest Books, 1956; originally published, 1928).

defied the gender binary, having and developing qualities as much feminine and masculine, "of vigour and sinuosity, of pertinacity and vacillation ... what her case required."[96] She would, Strachey argues, "have been lost" if she followed "the approved pattern of the strong man of action, ... taking a line and sticking to it."[97] "Her femininity saved her,"[98] because, unburdened by conventional ideals of male honor, she could avoid "the appalling necessity of having, really and truly, to make up her mind," escaping "the pressure that came upon her from every side."[99] But she also had the courage to reject "the ways of strength"[100] of patriarchal masculinity, in particular, avoiding war and keeping the peace for thirty years.

What made Elizabeth's love for Essex late in her life tragic is that Essex brought to his love for Elizabeth all the conventional patriarchal assumptions in this period,[101] a patriarchal psychology that disabled him from seeing or understanding Elizabeth's gifts and achievement as a monarch, insisting, at the end, that he must rule as king when, as Elizabeth came to see, he lacked the qualities to be a good ruler. Strachey understands this tragedy in terms of the way patriarchy kills the love of equals, perhaps his deepest observation about the ravages patriarchy imposes on intimate life. This already-riveting narrative ends with yet another brilliant turn in Strachey's analysis as he offers a psychoanalytic explanation of how Elizabeth could order the death of the man she loved: she comes to see in Essex her own patriarchally jealous and homicidal father, Henry VIII, who ordered the death of his wife Ann Boleyn, probably on trumped up charges of adultery,[102] Elizabeth, a trauma victim but now exercising the power of her father, sought revenge on her father by doing to him (Essex) what Henry had done to her mother. In 1928, Freud himself, after reading the book, wrote an admiring letter to Strachey: "you have moved me deeply, for you yourself have reached greater depths ... you have approached one of the most remarkable figures in your country's history, you have known how to trace back her character to the impressions of her childhood, you have touched upon her most hidden motives with equal boldness and discretion, and it is very possible that you have succeeded in making a correct reconstruction of what actually occurred."[103]

---

[96] Ibid., p. 12.
[97] Ibid., p. 13.
[98] Ibid., p. 13.
[99] Ibid., p. 13.
[100] Ibid., p. 13.
[101] On this point, see ibid., pp. 128, 162, 172, 177.
[102] On this point, see ibid., pp. 263–4.
[103] Cited in Holroyd, *Lytton Strachey*, at p. 615.

Strachey had found his vocation through and in resistance to patriarchy. The other members of this resistance group, who were subject to conscription, also opposed World War I. None of them served. Some of them, like Leonard Woolf, who had a lifelong tremor, were exempted on health grounds. Maynard Keynes privately opposed the war but refused to resign his post at the treasury. He was, however, effective in supporting the claims for conscientious exemption and alternative service of James Strachey, Duncan Grant, and David Garnett.

Although Keynes was criticized by his friends, including Lytton Strachey, for not protesting World War I more publicly, he would win Strachey's acclaim after the war for the analysis of *The Economic Consequences of the Peace*.[104] As a member of the British delegation, Keynes had attended the Paris conference at Versailles after World War I, leading to the terms of the peace treaty. What impressed Strachey and others was Keynes's piercing account of the psychology of the three allied leaders at the conference, Woodrow Wilson of the United States, Lloyd George of Great Britain, and Georges Clemenceau of France. Keynes's picture of Lloyd George is of a wily politician who, because of the "political immorality"[105] of calling and winning a General Election in Britain before the conference, had made election promises to the British electorate about a highly retributive peace treaty, calling for the trial of the kaiser, punishment for all atrocities, the fullest indemnities from Germany, and the like.[106] Clemenceau is portrayed as determined to exact the maximum retribution from Germany he was able to secure. What Keynes shows us is that Wilson, despite the idealism of the Fourteen Points and the decisive economic and military power of the United States to determine the direction of the conference, not only arrived unprepared for the discussions of the conference but was also psychologically unable to deal effectively with either the agility of Lloyd George or the retributive intransigence of Clemenceau. At the end, even Lloyd George's last-minute attempts to rectify some of the mistakes in the Treaty of Peace hit the psychological wall of Wilson's embattled stubbornness.

Writing long before Freud and Bullitt's not dissimilar psychological analysis of Wilson's incompetence at Versailles,[107] Keynes finds, like them, the roots of Wilson's psychological problems is his patriarchal religion: "The President

---

[104] John Maynard Keynes, *The Economic Consequences of the Peace* (U.S.A.: ReadaClassic.com, 2010) (originally published, 1919).
[105] Keynes, *Economic Consequences of the Peace*, p. 61.
[106] Ibid., p. 64.
[107] See Sigmund Freud and William C. Bullitt, *Woodrow Wilson: A Psychological Study* (New Brunswick, NJ: Transaction Publishers, 1999; originally published, 1967).

was like a Nonconformist minister, perhaps a Presbyterian. His thought and his temperament were essentially theological and intellectual, with all the strength and the weakness of that manner of thought, feeling, and expression."[108] Wilson had proposed a League of Nations and the Fourteen Points as abstract norms, but, to the surprise of Europeans, he had not come to the conference with any detailed plans for the League, nor for how the Fourteen Points would be embodied in the Peace Treaty. The president could speak from on high but was not agile in discussion with others and not well informed about European conditions. He clearly had the power to impose his view of the Peace Treaty but having decided that some concessions were unavoidable, he insisted that the Fourteen Points were absolutely binding on him, becoming "a document for gloss and interpretation and for all the intellectual apparatus of selfdeception, by which, I daresay, the President's forefathers had persuaded themselves that the course they thought it necessary to take was consistent with every syllable of the Pentateuch."[109] When the Germans protested that the resulting Treaty of Peace was inconsistent with the promises made, "every instinct of his stubborn nature rose in selfprotection," suggesting to Keynes "a Freudian complex. It was a subject intolerable to discuss, and every subconscious instinct plotted to defeat its further exploration."[110]

What is, of course, remarkable about Keynes's analysis is its probing insight into the insular, embattled psychology of threatened patriarchal manhood, which responds by repressing any voices or arguments that challenges its legitimacy. Keynes writes *The Economic Consequences of the Peace* as an act of resistance to such patriarchal insularity, offering compelling arguments for why such unjust, humiliating terms cannot be a reasonable basis for lasting peace in Europe. To the contrary, as we know, it was precisely such humiliating peace terms that set the stage for the catastrophic violence of fascist Germany in World War II. Patriarchy has, Keynes suggests, blinded us to the ethical dimensions at stake at Versailles – namely, that the cure of Europe's problems "lay in magnanimity," "prudent generosity instead of imbecile greed."[111] Keynes, like his friend Lytton Strachey, centered his life in loves for men and women that, in resisting the patriarchal Love Laws, enabled and enhanced an ethical intelligence that could think and feel beyond the patriarchal blinkers of friends versus enemies, blinkers that, in a contemporaneous letter to Duncan Grant at the time of the peace conference, resulted in the allies, who

---

[108] Keynes, *Economic Consequences of the Peace*, p. 22.
[109] Ibid., p. 26.
[110] Ibid., p. 27.
[111] Ibid, p. 65.

"had a chance of taking a large or at least a humane view of the world but unhesitatingly refused to sign it. Wilson, of whom I've seem a great deal more lately, is the greatest fraud on earth."[112]

If patriarchy, as I have suggested, impairs our ethical relationality, resistance may leave our relationality intact, which explains why Keynes, like Strachey, is such a penetrating analyst of human psychology. This may further explain how and why "[e]ven his sexual ambivalence played its part in sharpening his vision,"[113] in particular, both his ethical intelligence and his attention to human psychology, a gift that extends as well to his other work as one of the most creative economic thinkers of his age."[114] For example, Keynes came to disagree with the sense of probability (an empirical or frequency theory of probability) that G. E. Moore assumed in arguing in *Principia Ethica* that, in light of our ignorance of the future, we could depend on immediate consequences, as embodied in the rules of conventional morality, and not assume future consequences would reverse our calculations."[115] Keynes thus developed and published in 1921 *A Theory of Probability*, on which he was working while he lived with Duncan Grant (who was painting as Keynes worked on his manuscript), in which he argued probability statements should be analyzed in terms of the evidence available to an agent, which is not affected by later events. Keynes thus questioned the weight Moore accorded conventional rules of ethics, in favor of "the circumstances of an action," which "become the most important consideration in judgments of probable rightness."[116] It was Keynes's understanding of probability and his doubts in certainty about the future that led to his lifelong skepticism about doctrinaire forms of socialism (including Marxism) that claimed certainty about the laws of history. Keynes's economics was never intended to replace free market capitalism but rather to make corrections based on what Keynes believed was a better psychology of market behaviors[117] – namely, "the urge to consume which pushes economic activity forward, and the urge to not-consume which holds

---

[112] Quoted in Robert Skidelsky, *John Maynard Keyes Hopes Betrayed 1883–1920*, at p. 372.
[113] Robert Skidelsky, *John Maynard Keynes The Economist as Savior 1920–1937* (New York: Allen Lane, 1994), p. 537.
[114] For another exploration of this theme, see Bill Maurer, "Redecorating the International Economy: Keynes, Grant, and the Queering of Bretton Woods," in *Queer Globalizations: Citizenship and the Afterlife of Colonialism*, edited by Arnaldo Cruz-Malave and Martin F. Manalansan IV (New York: New York University Press, 2002), pp. 100–33.
[115] G. E. Moore, *Principia Ethica*, pp. 152–3.
[116] Robert Skidelsky, *John Maynard Keynes the Economic as Savior*, p. 154.
[117] On this point, see Roger F. Backhouse and Bradley W. Bateman, *Capitalist Revolutionary John Maynard Keynes* (Cambridge, MA: Harvard University Press, 2011).

it back."[118] The propensity to save was not, Keynes believed, always rationally connected to future economic advantage, but psychologically determined by "a generalized anxiety about the future as well as to a lack of capacity to enjoy the present."[119] For this reason, the market was not always self-correcting: consumption demand was too weak, investment demand too strong, resulting in a low effective demand and massive unemployment. The problem could, however, be corrected by prudent government action in light of these facts.[120]

Keynes was an economist but one deeply absorbed in the arts and in artists (his most serious lovers were flamboyant artists, Duncan Grant and Lydia Lopokova). The role that resistance played in Strachey's biographies and Keynes's economics crucially framed the work of the artists in our resistance group as well, in none of its members more profoundly than Virginia Woolf. Her *Mrs. Dalloway*[121] and *To the Lighthouse*[122] are among the most astonishing and revelatory artistic explorations of the power of patriarchy in the lives of women and men. Like *A Farewell to Arms* and *Lady Chatterley's Lover*,[123] they explicitly evoke the violence and trauma of World War I. Woolf's great plea for resistance to patriarchal violence, *Three Guineas*, written in the 1930s, directly explores what her novels exposed: the patriarchal roots of the fascist violence that would shortly erupt in the cataclysm of World War II. At this point, artistic resistance becomes political resistance.

What Woolf shows us so astutely in *Mrs. Dalloway* is the trauma of patriarchy, the losses inflicted on women and men. The novel pivots around a woman and a man who never meet – Mrs. Dalloway and Septimus Warren Smith – yet whose lives have been truncated by the patriarchal roles they have played. Mrs. Dalloway, the name capturing her evisceration as patriarchal wife and mother, has in effect lost her voice and her self. It is only in the very last word of the novel that we hear her name, as she finally appears as herself: "There she was: Clarissa." By this point, she has learned of the suicide of Septimus, the World War I soldier, traumatized by the loss of Evans, the comrade he loved.

---

[118] Ibid., p. 541.
[119] Ibid., p. 542.
[120] See John Maynard Keynes, *The General Theory of Employment, Interest, and Money* (New York: Palgrave Macmillan, 2007; originally published, 1936).
[121] Virginia Woolf, *Mrs. Dalloway* (San Diego, CA: Harvest Books, 1997; first published, 1925).
[122] Virginia Woolf, *To the Lighthouse* (San Diego, CA: Harvest Books, 1981; originally published 1927).
[123] For discussion of these novels, see Gilligan and Richards, *The Deepening Darkness*, pp. 201–3, 217–24.

The loss of love, or rather the relinquishment of love, has similarly traumatized Clarissa. As a young woman, she had been in love with her friend Sally Seton and also with Peter Walsh, a lively threesome joined in their resistance to patriarchy. In choosing to forgo these loves to marry the emotionally constricted "Dalloway" (as Sally insists on calling him), she opts to play her required role as the wife of a successful politician, spending her day preparing to give the dinner party that ends the novel. But Mrs. Dalloway is no Leopold Bloom. She is deeply lonely and unhappy, cut off emotionally from her daughter as well as from her husband and from herself. Woolf shows us the underlying psychology of loss that has turned the vibrant Clarissa into Mrs. Dalloway. Both Peter and Sally show up at the party, but in their own ways they too have succumbed. There is seemingly no way of avoiding the power of patriarchy. But Woolf also alludes to the loss of a story about love that had shown a way out.

In the middle of the day that ends with Septimus's suicide and Clarissa's recognition of her own despair, Woolf suddenly introduces an Apuleian reference. Crossing a busy street in London, Peter Walsh and also Septimus and his wife, Rezia, hear an old woman singing in a public garden, "the voice of no age or sex, the voice of an ancient spring spouting from the earth . . . singing of love – love which has lasted a million years . . . love which prevails and millions of years ago, her lover" (p. 47). The reference suggests the old woman in Apuleius's *Metamorphoses* who tells the despairing Charite the story of Cupid and Psyche. But although the subject – love – is unmistakable, the story itself has become incomprehensible, the path of resistance reduced to fragmented syllables.

Long before Judith Herman and other students of trauma had seen the analogies and drawn the connections between the lives of shell-shocked soldiers and battered women,[124] Woolf forged the link in *Mrs. Dalloway*. When the news of Septimus's suicide slices into Mrs. Dalloway's party, she feels for the first time the depth and force of her own despair. She thinks of committing suicide herself, but in the end she resists, emerging finally from the shell of her marriage to appear, at least to herself, as Clarissa. In showing us the different but analogous role that traumatic loss plays in the psychology of the women and men who take up their patriarchal destiny as wives and soldiers, Woolf also hints at the different capacities of men and women to resist and survive such trauma.

To the Lighthouse, Woolf's most autobiographical novel, portrays the patriarchal marriage of her remarkable parents, but also, in the character of Lily

---

[124] See Judith Herman, *Trauma and Recovery* (New York: Basic Books, 1997).

Briscoe, the role of the artist as resistor – the one who paints the portrait. At the center of Woolf's canvas we see Mrs. Ramsey, a woman so completely identified with her patriarchal role that she has no name, so selfless that she has no self, yet so compulsive in her enactment of the patriarchal narrative that "she was driven on, too quickly she knew, almost as if it were an escape for her too, to say that people must marry; people must have children" (p. 60). The portrait of Mr. Ramsey, off to one side, shows a man physically present but emotionally distracted in the midst of a family life centered on facilitating and supporting his compulsive work on his encyclopedia:

> It was a splendid mind. For if thought is like the keyboard of a piano, divided into so many notes, or like the alphabet is ranged in twenty-six letters all in order, then his splendid mind had no sort of difficulty in running over those letters one by one, firmly and accurately, until it had reached, say, the letter Q. He reached Q. Very few people in the whole of England ever reach Q. (p. 33)

Yet, Mr. Ramsey is obsessed with getting to the letter R. The patriarchal burdens weighing on him are such that despite his accomplishment, he is left with a gnawing sense that "he had not done the thing he might have done" (p. 45).

If *Mrs. Dalloway* reveals the shattering effects of trauma on the psyches of women and men under patriarchy, *To the Lighthouse* captures its blighting effects on creativity. Patriarchal violence, the implicit subject of both novels, moves to center stage in Woolf's late essay, *Three Guineas*. Her beloved nephew, Julian Bell, had been killed in the Spanish Civil War in 1937, the year Neville Chamberlain became prime minister of Great Britain. What Woolf came to see, in the rise of an aggressively violent fascism in Spain, Germany, and Italy – a fascism that had killed her nephew – was something Winston Churchill had also seen, leading him to call for resistance before it was too late: the aggressive violence of fascism was rooted in humiliated manhood.[125] Woolf brilliantly carries Churchill's insight one step further analytically to expose the patriarchal roots of fascist violence and explore the possibilities for resistance on the part of the daughters of educated (read patriarchal) men.

What makes the analysis of *Three Guineas* so astonishing is not only Woolf's pathbreaking analysis of the patriarchal origins of fascist violence but also her larger call for a resistance in which women join with men, as she had been joined by Lytton Strachey and her husband, Leonard Woolf (her description of the great procession of patriarchal men in British culture certainly echoes

---

[125] On this point, see David Richards, *Disarming Manhood*, pp. 198–218.

Strachey's critique of "eminent victorians"[126]). At issue, she argued, was what Josephine Butler called "the great principles of Justice and Equality and Liberty." Addressing men, Woolf comments:

> The words are the same are yours; the claim is the same as yours. The daughters of educated men who were called, to their resentment, "feminists" were in fact the advance guard of your own movement. They were fighting the same enemy that you are fighting and for the same reason. They were fighting the tyranny of the patriarchal state as you are fighting the tyranny of the Fascist state. (p. 121)

The same moral and political values justify resistance to both patriarchy and fascism: namely, the values of democracy, "the democratic ideals of equal opportunity for all" (p. 119). Woolf clearly sees and states as well the antidemocratic injustice and violence of what I have called moral slavery, the common patriarchal roots of anti-Semitism, racism, and sexism.[127]

Woolf frames her argument, however, by focusing on "the daughters of educated men" (p, 16), whom she sees as having an independence men do not have, caught up as they are in the great patriarchal processions of British professional and public life.[128] This independence reflects the four teachers of women who have historically resisted the patriarchal demands imposed on them: poverty, chastity, derision, and freedom from unreal loyalties. Women's resistance to patriarchy has, Woolf suggests, certain advantages in part because the disadvantages heaped on their resistance – their four teachers – render them more impervious to its seductions and threats. Even the injustice done to women in the area of sexuality ("how great a part chastity, bodily chastity, has played in the unpaid education of our sex") can be reinterpreted to the advantage of women's resistance: "It should not be difficult to transmute the old ideal of bodily chastity into the new ideal of mental chastity – to hold that if it was wrong to sell the body for money it is much more wrong to sell the mind for money, since the mind, people say, is nobler than the body" (p. 99). For this reason, she calls upon women to pledge "not to commit adultery of the brain because it is much more serious than the other" (p. 112).

Woolf anchors her call for women's resistance in a recognition of difference: it is because women are "[d]ifferent... as facts have proved, both in sex and in education," that "our help can come, if help we can, to protect liberty, to prevent war" (p. 123). Their distinctive strengths can flourish as grounds for resistance if women who gain access through education and the professions

---

[126] See, Virginia Woolf, *Three Guineas* Jane Marcus edition (Orlando, FL: Harvest Books, 2006) (originally published, 1938), pp. 18–39.
[127] On this point, see Woolf, *Three Guineas*, p. 122.
[128] See ibid., pp. 23–28.

form an "Outsiders' Society," finding their own voices as moral agents and speaking in <u>a different voice, a voice nourished by their own "unpaid-for education" – the relational experience and emotional intelligence that would lead women to question and to resist patriarchal demands on men as well as on themselves:</u>

> The Society of Outsiders has the same ends as your society – freedom, equality, peace, but it seeks to achieve them by the means that a different sex, a different tradition, a different education, and the different values which result from those differences have placed within our reach. (p. 134)

Woolf thus concludes by suggesting that women can best help men prevent war "not by repeating your [men's] words and following your methods but by finding new words and creating new methods" (p. 159). In doing so, women will refuse the function Woolf had earlier observed them playing in patriarchy, a function to which men had become addicted:

> Women have served all these centuries as looking-glasses possessing the magic and delicious power of reflecting the figure of men at twice its natural size. Without that power probably the earth would still be swamp and jungle. The glories of all our wars would be unknown.[129]

In *Three Guineas*, Woolf seeks to break the hypnotic spell of a patriarchally rooted male narcissism – the wounded honor or shame that fueled the mass appeal of Hitler and Mussolini.[130] What makes her argument pathbreaking is the way she connects the forms of public and private violence she had examined so sensitively in *Mrs. Dalloway* and *To the Lighthouse* to the aggressive fascism Britain faced in the 1930s, as well as the importance she accords to this linking of public and private worlds and tyrannies. To examine these connections critically, she urges that "it is time for us to raise the veil of St. Paul and to attempt, face to face, a rough and clumsy analysis" of how the Christian tradition has treated women.[131] Finally, in recognizing how far women have come in resistance to patriarchy, she observes how aggressive the response has been to such resistance.

Many of my central points in this book were first stated or at least suggested by Woolf. Once again, we are aware how deeply artists can see into the problematics of patriarchy, even when the religion, politics, and psychology around them are in thrall to its conceptions and institutions. In Woolf's terms,

---

[129] Virginia Woolf, *A Room of One's Own* (San Diego, CA: Harvest Books, 1981; originally published, 1929), p. 35.
[130] On this point, see Woolf, *Three Guineas*, pp. 132, 135.
[131] Ibid., p. 153.

women are, or can be, "a society of outsiders," with perhaps unique insights as to how to stand at once within and apart.

Why were Lytton Strachey and Virginia Woolf, in particular, able to carry their implicit or explicit criticisms of patriarchy so far, including their criticisms of British imperialism and, in Woolf's case, German fascism? One clue might be Strachey's remarkable "freedom of mind and expression," for example, the famous incident, recorded by Virginia, when, as Lytton entered the drawing room at Gordon Square, he "pointed his finger at a stain on Vanessa's dress and inquired 'Semen?' Could one really say it, they wondered, '& we burst out laughing.'"[132] Such freedom of speech enormously relieved the common grief shared by the sisters, Vanessa and Virginia, and Lytton at the death of Thoby, the beloved brother of the sisters and friend of Strachey, at the same time releasing Vanessa in particular "from guilt and the need to conform."[133] Such uninhibited speech may have approximated in conversations among these friends the kind of free association so central to psychoanalysis. Leonard Woolf, in this connection, observes that he and Strachey while at Cambridge, "long before we had any knowledge of Freud," developed a method of "psychological investigation applied to the souls of one's friends," "a kind of compulsory psycho-analysis."[134] It is surely no accident in this connection that Adrian, the sisters' other brother, became a psychoanalyst and that Lytton's brother James and his wife, Alix, were also psychoanalysts. In fact, Alix wrote an important psychoanalytic treatment of motives to war,[135] and, as noted earlier, James was the translator of the works of Freud into English for the Woolf's Hogarth Press.[136] Virginia only read Freud late in life,[137] but her artistic method of stream of consciousness in her novels is free associative and suggests that both she and Strachey may have achieved their remarkable insights into the deadening psychological hold of patriarchy on the British mind, including its best liberal minds (John Stuart Mill), through a psychological method of expression and conversation quite like free association and with similar revelatory consequences.

If Strachey, Keynes, and Virginia Woolf question the impact of patriarchy on British imperialist psychology, Leonard Woolf, following John A. Hobson,[138]

---

[132] See Hermione Lee, *Virginia Woolf*, p. 171.
[133] Quoted from Vanessa's biographer, Frances Spalding, at Hermione Lee, *Virginia Woolf*, p. 171.
[134] Leonard Woolf, *Sowing*, p. 114.
[135] See Alix Strachey, *The Unconscious Motives to War: A Psycho-Analytical Contribution* (New York: International Universities Press, 1957).
[136] See Hermione Lee, *Virginia Woolf*, p. 372.
[137] Ibid., p. 722.
[138] See J. A. Hobson, *Imperialism: A Study* (New York: Cosmo Classics, 2005) (originally published, 1902).

questioned both the economic good sense and morality of British imperialism itself.[139] Hobson had developed an early critique of British capitalism as involving underconsumption and overinvestment similar to ideas Keynes was later to develop. Hobson later covered the Second Boer War in South Africa as a journalist and came to oppose the war and condemn imperialism through his observation of the way Cecil Rhodes advanced imperialism as a way of securing wealth in the Transvaal. His classic study, *Imperialism: A Study*, published in 1902, connected a critique of unjust distribution under British industrial capitalism to imperialism, capitalists seeking higher profits by finding new markets and resources abroad. Lenin would construct his own Marxist critique of imperialism on the basis of Hobson's work.[140]

Leonard Woolf in *Empire and Commerce in Africa*[141] elaborated Hobson's critique with particular attention to Leopold II of Belgium, "who combined the business of a monarch with the profession of knight-errant of Christian civilization, and the profession of a crusader with the business of an extreme shady company promoter,"[142] subjecting "his African subjects to the most ruthless system of exploitation which even Africa has known."[143] It was "the savage and atrocious system" of European imperialism "applied in the Belgian Congo, the French Congo, and German South-West Africa, . . . which led to the extermination of large numbers of the inhabitants."[144] In sum, "[t]he aggressive imperialism of Europe helped to throw the whole power in Japan into the hands of militarist imperialists and these statesmen-soldiers laid their plans well."[145] At the end, Woolf appeals to a new conception of liberalism of universal human rights that embraces all the peoples now unjustly subject to imperial rule, one that treats each of them "as a human being with a right to own his own land and his own life, with a right even to be educated and to determine his own destiny, to be considered, in that fantastic scheme of human government which men have woven the world, an end in himself rather than in instrument to other people's ends."[146] Woolf was to continue to play an important role among the critics of British imperialism as Secretary for the Labour Party's Advisory Committee on Imperial Questions, which influenced Labour Party policy; Woolf distinguished himself among such

---

[139] Leonard Woolf, *Imperialism and Civilization* (London: The Hogarth Press, 1928).
[140] See V. I. Lenin, *Imperialism: The Highest Stage of Capitalism* (New York: International Publishers, 1939).
[141] Leonard Woolf, *Empire and Commerce in Africa: A Study in Economic Imperialism* (Lexington, KY: Cornell University Library Digital Collections, 2011; originally published, 1920).
[142] Ibid., p. 37.
[143] Ibid., p. 310.
[144] Leonard Woolf, *Economic Imperialism* (London: Swarthmore Press, 1920), p. 65.
[145] Id., p. 95.
[146] Leonard Woolf, *Empire and Commerce in Africa*, p. 369.

critics by the emphasis he placed on the expansion of higher education in the colonies.[147]

If the injustice of British imperialism was, as Hobson had shown, connected to distributive injustices within British industrial capitalism, questions had to be raised not only about British democracy but about the international system of competitive imperialism that had led to the catastrophic injustice of World War I. Woolf was, for this reason, an important advocate of democratic socialism in Britain as well as of new forms of international organization (such as a League of Nations), publishing important studies for the Fabian Society and the recently founded Labour Party.[148] Similar analyses both of the war and the need, explicitly, for a League of Nations were published by the Cambridge don and Apostle, Goldsworthy Lowes Dickinson, a close friend of E. M. Forster (who wrote a biography of his friend) and, like Forster, a gay man.[149] The League of Nations failed, and, as Keynes predicted, the unjust terms of the Peace Treaty elicited the even more monstrous violence of German fascist imperialism. Both Leonard and Virginia were alarmed by the rise of German fascism and, surprisingly, in light of Leonard's being a Jew, visited Germany to observe the pathologies of fascist politics at close hand, leading to two studies calling for resistance, *Quack! Quack!*[150] and *Barbarians at the Gate*.[151] (Both the bombing of Britain and the likelihood of German invasion, which she knew would mean the death of her Jewish husband and herself, may have been important ingredients of the not wholly irrational suicidal despair – reflected in her sense that her creative voice had "no echo... only waste air"[152] – she reveals in her last letter to Leonard). After World War II, Woolf argued that the catastrophe required a complete rethinking of Britain and European politics as well as international politics, discussing forms of federation (analogous to the European Union) and an international order that instituted a body not marred by the defects of the League of Nations.[153] Finally, Woolf worked on

---

[147] For an overview of the critics and their influence, see Nicholas Owen, "Critics of Empire in Britain," in *The Oxford History of the British Empire*, Vol. IV. *The Twentieth Century*, edited by Judith M. Brown and Wm. Roger Louis (Oxford: Oxford University Press, 1999), pp. 188–211; on Woolf, in particular, see ibid., pp. 194–5.

[148] See Leonard Woolf, *Socialism and Co-operation* (London: The National Labour Press, 1921); Leonard Woolf, *International Government: Two Reports* (London: Fabian Society Bookshop, 1916).

[149] For further discussion, see E. M. Forster, *Goldsworthy Lowes Dickinson* (London: Edward Arnold, 1973; originally published, 1934), pp. 129–62.

[150] Leonard Woolf, *Quack! Quack!* (New York: Harcourt Brace and Company, 1935).

[151] Leonard Woolf, *Barbarians at the Gate* (London: Victor Gollancz, 1939).

[152] Hermione Lee, *Virginia Woolf*, p. 755.

[153] See Leonard Woolf, *The War for Peace* (London: The Labour Book Service, 1940).

and published a multivolume study of the historical development of British democratic politics, calling for a better understanding and defense of the values of secular liberal democracy.[154] In light of Woolf's arguments in the wake of World War II, as the British Empire unwinds, Woolf's strands of liberal resistance may play some significant role not only in why Britain resists German fascism in World War II but in the role thereafter Britain plays in calling for protections of human rights in the European Convention.[155]

Leonard was brought to resist British imperialism through both his seven-year experience as a British civil servant in Ceylon and his breaking the Love Laws by marrying Virginia, clearly his equal, very much for love.[156] The feeling he shows for native Ceylonese in his first novel, *The Village in the Jungle*, reveals a remarkable relationality in his understanding and feeling for others, including the foreign and the alien. It is striking, in this connection, that when Virginia expresses her doubts about marriage to Leonard, she mentions his Jewishness as a mark of foreignness, so that, in breaking the Love Laws, she is also drawn by love, revealing her own capacity for relationality across patriarchal divides. The relationality of *The Village in the Jungle*, which he is working on at the time of their marriage, may have been enhanced by having found a resonance in Virginia, also an artist working on her first novel and finding a resonance in the same way in Leonard. Virginia also read and admired Leonard's books critical of British imperialism,[157] and her novels and essays, as we have seen, closely analyzed the ways in which patriarchy in Britain sustained the injustice of its imperialism.[158] In an argument with the Nicolsons (including Vita Sackville-West) who claimed the British had a genius for colonization, Virginia opposed them, "'Why not grow, change?' I said. Also, I said, recalling the aeroplanes that had flown over us, while the portable wireless played dance music on the terrace, 'can't you see nationality is over? All divisions are now rubbed out, or ought to be.'"[159]

---

[154] See Leonard Woolf, *After the Deluge: a Study of Communal Psychology* Vol I (London: The Hogarth Press, 1953): Leonard Woolf, *After the Deluge: a Study of Communal Psychology* Vol. II (London: The Hogarth Press, 1953); Leonard Woolf, *Principia Politica: A Study of Communal Psychology* Being Volume 3 of *After the Deluge* (London: The Hogarth Press, 1953).

[155] On this point, see A.W. Brian Simpson, *Human Rights and the End of Empire: Britain and the Genesis of the European Convention* (Oxford: Oxford University Press, 2004).

[156] On Leonard Woolf's anti-imperialism and its impact on his wife, see Elleke Boehmer. *Empire, the National, and the Postcolonial 1890–1920: Resistance in Interaction* (Oxford: Oxford University Press, 2002), pp. 180–91, 201–14.

[157] See Kathy J. Phillips, *Virginia Woolf against Empire* (Knoxville: The University of Tennessee Press, 1994), pp. viii, xxxi–xxxv.

[158] See, for good general treatments, Kathy J. Phillips, *Virginia Woolf against Empire*; Jane Marcus, *Virginia Woolf and the Languages of Patriarchy* (Bloomington: Indiana University Press, 1987).

[159] Cited in Hermione Lee, *Virginia Woolf*, at pp. 509–10.

Like his wife's piercing explorations of how patriarchy destroyed love in her novels (for example, *Mrs. Dalloway*), Leonard also connected the psychology of British imperialism to sexual repression in Britain, as did another of our resistance group, E. M. Forster. An Indian nationalist, Mulik Raj Anand, had asked Leonard to meet the author of *A Passage to India*, so Leonard asked both Forster and the nationalist to drinks:

> The talk centered on British prudery and sexual repression, which led, Leonard said, to the British "compensating for our guilts by going and bossing other people," and to young Englishmen on tea plantations behaving appallingly when they got the chance; they had been brought before him for rape in Ceylon. D.H. Lawrence had it right, said Leonard, about sex. Mulik made copious diary notes. He saw the two friends that evening as "two pioneers of freedom and intimacy"... "with the bluff of white Sahib superiority." In the smoky London sunset, he thought he saw Leonard's eyes, "filled with nostalgia for the tropic light of Ceylon evenings... his forehead lined with furrows of doubt."[160]

E. M. Forster's role in resistance connects his resistance to the patriarchal condemnation of his homosexuality to his exposure of the sexual lies and hypocrisies that, as he came to see, rationalized British imperialism. Travel abroad historically has, as earlier observed, played in important role in the lives of a number of British gay men besides E. M. Forster, for example, Edward Carpenter, J. R. Ackerley, and Christopher Isherwood. All of these men, including Carpenter, spent significant amounts of time in India. There is little doubt that the interest in India is in part rooted in the search for an alternative belief system to the hegemonic Christian homophobia they experienced in Britain – for Isherwood, Hinduism[161] (for the American gay poet, Allen Ginsberg, Buddhism[162]); for Carpenter, his own original synthesis of Indian and other influences.[163] Both Forster[164] and Ackerley[165] wrote novels based on their experiences in India, and, in the case of Forster, the novel, *A Passage to India*, is an important exposure of the sexual hypocrisy that

---

[160] Victoria Glendinning, *Leonard Woolf*, p. 234.
[161] On this point, see Christopher Isherwood, *My Guru and His Disciple* (Minneapolis: University of Minnesota Press, 1980).
[162] See Barry Miles, *Allen Ginsberg: Beat Poet* (Croydon, UK: Virgin, 1989), pp. 295-336, 435-79.
[163] See David A. J. Richards, *Women, Gays, and the Constitution*, pp. 317-27.
[164] E. M. Forster, *A Passage to India* (San Diego, CA: Harvest Books, 1984; originally published, 1924).
[165] J. R. Ackerley, *Hindoo Holiday* (New York: New York Review Books, 2000; originally published, 1932).

he came to see as underlying British imperialism in India, including sexual desire across the ethnic boundaries defined by the patriarchal Love Laws that separated the English imperialists, men and women, from any possibility of real connection.[166]

Forster shows us how the patriarchal Love Laws are maintained through the experience of an otherwise open-minded British woman, Miss Adela Quested, who comes to India with her mother-in-law-to be, Mrs. Moore, ostensibly to be married to Ronny, a British civil servant, a judge, in India. Both women are shocked by the how even Ronny conforms to the strict hierarchy that separates the British from the Indians. It is the oversolicitous relationship of Dr. Aziz, an Indian Muslim, to Miss Quested and Mrs. Moore, trying to break through this barrier, that is at the heart of the novel. Aziz insists on taking the British women to visit the Marabar Caves, at which Mrs. Moore has a vision of life's nothingness and Ms. Quested a hallucination that Dr. Aziz raped her, which is the basis of a scandalous public trial of Aziz for rape. What Forster shows us is the impact of the patriarchal racialized pedestal on the lives and experiences of the women subject to its idealizing demands. The white woman on the pedestal is idealized as asexual and good and the women of color are denigrated as highly sexual and bad. Accordingly, for the British community, any idea that Adela Quested may herself have been sexually attracted to a man of color, Dr. Aziz, is unthinkable, whereas it is thought highly probable that such a man of color may have raped a white woman. Only when Adela comes to realize that the rape did not take place and so testifies does she expose as probable what British racism deemed unthinkable, that she may have been attracted to Aziz, and that a false rape charge was a way of keeping such a thought unthinkable, even from herself as a woman.

Paul Scott's remarkable novels, *The Raj Quartet* (published in the 1960s and 1970s),[167] about the British experience in India at the end of the Raj, explicitly explores several homosexual characters. (Scott had spent considerable time in India in the civil service and had had homosexual relationships

---

[166] For an illuminating study of Forster's novel and comparison with those of Edward Thompson, see Harish Trivedi, *Colonial Transactions: English Literature and India* (Manchester, U.K.: Manchester University Press, 1995), at pp. 139–173.

[167] See Paul Scott, *The Jewel in the Crown: The Raj Quartet 1* (Chicago: University of Chicago Press, 1998; originally published, 1966); *The Day of the Scorpion: The Raj Quartet 2* (Chicago: University of Chicago Press, 1998; originally published, 1968); *The Towers of Silence: The Raj Quartet 3* (Chicago: University of Chicago Press, 1998; originally published, 1972); *A Division of the Spoils: The Raj Quartet 4* (Chicago: University of Chicago Press, 1998; originally published, 1975). See also Paul Scott, *Staying On* (Chicago: University of Chicago Press, 1998; originally published, 1977).

before marrying rather unhappily.[168]) The lead homosexual character, Ronald Merrick, is a British police officer serving in India who experiences sadistic sexual release, including torture, of an Indian man, Kumar, who been brought up and schooled in Britain and had developed a British mind and values that alienated him from fellow Indians. Kumar sexually loved a British woman, Daphne Manners, breaking the Love Laws. Scott, like Forster, shows us the incendiary violence under patriarchal imperialism of violating the Love Laws: Daphne is raped by young Indians (later dying in child birth), and Kumar is sadistically raped by Merrick. The rest of the tetralogy draws out the consequences of these horrors, as Merrick is pursued by Indian nationalists to exact revenge for his sadism as he achieves much higher rank in the British imperial service than he possibly could have achieved in more class-bound Britain and covers his homosexuality by marrying. Merrick makes clear that, once the Raj ends, he will remain in India where he will continue to have much higher status than he would in Britain. The horror for Merrick is that when he comes to fall in love, with all that means, with one of the Indian youths he has sex with, he lets down his guard, then realizes the youth is a decoy of the Indian nationalists, who then murder Merrick.

Both Forster and Scott place the patriarchal Love Laws at the center of their penetrating explorations of the psychology of British imperialism to explain its violent racism and suggest that resistance to the Love Laws is the key to releasing oneself from an imperialism that corrupts both love and politics. Why should gay men be capable of such insights? E. M. Forster's entire life was preoccupied with his struggle to love as a gay man, inspired by Carpenter's lifetime partnership with another man, and apparently experienced his first deeply felt sexual relationship with an Egyptian tram driver, Mohammed, whom he met on his travels abroad.[169] Forster fell in love with Mohammed, who later died; in contrast, another liaison, arranged by the sympathetic maharajah, with a court barber in India was understood by Forster as a connection based only on sex.[170] Loving across the ethnic and gender and class boundaries of the Love Laws was central to Forster's own struggles to dignify his life as a gay man, but the experience also opened his heart and mind, his ethical relationality, to the

---

[168] See Hilary Spurling, *Paul Scott: A Life of the Author of The Raj Quartet* (New York: W.W. Norton, 1991).

[169] For two excellent studies, see Wendy Moffat, *A Great Unrecorded History: A New Life of E. M. Forster* (New York: Farrar, Straus & Giroux, 2010); P. N. Furbank, *E. M. Forster: A Life* (San Diego, CA: Harvest Books, 1977).

[170] Peter Parker, *Ackerley: A Life of J. R. Ackerley* (New York: Farrar, Straus & Giroux, 1989), p. 50. For Forster's own account of his relationship with this maharajah, see E. M. Forster, *The Hill of Devi* (New York: Harcourt Brace and Company, 1953).

person, the individual he loved, including as a subject of what Forster came to see as unjust British racist imperialism.

What Forster experienced as a gay man may seem quite different from what Roger Casement, an Irish nationalist who had served Britain in its civil service, experienced as a British civil servant in his carefully recorded, rather promiscuous sexual affairs with men of color in South America and Africa.[171] Nonetheless, his experiences may have enabled Casement to see clearly and resist what most Europeans refused to see: the atrocities inflicted by Leopold II in the Belgian Congo, inspiring Joseph Conrad to write his greatest novel, *The Heart of Darkness*.[172] The subject of an important recent biographical novel by Mario Vargas Llosa,[173] Casement came to see a common injustice in the imperialism he had seen abroad (publicly attesting, as he did for the British, to racist atrocities in the Belgian Congo and Amazonia) and British colonialism at home in Ireland. His resistance took the form of aiding the Germans during World War I.

There is something psychologically puzzling, not explored by Llosa, in Casement's wrath against the British and support for imperialist Germans when it was the British who had employed him in his work in Africa and Amazonia and sponsored his disclosures of imperialist atrocities. Yet, Casement evidently came to see World War I as the ultimate expression of the destructiveness of competing European imperialisms. This allowed him, as an Irishmen so sensible of the wrongs done to his people by British imperialism, to resist, rather romantically and, as it turned out, self-destructively, the imperialism he had ambivalently served for so long. Writing to a cousin, Casement observed that "this journey into the depths of the Congo has been useful in helping me to discover my own country and understand her situation. In these jungles, I've found not only the true face of Leopold II. I've found my true self: the incorrigible Irishman."[174] There is something even more puzzling in the way Joseph Conrad, who knew and learned from Casement in the Congo, could describe him in a letter to John Quinn as "a man, properly speaking, of no mind at all – all emotion"[175] and how Llosa came to regard Casement's diaries

---

[171] Jeffrey Dudgeon, *Roger Casement: The Black Diaries* (Belfast, Northern Ireland: Belfast Press, 2002).

[172] Joseph Conrad, *Heart of Darkness*, in *Youth/Heart of Darkness/The End of the Tether* (London: Penguin, 1995; first published, 1903), pp. 47–148.

[173] See Mario Vargas Llosa, *The Dream of the Celt*, translated by Edith Grossman (New York: Farrar, Straus & Giroux, 2012).

[174] Quoted in John Banville, "Rebel, Hero, Martyr," in *New York Review of Books*, vol. LIX, no. 16, October 25, 2012, pp. 35–7, at p. 37.

[175] Quoted in Colm Tóibín, "A Man of No Mind," in *London Review of Books*, vol. 34, no. 17, 13 September 2012, pp. 15–16, 18–19, at p. 16.

of his gay interracial affairs, often for money paid by Casement, as true only in small part, more fantasy than reality.

In an important review of Llosa's book, the Irish gay novelist Colm Tóibín expresses his admiration of many of Llosa's other novels but explores the failure of this novel based on Casement's life, which refuses to take seriously "an understanding of his [Casement's] sexuality in all its energy and compulsion and its connection to the energy and compulsion he showed in other areas of his life."[176] How, Tóibín queries, could Conrad, regard Casement as "a man... of no mind at all" when

> [Casement's] reports for the British government on atrocities in the Congo and Peru are written in language of restraint and sobriety. His indignation was deeply controlled. He used detail with cold care and was concerned with accuracy, with information that could not be disputed. He was no longer Conrad's man of "no mind at all" as he worked on his reports. Casement's legacy rests on this work, on his generosity and steely will. But Casement's legacy is more complex than the work he did as a humanitarian.[177]

Tóibín wants us to see Casement in all his complexity, including the connections of his remarkable and courageous humanitarianism to his sexuality, something both Conrad and Llosa refuse to see, let alone explore. It is striking that Conrad phrases his denial in the terms of the patriarchal gender binary: Casement has no mind (masculine) but only emotion (feminine). Tóibín shows us how false this description is with regard to Casement's achievement, which intelligently used "cold care and was concerned with accuracy, with information that could not be disputed" and his life combined "generosity and steely will," both feminine and masculine attributes (in the polarized terms of the gender binary, which Casement's life and work resisted). What gets in the way of Conrad and Llosa and their understanding of Casement may be homophobia, and it certainly shows the continuing power of the patriarchal gender binary over even our best artists. What Llosa does not appreciate when he understates and falsifies the importance of Casement's sexuality, is how it may well be Casement's experience of his homosexuality (breaking the Love Laws with men and indeed with men of color) that may have made him such a radical outsider to the patriarchal pieties of his age, so ethically sensitive to its inhumanities, and so courageous and effective in his resistance to injustice. The British government certainly came to see Casement's homosexuality as the central issue. Thus, the British – who had earlier homophobically turned

---

[176] See ibid., p. 19.
[177] Ibid., p. 19.

their ire on another defiantly resisting gay Irishman, Oscar Wilde – did so, more monstrously, on Casement: his execution for treason by the British was evidently facilitated by the disclosure of his florid gay sex life with natives.[178] George Bernard Shaw had drafted a speech for Casement to give at this trial, but Casement rejected it and spoke in his own voice:

> Self-government is our right. A thing born in us at birth, a thing no more to be doled out to us or withheld from us by another people than the right to life itself – than the right to feel the sun or smell the flowers, or to love our kind.... Where men must beg with bated breath for leave to subsist in their own land, to think their own thoughts, to sing their own songs, to garner the fruits of their own labours... than surely it is braver, a saner and truer thing, to be a rebel... than tamely to accept it as the natural lot of man.[179]

Casement's passion for freedom (including the freedom "to love our kind") extended to all peoples, and his speech entered rapidly into the annals of anti-colonialism. It made a deep impression on a young man, Jawaharlal Nehru, who would lead his people to independence: "It seemed to point out exactly how a subject nation felt."[180]

Gay sexual love is apparently at the heart of the matter, enabling the lover to feel for and enter into the experience of the beloved, feeling "exactly how a subject nation felt." It was certainly Forster's sexual love, breaking the Love Laws, that brought him to a stance of resistance to British imperialist patriarchy in India. It is the same love for a boy, Daroun, that brought T. E. Lawrence, another gay man, to his role in the Arab revolt. The dedication of Lawrence's *Seven Pillars of Wisdom* to the boy, now dead, could not be clearer:

> I loved you, so I drew these tides of men into my hands and wrote my will across the sky in stars
>
> To earn you Freedom, the seven pillared worthy house, that your eyes might be shining for me
>
> When we came.
>
> Death seemed my servant on the road, till we were near and saw you waiting;
>
> When you smiled, and in sorrowful envy he outran me and too you apart;
>
> Into his quietness.

---

[178] For an illuminating discussion, see Adam Hochschild, *King Leopold's Ghost* (Boston: Houghton Mifflin Company, 1999), at pp. 195–208, 267–70, 284–7.
[179] Ibid., p. 286.
[180] Ibid., p. 286.

Love, the way-weary, groped to your body, our brief wage ours for the moment
Before earth's soft hand explored your shape, and the blind worms grew fat upon

Your substance.

Men prayed me that I set our work, the inviolate house as a memory of you.

But for fit monument I shattered it, unfinished; now

The little things creep out to patch themselves hovel in the marred shadow

Of your gift.[181]

It is the tragedy of T. E. Lawrence, himself the product of a marriage that broke the Love Laws, that, unlike his parents, he found no comparable fulfillment (his beloved Daroum had died).

Virginia Woolf, in conversation with Forster, questioned whether he was really a novelist, a proposition with which Forster agreed. What Woolf did not know was the explicitly gay fiction, including *Maurice*,[182] that Forster never published in his life time.[183] Forster wrote and published novels to the point they clarified the great struggle of his life within the limits British prudery imposed, and he stopped writing, remarkably early in his life, once he found the life and the man that met his deepest needs for love as a gay man. That man, Bob Buckingham, was a policeman, who eventually married a remarkable woman, May, who may have understood her husband's loving sexual relationship to Forster better than he did and warmly incorporated Forster into their family life as they had children; Forster died in their house, holding May's hand until he died.[184]

No one was more peculiarly local and British than Forster, and yet – in the midst of the rise of fascism and its challenge to British values – Forster spoke in the voice of a universalistic liberalism centered on friendship and love: "I hate the idea of causes, and if I had to choose between betraying my country and betraying my friend, I hope I should have the guts to betray

---

[181] T. E. Lawrence, *Seven Pillars of Wisdom: A Triumph* (New York: Anchor Books, 1991 (originally published, 1926). For an illuminating study of Lawrence the man, see John E. Mack, *A Prince of Our Disorder: The Life of T. E. Lawrence* (Cambridge, MA: Harvard University Press, 1998), especially pp. 96–8, 189, 192.

[182] E. M. Forster, *Maurice* (Toronto: Macmillan of Canada (1971; novel begun and finished, 1913–14).

[183] See Wendy Moffat, *A Great Unrecorded History: A New Life of E. M. Forster* (New York: Farrar, Straus, & Giroux, 2010), p. 194.

[184] See Wendy Moffat, *A Great Unrecorded History*, pp. 220–36, 321–2.

my country."[185] Forster defended democracy because of the value it placed on liberty in general and on free speech in particular, but he introduced his discussion, citing Shelley, turning to "Democracy, 'even Love, the Beloved Republic, which feeds upon Freedom and lives.'"[186] Forster wrote these words before gay rights had become a live issue in British politics, and he accordingly resisted the association of Democracy with "the Beloved Republic." In his greatest novels, Forster had written both of how deep relational love was in our natures and yet how difficult it was under patriarchy to take it seriously:

> It did not seem so difficult. She need trouble him with no gift of her own. She would only point out that salvation that was latent in his own soul, and in the soul of every man. Only connect! That was the whole of her sermon. Only connect the prose and the passion, and both will be exalted, and human love will be seen at its height. Life in fragments no longer. Only connect, and the beast and the monk, robbed of the isolation that is life to either, will die.[187]

But in the light of what has happened since Forster wrote, we may see Forster's liberalism as resting on the voice he had found through according gay love the dignity it had achieved in living the life and relationships he chose. So the closer study of how arguments for gay rights come to be made and to find a resonance requires us to take seriously both the local and the universalistic, joined, as they are, in the struggle of gay men and women to come to see the dignity of their relationships.

---

[185] E. M. Forster, *Two Cheers for Democracy* (New York: Harvest Books, 1938), at p. 68.
[186] Ibid., at p. 69.
[187] E. M. Forster, *Howards End* (New York: Vintage International Edition, 1989), at p. 195.

4

The Fall of Empire

The connection between the rise of gay rights to the fall of empire must be discussed in two stages. First, there is the period running from the rise of gay rights to World War II up to the 1967 decriminalization of gay sex in Great Britain. Second, there is the period after the 1967 decriminalization. I divide the discussion in this way because the concept of gay rights, as I explored in some depth in Chapter 3, came alive and became the subject of creative public work under the radar of repressive British censorship and the criminal penalties for gay sex that had destroyed the life of Oscar Wilde. Much of that work, as we have seen, questioned and criticized, either explicitly or implicitly, British imperialism, including not only resistance to service in World War I, but British imperialism itself after the war. We can see its impact during this period in the growing debate within Britain about giving up the Raj in India, the Jewel in the Crown of the British Empire, together with the impact Gandhi's activism increasingly had on British public opinion, much to Winston Churchill's furious objection to this "seditious Middle Temple lawyer, now posing as a fakir of a type well known in the East."[1] (Britain, after delaying much too long, rather precipitously gave India its freedom in 1947.[2]) Further evidence is seen in the willingness of Britain finally to free Ireland from colonial rule in 1922 (Gladstone's 1885 proposal of Irish Home Rule had earlier failed[3]). But because gay rights during this period was not yet on the public stage, its impact on British ethics and politics was not yet publicly known and discussed. For example, the leading biography of John Maynard

---

[1] Cited in Roy Jenkins, *Churchill: A Biography* (New York: Farrar, Straus & Giroux, 2001), at p. 436.
[2] On the disastrous consequences, see Yasmin Khan, *The Great Partition: The Making of India and Pakistan* (New Haven, CT: Yale University Press, 2007).
[3] See Roy Jenkins, *Gladstone*, pp. 539–62.

Keynes by Roy Harrod, published in 1951, contained no discussion at all of the long, decisively important period of his living and loving as a gay man.[4] The recommendations of the 1957 Wolfenden Commission, which proposed the decriminalization of gay sex, never did so on the grounds that would have been urged by Lytton Strachey or Virginia Woolf – namely, that gay or lesbian love, breaking the Love Laws, was a human and ethical good, making possible the levels of ethical intelligence that we see in the works of, among others, Strachey, Virginia Woolf, Keynes, and E. M. Forster. What marks the second period, from the 1967 decriminalization of gay sex to date, is the loosening of censorship in Britain, making possible the public knowledge we now have of the rise of gay rights in all its complexity (see Chapter 3) as well as the much more public role gay rights now plays in Britain, the United States, and elsewhere.

The decisive turning point between the rise of gay rights and the fall of empire is, I believe, the impact of World War II – in particular, on the United States and Britain. Two important plays written after World War II give us a sense of the very different worlds Americans and Britons faced after World War II: Tennessee Williams's *A Streetcar Named Desire*, which opened in New York City in 1947, and John Osborne's *Look Back in Anger*, which opened in London in 1956.

Williams, a gay man, anatomizes the impact of World War II on American sexuality and gender roles long before these issues would emerge in American politics in the Civil Rights movement, feminism, and gay rights, anticipating, as great artists do, the increasingly important role resistance to injustice would play in American life and politics. At the center of his narrative of resistance is a woman, Blanche DuBois, who had once been the classic Southern good girl on her idealized pedestal, devoted to care of her declining, formerly rich Southern family and marrying a young poet she also idealized and almost worshipped. Blanche's self-sacrifice, however, led to traumatic loss, the deaths of her family and the suicide of her husband when Blanche confronts him with his homosexual connection to an older man. In despair, Blanche, an English teacher, steps down from her self-sacrificing pedestal, becoming sexually active with soldiers and even a student of hers. Because she has violated the code of womanly honor in which she once believed, Blanche becomes the object of opprobrium in her Southern community and, after the affair with a student, loses her job. As the play opens, Blanche, exhausted and an alcoholic, comes to stay with her sister, Stella, who lives with her husband, Stanley Kowalski, in a small two-room apartment in New Orleans. Stella, in contrast to Blanche,

---

[4] On this point, see Robert Skidelsky, *John Maynard Keynes Hopes Betrayed*, p. xv.

had left her family and sought a job in New Orleans, meeting and falling in love with Stanley, who takes pride in having taken Stella off her pedestal and explored with her a deeply sexual, mutually satisfying love. Stanley had been in World War II with several of his buddies, including Mitch, with whom he currently works. His anger, which explodes at several points in the play, may be connected to traumatic experiences in war. He is portrayed in the play as, in Stella's words to her sister, a "different species"[5] from the men they had known, the most ambitious and driving of his friends, but also as the most patriarchal, exploding whenever his wife gives him an order and self-consciously invoking a new found sense of American patriarchal manhood, "Every Man is a King!"[6]; "one hundred percent American, born and raised in the greatest country on earth and proud as hell of it."[7]

The dramatic agon at the center of the drama is Blanche's growing dismay first at Stanley's bad manners and then at his violence (hitting his wife when she challenges his authority) and Stanley's indignation at Blanche's pretensions to sexual purity and the way she racializes him, as Polish, even as subhuman.[8] Stanley finds out the truth about Blanche's past and ruins her chance to marry Mitch, his friend. When Stella is taken to the hospital to have a baby, he rapes Blanche. No one, including her own sister, will believe Blanche, who is hospitalized at the end of the play as insane. The exchange between Stella and her friend, Eunice, on this point is piercing:

STELLA: I don't know if I did the right thing.
EUNICE: What else could you do?
STELLA: I couldn't believe her story and go on living with Stanley.
EUNICE: Don't ever believe it. Life has got to go on. No matter what happens, you've got to keep on going.[9]

There is no doubt Blanche has been unjust in her slurs at Stanley's background; likewise, there is no doubt she is the only person in the play who resists Stanley's patriarchal violence – and pays the price of such resistance when she is raped and her own sister is complicitous by refusing to hear Blanche's truthful story. Williams thus shows us how American patriarchal violence is sustained ("I couldn't believe her story and go on living with Stanley") and how difficult resistance to it will be.

[5] Tennessee Williams, *A Streetcar Named Desire* (New York: New Directions, 1957).
[6] Ibid., p. 124.
[7] Ibid., p. 126.
[8] Ibid., pp. 80–1.
[9] Tennessee Williams, *A Streetcar Named Desire* (London: Penguin, 1975), p. 99.

In John Osborne's *Look Back in Anger*, the central figure of resistance is Jimmy Porter, who broke the British patriarchal Love Laws when he married his upper-class wife, Alison, the daughter of Colonel Redfern, who served in India with the British military. Alison's mother had taken extraordinary steps to try to prevent the marriage. Porter's resistance in the play is centered, paradoxically, on tirades against his wife, who will not speak to him in her own defense and is now, unknown to Jimmy, pregnant. On one hand, Porter takes pride in having taken his wife off her idealized asexual upper-class pedestal in a relationship portrayed as highly sexual and satisfying to both (like that of Stella and Stanley in *Streetcar*), but Alison, like Blanche, has not yet found an alternative way of living, having, in effect, lost her voice in relationship. Jimmy's anger centers at that loss of voice, identifying Alison with her patriarchally controlling mother, "the White Woman's Burden,"[10] "this monument of non-attachment... like some fleshy Roman matron."[11] The allusion to Roman patriarchal imperialism and the role of women in sustaining it are not accidental but part of the play's critical study of how patriarchy, especially in a period of transition at the fall of empire, continues to destroy the only kind of love that could sustain resistance to patriarchy, the love of equals with equal voice in relationship and in politics generally. Alison leaves Jimmy, allowing Alison's actress friend, Helena, to have an affair with him. When Alison leaves, we meet Colonel Redfern, her father, who agrees with what Alison calls Jimmy's description of him, "One of those sturdy old plans left over from the Edwardian Wilderness that can't understand why the sun isn't shining any more."[12] He explains how much he loved imperial service in India. His daughter comments that he is "hurt because everything is changed. Jimmy is hurt because everything is the same."[13] Jimmy's sense of purposelessness has been expressed by him as this "dreary living in the American Age"[14] when Britons have "no convictions and no enthusiasm."[15] He observes later, "There aren't any good, brave causes left."[16] For this reason, Alison describes her husband's moralism to Helena as, ironically (invoking Strachey), "an eminent Victorian."[17] At the end of the play, Alison returns to Jimmy, having lost her baby and her capacity to have other children. She is abject and broken, as Jimmy, in one of his earlier

---

[10] John Osborne, *Look Back in Anger* (New York, N.Y., Penguin, 1982), at p. 11.
[11] Ibid., p. 21.
[12] Ibid., pp. 66–7.
[13] Ibid., p. 68.
[14] Ibid., p. 17.
[15] Ibid., p. 17.
[16] Ibid., p. 84.
[17] Ibid., p. 90.

tirades, had hoped she would someday be. She is now as broken and damaged as Jimmy, which makes possible the play's ending, a reconciliation in which they can express their love by portraying themselves as animals, a bear and a squirrel.

What both these remarkable plays share is their sense after World War II of wholly new challenges to American expansiveness and British withdrawal. For the American, Tennessee Williams, the worry is a resurgent American patriarchy and its violence, as well as the need for and difficulty of resistance; an additional concern is the sense that resistance would be found in women resisting patriarchy and speaking in a new ethical voice. For the Briton, John Osborne, the worry is loss of meaning as the British Empire declines, the loss of "good, brave causes," but the deeper worry is about the possibility of love in a postimperial world. On the issue of gay rights, it is striking that whereas Williams, the American gay man, gives a central role to closeted homosexuality in Blanche's tragedy, Osborne, a straight man, comments, speaking through Jimmy, that at least homosexuals "have a good cause"; indeed, "plenty of them do seem to have a revolutionary fire about them."[18] Resistance, Osborne suggests, may come from gay rights.

THE FALL OF EMPIRE FROM THE RISE OF GAY RIGHTS TO THE 1967 DECRIMINALIZATION

There are many causes for the fall of empires, and I certainly do not claim that what we explored in Chapter 3 as the rise of gay rights was the only or even the main explanation for the fall of the British Empire, let alone the German Empire of Hitler or the Empire of Japan. The main reason for the fall of the imperialisms of Germany and Japan was defeat in World War II, a defeat that fortunately did not, unlike the peace treaty ending World War I, lead, as Keynes suggested it might, to an even worse, more aggressive form of imperialism. World War II, in which Britain was victorious, paradoxically was crucially responsible, as we shall see, for the rather rapid dissolution of the British Empire.

Imperialism did not, however, end magically with the defeat of fascism. The Soviet Union, in the wake of its role in the allied victory in World War II, used its Marxist ideology, as a form of patriarchal state religion, to rationalize its own form of continuing the Russian imperialism of the czars. Marxism-Leninism was to the imperialism of the Soviet Union, what Russian orthodoxy was to the Russian Empire: Lenin and later Stalin were the high

[18] Ibid., p. 35.

priests of its patriarchal imperialism as much as the czars ("caesars") were the religious-political autocrats of Orthodox Catholicism. Mao played a similar role in Communist China. What all these imperialisms despised was liberal democracy.

I am, however, concerned with the fall of the British Empire and the connections of that fall to the increasingly powerful political role played by the United States in international politics as Britain and the United States and others joined in alliances to contain the imperialism of the Soviet Union. I do not, like Niall Ferguson, mourn the fall of the British Empire,[19] and I certainly do not agree with him that the mantle, no longer worn by Britain (as the most successful imperial power of the modern world), should now be worn by the United States.[20] On the other hand, I recognize that American power after World War II can sometimes be reasonably interpreted as reflecting imperialist pretensions, including the war in Vietnam and the more recent war in Iraq. I want critically to examine both how and why such imperialism led to these mistakes and connect that discussion to the question of resistance, including the successful American resistance that ended the Vietnam War. In the discussion of all these points, I believe gay rights plays an important role as a resistance movement that, joining its voice to and empowered by other resistance movements, questions and subverts imperialism both at home and abroad.

I have shown in Chapter 3 the important connections between the American prophet of gay rights, Walt Whitman, and the resistance movement in Britain. Except for Edward Carpenter, who published about gay rights and lived openly as a gay man, most members of the resistance movement stayed under the radar of British homophobia and lived quietly among themselves openly gay or lesbian lives in ever-changing configurations. Though always drawn together by the love and friendship they shared, none of them wrote publicly, as had Carpenter, about the dignity of gay love. Breaking the Love Laws was a common feature of their creativity as writers and artists, enabling them, in their work, remarkably to challenge British patriarchy at home and abroad and thus to challenge British imperialism. They lived gay rights, and this was, I argue, the key to their remarkable achievements; they did not, however, preach gay rights. In fact, it was only after the 1967 British decriminalization of gay sex in Britain that books were published revealing to a general public what had gone on. And then, of course, drawing inspiration from the resistance

---

[19] Niall Ferguson, *Empire: The Rise and Demise of the British World Order and the Lessons for Global Power* (New York: Basic Books, 2002).
[20] Niall Ferguson, *Colossus: The Price of America's Empire* (New York: Penguin Press, 2004).

movements in the United States and the growing historical understanding of their resistance movement at home, gay rights, as a political movement, took off in Britain and elsewhere.

Nonetheless, it seems to me quite clear that the group I have investigated was a resistance group, and their resistance centered in the ways they self-consciously broke the patriarchally enforced Love Laws that hold patriarchy in place by condemning any form of love across the barriers of class or religion or ethnicity or race or gender on which patriarchy depends. These barriers are enforced by the dehumanizing stereotypes patriarchy never questions, or allows to be reasonably questioned, on the basis of experience. Why loving across these barriers is so liberating to creative ethical intelligence is because loving means coming to see and value the beloved for the individual person she or he is in all that person's complexity; it thus implies coming to see the falsity of the stereotypes that forbade such love. Such stereotypes rationalize irrational prejudices – extreme religious intolerance (for example, anti-Semitism), racism, sexism, and homophobia – that in turn rationalize injustice. The forms of love seen in our resistance group are so important to understand because they show, in the personal and creative lives of these remarkable friends and lovers, how resistance to the Love Laws is grounded in love, and how love enlarges the expression of our ethical relationality and allows us to see and challenge the irrational prejudices that have confined and deadened our relationality. If I am right about this, then the resistance we see in them advances understanding of one of the most important forms of moral growth a people may experience. This moral growth shows itself in the new forms of creative voice with which members of this group, as we have seen in Chapter 3, challenged British patriarchy and thus British imperialism.

One of the features of patriarchy, when it is hegemonic, is its quashing of resisting voice, so that the injury patriarchy inflicts on love and relationship is supposed to be in the nature of things, what it is to be a good man or woman. The patriarchal story is that manhood requires a heroic sacrifice of personal life (as Aeneas leaves the woman he loves as an equal, Dido, to do his patriarchal duty as the founder of Rome). What marks the work of a great artist like Vergil in *The Aeneid*, what so moved imperialistic Romans like Augustus for whom he wrote it, is that he shows us the traumatic terms of such terrible loss in love, indeed psychologically connecting such loss to what turns "pious" Aeneas into the "savage" Aeneas, whose illimitable violence in war ends the epic. What made this possibly subversive narrative so moving to the Romans and to the British imperialists who later read it in their public schools and elite universities is that they could reasonably read the narrative as clarifying what made imperialistic heroism heroic. As we saw in our earlier discussion of British patriarchy (Chapter 2), the mode of education central to imperial service called for a public school and elite university education (with emphasis on athletic prowess and study of classics or history) that required not only traumatic breaks with parents but a hierarchical bullying in public schools, traumatic experience that made psychologically possible identification with the kind of patriarchal authority the imperial elite exercised when abroad. Kwasi Kwarteng, in his important book *Ghosts of the Empire*,[21] underscores with great force that it was not money nor even birth or status that made this imperial ruling elite psychologically possible; rather, it was this kind of education,[22] which the imperial elite shared and was the basis for their solidarity and isolation from native peoples when abroad, a phenomenon E. M. Forster and Paul Scott trenchantly observe in their great novels about the British ruling elite in India. The consequence of such trauma, under both Roman and British patriarchy, was a certain shallowness in personal relations between parents and children and in couples, leading in the imperial elite to sexual austerity (bachelors were preferred in the imperial civil service,[23] which may explain why, for Leonard Woolf, his marriage to Virginia precluded continuing imperial service in Ceylon).

What Kwarteng shows us is several important features of British imperial patriarchy that advance understanding of distinctive features of British imperialism: first, the individualism of the elite once abroad, leading to quite different approaches to imperial rule over time depending on the temperament and personality of the person in charge; second, the political independence they were largely, although not always, accorded[24]; and third, the aristocratic character of the imperial elite when abroad (often not at all in line with their station when in Britain), leading to their lack of interest in advancing democracy and democratic values in the peoples they ruled. Rather, the pattern of indirect rule through local rulers led the British elite to search for and sometimes put in power monarchs who were as politically hierarchical as they, or themselves to rule as despotic autocrats in a way that would have been unthinkable in Britain. Kwarteng shows in some depth how disastrous these choices often were for the nations that were formerly parts of the British Empire (including Iraq, Kashmir, Burma, Sudan, Nigeria, and Hong Kong).

---

[21] See Kwasi Kwarteng, *Ghosts of Empire: Britain's Legacies in the Modern World* (New York: Public Affairs, 2011).
[22] On this point, see ibid., pp. 237–9, 292–3, 335–6.
[23] Ibid., p. 242.
[24] A notable exception was the role of Randolph Churchill in securing the annexation of Burma; see ibid., pp. 145–270.

148   The Rise of Gay Rights and the Fall of the British Empire

What these features clarify is how and why it was that the British Empire should have grown and prospered on these terms during a period of increasing democratization and liberalization in Britain itself: there was an institutional disconnect between growing British liberal democracy at home and the antidemocratic terms on which Britain ruled the British Empire. Of course, the British imperial expansion was always in service of British industry at home and commerce abroad. And as long as British prosperity could be politically explained as advanced by the empire, even the increasingly politically powerful British public (after the Second Reform Bill in 1867, the Third Reform Bill in 1884, the extension of the franchise to all adult males in 1918, the granting of votes for women at the same age as men in 1928, and the lowering of the voting age to eighteen in 1967) could be persuaded, as by Disraeli with the support of Queen Victoria, enthusiastically to support it.[25] Joseph Chamberlain, as secretary of the Colonial Office at the end of the nineteenth century, did not have the usual background of the British ruling class, being a successful businessman, but he shared their racism.[26] Moving from the left wing of the Liberal Party into alliance with the Conservatives, he became a strong supporter and quite popular democratic agent of British imperialism when he came to see that Britain's industrial power was now rivaled by the United States and Germany. He came to believe that only by extending Britain's supremacy in its empire (encouraging investment in infrastructure in the colonies and the like) could Britain maintain its competitive edge economically, including incurring even the financial and human costs of the Second Boer War.[27] As he put the point:

> Is there any man in his senses who believes that the crowded population of these islands could exist for a single day if we were to cut adrift from us the great dependencies which now look to us for protection and assistance, and which are the natural markets for our trade?[28]

It was strong democratic support for this view of imperialism that doomed Gladstone's abortive attempt to secure Home Rule for Ireland (which Chamberlain, in his turn to imperialism, came to oppose)[29] and later disastrously

---

[25] On this point, see John M. MacKenzie, "The Popular Culture of Empire in Britain," in *The Oxford History of the British Empire*, Vol. IV. *The Twentieth Century*, edited by Judith M. Brown and Wm. Roger Louis (Oxford: Oxford University Press, 2001), pp. 188–231.
[26] On this point, see Peter T. Marsh *Joseph Chamberlain: Entrepreneur in Politics* (New Haven, CT: Yale University Press, 1994), pp. 411–12.
[27] On this point, see ibid., pp. 406–522.
[28] Quoted in Richard Jay, *Joseph Chamberlain: A Political Study* (Oxford: Clarendon Press, 1981), at p. 189.
[29] See Roy Jenkins, *Gladstone: a Biography* (New York: Random House, 1997), pp. 536–8.

made possible the mobilization of the British people for military service in World War I.

This kind and level of support would not have been psychologically possible if patriarchy were not as hegemonic as it was in Britain during this period, quashing resisting voices. What makes the gay rights movement in Britain before World War II so remarkable is that, although the Empire continues during this period, their new forms of love, made possible by resisting the Love Laws, empowered the forms of creative voice they innovated as writers and artists. These voices broke the silence on which the hegemony of British patriarchy depended and thus offer us a model for understanding how resistance arises and is sustained and the impact it has on ethical and political culture cumulatively over time, as I now hope to show. At the heart of the matter is that their voices arose in resistance to the patriarchal roles British imperialism imposed on both men and women, including their remarkable resistance to World War I.

Lytton Strachey and his intimate friend Virginia Woolf illustrate such resisting voices. Strachey's whole life was a standing challenge to then-conventional conceptions of British imperial masculinity – he not only loved other men deeply as a gay man and made the search for such love the center of his life, but appreciated, listened to, loved, and supported women, like Virginia Woolf and Dora Carrington, on terms of equality. It is from this experience of love that his resisting voice came, a voice that challenged the destructive patriarchal masculinity and femininity he explored in his four "eminent Victorians," three men and one woman, as well as in his lives of Queen Victoria and Elizabeth I, which we considered in Chapter 3. The men's lives had been distorted by a rigidly defined and enforced conception of the gender binary that rationalized what Strachey came to see as unjust violence in religion, education, and war, grounded in patriarchal religion. In contrast, unconventional women like Florence Nightingale and Elizabeth I never fit the patriarchal conception of womanhood, which both of them challenged; a woman like Victoria who came to define her life even more patriarchally, after her husband's death, in terms of a self-sacrificing worship of her dead husband and thus more aggressively served and advanced the unjust ends of British imperialism.

Virginia Woolf found the loving support she needed in a marriage with a man very much her equal and sexual love in her lesbian passion for Vita Sackville-West. Not only did Virginia love on terms of equality, she resisted patriarchy by showing us in her novels, like *Mrs. Dalloway*, the ways in which gender roles destroyed men (Septimus) and women (Mrs. Dalloway) alike. As we saw in Chapter 2, no one wrote with greater force and precision than Woolf, who came from a patriarchal family, of patriarchy's deadening intrapsychic effects on women's imagination and intelligence. In Woolf's view, patriarchy imposes on "good" women a self-sacrificing, self-abnegating idea that kills a real human voice, the basis for creativity. In "Professions of Women," considering the psychological blocs she had encountered as a creative women, Woolf wrote of this image of women as "the Angel in the House," a presence she must kill "in self-defense. Had I not killed her she would have killed me."[30]

Woolf saw the dark side of patriarchy for women so powerfully because she had experienced sexual abuse in her own patriarchal family from her two half-brothers. What is remarkable is how she connected such patriarchal violence in family life to the violence of fascism. To resist the violence of patriarchy, women, Woolf argued, must refuse the function she had earlier observed them playing, a function to which men had become addicted:

> Women have served all these centuries as looking-glasses possessing the magic and delicious power of reflecting the figure of men at twice its natural size. Without that power probably the earth would still be swamp and jungle. The glories of all our wars would be unknown.[31]

In *Three Guineas*, Woolf seeks to break the hypnotic spell of a patriarchally rooted male narcissism – the wounded honor or shame that fueled the mass appeal of Hitler and Mussolini.[32] What makes her argument groundbreaking is the way she connects the forms of public and private violence she had examined so sensitively in *Mrs. Dalloway* and *To the Lighthouse* to the aggressive fascism Britain faced in the 1930s, as well as the importance she accords to this linking of public and private worlds and tyrannies.

What Strachey and Woolf and others made so clear in their lives and works is their questioning of the Victorian conception of "My Station and Its Duties," celebrated in Kantian, neo-Hegelian terms by the philosopher F. H. Bradley[33] and memorialized in Rudyard Kipling's 1899 plea to the Americans in the Philippines to, like Britain, accept "the white man's burden."[34] Strachey and Woolf suggest that this imperial conception of self-sacrificing duty rested on ethically indefensible ideas of gender and sexuality that turn a sensitive artist like Kipling into an apologist of racism imperialism, covering his sensitivity,

---

[30] Virginia Woolf, "Professions of Women," in Virginia Woolf, *Women and Writing* edited by Michele Barrett (Orlando, FL: Harvest Books, 1980), pp. 57–63, at p. 59.
[31] Virginia Woolf, *A Room of One's Own* (San Diego, CA: Harvest Books, 1981; originally published, 1929), p. 35.
[32] On this point, see Woolf, *Three Guineas*, pp. 132, 135.
[33] See F. H. Bradley, *Ethical Studies*, edited by Ralph G. Ross (New York: The Liberal Arts Press, 1959; first published, 1876), at pp. 98–147.
[34] See T. S. Eliot, *A Choice of Kipling's Verse* (Garden City, NY: Anchor Books, 1962; first published, 1941), pp. 143–5.

as Theodore Roosevelt had in the United States (see discussion, *infra*), with a brutal mask of imperialist manhood.[35] Such an ethics of duty indefensibly rested on the patriarchal enforcement of the gender binary (male as aggressive, female as sensitive), requiring a traumatic sacrifice of intimate life on terms of equality that made psychologically possible unjust racist violence against those who challenged the hierarchical terms on which enforcement of the gender binary divided us from one another. What made this criticism ultimately so reasonably appealing to many is its ethical objection to the required self-sacrifice of the love of equals, as itself a great human evil, and its associated ethical objection to a patriarchal violence, unleashed by any challenge to its sense of honor, as a catastrophic political inhumanity.

There can for the British have been no more cogent illustration of the political force of this criticism, only now it was based on their own searing experience as the victims of an imperialism run amok, than what they faced and, with the support of their allies, ultimately defeated in World War II: the aggressive patriarchal fascism of Nazi Germany, grounded in the scapegoating and genocidal murder of Jews and all other supposedly inferior groups. Understandably,

> [t]he Second World War was a period of great upheaval for the British Empire, British officials could see that, by fighting Nazi Germany, they were actually undermining their own position among the colonial peoples they governed. Lord Moyne, the Colonial Secretary, warned the Governor of Nigeria about the high expectations raised by one of Clement Atlee's speeches: "There is no doubt that in the minds of many coloured people we are fighting this war primarily to vindicate the doctrine of the equality of all races in contrast to the Nazi idea of the Herrenvolk." He added, "I feel that we must be very careful to live up to what is expected of us."[36]

The problem for the British was not simply one of ethical consistency; now, in a postwar world and with the advent of the Universal Declaration of Human Rights and the United Nations, antiracism was not just an ethical ideal but a matter of international public law.[37] Also, the British victory in World War II had not been easy and included many defeats: "The cataclysmic blows struck by the triumphant Japanese in Hong Kong, Malaya, Singapore, and Burma

---

[35] On Kipling's background and complexities, see Charles Allen, *Kipling Sahib: India and the Making of Rudyard Kipling* (London: Abacus, 2009). For an example of Kipling's sensitivity to Indian culture, see Rudyard Kipling, *Kim* (Oxford: Oxford University Press, 2008; first published, 1902).

[36] Kwasi Kwarteng, *Ghosts of Empire*, p. 298.

[37] See Mary Ann Glendon, *A World Made New: Eleanor Roosevelt and the Universal Declaration of Human Rights* (New York: Random House, 2002).

grievously undermined the myth of European invincibility. In the Far East, the British Empire 'depended on prestige,' wrote Sir Frederic Eggleston, the Australian Minister in Chunking at May 1942. 'This prestige has been completely shattered.'"[38] Churchill had written prophetically in his diary after the British defeat in Singapore: "If the Army cannot fight better than it is doing at present we shall deserve to lose our Empire."[39] After the devastation of World War II in Britain, the nation was economically weaker than it had ever been – and increasingly dependent on its American ally: "American assistance allowed the British Empire to revive before it collapsed. The American support of the British Empire was an arrangement that neither side cared to publicize, the British because it was humiliating to be so dependent on the United States, the Americans because the support of empire seemed at variance with historical principles."[40] In fact, the United States was quite hostile to Britain's continuing colonial enterprise, as it would later show when President Dwight Eisenhower refused to support Britain's war over Suez, leading to a humiliating sense of defeat in Britain, and here at the hands of its greatest ally.

If Britain, standing alone, no longer had the coercive power to enforce its will, that lack of power, the consequence of World War II (including the rising tide of anticolonial expectations in its colonies) may have had the same effect in precipitating the end of the empire that the lack of coercion had in the unexpected dissolution of the Soviet Union when Gorbachev "failed to realize that the USSR has been assembled from a collection of captured nationalities held together by coercion. As soon as the coercion was removed, almost all the non-Russian republics prepared to leave."[41] The role of the supposed legitimacy of coercion in imperialism should never be understated, and World War II, exhausting British military power and leading to a more broadly shared sense of a legitimation crisis about its imperialism, played an important role in the rapid dissolution of the empire that followed:

> The means by which the immense resources of the Empire were channeled into an extraordinary collective war effort unleashed social and political expectations that in the end could not be accommodated, even within a reformed colonial system such as that envisaged by Oliver Stanley and his successors in the Labour government. Paradoxically, the ultimate cost of

---

[38] See Keith Jeffery, "The Second World War," Judith M. Brown and Wm. Roger Louis, op. cit., pp. 306–28, at p. 318.
[39] Roy Jenkins, *Churchill: A Biography* (New York: Farrar, Straus & Giroux, 2001), at p. 681.
[40] Wm. Roger Louis, "The Dissolution of the British Empire," in Judith M. Brown and Wm. Roger Louis, op. cit., pp. 329–56, at p. 330.
[41] See Norman Davies, *Vanished Kingdoms: The Rise and Fall of States and Nations* (New York: Viking, 2011), at p. 721.

defending the British Empire during the Second World War was the Empire itself.[42]

There were certainly leading British politicians, notably Sir Winston Churchill, who resisted to the end the surprisingly rapid dismantling of the British Empire (starting with India in 1947).[43] In understanding the speed of the fall of the British Empire, it important to recall the earlier observed distinction between the increasing liberalization and democratization of Britain itself and the antidemocratic, hierarchal aristocratic elite in Britain that sustained the empire. The broad appeal of the empire in Britain had always been economic. But Britain could no longer economically afford or, what amounted to the same thing, militarily enforce the empire, and in a period of economic devastation and loss, the idea of supporting it, which was now so obviously an economic burden for the British people, could not be democratically sustained for long.[44] In fact, the empire ended more rapidly than British leaders had expected.[45] Why?

George Orwell, writing during World War II, refers to the changes wrought in the British people by the experience of World War II as the "English Revolution."[46] For Orwell, this revolution was a turn to democratic socialism (an analysis confirmed by the stunning victory of the Labour Party at the end of World War II). With his homophobic contempt for the "pansy-left,"[47] however, Orwell misses another point that had been made by Keynes, someone Orwell may have regarded as "pansy-left" – namely, that the economic prosperity of Britain under the empire unjustly depended on the undemocratic sacrifices that had been required of working people and others under industrial capitalism. According to Keynes, a more democratic sense of justice (wrought by the sense of shared sacrifice in World War II) would no longer exact such sacrifices, would share the gains of prosperity more broadly, and would give more

---

[42] See Keith Jeffery, "The Second World War," Judith M. Brown and Wm. Roger Louis, op. cit., pp. 306–28, at p. 327.
[43] On Churchill's unbending advocacy of not letting India go, see Roy Jenkins, *Churchill*, pp. 456–63.
[44] On this point, see Wm. Roger Louis, "The Dissolution of the British Empire," in Judith M. Brown and Wm. Roger Louis, op. cit., pp. 329–56.
[45] See, for a good general study, Piers Brendon, *The Decline and Fall of the British Empire 1781–1997* (London: Vintage, 2008).
[46] See George Orwell, "The Lion and the Unicorn: Socialism and the English Genius," in *Why I Write* (New York: Penguin, 1984; "Lion and the Unicorn" originally published 1941), pp. 33–94, at p. 64.
[47] See George Orwell, "Rudyard Kipling," in *A Collection of Essays* (Orlando, FL: Harvest Books, 1981; "Rudyard Kipling" originally published, 1942), pp. 116–32, at p. 117.

people access to life's pleasures.[48] Keynes thus elaborates an argument made earlier by Hobson and Woolf, questioning the unjust demands of self-sacrifice that had been rationalized in service of the British Empire. The empire was dead and dying, and so too were the demands of the patriarchal psychology that sustained it, the demands of "imperial manhood"[49] that now, in a more coherently liberal democratic Britain, were increasingly seen as pointless and even unjust.

It is at this point that I believe that the arguments of the Bloomsbury Group may have begun to have more broad democratic resonance among the British than ever before; arguments, once regarded as marginal, now had ethical and political appeal.[50] What Strachey and Woolf and others saw was the extraordinary psychological burden patriarchal masculinity and femininity imposed on British men and women. They asked questions about its connections to unjust patriarchal injustice and violence both at home and abroad. Such questions may have had greater resonance in the experience of many in Britain after World War II than ever been: why all this sexual/emotional repression and anxiety about sexual feeling (reflected, for example, in Gladstone's distracted, tormented preoccupation with pornography and prostitutes[51]). What price was to be paid for the propensities to unjust imperialist violence that increasingly looked to be rooted in racism, now discredited as a basis for law and policy? For many in Britain and Europe, World War II was the last step in discrediting the forms of racist imperialism that had dominated European and world politics for so long. If World War I – essentially a war among competing European imperialisms – were not enough, World War II (in which a humiliated German ethnic imperialism sought its apocalyptic revenge) was the last straw.

In understanding the surprising speed of the fall of the British Empire, it is not without causal importance that its unraveling expressed a now more broadly and democratically shared sense of a legitimacy crisis in British patriarchy and imperialism, a sense that drew on the arguments our resistance group had made. The fall of the British Empire could now be regarded as a good and just thing not only for the colonies but for Britain itself, as both Hobson and Leonard Woolf had argued in their criticisms of imperialism in general and British imperialism in particular and as Strachey and Virginia

---

[48] See John Maynard Keynes, "Economic Consequences for Our Grandchildren," in *Essays in Persuasion* (New York: Palgrave Macmillan, 2010), pp. 321–32; John Maynard Keynes, *The General Theory of Employment, Interest and Money*, pp. 372–84.
[49] Kwarteng, *Ghosts of Empire*, p. 179.
[50] On this point, see Noel Annan, *Our Age*.
[51] On this point, see Roy Jenkins, *Gladstone: A Biography*, at pp. 100–15.

The Fall of Empire

Woolf had shown in their revelatory criticisms of British patriarchy. What had emerged in our resistance group as an ethically creative discovery of new moral and political truths could be broadened and deepened in the moral growth of a free people, a growth experienced as a loss and questioning of previous certainties and an anxious search for a new order less burdened by the mistakes of the past. If patriarchy could be debunked and questioned here, why not elsewhere?

There is good evidence for such shifts in thought and feeling in the world John Osborne shows us in *Look Back in Anger*, which tells the story of a young husband and wife from different classes, whose sexual love cannot bridge the gap between them. The wife remains on her patriarchal pedestal, having no voice in the relationship, while the husband has lost all meaning in the causes that once moved him and feels desperately alone in this loss, unacknowledged as it is by the woman he loves. The barrier between them is her holding onto the patriarchal pedestal and his rejecting it, reflected quite clearly in his rejection of the patriarchal conception of the "gentleman" ("I hope you won't make the mistake of thinking for one moment that I am a gentleman"[52]), a conception at the very center of the roles required of the British imperial elite.[53] This would explain why the husband's violence is no longer directed at the aims of imperial British honor but takes the form of angry tirades against his wife and everything for which he takes her to stand. The play problematizes patriarchal gender roles in marriage, which the husband has come to resist more fully than his wife (she did, after all, break the Love Laws in marrying him, which bespeaks resistance). The only cause the husband acknowledges that may have some traction in this postimperial world is that of homosexuals.

Why homosexuals, and why at this point in British history? *Look Back in Anger* opened in London in 1956, which was followed the next year by the Report of the Wolfenden Commission, recommending the decriminalization of male adult homosexual relations. In the 1960s, Parliament would change British law in a number of domains: capital punishment, homosexuality, abortion, censorship of the press, divorce, and Sunday entertainment.[54] Homosexuality was decriminalized in 1967, ten years after the Wolfenden Commission Report.[55]

What, if anything, had changed things? As I have suggested, World War II led to a legitimation crisis for British imperialism, to which our resistance group,

---

[52] John Osborne, *Look Back in Anger*, p. 57.
[53] On this point, see Kwarteng, *Ghosts of Empire*, p. 179.
[54] For a comprehensive study, see Peter G. Richards, *Parliament and Conscience* (London: George Allen & Unwin, 1970).
[55] See ibid., pp. 63–84.

questioning patriarchy, made an important contribution. In the United States, which was much more homophobically repressive than Britain, historians have pointed to the experience of gay men and lesbians in the military, many away from home for the first time in their lives, and finding in military service with other gay men and lesbians a congenial environment for relationships; indeed, the impulse to resistance may have begun in these men and women when the military dishonorably discharged many of them because of their sexual orientation.[56] It is not clear that the same phenomenon occurred in Britain on this scale or with this significance, largely because gay and lesbian life in Britain may have flourished before the war, as long as it remained closeted, in a way it did not in the United States. Nonetheless, something of this sort may have occurred in Britain as well.

What accelerated these changes in Britain was the pressure World War II placed on the traditional supports of the British Empire both economically and politically. With the Empire now gone or at least on its way out,[57] the distributive injustices within Britain that had sustained the empire were no longer acceptable. These injustices included not only the enormous wealth and privilege of some at the expense of others but the remarkably permissive sexual lives within the aristocracy, as the life of Winston Churchill's mother, Jeannie, shows so vividly, which was deemed unacceptable in the lower classes.[58] (Winston Churchill's biographer, Roy Jenkins, observes: "George Moore, the Anglo-Irish novelist, said she [Jeannie] had 200 lovers, but apart from anything else the number is suspiciously round."[59]) Not only wealth and power but access to such pleasures should now be more equitably distributed. In particular, the demands of traditional morality, once thought to support the self-sacrifices, including sexual self-sacrifices, required by the patriarchal assumptions of the British Empire, were, with the end of the empire, exposed to the full force of British liberal democracy no longer constrained by the now anachronistic demands of patriarchy: hence, the liberal reforms of the 1960s. In particular, questioning patriarchy means questioning the polarized gender binary it enforces, and this in turn requires questioning condemnation of homosexuality as unmasculine or unfeminine (and also condemnation of contraception and abortion).

---

[56] See Allan Berube, *Coming Out Under Fire: The History of Gay Men and Women in World War Two* (New York: Free Press, 1990).

[57] On this point, see Keith Jeffery, "The Second World War," Judith M. Brown and Wm. Roger Louis, op. cit., pp. 306–28, at p. 327; Wm. Roger Louis, "The Dissolution of the British Empire," in ibid., pp. 329–56.

[58] On this point, see David A. J. Richards, *Disarming Manhood*, pp. 198–218.

[59] Quoted at ibid., p. 184.

If there were underlying shifts in the public understanding of gender and sexuality after World War II, they were not yet reflected in government policy – in fact, there were more aggressive prosecutions of gay male sexual relations in Britain after World War II.[60] More aggressive prosecutions of gay sex in Britain during this period reflected American pressure, to which an economically distressed Britain was at this time especially vulnerable. Some of this pressure was undoubtedly American homophobia, fomented by the McCarthy witch-hunts, made possible by the much more aggressive repression of any semblance of gay advocacy in the United States than in Britain (see Chapter 3, comparing Whitman and Carpenter).[61] But American concerns were also aroused by the 1951 escape to Moscow of two spies for the Soviet Union, Guy Burgess and Donald Maclean (another such spy, Kim Philby, would escape to Moscow much later, after earlier being exonerated on espionage charges, in 1963).[62] Burgess, in fact, was flamboyantly gay and had been at Cambridge with another gay man and, as later proved, Soviet spy, Anthony Blunt. Both Burgess and Blunt had been Apostles at Cambridge, the same discussion group that, at an earlier point, gave rise to the resistance group studied in Chapter 3.[63]

The Apostles had come a long way from the philosophical rigors of discussions with G. E. Moore and Bertrand Russell. In the meantime, the group had gravitated toward Marxism under the impact of the rise of fascism in the 1930s and the experience of the Spanish Civil War, in which the Soviet Union

---

[60] See Stephen Jeffery-Poulter, *Peers, Queers, and Commons: The Struggle for Gay Law Reform from 1950 to the Present* (London: Routledge, 1991), pp. 8–27. For an illuminating study of other reactionary prosecutions during this period including of Stephen Ward (who committed suicide), see Richard Davenport-Hines, An *English Affair: Sex, Class and Power in the Age of Profumo.* (London: Harper Press, 2013).

[61] See Barbara Epstein, "Anti-Communism, Homophobia, and the Construction of Masculinity in the Postwar U.S.," *Critical Sociology* 20 (1994): 21–44.

[62] See ibid., pp. 25–7.

[63] See Wikipedia entries online for Guy Burgess, Donald Maclean, Kim Philby, and Anthony Blunt. Alan Turing – the great British mathematician, inventor of the computer, and pivotal figure in the intelligence effort that was crucial to Britain's victory over Germany – was the most tragic victim of this homophobic period in Britain's post-war history. Turing had been at Cambridge, both as a student and fellow at Kings (the college of Keynes); but he was never a part of a group of close friends like that of the Bloomsbury Group; he was not, for example, an Apostle, and clearly rejected the Marxism of Burgess, and the others. Turing was, however, gay and sexually active with men not of his background and class, a fact he quite openly told the police when he was asked. For this reason, he was during this period (when his war service was a well-kept state secret) criminally prosecuted for consensual adult gay sex, the penalty calling for prison time or treatment with female hormones that would allegedly cure his homosexual desires (homosexuality being regarded as a disease or ailment); Turing, disastrously, chose the latter. Turing committed suicide in 1954. For a revelatory investigation of this brilliant gay man, treated so badly by the nation he had served so well, see Andrew Hodges, *Alan Turing: The Enigma* (Princeton: Princeton University Press, 2012; first published, 1983).

supported the republican government and fascist Germany and Italy supported Franco; both Britain and the United States remained neutral. Julian Bell, son of Vanessa, was at Cambridge and an Apostle, perhaps a lover of Anthony Blunt. He went to Spain to assist the republican forces as an ambulance driver and was killed, breaking the heart of his mother and her sister Virginia Woolf (his death inspired her writing of her antipatriarchal masterpiece, *Three Guineas*). The gay loves of these latter-day Apostles grounded their resistance to fascism, but their betrayal of Britain suggests a loss of the liberal good sense of their predecessors, all of whom, notably Leonard Woolf and Maynard Keynes, rejected Marxism as resting on indefensible ideas of apodictally certain laws of history. The homophobic Americans were not, however, capable of making such distinctions and certainly had no interest whatsoever in fairness to homosexuals. It sufficed for them that gay men from Cambridge University were a nest of treasonous vipers. Britain must get its house in order.

The more aggressive prosecutions in Britain, however, encountered something new in British experience: resistance and protest. One such successful 1954 prosecution of a peer, Lord Montagu and friends, for sex with two airmen, was followed, to the surprise of the defendants, by support and encouragement from crowds, something Oscar Wilde had certainly not experienced. The prosecution itself was condemned by *The Sunday Times* and other publications,[64] and questions soon followed in the House of Commons, followed by a full debate. Proponents of decriminalization put great weight on the recommendation to that effect of the Church of England Moral Welfare Committee (distinguishing sins from crimes proper) and called for the government to appoint a commission to study and report on the matter, known as the Wolfenden Commission.[65]

How and why did the Anglican Church play such an important role in justifying decriminalization? Many Christian churches had been and were under pressure to rethink their historical traditions after World War II in light of the Holocaust and the role Christian anti-Semitism played in rationalizing this atrocity. Consider the role Vatican II would play in the Catholic Church's repudiation of its traditional argument for persecution and opposition to political liberalism. The Church, however, drew the line at the traditional Catholic view of sexual morality: the papacy refused to reexamine traditional Catholic moral teaching, condemning contraception, abortion, and homosexuality. I argue in a coauthored book, *Patriarchal Religion, Sexuality, and Gender: A Critique of New Natural Law*,[66] that the attempt to defend, as a secular view, these

---

[64] See Stephen Jeffery-Poulter, *Peers, Queers, and Commons*, pp. 16–19.
[65] See ibid., pp. 19–27.
[66] Nicholas C. Bamforth and David A. J. Richards, *Patriarchal Religion, Sexuality, and Gender: A Critique of New Natural Law* (Cambridge: Cambridge University Press, 2008).

Catholic positions fails utterly and that the regressive views of the Catholic Church on these and other issues arises from its embattled insistence on papal patriarchal rule. In contrast, what distinguished the Anglican Church was both the initiative it took and the resonance it gave to the first twentieth-century extended treatment of homosexuality by an ecclesiastical body, which was later to be followed by its opening its clergy to women. This suggests a much better understanding in the Anglican Church of the ways in which Roman patriarchy corrupted Christianity. Under the guidance of an Anglican priest and theologian Rev. Dr. Derrick Sherwin Bailey, a group of clergy, doctors, and lawyers, known as the Church of England Moral Welfare Council, studied the existing materials on homosexuality. Together, they produced in 1954 a privately produced pamphlet titled *The Problem of Homosexuality*.[67] In 1955, Bailey published his own groundbreaking historical investigations in an important book[68] concerning how the condemnation of homosexuality arose within Christianity and questioning whether in contemporary circumstances this condemnation could be regarded as authoritative, even among Christians. The Moral Welfare Council of 1954–5 provided important conceptual guidelines for subsequent discussions about homosexuality.[69]

Arguments of this sort could be interpreted in one of two ways, both favorable to decriminalization of gay sex. First, we could, as Christians, come to see that gay sex was not a sin at all – indeed, that the traditional condemnation rested either on misinterpretations of biblical texts or on beliefs (e.g., homosexuality caused earthquakes) that were no longer credible. Second, in light of such studies, we may come, as Christians, to understand why gay sex is a sin but reasonably doubt whether other citizens should or would reasonably regard Christian views of sin as a legitimate basis for laws in a constitutional democracy committed to religious and moral pluralism as aspects of basic human rights of conscience.

It is striking that the arguments made in the 1957 Wolfenden Commission Report for decriminalization of gay sex all are made in terms of the second interpretation.[70] The report assumes, *arguendo*, that gay sex is sinful for Christians but then denies that it suffices for criminalization that an act is sinful. There is, however, a puzzle here. The Anglican Church was and remains the

---

[67] *The Problem of Homosexuality: An Interim Report by a Group of Anglican Clergy and Doctors*, produced by the Church of England Welfare Council by the Church Information Board (for private circulation, 1954).
[68] See Derrick Sherwin Bailey, *Homosexuality and the Western Christian Tradition* (Hamden, CT: Archon Books, 1975; originally published, 1955).
[69] See Jonathan Sinclair Carey, "D. S. Bailey and 'the Name Forbidden Among Christians'," *Anglican Theological Review* 70, n. 2 (1988): pp. 152–73.
[70] *The Wolfenden Report: Report of the Committee on Homosexual Offenses and Prostitution* (New York: Stein and Day, 1963).

established church in Great Britain, in contrast to the Untied States, where the First Amendment forbids established churches. But if the Anglican Church is and remains the established church of Britain, then its views, including its view of sin, may be regarded as binding on all British citizens and thus a legitimate basis for law. Interpretively, the Wolfenden Report argument would, on this view, be more sensible under the American than the British constitutional arrangements.

But interpretive charity to the report requires us to take seriously how expansive the British understanding of the principle of religious toleration, rooted in Lockean political theory (see Chapter 2), was by this time. It was no longer disqualifying from any political, educational, or other position (except being the monarch) that one was not Anglican. It is a reasonable interpretation of this development that the internal religious views of the Anglican Church can no longer be binding on all British citizens, so that; whether or not Anglicans regard gay sex as a sin, their views are not binding on others. Once the question of sin is thus put aside, the report focuses its argument not on any putative good of gay sex, let alone to a right to such sex, but on the harms criminalization inflicts, including discouraging homosexuals from seeking the therapeutic care they may need.

The Wolfenden Report opened the question of homosexuality to public debate and discussion, which may be its most enduring importance in the history of gay rights. A silence, constructed around the supposed unspeakability of homosexuality, was finally broken in Britain and the United States, and arguments had to be made as to why such consensual relationships were criminal and, eventually, why they were morally condemned, or, more to the point, the lack of argument on both points was to be exposed for what it was. The Tories had a substantial majority, however, and resisted change until public opinion shifted (with regard to prostitution, however, the government implemented its recommendations, rushing through the Street Offences Act of 1959, which decriminalized commercial sex but outlawed public solicitation). The Homosexual Law Reform Society and Albany Trust were formed in the spring of 1958 and played an important advocacy role urging the case for decriminalization with members of Parliament over the next ten years.[71] Antony Grey, a gay man who played an important role in such advocacy, writes powerfully about the slow process that was required,[72] noting the financial support given the Reform Society by E. M. Forster, now eighty-five, who had remarked, "I am the only bugger of us all who has any money."[73] With Labour

---

[71] Jeffrey Weeks, *Coming Out*, pp. 168–75.
[72] Antony Grey, *Quest for Justice: Towards Homosexual Emancipation* (London: Sinclair-Stevenson, 1992).
[73] Quoted at Grey, *Quest for Justice*, at p. 78.

now in power, what eventually had force and carried the day in 1967 was "the pragmatic ideology endorsed by the Wilson leadership of the Labour Party: a negative, utilitarian position: the law obviously did not work, so the best thing to do was change it."[74] As Professor Peter Richards observes, "A feature of the parliamentary debates on this subject is that the fundamental moral issue was consistently avoided," including, in a period anxious over the population explosion, whether the homosexual's "failure to reproduce ... is making a contribution to the welfare of society. Clearly, <u>it was not in the interests of the reformers to raise contentious issues of this sort. Their task was to arouse Christian compassion, not Christian controversy.</u> Their tactic was to keep public and parliamentary debate as rational and moderate as possible because of the danger that an upsurge of emotion and prejudice would ruin their chance of success."[75] The point was underscored by Lord Arran, one of the most eloquent supporters of the decriminalization in the House of Lords:[76]

> [I]n all the discussions we have had, and in all the speeches, no single noble Lord or noble Lady has ever said that homosexuality is a right or a good thing. It has been universally condemned from start to finish, and by every single Members of this House.[77]

This was the dominant tone. Lord Snow (C. P. Snow, the novelist), however, expressed incredulity at the "curious unworldliness" of such rhetoric:

> It has seemed to me, occasionally, the some noble Lords speak as though they have never met a homosexual, as though, these were something like the white rhinoceros – strange animals, difficult to observe. Yet every noble Lord here must have met many homosexuals ... some of [them] the most distinguished and, if I may say so, worthy of Englishmen.[78]

We can see the importance of this new kind of discussion in the justly famous Devlin/Hart debate in which a leading British judge (Patrick Devlin) and Britain's leading legal philosopher (H. L. A. Hart) wrangled over their disagreement over the Wolfenden Report, with Devlin opposing its recommendation and Hart supporting it.

What is remarkable about Devlin's argument is the lengths to which he was prepared to go to justify a morality of the criminal law that would continue to criminalize gay sex, including the consequences he contemplated from

---

[74] Jeffrey Weeks, *Coming Out*, p. 175.
[75] Peter G. Richards, *Parliament and the Constitution*, pp. 82–3.
[76] On this point, see Antony Grey, *Quest for Justice*, pp. 87–9.
[77] Quoted at Grey, *Quest for Justice*, p. 117.
[78] Quoted at Grey, *Quest for Justice*, p. 117.

decriminalization (even Devlin came to support the reform in 1967[79]). The Wolfenden Report distinguished sins from crimes, and argued that it did not suffice for making a private consensual act between adults a crime that it was sinful and argued less harm on balance would be done by continuing criminalization than decriminalization. Harm-based arguments of this sort are deeply rooted in British liberal thought, notably in John Stuart Mill's *On Liberty*. For Devlin, the issue is not whether homosexuality is a sin or whether it harms the homosexual or others, but whether it is central to the social morality that is distinctively part of the British moral tradition. To determine what that social morality is, we must consult the sentiments, including deep feelings of "intolerance, indignation, and disgust,"[80] of "the man in the Clapham omnibus,"[81] the judgments of immorality, citing Pollock, "we expect to find in a reasonable civilized man or reasonable Englishman, taken at random."[82] Homosexuality remains condemned by such judgments, based in "the Christian idea of marriage,"[83] central to British moral life, and should not be decriminalized because its moral condemnation "is built into the house in which we live and could not be removed without bringing it down."[84] It should thus remain criminalized for the same reason treason is criminal: it threatens the existence of society.[85]

H. L. A. Hart first responded to Devlin in his "Immorality and Treason" in 1959.[86] Hart found remarkable Devlin's conception of the public morality that the criminal law enforces, resting, as it does, on deep feelings of "intolerance, indignation, and disgust," a conception, as one critic of Devlin acidly observed, that would allow every kind of irrational fear, drenched in prejudice, as a basis for law: "We once burnt old women because, without giving our reasons, we felt in our hearts that witchcraft was intolerable."[87] What is quite shocking about Devlin's conception is how it detaches public morality from "reason, sympathetic understanding, as well as critical intelligence,"[88] raising for us

---

[79] See Jeffrey Weeks, *Coming Out*, p. 167. See also Patrick Devlin, "Judges and Lawmakers," 39 *Mod. L. Rev.* 1, 2 (1976).
[80] Patrick Devlin, "The Enforcement of Morals," in *The Enforcement of Moral* (London: Oxford University Press, 1965; originally published, 1959), pp. 1–25, at p. 17.
[81] Ibid., p. 15.
[82] Ibid., p. 15.
[83] Ibid., p. 9.
[84] Ibid., p. 9.
[85] Ibid., p. 13.
[86] H. L. A. Hart, "Immorality and Treason," reprinted in *Morality and Law*, edited by Robert M. Baird and Stuart E. Rosenbaum (Buffalo, NY: Prometheus Books, 1988), pp. 47–53 (originally published in *The Listener* [July 30, 1959]: pp. 162–3).
[87] Quoted at ibid., p. 51.
[88] Ibid., p. 52.

the real question whether views of this sort could even count as a morality, let alone the morality that may legitimately be enforced through the criminal law in a constitutional democracy. Finally, Hart quite rightly questioned the analogy to treason or sedition:

> [I]t is grotesque, even where moral feeling against homosexuality is up to concert pitch, to think of the homosexual behavior of two adults in private as in any way like treason or sedition either in intention or effect. We can make it *seem* like treason only if we assume that deviation from a general moral code is bound to affect that code, and to lead not merely to its modification but to its destruction.... But, we have ample evidence for believing that people will not abandon morality, will not think any better of murder, cruelty, and dishonesty, merely because some private sexual practice which they abominate is not punished by law.[89]

The moral power of this short essay may be contrasted with the rather different, more academic tone Hart adopted in his short book 1963 book, *Law, Liberty, and Morality*.[90] Hart is here concerned not only to show why the general form of Devlin's argument (including the similar argument made by James Fitzjames Stephens earlier against John Stuart Mill) rests on unacceptable premises like the disintegration thesis he earlier criticized but to explain his own reasons for modifying one of Mill's principles. (Mill apparently forbids the application of a criminal law solely based on paternalistic harms to the agent, whereas Hart believes some harms, like death, might be a ground for such laws.[91]) Nothing in Hart's modification affects his defense of the Wolfenden recommendation because the criminalization of gay sex cannot be justified on this ground. There is only one point in Hart's argument (discussing the criminalization of bigamy) in which he writes humanely about the issue at hand. Whereas laws criminalizing bigamy call for "very little sacrifice or suffering," "[t]he case is... utterly different from attempts to enforce sexual morality which may demand the repression of powerful instincts with which personal happiness is intimately connected."[92]

Why did Hart so forcefully engage these issues in the way he did? It may clarify his moral courage to understand its background. Nicola Lacey's remarkable biography of Hart may help us understand what it may have cost Hart to engage this issue at all and why his longer defense of the Wolfenden Report

---

[89] Ibid., p. 51.
[90] H. L. A. Hart, *Law, Liberty, and Morality* (Stanford, CA: Stanford University Press, 1963).
[91] See ibid., pp. 30–34.
[92] Ibid., p. 43.

has the more academic tone it has.[93] Hart was Jewish and, although probably sexually not active, regarded himself as homosexual and was deeply conflicted over these feelings until he met, fell in love with, and married Jenifer Williams, a well educated and sexually experienced woman, as well as a communist who modeled herself and her sexuality on Bloomsbury. They would have several children. A marriage of this sort might also have had the virtue in this still quite homophobic period of conferring a certain respectability on a man as ambitious as Hart, the chair in jurisprudence at Oxford, which he occupied, having a quasi-political status in British public life. <u>Marriages of this sort, however understandable, bury or seek to bury deep feelings and may for this reason impose their own costs on the psyche</u>. In fact, it was a difficult marriage. Where Jenifer was sexually active outside the marriage (including having an affair with one of Hart's best friends, Isaiah Berlin), it is not clear Hart ever was sexually active, although there may have been highly discreet homosexual attachments. Even a scholar as thorough and honest as Nicola Lacey cannot be sure. What we do know, however, is that at the end of his life, Hart suffered a debilitating depression, connected to revelations of his wife's early communism.

What this background suggests to me is that the role of public intellectual that Hart took up as the leading defender of the Wolfenden Report was never for him a mere academic exercise. It touched intimate sexual feelings, as well as the terrors of repression and condemnation, he knew at firsthand. Nothing required Hart to take the stand he did. Certainly, other Oxford academics, notably Maurice Bowra, who were homosexually active in a way Hart was not, did not take the kind of public position Hart did.[94] Indeed, Bowra refused at one point to join ceremonies giving an honorary degree to the French gay writer, Andre Gide, "one of the few examples of cowardice in Bowra's life."[95] In light of what we now know about Hart after Lacey's biography (including his struggle against English anti-Semitism and his struggles with homosexual feelings), the stance he chose to take in defense of the Wolfenden Report and against Devlin seems to me all the more remarkably courageous, itself an act of resistance against forces of British patriarchy Hart knew at first hand.

What Hart's work made possible in Britain and America was a wholly new form of responsible, public argument about an issue, homosexuality, that had never before been subject to any reasonable public discussion. It was the vacuum of such discussion, the radical silencing surrounding homosexuality, that

---

[93] See Nicola Lacey, *The Life of H. L. A. Hart: The Nightmare and the Noble Dream* (Oxford: Oxford University Press, 2004).
[94] Bowra did join other distinguished academics and public figures in publicly endorsing the Wolfenden Report. See Antony Grey, *Quest for Justice*, pp. 26–7.
[95] Leslie Mitchell, *Maurice Bowra: A Life* (Oxford: Oxford University Press, 2009), p. 127.

led to the lies, distortions, and an emotional loathing of gay men untethered to any sense of or basis in reason, let alone in experience. Once homosexuality was decriminalized in Britain and Wales in 1967, a new kind of resistance would eventually arise in Britain, one heavily influenced by resistance movements that had emerged in the United States. Public intellectuals like Hart had prepared the way. Now, gay men and lesbians would find and speak in their own voices.

THE FALL OF EMPIRE IN THE ERA OF GAY RIGHTS IN THE UNITED STATES AND BRITAIN

The 1967 decriminalization of gay sex acts in Great Britain marked an important stage in the recognition of gay rights – not only in Britain but in the United States and elsewhere. Nonetheless, it is important to see that even the most progressive defenders of the decriminalization, like H. L. A. Hart, never put their case in terms of the normative conception of gay rights that was later to develop. We see this normative conception certainly in the life and works of Edward Carpenter, and, at least implicitly, in the lives and works of the resistance movement in Britain we studied earlier (Chapter 3). What makes the normative conception important is the feminist grounds of its rethinking of human rights, which is seen in its resistance to the ways the patriarchal Love Laws divided not only religions and ethnicities but women from men, as well as women from women and men from men – all in terms of a rigid gender binary that enforced the divisions that make patriarchy possible. The idea of gay rights arises when the feminist challenge to the gender binary questions the traditional understanding of human rights as limited to the mind or consciousness in contrast to the body, or thought in contrast to feelings, all gendered as masculine versus feminine. In challenging these gendered dualisms, the scope of human rights can no longer be limited to thought or mind or abstract consciousness; it must embrace feelings, the body, and the depth in the human psyche of sexuality. This kind of rethinking justifies the normative conception that human rights extend to the sexual love of mature adults across all the barriers enforced by the Love Laws, whether related to ethnicity, religion, or gender. What makes this rethinking new – indeed, ethically revolutionary – is the centrality it accords to the criticism of patriarchal demands and its consequent focus on the consensual sexual love between equals as at the heart of the equal dignity that grounds human rights. Its criticism of traditional patriarchal demands on both men and women argues for a democracy of equal voice and against hierarchies that rest on the suppression of such equal voice, including imperialism. Its focus on equality in intimate personal life connects a psychology of loving and being loved to a psychology of gender less susceptible to the impulses of patriarchal violence at home and in public life.

I believe this normative conception emerges into more general ethical and political consciousness as a consequence of the links among several interconnected resistance movements that arose in the United States after World War II – the movements for the civil rights of persons of color, feminism, and gay rights, and against the Vietnam War. These movements, properly understood as forms of resistance to American patriarchy, led in the United States and elsewhere to a new understanding of human rights, with gay rights prominently among them. If, as I have suggested, British patriarchy was much in decline after World War II, leading to the fall of the British Empire and the rise of gay rights, the United States at this time faced an unprecedented prosperity and world dominance after a long period of depression and isolationism. If British decline is portrayed in *Look Back in Anger* as raising questions about whether personal love in Britain could now continue in its now discredited patriarchal forms, American triumph is shown by Tennessee Williams in *A Streetcar Named Desire* as leading, if anything, to violent forms of patriarchy in marriage that might rationalize and support American patriarchal violence abroad, serving unjust imperialistic ends inconsistent with the values of democracy.

Resurgent American homophobia after World War II supports the worry implicit in Williams's great play. I earlier observed (Chapter 3) that Edward Carpenter, who visited Walt Whitman in the United States twice, charitably interpreted Whitman's denial of his homosexuality as reflecting the state of press censorship in the United States under the influence of the powerful purity movement that was "ten times worse" than in Britain.[96] The American problem of censorship was to persist for some time, indeed until well after World War II, when the Supreme Court's liberalization of obscenity laws[97] was to make an open gay rights discourse possible in the United States. Until that time, such public advocacy was met with censorship and prison.[98] It is this context, in which there was no resistance group of the sort we have explored in Britain, that explains the political power of homophobia in the United States (reflected in a remarkable literature conflating communism and homosexuality as threats to the independence of American masculinity[99]) and why it should have expressed itself, at the beginning of the Cold War, by American demands that Britain more aggressively prosecute homosexuals. In fact, as we have seen, Britain moved to the liberalization of its anti-homosexuality laws in 1967. It

---

[96] On this point, see Richards, *Women, Gays, and the Constitution*, p. 304.
[97] See *Roth v. United States*, 354 U.S. 476 (1957).
[98] See Richards, *Women, Gays, and the Constitution*, pp. 327–37.
[99] See Barbara Epstein, "Anti-Communism, Homophobia, and the Construction of Masculinity in the Postwar U.S."

was two years later in 1969 that the Stonewall riot exploded in New York City's Greenwich Village, usually taken to mark the beginning of the gay rights movement in the United States. Almost all American states at this time criminalized gay sex (only Illinois had decriminalized gay sex in 1961).

American Resistance Movements

To understand how and why the gay rights movement in the United States came to have the significance it has had in Britain and elsewhere, we must first place it in the context of the other resistance movements in the United States after World War II. I begin with the civil rights movement led by Martin Luther King, Jr. and then turn to the antiwar and feminist movements, and, finally, gay rights.

King must be understood both as a person in himself who came to a powerful stance of resistance and as the leader of the nonviolent mass movement of protest for civil rights that he inspired.[100] More specifically for our purposes here, he is important for two reasons. First, he came to see the social movement that he led as a reformation and great awakening within Christianity that challenged the traditional religious, ethical, and political authority of the Christian churches in terms of a certain reading of Jesus of Nazareth. Second, he was a major twentieth-century leader of the struggle within the United States against the structural injustice of racism, a struggle that could reasonably be traced to the pre–Civil War radical abolitionist movement. Despite his advocacy of nonviolence, King always accepted the right of self-defense[101] and was a lifelong skeptic of pacifism. He was a Baptist preacher much within the Protestant tradition and – after much struggle over his vocation – a preacher in a black church in the deep, racist South. His originality lay in the prophetic ethical voice he found within this role, a voice that energized a remarkably disciplined social movement and spoke to the conscience of the nation as no black voice ever had.

No small part of the appeal of the prophetic ethical voice King discovered was the recognition by black women in his audiences of a religious and ethical nonviolence they now understood to have a wider scope, applicability, and resonance. Andrew Young, a leading figure in King's movement, observed that getting black men to accept nonviolence was always more of a struggle:

---

[100] See Taylor Branch, *Parting the Waters: Martin Luther King and the Civil Rights Movement 1954–63* (London: Papermac, 1988); see also Taylor Branch, *Pillar of Fire: America in the King Years 1963–65* (New York: Simon & Schuster, 1998).

[101] On this point, see Taylor Branch, *Parting the Waters*, pp. 56, 389, 390–1, 571, 589–9.

Throughout the movement, the men were usually the last to become involved, always using the reason that they didn't believe in a non-violent response to violent provocations. This was more an excuse than anything else. I began challenging the men as they went into the pool halls and bars, attempting to shame them for letting the women and children carry the movement.... Finally the men realized that their presence was essential.... Women and the elderly had borne the brunt of our demonstrations for far too long.[102]

But King was also speaking in a voice that challenged traditional manhood, including black manhood. His challenge appealed to two kinds of arguments, constitutional and religious.

Constitutionally, he took on board the remarkable successes of the NAACP's litigation strategy, arguing that African American protest rested on a more reasonable understanding of American constitutionalism than that held by its racist opponents, a fact shown by its appeal to the constitutional right to protest. By anchoring his movement for justice in nonviolence, King underscored the basis of his movement in an ethical voice, supported by constitutional principles of free speech. Indeed, under the impact of his movement, such principles were held by the Supreme Court to include conscientious dissent, requiring such dissenters to be protected by the state.[103] Because the police in Birmingham and Selma were conspicuous agents of state violence against conscientious dissenters, Americans during this period came increasingly to see that King's movement rested on constitutional principles.

Religiously, King appealed to the ethical voice of Jesus, within the Christian tradition. He was striking a chord he was to repeat throughout his career in suggesting that the racist persecution of African Americans was in principle the same atrocity as religious persecution, including the persecution not only of Puritans that drove them to New England but also of Christians under the Roman Empire.[104] King and his social movement thus signified an ethical reformation of Christianity against its corruptions as much as a movement for justice under American constitutional law.

In anchoring a mass movement of resistance in nonviolence, King took on the codes of male honor. A plausible interpretation of Jesus's injunction

---

[102] See Andrew Young, *An Easy Burden: The Civil Rights Movement and the Transformation of America* (New York: HarperCollins, 1996), p. 295.

[103] See, on this important constitutional development, Harry Kalven, Jr., *The Negro and the First Amendment* (Chicago: University of Chicago Press, 1965).

[104] On this point, see James M. Washington (ed.), *A Testament of Hope: The Essential Writings of Martin Luther King, Jr.* (San Francisco: Harper and Row, 1986), at pp. 50, 71, 88, 265, 266, 290, 294, 300, 328, 347, 349.

"if anyone strikes you on the right cheek, turn the other also" (Matt. 5:39) is an ethical skepticism about the ways in which insults to male honor trigger violence. King essentially rediscovered or reinvented this interpretation, one that would have great appeal to black men of the South who had suffered for centuries under a racist regime of white male violence, including lynchings, directed at black threats to white male honor. It also appealed to African American constitutionalism, which had come so far under the leadership of the NAACP by an insistence on pressing its constitutional rights of free speech and protest. By centering a mass social movement in nonviolence, King made central to the democratic experience of African Americans in general the exercise of their constitutional rights to protest that had hitherto figured largely only in the protest of black elites, including black lawyers and intellectuals.

King's most successful experiments in ethical voice were in Montgomery (with the bus boycott); Birmingham, leading to the Civil Rights Act of 1964; and Selma, leading to the Voting Rights Act of 1965. Apart from drawing on the achievements of African American constitutionalism (the Montgomery bus boycott was one year after *Brown v. Board of Education*), the appeal of King's nonviolent voice also drew importantly on the role of the black churches in the South. On one hand, his insistence on a nonviolent voice protesting the structural injustice of racism brought him into the very center of developing principles of American constitutionalism, including not only the recognition of the evil of racism as a violation of the Equal Protection Clause of the Fourteenth Amendment but also a muscular, speech-protective interpretation of the First Amendment, which the movement used, tested, and extended.[105] On the other hand, the authority of his voice drew on an interpretation of nonviolence in the life and teachings of Jesus – in particular, the Sermon on the Mount[106] – that justified participation in nonviolent civil disobedience as an ethical and religious duty. King's voice gave an ethically compelling sense to Jesus' injunction, "Love your enemies" (Matt. 5:44), to which he appealed as early as 1957 as the proof text for the demands of his movement. As he put the point:

---

[105] See, for a discussion of these free speech principles, David A. J. Richards, *Free Speech and the Politics of Identity* (Oxford: Oxford University Press, 1999); Harry Kalven, Jr., *The Negro and the First Amendment*.

[106] See, on the role of this text in King's statements, James Melvin Washington (ed.), *A Testament of Hope: The Essential Writings of Martin Luther King, Jr.* (San Francisco: Harper and Row, 1986), at pp. 38, 47, 90, 140, 216, 256, 297, 436, 447.

So this morning, as I look into your eyes, and into the eyes of all my brothers in Alabama and all over America and over the world, I say to you, "I love you. I would rather die than hate you." And I'm foolish enough to believe that through the power of this love somewhere, men of the most recalcitrant bent will be transformed. And then we will be in God's kingdom.[107]

The ethical voice that energized mass political protest also gave a strengthening resonance to white Southerners, who had seen the role that racism played in the South's political and economic backwardness.[108] King always emphasized how much blacks and whites shared in the South, the "network of mutuality"[109] or "single garment of destiny" that tied them to one another's lives, not only in economic relationships but also sometimes as children in playgrounds, sometimes as black caretakers in white homes, sometimes in easy social and even sexual relationships or in clandestine visits of whites to experience black dance or music. The dominant racist ideology required that such relationships not be recognized or accorded significance. King's ethical voice raised exactly the questions that – when heard – destabilized the hegemonic power that southern ideology had enjoyed for so long. What the nonviolence of the movement brought out with such clarity, when its moral dramaturgy was most successful, was that it was unjustly repressive violence – including the violence of public officials – that held this ideology in place.

King's appeal, both northern and southern, thus drew on something that American whites and blacks deeply shared – namely, a commitment to constitutionalism and a religion that was broadly Judeo-Christian. His voice carried great authority for African Americans and Americans generally, showing that ethical protests were not peripheral or marginal but a manifestation of core political and religious values. His insight that nonviolence was a way of working through racism's psychic injuries led to a strategic disarmament: by disarming themselves of violence to act out their hatred and eradicate shame, African Americans found an ethical voice to express feelings that might otherwise have seemed to compromise manhood. These feelings were deeply, centrally human and connected them to other Americans through what King unashamedly called love: "I love you. I would rather die than hate you."

That King's voice would be silenced by assassination and the movement he led would be contested in the name of Black Power underscores the volatile

---

[107] See Martin Luther King, Jr., "Loving Your Enemies," in Clayborne Carson and Peter Holloran, eds., *A Knock at Midnight: Inspiration from the Great Sermons of Reverend Martin Luther King, Jr.* (New York: Warner Books, 2000), pp. 41–6, at p. 59.
[108] On this point, see David L. Chappell, *A Stone of Hope: Prophetic Religion and the Death of Jim Crow* (Chapel Hill: University of North Carolina Press, 2004).
[109] On this point in King's statements, see James M. Washington (ed.), *A Testament of Hope*, pp. 210, 254, 269, 290, 474, 588, 594, 626.

gender dynamics still playing out in this protest against racial injustice. The advocacy of the pre–Civil War radical abolitionists and that of Martin Luther King illustrate the transformative power and appeal of free ethical voice, speaking out against injustices that affront the values of constitutional democracies. These historical examples are notable in that the voice of protest, although based on specifically Christian sources, is as much critical of the views of established Christian churches as of conventional politics as such. In *Letter from a Birmingham Jail*, King challenged the complacency of churchmen[110] who refused to take action against the violence that enforced southern racism. The ethical power and appeal of the radical abolitionists and King are distinguished by the way in which they found their free ethical voices at precisely the point where the violence deployed in support of injustice appeared to be so close to hand.

I have now examined the role the psychology of ethical resistance, rooted in an the ethics challenging patriarchal manhood, played in the life, appeal, and legislative successes of Martin Luther King, Jr. This psychology also explains how and why King came to resist the Vietnam War.[111] King saw a connection between the unjust violence directed at the civil rights movement and the unjust violence of America's war in Vietnam, because his ethics, grounded in a questioning of patriarchal manhood, led him to question in the same way how any threat to patriarchal American manhood elicited repressive violence whether against the challenges of Americans blacks to our cultural racism or the challenges of the people of color in Vietnam to a now discredited Western imperialism itself rooted in racism. The impact of the resistance movements starting in the 1960s – the civil rights and antiwar movements, second-wave feminism, gay rights – was both to expand the constitutional conception of American free speech to include the voices of people of color, women, and gays and lesbians and also to move the contemporary constitutional interpretation of the Reconstruction Amendments, most notably, the Fourteenth Amendment, much closer to the views of the antebellum abolitionist feminists.[112] The impact of these movements both on American constitutional law and politics also represent, I believe, the most profound challenge to patriarchy in American history, a success that sets the stage for understanding how and why a reactionary political movement emerged to limit or reverse these successes. I start with the resistance movements and then turn to their cumulative threat to American patriarchy.

---

[110] On this point, see Martin Luther King, Jr., "Letter from a Birmingham Jail," in James M. Washington, Jr., *A Testament of Hope*, at pp. 289, 292.

[111] See King, *A Testament of Hope*, pp. 231–44.

[112] For defense of this view, see Richards, *Women, Gays, and the Constitution*.

172   The Rise of Gay Rights and the Fall of the British Empire

The civil rights movement began as a resistance movement against American racism, entrenched in American institutions through laws requiring racial segregation and condemning miscegenation that had only recently been struck down as unconstitutional by the Supreme Court.[113] Martin Luther King, in leading this movement, spoke from a new voice in Christianity that challenged the role of Augustinian Christianity in the legitimation of religious persecution, including anti-Semitism, and soon directed his energies as well to an antiwar movement, opposing the Vietnam War. King's insistence on nonviolent civil disobedience (a strategy he had learned from Gandhi) gave expression to a conception of democratic manhood centered in voice, not violence, as a response to injustice. It is no accident that this antipatriarchal conception of manhood appealed to and empowered many women, black and white, who played important roles in the civil rights movement. Their activism, on the grounds anticipated by the radical abolitionists, soon led to the emergence of rights-based feminist arguments as well.[114]

As Carol Gilligan's study of women making the abortion choice shows, women in second-wave feminism challenged the traditional conception of patriarchal women as selfless, raising ethical questions about whether the imposition of the sacrifice of self on women deprived them of a responsible ethical voice, responsible for their relationships as a moral agent and as a free and democratic citizen.[115] In "Professions of Women," Virginia Woolf, considering the psychological blocks she had encountered as a creative woman, wrote of "the Angel in the House," an image of selflessness that a creative woman, finding her own voice, had to kill. "Had I not killed her she would have killed me."[116] Woolf gives expression to the crippling effect on women's creative voices of patriarchally imposed images of self-sacrifice and sexual purity that effectively cut them off from themselves, dissociating them from their minds and emotions. Women and men in the 1960s and similarly found their personal and ethical voices, as moral agents, by individual and collective resistance to these images and in speaking out against systematic injustices. In so doing, they successfully moved American constitutional law to recognize many of their claims, including not only *Roe v. Wade* but the increasingly

---

[113] See *Brown v. Board of Education*, 347 U.S. 483 (1954) (laws requiring racial segregation held unconstitutional); *Loving v. Virginia*, 386 U.S. 1 (1967) (antimiscegenation laws held unconstitutional).

[114] On this development, see Sara Evans, *Personal Politics: The Roots of Women's Liberation in the Civil Rights Movement and the New Left* (New York: Vintage Books, 1980).

[115] On this point, see Carol Gilligan, *In a Different Voice: Psychological Theory and Women's Development* (Cambridge, MA: Harvard University Press, 1982).

[116] Virginia Woolf, "Professions of Women," in Virginia Woolf, *Women and Writing* edited by Michele Barrett (Orlando, FL: Harvest Books, 1980), pp. 57–63, at p. 59.

demanding constitutional scrutiny of gender stereotypes to combat sexism on a par with the even more demanding scrutiny of ethnic stereotypes (combating racism).[117]

Men in the antiwar movement, many of whom had served with distinction in Vietnam, refused continuing complicity with a violence they had come to regard as unjust. Others found their voices in <u>questioning a sense of manhood that had crushed their sense of conscience</u>, leading them to serve in a war they always regarded as unjust.[118] Still others, like James Carroll, found a voice in themselves not only to resist as a priest but also to question the role their fathers played in supporting that war and, ultimately, their own vocation.[119] The intergenerational conflict between these young men and their fathers was over the issues of conscience that the Vietnam War posed for sons, who found an ethical voice resisting the patriarchal appeals of their fathers (reflecting sometimes their own war experience in World War II or Korea). These fathers often only came to appreciate their son's views much later. The success of their resistance in ending the war in Vietnam marked an important turning point in American history.

Men and women in the gay rights movement, which developed from the movement for women's liberation, also questioned a patriarchal conception of manhood and womanhood that warred on loving relationships between men and women of the same gender. Gay men in this situation, for example, found that resistance to the homophobic lies told about gay love was a necessary condition for experiencing love, for coming to trust themselves and others to live a life together in the truth of a loving relationship.[120] In so doing, such men come fundamentally to question patriarchy, which, imposing hierarchy not only between men and women but also between men and men, undermines the free and equal voice in relationship that makes mutual love possible and sustaining.

I regard these interconnected resistance movements as grounded in both the moral argument and the psychology of resistance offered in this book. At the heart of it is speaking in a different voice, one that by resisting the traditional

---

[117] For fuller exploration and defense of these developments, see Richards, *Women, Gays, and the Constitution*.

[118] See, for example, Tim O'Brien, *The Things They Carried* (New York: Broadway Books, 1990), pp. 39–61.

[119] See James Carroll, *An American Requiem: God, My Father, and the War That Came Between Us* (Boston: Houghton Mifflin Company, 2001).

[120] See, on these points, David A. J. Richards, *The Case for Gay Rights: From Bowers to Lawrence and Beyond* (Lawrence: University Press of Kansas, 2005). For an important early defense of gay rights, see Dennis Altman, *Homosexuality: Oppression and Liberation* (New York: New York University Press, 1993; first published, 1971).

authority enjoyed by patriarchy in the politics, religion, and psychology of Western culture speaks from the embodiment of our desires for love and relationship. The increasingly important role of women's resistance in these movements is not surprising, nor is the role of men who find and strengthen their resisting voices through relationships to such women. It is what the Cupid and Psyche story would lead us to expect: as women's resistance to the patriarchal objectification and dissociation traditionally imposed on them makes possible new kinds of relationships, including those between women and the men who love them.

At the heart of this transformative development were the morally empowered voices of groups that reasonably challenged the repressive force of patriarchy. The 1960s witnessed an ethical resistance to the corruption of the American constitutional protection of universal human rights that transformed American constitutional law. Perhaps more to the point, the resistance movements of the sixties questioned the patriarchal Love Laws, including not only antimiscegenation laws but those limiting reproductive autonomy and criminalizing harmless sex acts. Such resistance to patriarchy is historically quite remarkable, and the scale and broad front of interconnected movements opposing anti-Semitism, racism, sexism, and homophobia have not been fully honored or understood. A fundamentalist reaction moved to denigrate these achievements, as patriarchal reaction always does, in terms of a libertine sexualization that ideologically transformed movements of genuine ethical struggle into an era of "sex, drugs, and rock 'n' roll."[121] One cannot understand this political reaction unless we take seriously the degree to which the successes of the resistance movements of the 1960s and later put American patriarchy under greater threat than it had even been, as I now show.

Patriarchy has been around in human culture for a long time, and, as I argued in Chapter 1, has rationalized the autocratic rule of patriarchal priest-kings that dominated the high cultures of the Neolithic Age. It also persisted both in the Athenian democracy and the Roman Republic, both of which were important models in the deliberations of the American Founders. There is a tension between democracy (based on constitutional guarantees of free and equal voice) and patriarchy (requiring the repression of any voice that resists its authority). It has, however, been a notable feature of democracies,

---

[121] For a striking example of this ideological distortion, see the book review of David A. J. Richards' *Sex, Drugs, Death and the Law: An Essay on Human Rights and Overcriminalization* (Totowa, NJ: Rowman & Littlefield, 1982) by Mark V. Tushnet, "Sex, Drugs and Rock 'n' Roll: Some Conservative Reflections on Liberal Jurisprudence," *Columbia Law Review* 82, no. 7 (1982), 1531–43.

from Athens until today, that the tension, which in my view brings democracy disastrously in contradiction with itself, has not been acknowledged as the problem it is. Great artists (Aeschylus in democratic Athens, Vergil and Apuleius in Rome) often show us the conflicted psychology that supports the demands of manhood and womanhood in tension between democracy and patriarchy. But the usual view taken is that these conflicts do not reveal something that must be addressed for democracy to flourish but rather show us the inevitable burdens of civilization. Aeschylus, for example, concludes the *Oresteia* essentially by aligning democracy with patriarchy. The traumatic breaks in relationship between men and women that Aeschylus shows us are in the nature of things, and women and men must take their place in the Athenian democracy as patriarchy requires: women must traumatically lose their voices (the Furies must become the Eumenides, the good women) and sacrifice personal relationships, including to their children (Klytemnestra's relationship to her daughter Iphigenia must be sacrificed to uphold her husband's honor as leader of Greece's war on Troy). Thus they identify themselves, as wives and mothers, with the patriarchal demands imposed on them.

I call this phenomenon patriarchy hiding in democracy. Patriarchy could only successfully hide in this way, as it has in democracies since Athens, if a personal and political psychology made it possible for men, in particular, to naturalize patriarchy, as psychology largely has, including the psychology of Freud himself.[122] Intelligent and sensitive men, men like Freud who resisted anti-Semitism and Tolstoy, Gandhi, and King who resisted religious and ethnic/racial intolerance,[123] are nonetheless compromised and crippled in their resistance when, as men, they accept and enforce the patriarchally enforced gender binary, as they often do in their conflicted relationships to women. It is because the psychology of traumatic breaks in relationship occurs so early in boyhood that it enters so deeply into the psyche of men for whom challenging the gender binary remains so terrifying to their sense of themselves as men. What makes this so tragic for these men is that, in enforcing the gender binary, they cut themselves off from precisely the relationships to resisting women that would help them.

The beginning of wisdom is, I believe, to expose to the light of reason that what I call the tension between democracy and patriarchy is not in the nature of things but feeds a contradiction that has been and is destructive – indeed sometimes catastrophically so – to democratic values. What Carol Gilligan and

---

[122] On this point, see Gilligan and Richards, *The Deepening Darkness*, chapter 7.
[123] For fuller treatment of this point, see David A. J. Richards, *Disarming Manhood: Roots of Ethical Resistance*.

I argued about the Roman Republic in *The Deepening Darkness* – namely, that patriarchy destroyed whatever democracy Rome had – bespeaks a truth that holds over time.

The founding of American constitutional democracy, for example, was informed by a consciousness of the many experiments both in republican government and in forms of a federal state that had existed in human history, including republican Rome (with its balanced constitution) and its growing empire.[124] Vergil's *Aeneid* was, of course, read by the American Founders in their studies at university.[125] The founding of Rome was thus one of the historical precedents they had in mind when they reflected on their own establishment of an American republic in the Constitution of 1787, as amended by the Bill of Rights of 1791.[126]

For the Founders, the sense of themselves as establishing a new Rome carried with it a sense of the kind of heroic man (Aeneas) that they also inherited from Rome and its foundation narrative.[127] Benjamin Rush, for example, confessed that "[n]othing struck me more than the moving story of his [Aeneas'] leaving Dido at Carthage," bespeaking precisely "that manly heroism which the prospect of establishing a kingdom and being the author of an illustrious race of heroes in a distant country naturally fired his soul."[128] American constitutional law and development have come a long way since 1787–91, marked crucially by the second refounding of the Constitution in the Reconstruction Amendments of 1865–70 in the wake of the Civil War[129] and by the impact on the interpretation of the Constitution of the resistance movements starting in the 1960s.[130] But persistent American problems with patriarchy undoubtedly date from the uncritical incorporation of Aeneas as founder as one among the sources of our founding. The tension between patriarchy and democracy has long existed in America. Examples include the degree to which it may underlie many of our most damaging and disastrous inconsistencies, including our treatment of the native Amerindians and the

---

[124] On the classical education of the Founders, Carl J. Richard, *The Founders and the Classics: Greece, Rome, and the American Enlightenment* (Cambridge, MA: Harvard University Press, 1994), pp. 13, 17–25, 33–5, 221.
[125] On the classical education of the Founders, Carl J. Richard, *The Founders and the Classics*, pp. 13, 17–25, 33–5, 221.
[126] On this point, see Gilligan and Richards, *The Deepening Darkness*, pp. 225–6.
[127] On this point, see Hannah Arendt, *The Life of the Mind*, one-volume edition (New York: Harcourt Brace Jovanovich, 1978), pp. 195–217; Carl J. Richard, *The Founders and the Classics*, pp. 23, 55, 182, 207, 224.
[128] Quoted in Richard, ibid., p. 207.
[129] See David A. J. Richards, *Conscience and the Constitution: History, Theory, and Law of the Reconstruction Amendments* (Princeton, NJ: Princeton University Press, 1993).
[130] On this point, see Richards, *Women, Gays, and the Constitution*.

The Fall of Empire

persistence of American slavery long after it was abolished elsewhere. Consider too slavery's legacy, after its abolition by the Thirteenth Amendment, in the persisting patterns of American racism, not to mention sexism and homophobia.

There were, of course, important differences between Roman and American slavery. Roman slavery was not racially or ethnically defined, as American slavery tragically was, and manumission to freedom was much more easily available in Rome than in antebellum America. Furthermore, freedom in Rome could lead to a kind of mobility and opportunity not available in racist America.[131] However, Roman patriarchy played a central role in the legitimation of the treatment of Roman slaves as lacking basic human dignity[132] in precisely the same way that the patriarchal family in the antebellum South rationalized the racist dehumanization of people of color held in slavery. They were seen as so lacking in human feeling that they were incapable of family relations and, thus, allegedly bore easily the separations (through sale of family relatives) common under American slavery.[133] One can see the stark force of such patriarchally rooted racism in the infamous 3/5 Clause of the U.S. Constitution that accorded the southern states disproportionate political power (each slave being accorded three-fifths the representative weight of a citizen) until the Civil War.[134]

It is such disproportionate political power that made possible the growing importance, under the intellectual and political leadership of John Calhoun, of proslavery constitutionalism, a view that constitutionally entrenched slavery not only in the states that allowed it but in the territories as well (a constitutional interpretation accepted by the Supreme Court of the United States in the infamous *Dred Scott v. Sanford*).[135] No historical precedent was more important to Calhoun than the central place of slavery both in the Athenian democracy and in the Roman Republic, which makes clear how important Roman patriarchy and slavery were in both the design and interpretation of the U.S. Constitution, including the extraordinary and deadly polemical force that proslavery constitutionalism enjoyed among southerners, legitimating, in

---

[131] On these points, see William D. Phillips, Jr., "Continuity and Change in Western Slavery: Ancient to Modern Times," in M. L. Bush, ed., *Serfdom and Slavery: Studies in Legal Bondage* (London: Longman, 1999), at pp. 71–88.

[132] On this point, see Richard Saller, "The Hierarchical Household in Roman Society: A Study of Domestic Slavery," ibid., pp. 112–29.

[133] On the classical education of the Founders, see Carl J. Richard, *The Founders and the Classics*, pp. 13, 17–25, 33–5, 221.

[134] On this point, see Richards, *Conscience and the Constitution*, at pp. 24, 92, 120.

[135] *Dred Scott v. Sanford*, 19 Howard 393 (1857). For commentary, see Richards, *Conscience and the Constitution*, at pp. 41, 54–5, 78, 81, 106, 113, 120, 125, 129, 137, 200, 217, 258.

their view, secession and the fratricidal violence of civil war.[136] In contrast, abolitionist constitutionalists in the antebellum period rejected the continuing historical authority of slavery in ancient Greece and Rome because the fundamental American constitutional value of universal human rights rendered slavery illegitimate in principle.[137] No war in American history was more rooted in the defense of its patriarchal honor, identified by the South with slavery,[138] and no war, as my argument suggests and explains, was, in consequence, more violent and costly in American lives. It is when patriarchy most uncritically consumes us that our putative constitutional piety (to which all sides in the Civil War appealed) turns us, like Aeneas, into savages.

In contrast, the abolitionist feminists, the most radical antebellum critics of American slavery and racism, thus analyzed the roots of American slavery and racism as the same as those of the American subjection of women and sexism – namely, patriarchy.[139] Nathaniel Hawthorne's *The Scarlet Letter*, written under the influence of the abolitionist feminists, also critically examines his persecutory Puritan ancestors in terms of their "patriarchal" character.[140] In fact, it carries their criticism a step further, portraying in Hester Prynne a prophetically antipatriarchal ethical voice, rooted in her freer sexual voice and life that the New England patriarchy so condemned.

The criticism of patriarchy as being at the root of the constitutionally contradictory evils of slavery and racism is thus hardly historically novel, as both the abolitionist feminists and Hawthorne's art make quite clear.[141] Yet, our patriarchal assumptions have been so powerful that the antipatriarchal core of the abolitionist feminist criticism of both racism and sexism was marginalized inasmuch as the Reconstruction Amendments emancipated both black men and women from slavery but emancipated black women into patriarchy. Elizabeth Stanton, who had been a crucial figure in securing ratification of the Thirteenth Amendment, opposed both the Fourteenth and Fifteenth Amendments for this reason (the Fifteenth Amendment gave the vote to black

---

[136] For an extended treatment of proslavery constitutionalism, see Richards, *Conscience and the Constitution*, pp. 28–42. Abolitionist constitutional thought, in contrast, argued that Roman and Greek slavery were inconsistent with the fundamental American constitutional commitment to universal human rights. See ibid., pp. 61–2, 91, 130, 132.
[137] See Richards, *Conscience and the Constitution*, 61–2, 91, 130, 132.
[138] See Bertram Wyatt-Brown, *Southern Honor: Ethics and Behavior in the Old South* (Oxford: Oxford University Press, 2007).
[139] For extended treatment of this argument, see David A. J. Richards, *Women, Gays, and the Constitution*.
[140] See Nathaniel Hawthorne, *The Scarlet Letter* (New York: Penguin, 1983; originally published, 1850), at p. 15; see also ibid., pp. 12–14, 18, 20, 132, 190.
[141] On the abolitionist feminists, see Richards, *Women, Gays, and the Constitution*.

The Fall of Empire

men but not to women, including black women).[142] In effect, black women were no longer black but were only women. Thus, even the Reconstruction Amendments were compromised by patriarchal assumptions at war with their deeper ethical principles.

We can also see the continuing destructiveness of American patriarchy in American foreign policy after the Civil War on a man as educated and literary and sensitive as Theodore Roosevelt. It was precisely these features of Roosevelt's background, combined with his "high-pitched, Harvard-tinged voice," that led Roosevelt's assembly colleagues in Albany to apply to him "the demeaning nickname 'Oscar Wilde' ..., a mocking reference to the disgraced British homosexual."[143] It was decisively to rebut these impressions that Roosevelt became so aggressive, so strutting an imperialist, accepting uncritically the dominant racism of the age that rationalized such imperialism.[144] Roosevelt would for this reason play an important role in the Spanish-American War and later in urging America to enter World War I.[145] His racism also led him to interpret the resurgent Japanese as less inferior than other Asians and thus, as president of the United States, to encourage their own aggressive imperialism that was to culminate in World War II.[146]

Roosevelt interpreted the Japanese through a patriarchal lens that blinded him, like so many others later, to the dangers to world peace from the forms of patriarchal autocratic nationalism that were developing in Japan and were to develop in fascist Italy and Germany, rooted, as they were, in reviving Roman patriarchal manhood (see Chapter 2). It was in part because during these periods Americans were themselves so patriarchal that, not seeing the tension between democracy and patriarchy at home, they could not see it abroad as well. Their failure was, of course, catastrophic, failing to take seriously Churchill's remarkable prescience in urging that German aggressive fascism be stopped early when it could be stopped at comparatively little cost compared with the catastrophe that, in fact, followed. If Churchill could see it, why couldn't Americans?[147]

---

[142] On this point, see *Women, Gays, and the Constitution*, pp. 138–9.
[143] James Bradley, *The Imperial Cruise: A Secret History of Empire and War* (New York: Little, Brown and Company, 2009), at p. 50.
[144] See James Bradley, *The Imperial Cruise*, at p. 48.
[145] See Evan Thomas, *The War Lovers: Roosevelt, Lodge, Hearst, and the Rush to Empire, 1898* (New York: Little, Brown & Company, 2010); Gregg Jones, *Honor in the Dust: Theodore Roosevelt, War in the Philippines, and the Rise and Fall of America's Imperial Dream* (New York: New American Library, 2012).
[146] See, in general, James Bradley, *The Imperial Cruise*.
[147] On the antipatriarchal roots of Churchill's psychology that explain his intelligence on this point, see David A. J. Richards, *Disarming Manhood*, chapter 5.

The victory of the United States and its allies in World War II set the stage, both in America and Europe, for a rebirth of democratic constitutionalism. Having achieved victory over aggressively racist powers hostile to the very idea of universal human rights, the United States was compelled to question the degree to which its constitutional law, grounded in the protection of such rights, had failed to protect the rights of people of color and many others as well. A growing American sensitivity to antipatriarchal voices arose from revulsion at the violence of political fascism, itself grounded, as we saw in Chapter 2, in Roman patriarchal manhood. Martin Luther King, Jr.'s strategy of nonviolence was so appealing and successful because through nonviolence, he made his point that his advocacy was rooted in American constitutional values of free speech and voice and that it was his racist opponents who exploded in violence, a repressive violence directed at the exercise by fellow Americans of their basic rights of free speech.

The other resistance movements of the 1960s and later carried, if anything, the criticism of American patriarchy even further, as many American men serving in Vietnam, inspired by King, came to question a patriarchal manhood that had quashed their own sense of conscience in participating in an unjust war. And women and men in the feminist and gay rights movements challenged the role the patriarchally enforced gender binary had traditionally played in supporting the interlinked injustices of American racism, sexism, and homophobia. It was an extraordinary moment in American constitutional and political history; these movements led to the constitutional attack on the patriarchally enforced Love Laws, the laws about whom and how one might love that had been so crucial to the ways in which patriarchy had historically killed the human relationality that is the basis of the ethics of care, a relationality that moves naturally across the artificial barriers of religion, ethnicity, gender, and sexual orientation that patriarchy traditionally imposes in its way. John Rawls's *A Theory of Justice*, published in 1971, grounds and supports this development, one of worldwide ethical importance, in an ethics of care, and Carol Gilligan's work on moral development has, advancing beyond Rawls, shows how and why the resistance of these movements crucially connects to questioning the gender binary, an idea at best implicit in Rawls's thinking.[148]

Such resistance rests on a normative conception of free and equal democratic voice that is fundamentally at odds with the traditional place of patriarchy in our lives. Indeed, I would generalize the point in terms of a contradiction,

---

[148] On this point, see David A. J. Richards, *Resisting Injustice and the Feminist Ethics of Care in the Age of Obama: "Suddernly, ... All the Truth Was Coming Out"* (forthcoming 2013).

both normative and psychological, between democracy and patriarchy. Constitutional democracy has at its core a normative conception of respect for equal human rights that include, prominently, equal respect for free voice speaking from conviction, a right protected constitutionally in the United States by the guarantees of the First Amendment (including the protection of conscience from improper exercises of state power in a secular state, as well as the protection of speech expressing conscience). <u>Such guarantees of free and equal voice are in tension with the hierarchical conception of authority required by patriarchy</u>. Indeed, the stability of patriarchy rests on the violent denial and abridgement of such voices – in particular, the voices of those who would most reasonably challenge its authority.

Given this tension, indeed contradiction, between democracy and patriarchy, resistance movements to the continuing role of patriarchy in our lives must be regarded as both democratic and democratizing: they both assert a basic right to equal voice and deliberatively seek to persuade others to eliminate patriarchal institutions that rest on an antidemocratic suppression of voice. <u>What makes such resistance psychologically possible and appealing – in the face of the traditional power of patriarchy – is the way it breaks a silence imposed on the psyche, breaking the taboo on seeing, knowing, and speaking about love.</u> We resist because only through resistance can we come to know and realize the value of loving relationship in a human life. Both the force and historical endurance of such resistance comes from its grounding in our human nature, as research in developmental psychology, evolutionary psychology, and neurobiology now show. The resistance movements in question could not have gotten as far as they did if their claims did not find a resonance in the hearts and minds of their fellow Americans.

Impact on Britain and Elsewhere

What is of interest to my current study is that these American movements had a resonance abroad as well, particularly in Britain. In light of our earlier argument about the Wolfenden Report, the Devlin-Hart debate, and the 1967 parliamentary decriminalization of gay sex in England and Wales, on the issue of gay rights, Britain may reasonably be regarded as much advanced over the United States, certainly in 1969 when the Stonewall riot takes place in New York City's Greenwich Village. Moreover, as now studied in some depth, a gay rights resistance movement existed and flourished in Britain, and two of its leading figures, Lytton Strachey and Virginia Woolf, implicitly made the case for gay rights, connecting it to a criticism of British patriarchy, which led them and others to resist World War I and question British imperialism more generally. Although I regard the historical recovery and fuller understanding of this resistance movement as being of extraordinary ethical and political importance in the emergence of and defense of gay rights, it was a resistance movement consisting of a relatively small group of lovers and friends, who, through breaking the patriarchal Love Laws, came to live and to work as writers and artists. Through their lives and work, they exposed to ethical criticism how the patriarchally enforced gender binary had rendered the love of equals problematic if not impossible. This gender binary also supported the unjust imperialism that rested on the irrational prejudices (religious intolerance, racism, sexism, and homophobia) that patriarchy used hierarchically to divide people. Although this resistance group came to the same conclusions as the later American resistance movements, the underlying character of the Bloomsbury Group's lives and works were not well known until the more permissive environment initiated by the 1967 decriminalization made possible the remarkable biographies of Lytton Strachey, Virginia Woolf, and others, revealing the importance in their lives of the love of equals in general and homosexual love in particular (see Chapter 3). A resistance movement without free speech operates always through euphemism and with a lack of direction, limiting public understanding of its claims and marginalizing any just impact on the policies of unjust imperialism (for example, opposition to World War I) they could have had. A movement operating under these conditions undoubtedly casts some light on what would otherwise be the patriarchal darkening of public intelligence, but it remains in the shadows.

The British courts, in contrast to the American Supreme Court, did not develop expansive conceptions of free speech to empower resistance movements in Britain. Quite to the contrary. In a remarkable and much criticized case, the House of Lords in a 1961 opinion, *Shaw v. Director of Public Prosecution*,[149] held a common law charge of conspiracy to corrupt public morals against the defendant, who had published "The Ladies' Home Directory," which advertised the services of commercial sex workers to interested clients. It did so even though Parliament had expressly decriminalized commercial sex in 1959. The role of Lord Devlin, in leading the charge against the Wolfenden Report, suggests the conservative bent of British judges who certainly would provide no aid or comfort to the reform movements now active in British political culture. What in the United States was achieved through the Supreme Court's recognition of basic rights to contraception, abortion, and gay/lesbian sex would in Britain be matters for Parliament, not its conservative

---

[149] House of Lords [1962] A.C. 220.

judges.[150] If Parliament wanted to protect a new human right, it could do so. The courts would not.

During the debates over the 1967 decriminalization, twice Lady Wootton, an important liberal jurist, tabled amendments to ensure that such conspiracy charges would not be brought against people seeking to commit the now decriminalized sex acts. Each time she failed with the result that "within a few years, charges of conspiracy to corrupt public morals were successfully brought against the 'underground' paper IT (*International Times*) for carrying homosexual contact advertisements, and unsuccessfully against *Oz*. Later in the 1970's they were used against a new wave of homosexual magazines."[151] It was in this environment that, even after the decriminalization, gays and lesbians in Britain not only did not enjoy judicial support for their claims but confronted a judiciary, like that in *Shaw*, likely to be outright hostile, in effect, seeing its role as continuing to enforce an anachronistic, now democratically discredited public morality.

In contrast, the resistance movements in the United States that began with Martin Luther King, Jr.'s civil rights movement were made possible by the much freer regime of free speech that the U.S. Supreme Court came to impose during this period, often in response to the more expansive understanding of free speech that these resistance movements demanded. Free speech made possible not only the discussion of new topics (for example, the evil of racism) but new ethical voices, like that of King, that had previously been silenced, and the growing resonance accorded those voices in American political life with the passage of the Civil Rights Act of 1964 (forbidding discrimination in employment on grounds of race and gender) and the Voting Rights Act of 1965. Moreover, the antipatriarchal character of that voice became evident when King led his movement into opposition to the Vietnam War and when the antiwar movement, initially quite unpopular, eventually changed American public opinion, leading many to demand an end to what Americans had come to regard as an unjust, imperialistic war. The damage done by patriarchy both to the human psyche and to ethics and politics could now be seen in a much brighter light.

The American resistance movements thus became powerful cultural and political movements, soon joined by the feminist and gay rights movements, in which the now liberal American constitutional platform of free speech opened the American mind to both new issues (the evils of sexism and homophobia) and new voices – voices that had previously been repressed. As we have seen,

---

[150] On the British development, see Peter G. Richards, *Parliament and the Constitution*.
[151] Jeffrey Weeks, *Coming Out*, p. 177. See also Antony Grey, *Quest for Justice*, pp. 115–16, 163.

patriarchy always depended on the repression of the voices of those who most reasonably might challenge its justice for its continuing hegemonic power, including, as Virginia Woolf observed about the impact of the Angel in the House on women, the silencing and deadening of an independent resisting ethical voice and creativity, coming to see the world exclusively through a rigid patriarchal lens. What marked the American resistance movements was not their common resistance to patriarchy (the British resisting movement had discovered this earlier) but their broader and deeper impact on the American psyche, as women and men found their own ethical voices through resistance to the patriarchal Love Laws. Gay rights in the United States thus took the form of claiming the equal dignity of gay love with all forms of love that resist patriarchy, as a great human and ethical good. Although progress was slow and uneven in the United States, its goals were not defeated even by the AIDS crisis, which, if anything, revealed not only the extent of gay sexual activity but the humanity with which gay men and their friends cared for one another and dealt with terrible loss. Thus, its claims extended beyond decriminalization to nondiscrimination and the legal recognition of same-sex partnerships.

The impact of these movements abroad is evident in their impact on British law and policy. For example, "throughout the 1960's, the political conflict and violence associated with civil rights struggles in the US formed the backdrop for a discussion of race and immigration in Britain. Moreover, US models of discrimination law had a more direct impact on the form and content of domestic discrimination law."[152] Leading British academics closely studied the American developments and urged changes in the British law of racial discrimination that took these developments seriously.[153] There was a comparable American influence on the British development of its law of discrimination dealing with gender, religion, age, and disabilities both directly and indirectly through the impact of American experience on the discrimination law of the European Union (which Britain joined in 1973)[154] and the evolving European law of human rights under the European Convention on Human Rights, which came into force in 1953 after signature in 1950 through the Council of Europe in which Britain was a prominent founding member.[155]

---

[152] See Nicholas Bamforth, Maleiha Malik, and Colm O'Cinneide, *Discrimination Law: Theory and Context* (London: Sweet & Maxwell, 2008), p. 781.
[153] See Christopher McCrudden, "Institutional Discrimination," 2 Oxford J. Legal Stud. 303 (1982).
[154] For an illuminating general study, see Nicholas Bamforth et al., *Discrimination Law*.
[155] See A. W. Brian Simpson, *Human Rights and the End of Empire: Britain and the Genesis of the European Convention* (Oxford: Oxford University Press, 2004).

The American gay rights movement energized a similar movement in Britain and elsewhere. As Jeffrey Weeks observes,

> In June 1970, when I read about the Christopher Street Gay Pride march in New York, I remember feeling that *that* could never happen in London – and a good thing too. But by November of that year I was enthusiastically attending meetings of the London GLF and feeling my whole outlook and life were being transformed.[156]

Although the emergence of the gay rights movements in the United States thus influenced the development of such a movement in Britain and Europe, the legal protection of gay rights has been and continues to be much more advanced in Britain and Europe than in the United States.[157] Britain itself decriminalized gay sex in England and Wales in 1967, and in 1982 the European Court of Human Rights struck down the criminalization of gay sex in Northern Ireland in *Dudgeon v. United Kingdom*[158] as a violation of the constitutional right of privacy guaranteed by the European Convention (it would take until 2003 for the U.S. Supreme Court to strike down such laws). Similarly, the law of nondiscrimination on grounds of sexual orientation is much more highly developed in Britain and Europe than in the United States[159] and has led as well to both the legal recognition of same-sex partnerships (Britain) and, in several nations, gay marriage (Belgium, the Netherlands, Norway, Portugal, Spain, Sweden).

Conservative Reaction in the United States

Why this difference between the United States and Great Britain as well as Europe? The success of the various resistance movements in the United States challenged American patriarchy more profoundly than ever before. This led to a reactionary politics of threatened patriarchy charged with reversing or limiting these advances.[160]

---

[156] Jeffrey Weeks, *Coming Out*, p. 189.
[157] On 1970s developments in Britain, see Lisa Power, *No Bath but Plenty of Bubbles: An Oral History of the Gay Liberation, 1970–73* (London: Cassell, 1996); on 1980s developments in Britain, see Davina Cooper, *Sexing the City: Lesbian and Gay Politics within the Activist State* (London: Rivers Oram Press, 1994).
[158] *Dudgeon v. United Kingdom* (A/45)(1982) 4 E.H.R.R. 149, ECHR.
[159] On this point, see Nicholas Bamforth et al., *Discrimination Law*, pp. 653–754.
[160] See, for example, George Lakoff, *Moral Politics: How Liberals and Conservatives Think*, 2nd ed. (Chicago: University of Chicago Press, 1996, 2002); Mark J. Hetherington and Jonathan D. Weiler, *Authoritarianism and Polarization in American Politics* (Cambridge: Cambridge University Press, 2009); Naomi Cahn and June Carbone, *Red Families v. Blue Families: Legal*

It is important to keep in mind a period of division among liberals that arose during the 1960s. Consider the alliance between Martin Luther King, Jr. and President Lyndon Johnson that had led to the stunning political successes of the civil rights movement. Their cooperation collapsed over the Vietnam War, which Johnson, tragically, supported and King opposed. Johnson, who championed civil rights and a war on poverty that called for attention to matters of redistributive justice, was politically destroyed by his escalation of the Vietnam War. The Cold War was at this time a live political issue in the United States, largely supported by a bipartisan political consensus that had opposed the aggressive claims and advances of communist states in Europe after World War II, in the Korean War, and in the Cuban Missile Crisis. Johnson's sense of political manhood was clearly threatened by the very existence of the communist regime in Hanoi and its essentially nationalistic civil war in the South, a war that never aggressively threatened the United States. Patriarchal manhood thus imaginatively transformed an internal civil war into an aggressive threat. This failure of judgment on Johnson's part, however understandable and once broadly shared, rationalized an aggressive escalation of American fighting forces in Vietnam that eventually came to be widely condemned by Americans as unjust both in its ends and its means. King was among those who condemned it. What he saw that Johnson could not was that the same implicit questioning of patriarchy that mobilized the nonviolent civil rights movement also questioned the patriarchal violence of an unjust war. King was, however, opposed by more conventional men of color, including the Black Power movement, who regarded the use of violence against America's racism as their patriarchal right as men and indeed denigrated nonviolence as unmanly. King was assassinated in 1968, and his astonishing heritage of nonviolence was covered over in the American public mind by race riots.

As we have seen, patriarchy has been a powerful force in American democracy for a long time, hiding quite successfully in democracy just as it has in most democracies since Athens. King's resistance, its appeal, and its success suggested that American patriarchy, although powerful, could now reasonably and indeed successfully be resisted in ways not possible in the past. Americans now responsibly faced, perhaps for the first time in our history, the injustice of our cultural racism, long supported by segregation and antimiscegenation

Polarization and the Creation of Culture (Oxford: Oxford University Press, 2010). See also Bob Altemeyer, *The Authoritarian Specter* (Cambridge, MA: Harvard University Press, 1996); Bob Altemeyer, *Right-Wing Authoritarianism Right-Wing Authoritarianism* (Winnipeg, Canada: University of Manitoba Press, 1981).

The Fall of Empire

laws that the Supreme Court had validated for more than sixty years and only recently struck down. But King's resistance to patriarchy, which grounded his leadership of the civil rights movement and his opposition to the Vietnam War, was itself partial and was itself questioned not only by other people of color but by white liberals like Johnson who could not follow him in opposition to the Vietnam War. American patriarchy remained powerful. It was at this point of increasing division among liberals, as their leaders could not agree among themselves and were forced to leave politics (Johnson), were murdered (King, President John Kennedy, and his brother, Robert Kennedy), or were discredited and defeated (President Jimmy Carter) that a reactionary conservative politics developed in the United States. <u>Patriarchal religious fundamentalism</u> would play an increasingly important role in this development.[161]

Politicians are by nature often highly opportunistic, and it is certainly not surprising that conservative politicians would have understood the disarray among liberals as giving them an opening to be more successful in American politics than they had been for some time. The degree of their success has, however, been remarkable in ways that require a sharper and more cogent explanation than has yet been given. It is a distinctive feature of American conservatives that they are trying to conserve a tradition in which liberal democracy is in tension with patriarchy.[162]

The psychological basis of its reactionary politics is seen in its aggressive focus on any challenge to the gender binary, apparent in the resistance movements of the 1960s and later. An illuminating way to see the reactionary force of the gender binary in action in this connection is to explore its role in the life and art of Ayn Rand, the novelist whose ideology, known as objectivism, has been such an influence on American libertarians (including Alan Greenspan who, as Fed chairman, campaigned for repeal of much of the regulation of the banking industry that led to our recent financial crisis[163]) as well as many American businessmen grateful to her for freeing capitalists from guilt.[164] Rand was an émigré from the early Soviet Union, whose contempt for the American left (including Roosevelt's New Deal) was formed by her insider's knowledge that

---

[161] See Dominic Sandbrook, *Mad as Hell: The Crisis of the 1970s and the Rise of the Populist Right* (New York: Alfred A. Knopf, 2011).

[162] For fuller development of the argument that follows, see David A. J. Richards, *Resisting Injustice and the Feminist Ethics of Care in the Age of Obama*.

[163] On this point, see Louis Uchitelle, "Volcker, Loud and Clear," *The New York Times*, Sunday, July 11, 2010, pp. 1, 7.

[164] See, in general, Jennifer Burns, *Goddess of the Market: Ayn Rand and the American Right* (Oxford: Oxford University Press, 2009).

its sometimes uncritical admiration for the Soviet Union was, to say the least, unjustified. Rand, a Jew, came to the United States alone, experiencing what must have been a traumatic break in her relationship to her parents and two sisters; she was never to see them again. The psychological consequence was that she came aggressively to identify with a patriarchally idealized Hollywood image of American women and men defined by the gender binary with which she passionately identified in the works of her favorite philosopher, Friedrich Nietzsche. She absorbed from Nietzsche his patriarchal rage against liberal equality, including feminism. Her life, both as a woman and artist, played out highly patriarchal ideals of superior men who dominated women, who realized their natures in abject man worship,[165] an idealization of men and denigration of women completely inconsistent with Rand's actual relationships to men, both her long-suffering and economically dependent husband and her worshipful and much younger lover. Consistent with the rather rigid form of the gender binary she assumed, Rand's ideology centered on reason and a contempt for emotions, which led to the objectivist theory of love as resting not on emotion but on the value of the beloved; it is for this reason that she tragically misread her young lover's eventual lack of sexual interest in her as a kind of heretical moral betrayal, not tracking her supreme objectivist value as artist and philosopher.[166] It is precisely because Rand naturalized patriarchy into a metaphysical principle that her objectivism had no place for the ethics of care, celebrating selfishness in the pursuit and perfection of one's talents as the only objectivist value. Ethical egoism is often a preferred way to support on secular grounds patriarchal demands, as it was for Hobbes. What is of interest, from my perspective, is how Rand's personal and political psychology, rooted in trauma and patriarchal identification, expresses itself in the rejection of any form of social democracy, whether guaranteeing an economic and social minimum, redistributive taxation, or reasonable regulation of markets. Unlike other reactionary conservatives, however, Rand completely rejected religion in politics, opposed the war in Vietnam,[167] and was appalled by Reagan's attack on the constitutional protection of the right to an abortion.[168] Rand came to her reactionary views on social democracy not in the way fundamentalist religious believers came to their views on social issues, but both did so, nonetheless, through the lens of patriarchy, construing the aims of social democracy (for

---

[165] On this point, see Burns, *Goddess of the Market*, at pp. 226–7, 240, 264–5.
[166] On this point, see Jennifer Burns, *Goddess of the Market*, pp. 224–7.
[167] See Jennifer Burns, *Goddess of the Market*, pp. 228–9.
[168] See Jennifer Burns, *Goddess of the Market*, p. 263.

example, adequate health care) as feminine and thus not properly a legitimate public purpose.

What is extraordinary is the continuing appeal for many Americans of Rand's ideological farrago, which suggests that her reactionary conservatism touches a deep patriarchal chord in the American psyche. How could the demands of the ethics of care, including its social democratic requirements, be so guiltlessly repudiated? It is easy to see why the demands of the ethics of care extend to social democracy. Rand herself, like many of her fellow conservatives, certainly accepted many ethical demands grounded in the moral ideal of treating people as equals, for example, no one has the right to initiate the use of force against others.[169] But believers in laissez-faire, like Rand and others, apparently believe that unconstrained markets, in which people are free to buy and sell their labor as they want and can, respect the moral ideal of equal concern. But anyone living in poverty can reasonably ask whether the laws inherent to this type of system treat them as equals. It is not a reasonable response that the system respects personal choice and responsibility. People are not responsible for much, including genetic endowment and early care and education, of what determines their place in such an economy. There is nothing in the principle of responsible care for oneself and others that justifies such inequality.

Nonetheless, many Americans find views like those of Rand deeply appealing. Why?

What is at work here is not ethical argument but a still-powerful American patriarchal psychology, which Rand, the Russian émigré, came passionately to accept. What makes Rand interesting, from my perspective, is that her life and work so clearly illustrate how this sort of patriarchal psychology self-consciously expresses itself through insistence on a form of the gender binary. This may be tracked in Rand's case to her devotion to Nietzsche, which regards crass mercenary success in the unconstrained American marketplace as an absolute objectivist value. By the same token, any reasonable constraint or regulation of successful moneymaking is as bad as rape or slavery. A feature of traumatic loss empowers this psychology, a psychology that expresses itself in a repressive rage at anyone who might reasonably challenge its patriarchal demands, thus scapegoating those who are outsiders and potential dissenters. Because the psychology frames its self-understanding within a rigid form of the gender binary, it expresses itself in highly gendered ideals of what a successful or strong man is and must be, and, correspondingly, ideals of what an appropriately abject and worshipful woman is and must be. Such gender ideals, enforced in the

---

[169] On this point, see Jennifer Burns, *Goddess of the Market*, p. 212.

United States through highly patriarchal forms of religion and family life, define self-respect in terms of mercenary success and correspondingly experience a shaming humiliation when such success is challenged or questioned. Out of such humiliation, grounded in traumatic loss, comes the propensity to denigrate and demonize those who are "failures" in its terms of success or, even worse, those who question its terms of success.

Such a patriarchally grounded vulnerability to shame often expresses itself in forms of unjust violence grounded in irrational prejudice, as it did, for example, in the way Hitler mobilized and harnessed irrational political anti-Semitism to his political ends, including the genocidal murder of six million European Jews. What makes patriarchy so catastrophically dangerous in politics, as Hitler's totalitarianism clearly shows, is that by inculcating gendered ideals of manhood and womanhood, anyone regarded as a challenge to those ideals is regarded as a shameful humiliation, and humiliation expresses itself in murderous violence. Patriarchy thus forges a gendered sense of shame that covers over, marginalizes, and sometimes successfully represses the healthy sense of moral guilt that would otherwise actuate resistance to unjust murder of the innocent. The ethical, religious, and philosophical traditions of Germany certainly supported such a sense of guilt, but Hitler's patriarchal mobilization of shame proved stronger, showing how dangerous and corrupting the political mobilization of patriarchally grounded shame has been and can be. Japan's mobilization to a murderously aggressive fascism in World War II is yet another example.[170]

Ayn Rand was, of course, no Hitler, but she played a powerful political role in America by expressing, through a patriarchal psychology many Americans uncritically accepted, what patriarchal Americans wanted to hear, massaging their ethical complacency about the evils of inequality in American economic and social life. Although Rand published ostensibly philosophical works, her impact on the culture came not through argument but through the highly idealized gender stereotypes of her two best-selling novels, *The Fountainhead* and *Atlas Shrugged*.[171] *The Fountainhead* was adapted by Rand into a movie starring Gary Cooper, introducing an additional audience to her philosophy and creating a Hollywood mythology of the erotically charged gender wars in which strong and talented men triumph and women abjectly submit, more patriarchal rape victims than passionate and tender egalitarian lovers. Rand

[170] For exploration of these points, see Ian Buruma, *The Wages of Guilt: Memories of War in Germany and Japan* (New York: Meridian, 1995); Ian Buruma, *Behind the Mask: On Sexual Demons, Sacred Mothers, Transvestites, Gangsters, and Other Japanese Cultural Heroes* (New York: Meridian, 1984).
[171] See, on these novels, Jennifer Burns, *Goddess of the Market*.

was an actress, mindlessly acting out the patriarchal American gender binary as much as former actor Ronald Reagan did as president, and often (although not always) to similar effect (Rand was much more intellectually coherent than Reagan); and, of course, both were similarly popular. Her life and work were irresponsibly celebrated as an ultimate objectivist value – crass mercenary success in the American marketplace, and any limit, regulation, or ethical questioning of this success gave rise to a gendered sense of humiliation, imaginatively transforming victims of injustice (those unjustly treated by American inequality) into aggressors (totalitarian communists). Patriarchally grounded shame has in this way corrupted in many Americans a sense of what ethics is.

It is against this background that we may better understand the distinctive role irresponsible politicians played in fomenting the reactionary politics of the Republican Party. Never before in American history had the traditional role of American patriarchy, hiding in democracy, been so exposed, so fundamentally questioned, or so successfully addressed as a blight on our democratic constitutionalism than it was in the 1960s. What the resistance movements of the sixties and later show is that when people come to see the violence and lies that enforce patriarchy, they not only resist but can, against sometimes overwhelming historical odds, reasonably persuade others to join them to forge a more perfect democratic union based on justice.

What American conservatives confronted in these resistance movements was the most successful questioning of American patriarchy in our history, and what distinctively marks their conservative politics, I believe, were the ways in which they mobilized a political movement that was essentially reactionary, seeking to preserve an American patriarchy now very much at threat by insisting, sometimes violently, on the gender binary that the resistance movements had questioned. Patriarchy has dominated human politics, ethics, and religion for a long time, and as we have seen, even democracies, as the Athenian democracy conspicuously did, have lived in the contradiction between democracy and patriarchy, a tension revealed and yet covered over in their greatest works of art, such as the *Oresteia*. Patriarchy has enjoyed the level of support it has because it relied on and reinforced a political psychology of traumatic breaks in relationship, replacing relationship with honor codes of gender binary and expressing itself in violence directed at any threat or resistance to its demands, including the use of scapegoats. American conservative politicians during this period forged and mobilized a politics based on the repressive impulses in an American patriarchy still broadly shared among the American people. Their politics was thus shaped to cover, distort, discredit, and marginalize the achievements of the resistance movements of the 1960s and beyond, a politics that conspicuously featured, indeed took as its aims, the two marks of trauma, loss of memory and voice – in particular, distorting the memory and crushing the ethical voice of these resistance movements.

We must now examine more closely how the psychology of patriarchy under threat clarifies the continuing appeal of this reactionary politics. I believe that the crux of the matter is that much thought on the subject of ethics, even by so profound a moral philosopher as Kant, has been distorted by the uncritical impact of patriarchy on our religious, ethical, and political lives since the rise of high civilizations in the Neolithic. Accordingly, when Kant, followed by Rawls, analyzed ethics in terms of a stance of responsible care for oneself and others, it becomes important to criticize those features of the view that support this stance, and those that do not, in particular, those that reflect not its defensible moral ideals, but instead the long history of how patriarchy has destroyed the relationality central to ethics as such and indeed democracy. Carol Gilligan's groundbreaking work on women making the abortion decision after *Roe v. Wade* brilliantly observes this process; expressing their sense of ethical responsibility for themselves and others in relationship, women came to question and reject the patriarchally enforced conception of women's selflessness as a denial of their moral weight and agency.[172] Patriarchy arises, of course, precisely from the unjust denial of the voices of the women and men who would otherwise reasonably question its authority. It is precisely when women, as Gilligan's study shows, are empowered responsibly to speak or think in such a contesting voice that they speak or think in the different voice that rejects patriarchy.

The so-called cultural war that underlies the polarization of contemporary American political life occurs precisely at the fault line between the older patriarchal conception of moral values and the democratic conception of ethics as responsibility for self and others that Rawls and Gilligan regard as the ethics of care, the only ethics responsibly rooted in our human natures and circumstances as democratic equals. It is for this reason, as George Lakoff's important study of American politics makes quite clear, that the disagreement is one of moral politics, or what should count as morality in politics.[173] Everything we have learned about such patriarchal families is that they display what George Lakoff calls "a Strict Father model,"[174] enforced by corporal

---

[172] See Carol Gilligan, *In a Different Voice: Psychological Theory and Women's Development* (Cambridge, MA: Harvard University Press, 1982).

[173] See George Lakoff, *Moral Politics: How Liberals and Conservatives Think*, 2d ed. (Chicago: University of Chicago Press, 1996, 2002).

[174] Ibid., p. 33.

punishment[175] and a hierarchical "Moral Order" that valorizes strength and success[176] and rejects as illegitimate a moral authority, like the federal government, that seeks to question or constrain such success, for example, by redistributive taxation or social programs[177] or by regulation[178]; the model also expresses itself in a high retributive conception of criminal law, including the death penalty.[179] Lakoff contrasts such views with the quite different liberal views on all these and other questions of "the Nurturant Parent model"[180] and its "Nurturant Parent Morality,"[181] which he quite explicitly roots in what I have called here the ethics of care, citing Carol Gilligan's work on developmental psychology.[182] I believe the psychology of patriarchy under threat explains developmentally what Lakoff offers as a static model of the polarized views underlying America's divided politics. All of the views Lakoff describes in the Moral Order of the Strict Father model track or can be explained in terms of the patriarchally enforced gender binary: for example, valuing moral virtue in terms of strength (masculine) in contrast to empathy (feminine), or valuing morality (masculine) in terms of a strict father or a nurturant parent (feminine).

I earlier showed how Ayn Rand's life and work expose the reactionary psychology of American conservatism. However, what really made the conservative reaction in the United States so powerful was not Rand (who objected certainly to religious fundamentalism in any form), but the irresponsible national politicians, largely of the Republican Party, who saw a political opening both in the successes that liberals achieved and in the divisions among liberals starting in the 1960s about the resistance movements discussed earlier (for example, the division between Johnson and King over the Vietnam War). The two great legislative successes of the civil rights movement, the Civil Rights Act of 1964 and the Voting Rights Act of 1965, ended the racist disempowerment of people of color in the American South but made possible Nixon's and Reagan's Southern strategy, leading to a shift in political power in the South from Democrats to Republicans. The civil rights movement had been nonviolent (the key to its successes), but other activists were less disciplined; race riots erupted, and Americans were faced with assassinations of high-level

---

[175] Ibid., pp. 197–8, 339–49.
[176] Ibid., pp. pp. 71–6, 81–4.
[177] Ibid., pp. 179–96.
[178] Ibid., pp. 210–221.
[179] Ibid., pp. 197–209.
[180] Ibid., pp. 33–4.
[181] Ibid., p. 105.
[182] Ibid., at p. 300; see also p. 418.

political figures (including that of King) and violent conflict between police and citizens in the center of the best-known cities of America.

It is against this background that we can understand the political strategy rooted in patriarchy under threat that brought Richard Nixon to power. Nixon's law-and-order message was the dominant issue during his successful campaign of 1968, although, in fact, Nixon's policies were to increase levels of homicide and suicide "into the epidemic stratosphere."[183]

Ronald Reagan was more successful than Nixon at elaborating the political strategies Nixon had developed, but in the service of Reagan's much more conservative politics. As governor of California, Reagan had an early experience with the usefulness of the crime issue in politics, making the death penalty for murder "one of the signature differences in his 1966 campaign against incumbent governor Pat Brown."[184] But Reagan brought to American conservative politics something Nixon, despite his greater intelligence, did not – namely, an honest moral voice, based on his beloved mother's evangelical religion, that believed in and accepted, as his official biographer Edmund Morris observed, many of the tenets of American fundamentalist patriarchal religion:

> God wrote the Bible, and the Bible condones capital punishment. "Sodomy" is a sin. However, homosexuals have a Constitutional right to teach in public schools. Abortion is murder. Property is sacrosanct; so is privacy. Men may bear arms. Women are superior to men, therefore equal rights will downgrade them. Art should affirm moral values. Hard work is mandatory, boredom impermissible. Charity begins at home. Communism is evil because it saps the individual will.[185]

Despite or perhaps because of his father's alcohol abuse, Reagan formed his identity as a man around institutions embodying these patriarchal values, and lived them out, expressing them in an essay he wrote while a high school student that, as his son put it, "love of school has become a religion with him"[186] and only those playing on a football team know what "love and loyalty" are.[187] He also describes saving lives as a local hero while working during summers as

---

[183] See James Gilligan, *Why Some Politicians Are More Dangerous than Others* (Cambridge: Polity Press, 2011), p. 17.
[184] See Jonathan Simon, *Governing through Crime: How the War on Crime Transformed American Democracy and Created a Culture of Fear* (Oxford: Oxford University Press, 2007), at p. 56.
[185] Edmund Morris, *Dutch: A Memoir of Ronald Reagan* (New York: Modern Library, 1999), p. 415.
[186] See Ron Reagan, *My Father at 100: A Memoir* (New York: Viking, 2011), p. 112.
[187] Cited in Edmund Morris, *Dutch*, p. 94.

a lifeguard at Lowell Park[188] and going on to church-affiliated Eureka College "motivated by love for a pretty girl and football."[189]

In his first autobiography, written at the end of his career as a Hollywood actor, Reagan described his earlier self as a "a near-hopeless hemophilic liberal,"[190] who voted Democratic like his father for both Roosevelt and Truman. What Reagan calls his "disillusionment with big government" arose from "the ideals that suddenly sprouted and put forth in the war years."[191] Reagan describes how, as president of the Screen Actors Guild, he confronted the bullying tactics of American communists, then closely allied with the Soviet Union, that, in their grandiose aims to turn Hollywood into a communist propaganda mill, repelled Reagan both because of their means and ends.[192] What Reagan came to see as "the seamy side of liberalism"[193] was its incompetence at seeing communism for the evil it was and resisting it. Several traumatic events in Reagan's personal life also take place at this juncture that psychologically illuminate broken relationships, giving rise to identification with patriarchal stereotypes, a shift in views that surprised friends: a nearly deadly attack of acute viral pneumonia,[194] the death of the daughter born to him and his then wife Jane Wyman,[195] the deterioration and end of his marriage to Wyman (a much more successful actor then her husband, winning the Best Actress Academy Award for *Johnny Belinda*),[196] breaking his thigh in a charity baseball game, and lack of work, making this "Ronald Reagan's *annus horribilis*."[197] Such trauma shows itself in his expressed sense that his former liberalism cannot take the evil of communism seriously, a psychology very like that of Ayn Rand, who – traumatically leaving her family behind in the Soviet Union – repudiates an American liberalism that cannot take seriously the evil, as she knew it at firsthand, of the totalitarianism of the Soviet Union. Rand, like Reagan, may through experience have had a better understanding of the evils of communism than many American liberals during this period before the enormities of Stalin and Mao had been made quite clear. But, like

---

[188] Cited in Ron Reagan, *My Father at 100*, at p. 119.
[189] Ronald Reagan, *An American Life: Ronald Reagan* (New York: Simon & Schuster, 1990), p. 45.
[190] Ronald Reagan, *Where's the Rest of Me?: The Autobiography of Ronald Reagan with Richard G. Hubler* (New York: Karz Publishers, 1965), p. 139.
[191] Ibid., p. 139.
[192] On this period see ibid., pp. 153–75.
[193] Ibid., p. 169.
[194] Edmund Morris, *Dutch*, p. 249.
[195] Ibid., pp. 250–2.
[196] Ibid., pp. 252–9.
[197] Ibid., *Dutch*, p. 278.

Rand, the trauma Reagan endured led to a deeper identification with what he took to be the harder, more masculine values of patriarchal America, repudiating a liberalism he had himself described as a more feminine bleeding heart ("a near-hopeless hemophilic liberal"). The evident trauma of broken relationship, of not being loved or having someone to love,[198] was resolved by his political shift, followed by his marriage to Nancy Davis and by his role for eight years as host for television's popular *General Electric Theater* and touring giving speeches at GE plants around the country. It was in this latter role that Reagan experimented with, developed, and found his moral voice in politics, finding a resonance for views that became so controversially politically conservative that GE terminated his contract.

The key to the political appeal of Reagan's voice, winning election in 1966 as governor of California and again four years later, was the hard line he proposed to take – and did take – with the student protests at California universities, Berkeley and elsewhere.[199] The Ronald Reagan, who had written that "love of school has become a religion with him"[200] and had been so happy playing football at the church-affiliated college to which he went, reacted with a genuine sense of indignation to the increasingly disruptive protests at the distinguished California public universities, which were the pride of the state. In his illuminating memoir of his father, Ron Reagan describes his father as

> not at what I'd consider his personal best during this period. Outraged by college students protesting a war he never realized was a disastrous sham, flummoxed by the cultural transformation erupting on all sides (including within his own household), he became pinched and defensive. Looking at pictures from his governorship, I can see it in his face: lips compressed, left eyebrow arched, jaw tensed as if he were always choking back anger.[201]

During this crucial period of his entrance into politics, Reagan was not the genial person he was later to become. Sincerely angry himself, he mobilized a politics of patriarchal rage in others, in part because both universities and students questioned the patriarchal judgment of their government and fathers about a war but, more centrally, because the highly privileged students who attended California's public universities resisted even the authority of their universities, disrupting education. Reagan's rage reached, however, beyond their political resistance to their lifestyle. Reagan thus himself scripted his

---

[198] On this point, see ibid., at p. 266.
[199] For an excellent treatment of these protests, see W. J. Rorabaugh, *Berkeley at War: The 1960s* (New York: Oxford University Press, 1989).
[200] Ron Reagan, *My Father at 100: A Memoir* (New York: Viking, 2011), p. 112.
[201] Ibid., p. 204.

The Fall of Empire

own one-liners, to surefire applause: "Their signs said, 'make love, not war,' but it didn't look like they could do either."[202] Or, a staple of Reagan's 1967 speeches outside the state was: "We have some hippies in California. For those of you who don't know what a hippie is, he's a fellow who dresses like Tarzan, has hair like Jane, and smells like Cheetah."[203] Patriarchy at threat thus directs its venom quite pointedly at resistance to the gender binary enforced by patriarchy.

Reagan named Edwin Meese as his second attorney general. Meese was a career prosecutor, and his political career was tied to crime. Notably, he had been assistant attorney general in Alameda County, California, which included the volatile cities of Oakland and Berkeley during the period of radical political activity and conflict with the police during the 1960s. "Reagan picked Meese out of relative obscurity in part because of his public war with Berkeley. Meese became a political advisor to Reagan and an intermediary to the growing grass roots of right-wing property owners in California and nationally for whom crime was a major concern."[204]

If Nixon had developed the wars on crime and on drugs as ways of expressing patriarchal rage at student war resistance, Reagan – who found a resonance for his authentic moral voice in attacking student protest at California public universities – more aggressively mobilized the "war on drugs" as an expression of patriarchal rage at them, aligning the government with parents' fearful of loss of control of their children. Carlton Turner, asked by Reagan to implement this policy, quite clearly justified its criminalization of marijuana use not in terms of harms in the substance itself but because

> drug use is a behavioral pattern that has sort of tagged along during the present young-adult generation's involvement in anti-military, anti-nuclear power, anti-big business, anti-authority demonstrations; of people from a myriad of different racial, religious or otherwise persuasions demanding 'rights' or 'entitlements' politically while refusing to accept corollary civil responsibility.[205]

What this reveals is that the increasingly aggressive criminalization of drugs, as well as its connections to the escalation of sentencing and imprisonment more generally, was never justified on the basis of any reasonable argument about harms to self and others, which clarifies why these policies, based on

---

[202] Cited at Lou Cannon, *Governor Reagan: His Rise to Power* (New York: Public Affairs, 2003), at p. 285.
[203] Cited at Lou Cannon, *Governor Reagan*, p. 285.
[204] Jonathan Simon, *Governing through Crime*, p. 56.
[205] Dan Baum, *Smoke and Mirrors: The War on Drugs and the Politics of Failure* (Boston: Little, Brown & Company, 1997), at p. 154.

nothing legitimate, have been, as we shall later see, so destructive. Rather, the appeal of these laws rests on the political psychology of patriarchy at threat, making scapegoats of those, in particular, students, who have dared to resist the patriarchal demands of fighting an unjust war.

Is there perhaps a connection between Reagan's attack on social democracy (as communism) and the role played in his politics by supporting the wars on crime and drugs? Reagan clearly linked the two questions, advocating, as Katherine Beckett shows, that "public assistance is an 'illegitimate' state function, whereas policing and social control constitute its real 'constitutional' obligation."[206] Here is Ronald Reagan speaking in his own words at a fundraising event:

> This is precisely what we're trying to do to the bloated Federal Government today: remove it from interfering in areas where it doesn't belong, but at the same time strengthen its ability to perform its constitutional and legitimate functions. . . . In the area of public order and law enforcement, for example, we're reversing a dangerous trend of the last decade. While crime was steadily increasing, the Federal commitment in terms of personnel was steadily shrinking.[207]

In his important book *Why Some Politicians Are More Dangerous than Others*,[208] psychiatrist James Gilligan offers a powerful causal argument that the Republican Party's conservatism on social democratic questions is responsible for significantly higher rates of homicide and suicide when they are in power in contrast to the social democratic policies of the Democratic Party when they are in power. Gilligan's causal thesis is that the economic and social inequalities endorsed by Republicans so humiliate the men disadvantaged by these policies, for example, losing their jobs, that homicidal violence to others and self are much more likely. So, it is precisely the antisocial democratic policies Ronald Reagan advocated that elicited higher rates of homicide and suicide (harms if anything is), whereas the war on drugs (for example, marijuana use) never rested on any coherent or defensible evidence of harms, which means that these laws lack the only justification that can be acceptable in a secular constitutional democracy like the United States. Why haven't we seen this earlier?

---

[206] Citing Katherine Beckett, Bernard E. Harcourt, *The Illusion of Free Markets: Punishment and the Myth of Natural Order* (Cambridge, MA: Harvard University Press, 2011), at p. 40.
[207] Quoted in Bernard E. Harcourt, *The Illusion of Free Markets*, at pp. 40–1.
[208] James Gilligan, *Why Some Politicians Are More Dangerous Than Others* (Cambridge, U.K. Polity Press, 2011).

If legal or ethical logic were the stuff of American politics, we would or should all see, as rational and reasonable citizens, that there is something at least paradoxical and at worst contradictory in a politics that is libertarian when it comes to the economy (calling for lower taxes, and the end of social democratic programs) – causing, as Gilligan shows, real harms of homicidal violence to self and others, but illiberal when it comes to the criminal law (criminalizing the use of marijuana in the absence of harms to self and others). Yet, Reagan's politics – incoherent and illegitimate in all these ways – was enormously appealing to the American people, reshaping the political consensus in the United States in ways that persist today.

There is, however, a psychological logic here if we take seriously the role of patriarchy at threat in understanding this politics. What strikes me about the politics of the "war" on crime in general and the "war" on drugs in particular is the background conception of patriarchal manhood and womanhood to which, apparently successfully, it has appealed and continues to appeal (even Obama, the candidate opposed to the incursion into Iraq, endorsed the death penalty[209]). It is striking that President Johnson, who first proposed a "war" on crime after his defeat of Barry Goldwater,[210] did so in part to make a statement countering rising resistance to his policies in Vietnam (in particular, by the men who served in Vietnam), and President Nixon's proposal of a "war" on drugs, elaborated aggressively by Ronald Reagan, has the same roots. There is, in fact, no reasonable relationship between the ever escalating sanctions of the American "war" on crime (including mass incarceration disproportionately of people of color, solitary confinement, and the death penalty) and any effectiveness in lowering crime rates,[211] and the very rhetoric of the "war" on drugs reveals the patriarchal values at threat, transforming a self-regarding act by young people (often, young people of color) – often no worse and sometimes less harmful than the alcohol abuse of an older generation – into armed aggression. In fact, the war on drugs has done so much more harm than good that alternatives, including legalization, now "could hardly fail more spectacularly than has prohibition"[212] and seem clearly advisable as a matter

---

[209] Barack Obama, *The Audacity of Hope: Thoughts on Reclaiming the American Dream* (New York: Three Rivers Press, 2006), at p. 58.
[210] On this point, see Jonathan Simon, *Governing through Crime*, pp. 89–103.
[211] On this point, see ibid., p. 271; David Garland, *The Culture of Control: Crime and Social Order in Contemporary Society* (Chicago: University of Chicago Press, 2001), at p. 146.
[212] Robert Perkinson, "Drug of Choice," *The New York Times Book Review*, August 1, 2010, at p. 21 (reviewing Tom Feiling, *Cocaine Nation: How the White Trade Took Over the World* (Pegasus Books, 2010).

of good public policy.²¹³ When a public policy is so expensive and so clearly counterproductive and indeed illegitimate yet so enormously popular, I see a psychological logic of patriarchy at threat that conceals itself in democracy. I observe the same dynamic when, in Foucault's study of the rise of the prison in democratic America and republican France, that the institution became more disciplinary than humane; what strikes me, in Foucault's account, is that the model for republican government in France was the highly patriarchal Roman republic, showing yet again how patriarchy, hiding in democracy, undermines democratic values.²¹⁴ In the United States, we see another variation on the same theme. The threat to patriarchy from the successes of the resistance movements of the sixties – in particular, the civil rights and antiwar movements – imaginatively transformed changes achieved through largely nonviolent, democratic dialogue, which are coded feminine, as a breakdown of order, meaning patriarchal order, leading to a fear of disorder, which must be met, defensively, by force and strength, coded as masculine (thus, the call to "war"). The consequence, especially during the period 1973–2008, has been a "massive expansion of the carceral sphere during which free-market ideas and privatization flourished."²¹⁵

What was at the heart of Reagan's remarkable appeal, as Daniel Rodgers has shown in his close study of Reagan's speeches,²¹⁶ was his authentic moral voice calling for a kind of expansive freedom, taking the government as the only thing limiting our limitlessness, unencumbered by any sense of the collective rights and responsibilities central to the ethics of care, a topic on which Reagan was silent. James Gilligan quite correctly ascribes the appeal of this voice to the shame ethics of patriarchal manhood and womanhood, cultivating a sense of humiliation at the role resistance to the gender binary played in the resistance movements of the sixties. We have seen the appeal and force of this shame ethics before, as the mode through which irrational prejudices, grounded in patriarchy, attack and sometimes kill the relationality of the ethics of care, and thus the capacity for guilt and remorse central to this ethics.²¹⁷ Like Ayn Rand, Reagan released American greed from any sense of ethical constraint

---

[213] On this point, see Tom Feiling, *Cocaine Nation: How the White Trade Took Over the World* (Pegasus Books, 2010).
[214] On this point, see Michel Foucault, *Discipline and Punish: The Birth of the Prison*, translated by Alan Sheridan (New York: Vintage Books, 1995).
[215] Bernard E. Harcourt, *The Illusion of Free Markets*, p. 42.
[216] See Daniel T. Rodgers, *Age of Fracture* (Cambridge, Mass.: Belknap Press of Harvard University Press, 2011), pp. 22–41.
[217] See James Gilligan, *Why Some Politicians Are More Dangerous than Others*, pp. 123–54.

and supported deregulation that removed any legal constraint, unleashing the forces that led to the economic crisis of 2008 from which, at the time of this writing, we have not yet recovered.[218] It is supremely ironic that Reagan, who was nothing if not an authentic moralistic conviction politician, should have found his moral voice in a patriarchal politics whose appeal and success rested on deadening the ethical intelligence and sensitivity of the American people. Reagan's politics could not have had the appeal they did if they had not fomented and mobilized a sense a patriarchy at threat that turned repressively on those who had resisted American patriarchy and would turn, with comparable ferocity, on the resistance movements, feminism and gay rights, that, if anything, resisted American patriarchy more fundamentally – at its very core, the enforcement of the gender binary.

It was in this environment that religious fundamentalism, very close to Reagan's own views, aggressively entered into American politics, mobilized by attempts to limit further advances in racial equality (the attack on affirmative action) and, in particular, in angry reaction to successes of the antiwar and feminist movements and to claims of the incipient gay rights movement. It was during the administration of President Reagan that the political alliance between religious and legal fundamentalism took the form of Ed Meese's endorsement of "originalism" (constitutional interpretation must never depart from the things in the world to which constitutional text would have been applied when drafted and ratified) as the only valid mode of constitutional interpretation, expressed in the successful nomination to the Supreme Court of Antonin Scalia and the abortive nomination of Robert Bork. The same political alliance supported President George H. W. Bush's successful nomination of Clarence Thomas, an originalist, to the Supreme Court, and President George W. Bush's appointments of Chief Justice John Roberts and Justice Samuel Alito.[219]

There is no clearer example of the problem of patriarchal psychology than the war of American Christian fundamentalists, supported and fomented by conservative politicians, on now constitutionally recognized rights to abortion[220] and homosexuality.[221] Thus, the right of women, rather than their

---

[218] Jeff Madrick, *Age of Greed: The Triumph of Finance and the Decline of America, 1970 to the Present* (New York: Alfred A. Knopf, 2011).

[219] On this alliance and its impact on judicial appointment, see David A. J. Richards, *Fundamentalism in American Religion and Law: Obama's Challenge to Patriarchy's Threat to Democracy* (Cambridge: Cambridge University Press, 2010), pp. 218–30.

[220] *Roe v. Wade*, 410 U.S. 113 (1973).

[221] *Lawrence v. Texas*, 539 U.S. 558 (2003).

fathers or husbands, to decide whether to bear a child and the right of gays and lesbians to love become incendiary, lawless passions that defy patriarchal control. Such loss of control arouses fear and then the anger that leads to violence. Thus, abortion and gay marriage have become lightning-rod issues in American elections.

We can only understand this reactionary politics if we take seriously its roots in the personal and political psychology of patriarchy, which has a long history in the United States of hiding patriarchy in democracy. American religions have played an important role in this process because some of them are so uncritically patriarchal. We need to remember that patriarchy, as we have defined it, is the hierarchical rule of priests-fathers over other men and all women, which places religion at the heart of the problem of patriarchy to the extent religions are themselves patriarchal. Three such religions in the United States are Roman Catholicism, Protestant Evangelicals, and Mormonism. These religions disagree on fundamental matters of religious conviction, but they share a common patriarchal structure of a rigidly enforced male priesthood that has led them to agree on a common political position that politicians have been able to mobilize into a powerful conservative politics.[222] It is this reactionary politics that explains what many commentators have observed about contemporary American politics – namely, its highly polarized character, divided between red and blue states, a polarization rooted in different conceptions of family life.[223]

This polarization of American politics, in which gay rights is one of the wedge issues skillfully used by conservatives like President George W. Bush, has made the progress of gay rights slower and certainly more controversial than it has been in Europe and Britain. Against all odds, including the AIDS health crisis, it has, nonetheless, continued to make progress both through the courts, state and federal, and even politically (the Congressional repeal of "Don't Ask, Don't Tell" and New York State's passage of a gay marriage bill).

---

[222] For fuller discussion and defense, see David A. J. Richards, *Fundamentalism in American Religion and Law*.

[223] See, for example, George Lakoff, *Moral Politics: How Liberals and Conservatives Think*, 2nd ed. (Chicago: University of Chicago Press, 1996, 2002); Mark J. Hetherington and Jonathan D. Weiler, *Authoritarianism and Polarization in American Politics* (Cambridge: Cambridge University Press, 2009); Naomi Cahn and June Carbone, *Red Families v. Blue Families: Legal Polarization and the Creation of Culture* (Oxford: Oxford University Press, 2010). See also Bob Altemeyer, *The Authoritarian Specter* (Cambridge, MA: Harvard University Press, 1996); Bob Altemeyer, *Right-Wing Authoritarianism Right-Wing Authoritarianism* (Winnipeg, Canada: University of Manitoba Press, 1981).

Limited Impact on Britain and Elsewhere

It would be a mistake to think that Britain has not had its own share of such reactionary politics. After the 1967 decriminalization, there were the reactionary attacks of Mrs. Whitehouse on the Albany Trust[224] and the backlash of the 1980s.[225] It was, after all, Margaret Thatcher, the first female British prime minister, a kind of latter-day Ayn Rand, who aligned her politics, domestically and internationally, with that of Ronald Reagan. And that politics included passage of Section 28 of the Local Government Act 1988 in the United Kingdom, which prohibited local authorities from "intentionally promot[ing] homosexuality" or promoting "the teaching in any maintained school of the acceptability of homosexuality as a pretended family relationship."[226]

Nonetheless, such reactionary politics has not had the continuing force in Britain and Europe that it continues to have in the politics of the United States. In the 1990s in Britain, public gay rights advocacy on the American model became increasingly important features of public life in Britain, including both Stonewall[227] and Peter Tatchell's Outrage[228]; and in 1995, the gay man and barrister Martin Bowley gave the first Stonewall lecture, calling for greater recognition of gay rights in the legal profession and society generally. Indeed, the gay rights movement is now alive worldwide.[229]

The impact of such American-style activism on British political argument dealing with homosexuality can be seen by contrasting the terms of parliamentary debate, earlier discussed, leading to the 1967 decriminalization (in which there was substantial agreement on the wrongness of gay sex) with the terms of the 1994 debate in the House of Commons over changing the age of consent for gay sex from twenty-one to either eighteen or sixteen (the age of consent for heterosexual sex). The vote was a free vote in which members could vote their consciences. What is remarkable about the debate is the terms in which it was conducted, including the defense of changing the age of consent to sixteen by its proponent, Mrs. Currie:

> The image of gay men is at last changing. They are men whom we know, work with and whose work we admire. They are businessmen, civil servants, artists,

---

[224] Antony Grey, *Quest for Justice*, p. 211.
[225] Ibid., p. 265.
[226] Nicholas Bamforth et al., *Discrimination Law: Theory and Context*, p. 7.
[227] See Stonewall.org.uk.
[228] See Outrage.org.uk, and Wikipedia, Peter Tatchell. See also Peter Tatchell, *We Don't Want to March Straight: Masculinity, Queers, and the Military* (London: Cassell, 1995).
[229] See, on this development, Barry D. Adam, *The Rise of a Gay and Lesbian Movement* rev. ed. (Farmington Hills, MI: Twayne, 1995).

actors, soldiers, judges, bishops, priests, peers, and Members of Parliament. We all know someone who is gay, even if he has not yet declared himself. It is time to take the dark shadow and turn it into a human being; it is time to seize our homophobic instincts and chuck them in the scrap heap of history where they belong. In a free society the onus to prove that restricting freedom is on those who would discriminate. That is impossible to prove. Equality is the only worthwhile and sustainable position. No compromises will satisfy those people whom they affect. There is no such thing as partial equality; people are either equal or they are not.[230]

Although there were a few homophobic outbursts and one such speech by Rev. Ian Paisley, the dominant tone could not be more different from the earlier 1967 decriminalization debates, including prominent support for the age sixteen change by both Neil Kinnock and Tony Blair. Kinnock observed that initially, he was in favor of lowering the age of consent for gay sex to eighteen, but, on reflection, he decided there was no scientific basis for distinguishing the developmental maturity of homosexuals and heterosexuals and therefore support the same age of consent for both, sixteen. Tony Blair argued that the only ground offered for a higher age of consent for gay sex was the likelihood of predatory conduct by older men of the young, but that there was reason to believe that young gay men would be more likely to seek counseling to avoid such predation if the age were sixteen and that, in any event, the same worries about predation applied to heterosexual sex. He concluded "the real objection is not reason, but prejudice."[231] Moreover, there was a gay voice in the debate. Mr. Chris Smith addressed an argument he had heard in the debates, a

> less worthy argument. It is that being gay is abnormal and therefore unnatural and illegitimate. To these people, I would say: Yes, we are different. We have a different sexuality. But that does not make us in any way less valid or less worthy citizens of this country. Yet the law says that we are. A century ago A. E. Housman wrote: "Oh who is that young sinner with the handcuffs on his wrists? And what has he been after that they groan and shake their fists? And wherefore is he wearing such a conscience-stricken air? Oh they're taking him to prison for the colour of his hair." In this country we do not discriminate against people on the ground of the colour of their hair. We do not discriminate against people because they happen to be left-handed. We do not discriminate against people because they are of a different race. But

---

[230] See http:/www.parliament.uk, *Hansard*, Session 1993–4, vol. 238, February 21 1994, at Column 81.
[231] Ibid., Column 99.

we do discriminate against them because of their sexuality. I argue that we should not.[232]

The proposal for age sixteen was defeated narrowly, 280–307. The age eighteen was then adopted.

With the return to power of the Labour Party in 1997, other legal reforms followed. The age of consent for straight sex, sixteen, was made the same as for gay sex in 2001. Section 28 of the Local Government Act 1988 was repealed in 2003,[233] and the Civil Partnership Act, extending partnership rights to gays and lesbians, was passed in Britain in 2004.[234] Under European Union Law, under the Treaty of Amsterdam in 1999, the Employment Equality Directive forbids discrimination on grounds of sexual orientation in employment,[235] which was implemented in Britain by the Employment Equality (Sexual Orientation) Regulations 2003[236] and by the Equality Act (Sexual Orientation) Regulations 2007.[237] Discrimination on grounds of sexual orientation is also now forbidden "in relation to the enjoyment of Convention rights under Article 14 of the European Convention on Human Rights."[238] The current Conservative Prime Minister of Britain, David Cameron, announced in 2011 his support of gay marriage and has argued that steps be taken against nations like Zimbabwe and Uganda who are aggressively hostile to gay rights.[239]

How should we understand the difference between Britain and Europe on gay rights and the United States? Change in the United States came, as we have seen, from an interconnected group of resistance movements, including feminism and gay rights, that, appealing to the U.S. Constitution, spoke in a different ethical voice, grounded in the criticism as unjust of the traditional force of patriarchal demands in American personal and political life. The U.S. Supreme Court of the United States afforded a hospitable forum of principle that recognized many of the claims of these resistance groups as based on constitutional rights and principles, grounded in equal respect for human rights. But because the claims of these resistance groups challenged

---

[232] Ibid., at Column 112–13.
[233] See Nicholas Bamforth et al., *Discrimination Law*, p. 721.
[234] See ibid., pp. 726–45.
[235] See ibid., pp. 681–96.
[236] See ibid., pp. 703–15.
[237] See ibid., pp. 716–20.
[238] Ibid., p. 633. I am grateful to Nicholas Bamforth for helping me understand the complexity of these developments in Britain.
[239] On this point, see Josh Kron, "Resentment Toward the West Bolsters Uganda's New Anti-Gay Bill," *New York Times*, Wednesday, February 29, 2012, p. A4.

American patriarchy more profoundly than it had ever been contested, conservative politicians fomented a highly successful reactionary politics grounded in anger that patriarchy had been contested, seeking to limit and, if possible, reverse whatever advances have been made. What has, I believe, crucially strengthened this politics in the United States has been the uncritical force patriarchy continues to exercise over American personal and political life and American religion. I see this in the conservative approach to constitutional interpretation, originalism, which is itself grounded in patriarchy and in the ways in which patriarchal religion endorses and reinforces this approach.[240]

Patriarchy, of course, persists in Britain and Europe, and certainly in its religions (Roman Catholicism, in particular[241]). But the devastating experience of World War II on Europe and Britain may have perhaps discredited many of the institutions, including churches, that did not play the kind of ethical role one might have expected from them in resisting fascism, culminating in the Holocaust. Both the European Union and the European Convention mark a striking departure in European practice, more secular and democratic and more respectful of human rights. European nations, like Sweden and Britain, also have established churches, but notably liberal ones, closely in tune with the liberal and social democratic ethos of these nations.

America, in contrast, has the oldest written constitution in the world, giving primacy in First Amendment to its Bill of Rights to the rights of free exercise of religion and the prohibition on established churches. These constitutional provisions, as their authors (Jefferson and Madison) thought they would,[242] empowered religion in the United States as an active force in the lives of many Americans, because religion depended on the voluntary will of people, not the state. But because patriarchal religion has remained so uncritically dominant in the United States, the power of religion has developed into an unfortunate sectarian politics (in contradiction to America's prohibition on established religion) that, as we have seen, American politicians have fomented and mobilized. Also, originalism, the force of which depends on what was specifically meant by Founders some two or more centuries ago, must have less plausibility in constitutionalisms, like those in Europe and the European Union and the European Convention of Human Rights, founded much more recently or constitutionalisms or religions (for example, the Anglican Church)

---

[240] On this point, see David A. J. Richards, *Fundamentalism in American Religion and Law*.
[241] On this point, see Bamforth and Richards, *Patriarchal Religion, Gender, and Sexuality*.
[242] On this point, see David A. J. Richards, *Toleration and the Constitution* (New York: Oxford University Press, 1986), pp. 111–16.

much more interpretively open to contemporary democratic experience as it bears on the understanding of basic human rights.

On gay rights in particular, whereas the United States wholly repressed such arguments until well after World War II, Britain, as we have seen, nurtured a group of friends and lovers whose lives and works enriched British culture with resistance to patriarchy grounded in a more democratic understanding of human rights – more democratic because it includes the ethical voices of women and men previously silenced by patriarchal repression. It is not surprising that such a democracy should more robustly embrace gay rights today, and indeed, as we shall see, challenge and criticize its former colonies for retaining British-imposed laws and policies that Britain, having now abandoned its imperialism, rejects as violations of human rights. Imperialism, based on patriarchy, is now more alive in these colonies than it is in Britain, as we shall see in the next chapter.

5

Gay Rights in Former British Colonies: Legacy of Empire?

Despite the arguments to the contrary of liberal apologists such as John Stuart Mill, the British Empire appears to have been little concerned with introducing liberal democracy into its colonies. Indeed, the attempt to justify British imperialism and related practices on such grounds may not unreasonably be urged as grounds for questioning liberalism as a defensible political theory.[1] There is a connection, and an important one, between the rise of gay rights in Britain and the serious questioning in Britain of its imperialism, but the connection, as we have shown, led to a criticism of practices of British patriarchy at home and abroad (enforcing the patriarchal Love Laws) as inconsistent with the deeper values of liberal democracy, as the British resistance group discovered through its experiments in living that the sexual love of equals, resisting the divisions imposed by the Love Laws, enabled them through such love to resist the ways patriarchy destroyed love and rationalized unjust violence at home and abroad (including the violence of World War I). So the rise of gay rights and British imperialism were very much at odds, as we can see clearly in Leonard Woolf, who moves from being a successful agent of British imperialism in Ceylon to, under the impact of his remarkable marriage to Virginia Woolf and friendship with Lytton Strachey, a stance of resistance, reflected both in the novel he wrote based on his experiences in Ceylon and his books criticizing imperialism. And what gay men like E. M. Forster and Roger Casement discovered in having sex with natives (breaking the Love Laws of both race and gender) was a liberation of ethical intelligence in seeking to expose to the wider world how racism rationalized not just unjust imperial hierarchies but genocide.

---

[1] On this point, see Domenico Losurdo, *Liberalism: A Counter-History* (London: Verso, 2011).

Gay Rights in Former British Colonies: Legacy of Empire?

We know there was a long pattern of resistance by colonized peoples to the claims made on them by the British Empire.[2] What interests me in this book is how such resistance arose within Britain itself and the important connections of such resistance to the rise of gay rights. From this perspective, the interesting tension is between patriarchy and democracy, and gay rights is an ethical movement within liberal democracy, one struggling against the ways patriarchy corrupts and undermines liberal democracy. Nothing in this argument would suggest that ex-colonies of Britain, where the British aristocratic elite never attempted to develop democratic values and institutions, would themselves develop democracy, let alone liberal democracy. More likely, because many of these ex-colonies assumed indigenous patterns of religiously based political patriarchy (which the British, if anything, legitimated by ruling through them as indirect rule), they would be hostile to liberal democracy. Gay rights, which arises from its challenge to patriarchy, would not only have no traction in such nations but might itself, as we shall see, be the object of what had once been the forms of violence and repression familiar in the West. If this were true as a general matter, we might end our book here. Happily, it is not true, or not as true as our argument would suggest it should be.

In some former British colonies in Africa (Zimbabwe and Uganda), there are remarkable examples of the fomenting of homophobic violence by politicians, sometimes influenced by Christian fundamentalist groups from the United States.[3] There are also a distasteful homophobic politics in Singapore (inconsistent with its vaunted economic liberalism)[4] and Malaya, a largely Muslim nation.[5] A Cameroon court recently upheld a three-year criminal sentence for homosexual conduct for sending a text message to another man, saying: "I'm very much in love with you."[6] Sometimes such homophobic violence is justified as resisting Western imperialism, gay rights being viewed as a form of imperialism, so that the credibility of Frank Mugisha, a remarkably courageous gay rights activist in Uganda, "means keeping a distance from

---

[2] See Richard Gott, *Britain's Empire: Resistance, Repression, and Revolt* (London: Verso, 2011); Robert J. C. Young, *Postcolonialism: An Historical Introduction* (Oxford: Blackwell, 2001).
[3] See, for example, Josh Kron, "Resentment Toward the West Bolsters Uganda's New Anti-Gay Bill," New York Times, Wednesday, February 29, 2012, p. A4; Alexis Okeowo, "Out in Africa: A gay rights struggle with deadly stakes," *The New Yorker*, December 24&31, 2012, pp. 64–70.
[4] See Wikipedia, "LGBT rights in Singapore."
[5] See Wikipedia, "LGBT rights in Malaysia," on criminal prosecution of leading politician Anwar Ibrahim, leading to nine-year sentence and release after 4 years upon acquittal by Federal Court of Malaysia.
[6] See AP, "Gay Man's 3-Year Sentence Upheld by Cameroon Court," *The New York Times*, Tuesday, December 18, 2012, at p. A15.

well-meaning American or European politicians and human-rights groups."[7] My argument shows, to the contrary, that gay rights arose in resistance to imperialism, and there is nothing to be said for the claim that the argument for gay rights is in its nature imperialistic. To the contrary, the argument for gay rights is antipatriarchal, and the homophobic war on gay rights arises, as in Uganda, not from "African" values but from patriarchal American fundamentalist religions that, increasingly reasonably rejected in America as in Britain, seek and claim imperial rule over nations abroad. What this exposes is how uncritically dominant patriarchy remains in these nations that claim to be but are not democratic. Imperialism is never more powerful than when, as in imperial Rome and Britain, it enforces its will by dividing its colonized victims from one another, in the name, absurdly, of resisting imperialism.

My argument about the rise of gay rights in the United States and Britain suggests that it should not be surprising if these arguments have a resonance beyond national borders. When Oscar Wilde and Edward Carpenter traveled to the United States to visit Walt Whitman, it was because Whitman's poetic voice resonated for them with its more inclusive conception of democracy in which gay rights would play an important part. When the British in the wake of the 1967 decriminalization of gay sex saw in the United States a social movement of gays and lesbians no longer reticent and closeted, they found both American arguments and authenticity touched something in their psyches, enabling them to stand proudly and openly as free people, on their own remarkable history of gay rights. So, although the ex-colonies' imperial connection to Britain should not lead us to expect them to support gay rights, they sometimes do so. I want now better to understand how this has happened in several of them: Canada, South Africa, and India.

CANADA

Political leadership on questions of gay rights is sufficiently uncommon that the role of Pierre Trudeau, probably the leading Canadian politician of his generation, merits some study.[8] Trudeau was the fifteenth prime minister of Canada from 1968 through 1979 and again from 1980 through 1984. From the late 1960s until the mid-1980s, he dominated the Canadian political scene and aroused passionate reactions. "Reason before passion" was his personal motto.

---

[7] Alexis Okeowo, "Out in Africa: A gay rights struggle with dead stakes," *The New Yorker*, December 24&31, 2012, pp. 64–70, at p. 70.
[8] See Wikipedia, "Pierre Trudeau."

Trudeau began his career campaigning for socialist ideals, but he eventually joined the Liberal Party. An associate professor of law at the Université de Montreal from 1961 to 1965, Trudeau's views evolved toward a liberal position in favor of individual rights counter to the state and made him an opponent of Quebec nationalism. Trudeau ran successfully for the Liberals in the 1965, entering parliament. Upon arrival in Ottawa, Trudeau was appointed as Prime Minister Lester Pearson's parliamentary secretary. In 1967, he was appointed to Pearson's cabinet as Minister of Justice.

As Minister of Justice, influenced by the Wolfenden Report of 1957 and British decriminalization in 1967, Pierre Trudeau was responsible for introducing the landmark Criminal Law Amendment Act, 1968–69, an omnibus bill with provisions including, among other things, the decriminalization of homosexual acts between consenting adults; the legalization of contraception, abortion, and lotteries; new gun ownership restrictions; and authorization of breathalyzer tests on suspected drunk drivers. Trudeau famously defended the decriminalization of homosexual acts by telling reporters, "there's no place for the state in the bedrooms of the nation," adding that "what's done in private between adults doesn't concern the Criminal Code."[9] Trudeau also liberalized divorce laws.

At the end of Canada's centennial year in 1967, Prime Minister Pearson announced his intention to step down, and Trudeau entered the race for the Liberal leadership. His energetic campaign attracted massive media attention and mobilized many young people, who saw Trudeau as a symbol of generation change (even though he was forty-eight years old). Having joined the Liberal Party only in 1965, he was still considered an outsider as well as too radical and outspoken. Some of his views, particularly those on divorce, abortion, and homosexuality, were opposed by a substantial segment of the party. Nonetheless, Trudeau was elected as the leader on the fourth ballot and was sworn in as Liberal leader and prime minister. Trudeau soon called an election, which benefited from an unprecedented wave of personal popularity, called "Trudeaumania." He won the election handily.

As prime minister in his first term, Trudeau defended vigorously the newly implemented universal health care and regional programs as a means of making society more just. He also implemented official bilingualism and a multiculturalism policy. In his second term, Trudeau had two significant accomplishments. The first was the defeat of the referendum on Quebec sovereignty. Trudeau promised a new constitutional agreement with Quebec

[9] Ibid., p. 5.

should it decide to stay in Canada, and the "No" side (No to sovereignty) ended up receiving approximately 60% of the vote.

Trudeau had attempted patriation of the Constitution earlier in his career, and returned to it now, his second accomplishment. Despite opposition, the patriation was achieved, known as the Constitution Act, 1982. It included the Charter of Rights and Freedoms within Canada's constitution, one of Trudeau's most enduring legacies to Canada. It is seen as advancing civil rights and liberties, and, notwithstanding a clause allowing parliament to ignore its decisions, has become a cornerstone of Canadian values for most Canadians. It also represented the final step in Trudeau's liberal vision of a fully independent and nationalist Canada based on fundamental human rights and the protection of individual freedoms as well as those of linguistic and cultural minorities.

Such broader political purposes were central to Trudeau's motivation in entrenching a charter. Reviewing the patriation effort in his later years, Trudeau interpreted that the goal of the charter was to strengthen national unity by "basing the sovereignty of the Canadian people on a set of values common to all, and in particular on the notion of equality among all Canadians."[10] Trudeau believed that the adoption of the charter was a reflection of the "purest liberalism" in which each individual is regarded as a "human personality" who has absolute dignity and infinite value. It follows that "only the individual is the possessor of rights" and that certain inalienable rights can never be interfered with by any collectivity, whether the collectivity be state, nation, or another group.[11] The moral theory was that the enactment of the charter would emphasize these common values of citizenship, and particularism of provinces, regions, or groups would be correspondingly diminished. The charter would serve as a major instrument in which Canadians could transcend such particularism and focus on a core set of values common to all – as he put the point in his *Memoirs*, "the focal point was not the state but the individual – the individual seen as a person integrated into society, which is to say endowed with fundamental rights and essential liberties, but also with responsibilities."[12]

Canada's first thirty years of experience with its Supreme Court's interpretation of the charter suggests that it has made a significant contribution to the sensitivity of Canadian law and politics to arguments grounded in the

---

[10] Pierre Trudeau, "The Values of a Just Society" in *Towards a Just Society: The Trudeau Years*, edited by P. Trudeau and T. Axworthy (Markham: Viking Books, 1990), 357 at 363.
[11] Ibid.
[12] Pierre Trudeau, *Memoirs* (Toronto: McClelland & Stewart, 1995), at p. 47.

basic human rights of small minorities, notably, gays and lesbians. Gay and lesbian activism had been increasingly visible in Canada,[13] but public interest organizations representing traditionally disadvantaged groups, including gays and lesbians, were notably successful in appealing to the Supreme Court for recognition of its constitutional rights. On the basis of the equality guarantee, the Supreme Court has ruled that Alberta's human rights legislation violates section 15 – and cannot be justified under section 1 – for failing to prohibit discrimination against gays and lesbians[14] and has also found that the definition of "spouse" in Ontario's Family Law Act is deficient because it fails to include same-sex partners.[15] In response to these decisions, same-sex marriage was adopted across Canada by parliament in 2005.

In the United States, it has been a long time since politicians like Lyndon Johnson on civil rights and Jimmy Carter on human rights have led the nation to a better and deeper understanding of what our rights are. To the contrary, American conservative politicians have fomented a reactionary politics based on the repression and denial of human rights. The life and work of Pierre Trudeau show us there are alternatives – brilliantly successful democratic politicians who lead their people to a deeper understanding of and commitment to respect for basic human rights, including gay rights. President Barack Obama in the United States, who now supports gay marriage, may well be such a man.

SOUTH AFRICA

Both the construction and interpretation of the Constitution of South Africa afford yet another example of the importance of political leadership on gay rights. Here, however, in contrast to Canada, the leadership in question arose from a resisting, indeed a revolutionary, political movement, the African National Congress (ANC) against the radical injustice of South African apartheid, which became entrenched in South Africa in a period, after World War II, where it would be discredited and abandoned everywhere else. South African apartheid was an affront to the civilized conscience of the postwar world, a common object of condemnation during the Cold War, condemned, as it was, both by the Western democracies and the Communist states. Many early supporters of the ANC were communists, including Albie Sachs, who

---

[13] For illuminating studies, see Gary Kinsman, *The Regulation of Desire: Sexuality in Canada* (Montreal: Black Rose Books, 1987); Didi Herman, *Rights of Passage: Struggles for Lesbian and Gay Legal Equality* (Toronto: University of Toronto Press, 1994).
[14] *Vriend v. Alberta* [1998], 1 S.C.R. 493, 156 DLR (4th) 385.
[15] *M. v. H.* [1999], 2 S.C.R. 3, 171 DLR (4th) 577.

lost an arm in an assassination attempt on his life by South African agents (his friend, Ruth First, was murdered). Sachs went on to write of his recovery and his role in the constitutional negotiations of the ANC with the National Party (the leading party of apartheid South Africa).[16] Sachs would later serve as a justice on the South African Supreme Court, concurring in a 1998 opinion for the Court that decriminalized gay sex (as violating the constitutional rights of homosexuals)[17] and writing for the Court in a 2005 opinion requiring the government to recognize same-sex marriage,[18] which it did.[19] How and why did an erstwhile revolutionary communist play the role he did both in constructing and interpreting one of the most liberal constitutions the world has seen, in which the issue of gay rights played an important role?

The Constitution of South Africa arose in two stages: first, the interim Constitution of 1993, which required that the final Constitution conform to the 34 Constitutional Principles that made up Schedule 4 of the interim Constitution; second, the final Constitution of 1996, which was valid only after the South African Supreme Court certified that it conformed to the requirements of the interim Constitution. The Constitutional Principles were key to the two-stage negotiating process, for they guaranteed to both parties (the ANC and the National Party) that their main objectives would be secured in the final Constitution. For this reason, Schedule 4 and the requirement that the Supreme Court certify that the Constitutional Assembly did conform to these principles in deciding on the final Constitution; were the only parts of the Constitution that could not be amended in a two-thirds majority; indeed, they "were set in stone as the core of the negotiated agreement."[20] In fact, the court did not certify the first Constitution, in part because it did not require a more demanding amendment procedure for the entrenchment of its Bill of Rights as opposed to other provisions.[21] When the Constitutional Assembly carefully redrafted the final Constitution to conform to the Supreme Court's requirements, the Supreme Court certified the Constitution in 1997.[22] Any

---

[16] See Albie Sachs, *The Soft Vengeance of a Freedom Fighter*, new ed. (Berkeley: University of California Press, 2000).

[17] *National Coalition for Gay and Lesbian Equality v. Minister of Justice* [1998] ZACC 15, 1989 (1) SA 6, 1988 (12) BCLR 1517.

[18] *Minister of Home Affairs v. Fourie* [2005] 2 ACC 19, 2006 (1) SA 524 (CC), 2006 (3) BCLR 355 (CC).

[19] For Sachs's reflections on his work as a justice, see Albie Sachs, *The Strange Alchemy of Life and Law* (New York: Oxford University Press, 2009).

[20] Heinz Klug, *The Constitution of South Africa: A Contextual Analysis* (Oxford: Hart Publishing, 2010), at p. 85.

[21] Ibid., at p. 94.

[22] Ibid., at pp. 96–7.

amendment to the Bill of Rights could now be achieved only by a 75 percent majority in the National Assembly and the support of six of the nine provinces (even at the height of its appeal, the ANC reached only a two-thirds majority).[23]

The Constitution, consistent with the thirty-four principles of Schedule 4 of the interim Constitution, explicitly provides for these principles as "one, sovereign, democratic state founded" on a particular set of values. These founding values include the following:

> human dignity, the achievement of equality and the advancement of human rights and freedoms, non-racialism and non-sexism; supremacy of the constitution and the rule of law; as well as the basic principles of an electoral democracy, universal adult suffrage, a national common voters role, regular elections, and a multi-party system of democratic government to ensure accountability, responsiveness, and openness.[24]

The equality guarantee of the Bill of Rights goes on to provide:

> The state may not unfairly discriminate directly or indirectly against anyone on one or more grounds, including race, gender, sex, pregnancy, marital status, ethnic or social origin, colour, sexual orientation, age, disability, religion, conscience, belief, cultural, language and birth.[25]

We know that, in the negotiating process over the thirty-four principles of Schedule 4 of the interim Constitution, there was discussion of whether to include sexual orientation explicitly among the forbidden grounds of constitutional discrimination. Personal contacts by gay rights activists were of particular importance at this point (including Edwin Cameron, an out gay man and law professor).[26] Sexual orientation was explicitly included. An important article by Cameron (his inaugural lecture as a law professor in 1992) was published in 1993 that addressed these discussions, identifying the need for such an explicit prohibition on the ground that "[g]ays and lesbians are notoriously uncohesive politically," and yet their claims against discrimination go "to the root of the ethics of our Constitution-making."[27] Cameron identifies the ethical wrong in terms of the larger wrong of what I have called the patriarchal Love Laws, laws that not only prohibit same-sex relations but relations between those of

---

[23] Ibid., at p. 107.
[24] Ibid., at p. 107.
[25] Cited in Sachs, *The Strange Alchemy of Life and Law*, p. 282.
[26] Carl F. Stychin, "Constituting Sexuality: The Struggle for Sexual Orientation in the South African Bill of Rights," 23 *J.L. & Soc'y* 455 (1966), at p. 458.
[27] Edwin Cameron, "Sexual Orientation and the Constitution: A Test Case for Human Rights," 110 *S. African L.J.* 450, 451 (1993).

different religions or ethnicities or races. Cameron observes: "Traditionally, disadvantaged groups such as women and blacks both constitute a majority of the South African population," but "[g]ays and lesbians, by contrast, are by definition a minority."[28] Moreover, the irrational prejudices and contempt directed at them impose "on them powerful incentives to continue to suppress or conceal their sexuality,"[29] rendering them more invisible and vulnerable to injustice. Yet sexual feeling, the heart of sexual orientation, is not something chosen, and

> [o]ur Constitution, if it is to have meaning in creating a plural society in South Africa, must honour variant life styles, and where no harm to others is involved it must guarantee people's autonomy to make choices affecting their own lives. Yet, it remains particularly repugnant and arbitrary from a moral point of view to discriminate against a person solely on the ground of a characteristic over which he or she has no choice.[30]

When Cameron roots his argument in "the ethics of our Constitution-making," he has in mind the value of equal dignity self-consciously invoked by the South African Constitution as the value that gives rise to human rights. Because discrimination against homosexuals is an unjust degradation of their equal dignity to have and conduct an intimate personal life, such discrimination must be explicitly acknowledged as forbidden, in particular, in favor of a group so unlikely otherwise to achieve politically what equal justice requires. Cameron's article was importantly used by a coalition of gay activists to persuade the Constitutional Assembly to retain the explicit prohibition of discrimination on grounds of sexual orientation.[31]

Cameron's article was even more important in laying the normative foundation for the illegitimacy of the criminalization of consensual same-sex sexual acts in the South African Constitutional Court's decision in *National Coalition for Gay and Lesbian Equality v. Minister of Justice* (1999) 1 S.A. 6 at paras. [20]-[31], [75] (Justice Ackermann) and [128] (Justice Sachs). The Constitutional Court later deployed similar reasoning in *National Coalition for Gay and Lesbian Equality v. Minister of Justice* (2000) 2 S.A. 1 (immigration rights and same-sex couples) and *Minister of Home Affairs v. Fourie* (2005) 1 S.A. 524 (same-sex marriage).

---

[28] Ibid., p. 458.
[29] Ibid., p. 459.
[30] Ibid., p. 460.
[31] On the general role of these activists in the constitutional debates, see Carl F. Stychin, "Constituting Sexuality."

Edwin Cameron is now a justice of the South African Constitutional Court, a court that, on the basis of the explicit prohibition of sexual orientation discrimination that Cameron urged earlier, has moved in all the areas Cameron urged it to decriminalization, discrimination, and the equal recognition of same-sex partnerships. Both his integrity and courage are shown in his book dealing with his personal struggle with AIDS and his discussion of the general issue of gay rights and constitutionalism.[32]

His existence and impact on South African constitutionalism reflect a larger fact of South African life – namely, a diverse and increasingly active and self-conscious gay rights movement in South Africa.[33] The apartheid regime, which had been so harsh to people of color had been harsh to gays as well, and we know that some gay men, including the actor/director Cecil Williams, a communist, knew and helped the then young Nelson Mandela (who acted as his chauffeur) to travel incognito around South Africa as the police were searching for him (before his imprisonment for life).[34] As portrayed in the excellent documentary, *The Man Who Drove with Mandela*,[35] contacts between the then ANC leadership and William's circles were natural, sociable, and easy, sharing so much as exiles and outlaws from apartheid South Africa and sharing as well common revolutionary goals (Williams eventually escaped to Britain). It is this kind of experience that may explain why Cameron's arguments for the constitutional rights of gays had the resonance for Mandela and Sachs that they apparently did.[36] We need to recall, in this connection, the injuries South African apartheid inflicted on family life, as husbands and wives were often compelled to work at some distance from one another with little opportunity for life together, and leaders like Mandela were separated from their families, in his case for the twenty-seven years of his imprisonment. It is not surprising that a moral imagination, informed by the ethical insults to the dignity of love and family wrought by apartheid, could and would extend to the ways in which homophobia, also enforced by the apartheid regime, had warred on gay love and relationships, as they saw in the lives of their gay comrades, like Cecil Williams, in antiapartheid.

---

[32] See Edwin Cameron, *Witness to AIDS* (London: I.B. Tauris, 2007).
[33] On this point, Mark Gevisser and Edwin Cameron, *Defiant Desire: Gay and Lesbian Lives in South Africa* (New York: Routledge, 1995).
[34] For Mandela's description of these events, see Nelson Mandela, *Long Walk to Freedom* (Boston: Little, Brown & Company, 1995), pp. 307, 311, 312–15.
[35] Greta Schiller, *The Man Who Drove with Mandela* (1998).
[36] On this point, Stephen Chan, *Southern Africa: Old Treacheries and New Deceits* (New Haven, CT: Yale University Press, 2011), at pp. 51–2.

It is useful and illuminating at this point to contrast these gay-sensitive constitutional developments in South Africa with the very different ways in which the issue of homosexuality has been dealt with by South Africa's neighbor, Zimbabwe, and its leader, Robert Mugabe. There is, after all, common ground in Mugabe's leadership of a revolutionary movement against the white-dominated regime of Rhodesia, then establishing an ostensibly democratic republic and the ANC's similar struggles in South Africa, which Mugabe had assisted. Mugabe, like Albie Sachs, was a communist but a Maoist whose guerilla movement had been assisted by the Chinese and, once in power in Zimbabwe in 1980, by the North Koreans.[37] In 1982, national television showed the "discovery" of arms caches in the west, and the Fifth Brigade, trained by North Koreans, was formed to quell "the insurrection. "The sadistic ingenuity of the Fifth Brigade in their killing of defenseless people makes their work a war crime."[38] Their aim was the use of state terror to suppress any possibility of dissent. Mugabe was inspired by the tactics used by President Hastings Banda in Malawi to suppress political opposition; his Malawian Young Pioneers had slaughtered some 6,000 Jehovah's Witnesses, using his cadres of impressionable youth.[39] The apartheid regime in South Africa had trained its own guerilla group (opposing the Marxist regime) in Mozambique, known as RENAMO, that "became a byword for brutality and atrocity. It became one of the first movements to use child soldiers and literally blooded them by forcing them to commit atrocities against their own communities, and even their own families."[40] In 1985, Mugabe, joined by the leaders of Mozambique and Tanzania, successfully initiated a military intervention to open up a rail corridor from Zimbabwe through RENAMO territory to the only working South African port not in apartheid hands.[41] This defeat for South Africa anticipated its even more devastating defeat in Angola by forces of the Soviet Union and Cuba in 1988 that set the stage for the fall of President P. W. Botha in South Africa, the election of F.W. de Klerk, the legalization of the ANC, and the freeing of Nelson Mandela in 1990.[42] Mugabe also sent troops into war in the Congo (Zaire), enriching his generals through mining concessions there,[43] and his troops in Mozambique enabled him to play an important role

---

[37] On this point, see Stephen Chan, *Robert Mugabe: A Life of Power and Violence* (Ann Arbor: University of Michigan Press, 2003), at pp. 22–3.
[38] Ibid., at p. 32.
[39] Ibid., pp. 20, 23–4.
[40] Ibid., p. 38.
[41] Ibid., pp. 39–41.
[42] Ibid., pp. 42–8.
[43] Ibid., pp. 135–7.

in negotiations there.[44] Mugabe, successful in war, unfortunately carried this mentality into internal politics, as if always "he were a man at war."[45] Mugabe tragically descended into a self-blinding black nationalism that led him to wreck the once prosperous economy of Zimbabwe (illegally seizing the farms of whites by gangs of youth and ex-soldiers,[46] an "agrarian racist enterprise"[47]) and to war on the democratic black opposition in Zimbabwe.[48] He used violence and vote rigging in elections to hold on to power when, in contrast, President Kenneth Kaunda of nearby Zambia had memorably showed there was a different, more democratic way: when defeated in elections, Kaunda left office.[49] In the same spirit, Mugabe harassed and threatened leaders of the Anglican Church in Zimbabwe, who questioned his policies.[50]

In their important historical and comparative study of the role of liberal democracy in facilitating economic prosperity, Acemoglu and Robinson show that it is only when democratic accountability is joined to respect for liberal freedoms (including facilitating creativity and innovation) that democracy in fact facilitates economic prosperity.[51] It is liberal democracy, thus understood, that breaks the vicious cycle of what Acemoglu and Robinson, following Robert Michels, call "the iron law of oligarchy," explaining

> [t]he internal logic of oligarchies, and in fact of all hierarchical organizations, is that, argued Michels, they will reproduce themselves not only when the same group is in power, but even when an entirely new group takes control. What Michels did not anticipate perhaps was an echo of Karl Marx's remark that history repeats itself – the first time as tragedy, the second time as farce.[52]

Acemoglu and Robinson brilliantly analyze the postindependence leadership of many ostensibly democratic African nations as illustrative of this tragedy and farce and discuss Mugabe's war on liberal democracy in Zimbabwe in

---

[44] Ibid., pp. 54–8.
[45] Ibid., p. 213.
[46] Ibid., pp. 175–8.
[47] Ibid., at p. 178.
[48] See Stephen Chan *Robert Mugabe*, pp. 186–215.
[49] Ibid., pp. 54–5.
[50] See, on this point, Celia W. Dugger. "Mugabe Ally Escalates Push to Control Church: Anglican Leaders Harassed and Threatened," *The New York Times*, Monday, May 30, 2011, A6.
[51] See Daron Acemoglu and James A. Robinson, *Why Nations Fail: The Origins of Power, Prosperity, and Poverty* (New York: Crown Business, 2012). See also Larry Diamond, *The Spirit of Democracy: The Struggle fo Build Free Societies throughout the World* (New York: Times Books, 2008).
[52] Acemoglu and Robinson, *Why Nations Fail*, p. 360.

these terms.[53] It is against this background that we may understand the role that ethnic nationalism has played and continues to play in Zimbabwe and elsewhere, rationalizing the subversion of, indeed the attack on, liberal democracy, including the ideological manufacture of scapegoats to rationalize such subversion.

Ethnic nationalism is, in its nature, antiliberal, extending, in its most extreme forms, to German fascism, the irrational violence of which turned on scapegoats like the six million European Jews it murdered. What distinguishes fascism is its mindless violence; as one of its most astute analysts, Robert Paxton, put the point, "The legitimation of violence against a demonized internal enemy brings us close to the heart of fascism."[54] Certainly, Mugabe's claim runs afoul of all the problems of ethnic nationalism that, in the fascism of Mussolini and Hitler and the Japanese Emperor, almost destroyed human civilization – flourishing, ironically, in the two nations – Italy and Germany – that had contributed so much to our understanding of the enduring values of civilized life. Fascism has no political theory, although it does have a distinctive political psychology, rooted, as Carol Gilligan and I have argued elsewhere,[55] in the violence of humiliated patriarchal manhood directed at the imagined threats to its sense of honor (thus, the toxic anti-Semitism of Hitler's genocidal fascism).

Mugabe's propensity for illegal and indeed immoral violence suggests a mentality of patriarchal manhood like that Josephus noted in the Romans, one in which "there cannot be an end to fighting"[56] and the need for violence, like Hitler's, is fastened on scapegoats. Mugabe's scapegoats are homosexuals, on whom he wars publicly as a Western evil and prosecutes criminally not only under existing sodomy laws but under new laws that criminalize acts by gays such as kissing or holding hands.[57] He also seeks constitutional changes, as George W. Bush did in the United States, that would have banned gay marriage.[58] Why gays? Mugabe here may himself be drawing on the highly patriarchal forms of Western religions that traditionally condemned homosexuality, in the same way homophobic American religious fundamentalists

---

[53] Acemoglu and Robinson, *Why Nations Fail*, pp. 368–73. For a similar analysis, see Larry Diamond, *The Spirit of Democracy*, pp. 247–7, 251, 258.
[54] Robert O. Paxton, *The Anatomy of Fascism* (New York: Vintage Books, 2004), at p. 84.
[55] See Carol Gilligan and David A. J. Richards, *The Deepening Darkness: Patriarchy, Resistance, and Democracy's Future* (Cambridge: Cambridge University Press, 2009), pp. 232–8.
[56] Stephen Chan, *Robert Mugabe*, at p. 183.
[57] See Wikipedia, "LGBT Rights in Zimbabwe"; see also Stephen Chan, *Robert Mugabe*, pp. 123–4, 143.
[58] See Stephen Chan, *Robert Mugabe*, p. 143.

have played such a role in Uganda[59] or local clergy have in Malawi.[60] If so, Mugabe paradoxically is appealing to precisely the now discredited and quite anachronistic values of British imperialism that first imposed such laws on its colonies.[61] Perhaps gays have come to mean to Mugabe and others what Jews meant to Hitler's anti-Semitism – namely, a traditionally despised group that had, through its appeals to political liberalism, achieved some measure of toleration. Certainly, it is psychologically revealing that, when confronted by the British Prime Minister Tony Blair's criticism of his policies, Mugabe responds homophobically: "Blair's government was not only colonial, but unnaturally stuffed with gay and lesbian ministers who were forced to marry each other."[62] So the attack, apparently against Jews or homosexuals, is really about liberal democratic values and the role they have played, however imperfectly, in securing respect for the human rights even of the most historically despised minorities. But Mugabe himself claims to be a democrat and has insisted on regular elections in Zimbabwe, however flawed, and also notably signed on to the 1991 Harare Declaration of Human Rights.[63] Mugabe's attack is then on values he claims to defend, democracy and human rights, and what motivates him is, in fact, democracy's enemy, patriarchy, now very much threatened, and rightly so. It was patriarchy that motivated European imperialism, and one may reasonably understand Mugabe and other such opponents of gay rights in the terms Tagore used against the aggressive ethnic nationalism of Imperial Japan: he is "infected by the virus of European imperialism."[64] Mugabe, a wounded patriarch, is at war with the values and arguments that condemn him as the illegitimate, antidemocratic ruler he has chosen to become.

There is no serious attempt here, when appealing to African values, to investigate what distinctive African political values might be. If there were, such investigation might show us what South African research into tribal

---

[59] See Josh Kron, "In Uganda, Push to Curb Gays Draws U.S. Guest," *The New York Times*, Monday, May 3, 2010, A9; Josh Kron, "Resentment toward the West Bolsters Uganda's New Anti-Gay Bill," *The New York Times*, Wednesday, February 29, 2012, A4; Alexis Okeowo, "Out in Africa: A gay rights struggle with deadly stakes," *The New Yorker*, December 24&31, 2012, pp. 64–70.

[60] Barr Bearak, "Some-Sex Couple Stir Fears in Malawi of a 'Gay Agenda' Promoted by the West," *The New York Times*, Sunday, February 14, 2010, p. 6.

[61] See, on this point, Michael Kirby, "Legal discrimination against homosexuals – a blind spot of the Commonwealth of Nations?," *E.H.L.R.* 2009, 1, 21–36.

[62] Stephen Chan, *Robert Mugabe*, p. 178.

[63] On this point, see Stephen Chan, *Robert Mugabe*, pp. 65–8.

[64] Quoted at Pankaj Mishra, *From the Ruins of Empire: The Intellectuals Who Remade Asia* (New York: Farrar, Straus & Giroux, 2012), at p. 239.

values of *ubuntu* shows – namely, that such values are themselves rooted in democratic values of dignity and human rights.[65]

It is a continual worry by some of the most serious and independent students of South African politics that black nationalism has been altogether too important there as well, affecting public policy as in President Mbeki's scandalously unscientific attitude about the AIDS health crisis in South Africa.[66] I share these worries. It is, however, the achievement of South African constitutionalism, grounded like that of Canada in a conception of enforceable human rights, that it pulls against, questions, and limits the force of such ethnic nationalism in South African politics. It is South Africa's more expansive conception of democracy and human rights that has made this possible, including its embrace of gay rights.

INDIA

My general thesis has been that, because the British never took seriously introducing democracy in its colonies, its ex-colonies would not have learned democracy from them, let alone constitutional democracy. Most did not.[67] I put aside, for this purpose, the colonies founded largely by British settlers (Australia and New Zealand) in which the settlers understandably adapt British institutions as independent states and have studied Canada because its settlers were both French and British, raising the question of how to deal with competing ethnic nationalisms (which Trudeau transcended through a nationalism based on human rights).

India is a special case; not, I believe, because Britain made an exceptional effort there to introduce democratic institutions but because its indigenous emerging leadership through its vehicle, the Congress Party, confronted with its sense of the backwardness and indeed injustice of Indian life, initiated a long process of resistance to British imperial rule that reasonably demanded what Mohandas Gandhi called *swaraj*,[68] self-government, that would also make possible social transformation of Indian life.[69] The most important of these

---

[65] On this point, see Drucilla Cornell and Nyoko Muvangua, *Ubuntu and the Law: African Ideals and Postapartheid Jurisprudence* (New York: Fordham University Press, 2012).
[66] For a general criticism along these lines, see R. W. Johnson, *South Africa's Brave New World: The Beloved Country since the End of Apartheid* (New York: Overlook Press, 2009).
[67] On this point, see Kwarteng, *Ghosts of Empire*.
[68] See Mohandas K. Gandhi, *Hind Swaraj and Other Writings*, edited by Anthony J. Parel (Cambridge: Cambridge University Press, 2000).
[69] For an important recent study of a range of less well-known Asian intellectual leaders opposing colonialism, see Pankaj Mishra, *From the Ruins of Empire: The Intellectuals Who Remade Asia* (New York: Farrar, Straus & Giroux, 2012).

leaders, Gandhi had studied in Britain for several years at University College, London, to become a barrister. Another important leader, who, in fact, inherited Gandhi's mantle, was Jawaharlal Nehru; Nehru had studied in Britain at Harrow and Trinity College, Cambridge. The talents and importance of these two leaders were quite different, although they were close friends (Gandhi, the older, was a kind of beloved father figure to Nehru, whose real father, Motilal, had been an early leader of the Congress Party).[70]

Gandhi was the inspiring leader of the Congress Party during the long period of its struggle for freedom from Britain after World War I, brilliantly developing and leading a political strategy of nonviolent resistance (*satyagraha*) to British rule that was <u>designed to appeal to British democratic public opinion, the power of which Gandhi had come to understand by living in Britain for several years as a student</u>. The strategy, which had proven its effectiveness during Gandhi's twenty-year stay in South Africa, was to prove even more successful in India, mobilizing Indian men and, more surprisingly, women (breaking *purdah*, requiring concealment of women from men) into democratic agents of nonviolent resistance that, over time, seared the British liberal conscience. Gandhi's own ethical, religious, and political views had been crucially shaped by his stay in Britain, experiencing there, for the first time, an interest in Indian thought that led him to develop what was, in fact, a highly original interpretation and synthesis of the Christian and Hindu traditions much under the influence of his study of Leo Tolstoy's Christian pacifism and of the critique of industrial civilization in Britain by the gay man and activist, Edward Carpenter, who had had such an impact on E. M. Forster (see Chapter 3). Gandhi acknowledged the influence on him and recommended to others, as a model of *swaraj*, Carpenter's *Civilization: Its Cause and Cure*.[71] The appeal of Carpenter's argument, for Gandhi, was its indictment of the price in ill health and spiritual disassociation that the British had paid for the "mere fetish-worship"[72] of the products of industrial civilization, and how much the British had to learn from the health and wholeness of the so-called less civilized peoples, like the Indians, whom the British unjustly colonized on racist grounds. What Gandhi learned from Carpenter was that liberals in Britain, like Carpenter, regarded its imperialism as being as bad for Britons as it was for colonized peoples and that

---

[70] For recent critical evaluations of these leaders, see Perry Anderson, "Gandhi Centre Stage," *London Review of Books* 34, no. 13 (July 5 2012): pp. 3–11; Perry Anderson, "Why Partition?" *London Review of Books* 34, no. 14 (July 19 2012), pp. 11–19.
[71] Edward Carpenter, *Civilization: Its Cause and Cure and Other Essays* (London: Swan Sonnenschein, 1906), pp. 2–50. For Carpenter's influence on Gandhi, see Robert J. C. Young, *Postcolonialism: An Historical Introduction* (Oxford: Blackwell Publishing, 2001), pp. 326–7.
[72] Carpenter, *Civilization*, p. 43.

a strategy of resistance to British rule that appealed to such people of liberal conscience might have resonance in British democratic politics. On the basis of this remarkable synthesis, Gandhi found his voice of ethical resistance to the injustice of British imperialism, a voice that found a resonance in the Indian people who began to forge themselves into a democratic people through participation in Gandhi's satyagrahas. Gandhi's resistance was not only to Britain but also to unjust aspects of Indian culture, in particular, a caste system that dehumanized untouchables. It is this internal criticism of Hinduism, calling for its reform and rebirth, that makes the resonance the Indian people gave his ethical voice so remarkable, suggesting to him and others that the struggle against British imperialism was also a struggle to a new conception of Indian democracy, which would reform Indians, for the first time in their history, into a democratic people. (It is no accident that Gandhi was murdered by a Hindu conservative, shocked by Gandhi's reinterpretation of Hinduism.) Gandhi's own views on the form such Indian democracy should take were profoundly antiindustrial, calling for a bottom-up revival of the *panchayat* tradition of local village agrarian democracy in which spinning homegrown cotton into cloth, which anyone could do, would be a central economic activity.[73]

Jawaharlal Nehru, the son of a wealthy Indian barrister and early Congress Party leader, was sent by his father for six years of education in Britain, first at Harrow, then at Trinity College, Cambridge. At Cambridge, he studied the natural sciences, imbibed the religious skepticism of many intellectuals of that period (influenced by the attacks on religion of Leslie Stephens, the father of Virginia Woolf), and was influenced by the Fabian socialism that the Webbs, George Bernard Shaw, and Leonard Woolf were developing at that time. Nehru ended his British education by studying to become a barrister at the Inner Temple in London and was a man of the broadest humane culture.[74]

Nehru devotedly followed Gandhi's leadership of the Congress Party until 1934 when Gandhi resigned from politics, and Nehru, with Gandhi's support, became the leader of the Congress Party. In response to Indian resistance, Britain had associated Indians with local self-government since the late nineteenth century, and "from the 1909 Government of India Act through those of 1919 and 1935, Indians came to play an increasing role in both the executive and legislative sides of provincial and central government. The members who

---

[73] On all these points, see David A. J. Richards, *Disarming Manhood: Roots of Ethical Resistance* (Athens, OH: Swallow Press, 2005), pp. 92–130.

[74] See, for example, Jawaharlal Nehru, *The Discovery of India* (New Delhi: Penguin, 2004; originally published, 1946), Jawaharlal Nehru, *Glimpses of World History* (New Delhi: Penguin, 2004; first published, 1934–45). See also Jawaharlal Nehru, *An Autobiography* (New Delhi: Penguin, 2004; first published, 1936).

had participated in these fields of government could not have exceeded several thousand, but their influence was considerable. They had learned to work the system well and to like it – despite the difficulties engendered by their lack of final authority."[75] This experience in self-government under forms of British constitutionalism undoubtedly influenced Indians to think of self-government in terms of Western models, most notably, British and American constitutionalism.

The opposing figure to these models was always Gandhi, who continued to press his point of view on Nehru and others until his murder in 1948 (India was freed from Britain in 1947, and the Constituent Assembly would debate the form and content of the Constitution from 1947 to 1950). Nehru never took Gandhi's views on government seriously. Some changes to the proposed Constitution were made to acknowledge promotion of Gandhi's idea of home spinning in the Directive Principles,[76] but the model for the Constitution was British parliamentary democracy in a rather centralized federal system and an American-style judiciary to protect basic constitutionally guaranteed rights.[77] In light of his long education in Britain, with emphasis on the natural sciences, Nehru may have come to believe that what the two great Western democracies, Britain and the United States, had discovered in the natural sciences extended to government and economics and even ethics as well. In the long debates in the Constituent Assembly on the language question, Nehru finally intervened:

> We stand on the threshold of a new age.... What sort of India do we want? Do we want a modern India – with its roots steeped in the past... in so far as it inspires us – do we want a modern India with modern science and all the rest of it, or do we want to live in some ancient age, in some other age which has no relation to the present? You have to choose between the two. It is a question of approach. You have to choose whether you look forward or backward.[78]

There is no doubt where Nehru looked.

Nehru certainly shared Gandhi's view that self-government must lead to changes in Indian culture, including the inhuman treatment that the caste system inflicted on the untouchables (untouchability is forbidden by the

---

[75] Granville Austin, *The Indian Constitution: Cornerstone of a Nation* (Oxford: Oxford University Press, 2011; originally published, 1966), pp. 40–1.
[76] Ibid., pp. 81–2.
[77] See, in general, Granville Austin, *The Indian Constitution*. See also Granville Austin, *Working a Democratic Constitution: A History of the Indian Experience* (Oxford: Oxford University Press, 1999).
[78] Quoted in Granville Austin, *The Indian Constitution*, p. 304.

Constitution[79]). What about the caste system itself, which is at the heart of Hinduism?[80] Its entrenchment of hierarchical inequalities is, of course, profoundly patriarchal, including its enforcement of the Love Laws, requiring arranged marriages within one's caste and forbidding all marriages across caste lines, and purity rules which limit many forms of basic liberties – not only sexual liberties but associational liberties generally including eating, and liberties of choice of occupation.[81] It is striking, in this connection, that "[t]he Supreme Court first appeared in the proceedings of the Assembly in its role as guardian of the social revolution; even before a committee was established to inquiry into its functions; it was called upon to safeguard civil and minority rights."[82] The appeal of these provisions is an ethical conception of basic human rights whose protection requires an alternative, morally independent judicial forum "for adjudication of disputes outside society's repressive hierarchy."[83]

Indeed, the very conception of a universal political franchise, every Indian citizen having an equal right to vote, rests on the values of political equality, which appealed to Indian leaders like Nehru and others because it "made possible new allegiances, national instead of local, thus creating an alternative to the caste and other purely local loyalties that impeded national unity."[84] Unfortunately, "direct elections and the growth of political parties has abetted caste consciousness, thus promoting what the constitution was designed to defeat."[85]

In his magisterial treatment of how the Indian Constitution has operated over time, Granville Austin concludes with a probing discussion of the role caste hierarchy has played in India in impeding the realization of constitutional values.[86] "[T]he Constitution's concept of individual freedom is spreading to rival *karma*'s determinism," but such an ancient belief leads even the government "to look down on the people as objects whose affairs it is to manage," leading to unjustified paternalism and centralization.[87] Even more

---

[79] Section 17 of the Indian Constitution reads: "'Untouchability' is abolished and its practice in any form is forbidden," The Constitution of India: http//lawmin.nic.in/olwing/coi/coi-english/col-indexenglish.htm.

[80] See, in general, Wendy Doniger, *The Hindus: An Alternative History* (New York: Penguin, 2009).

[81] See, on this point, Carol Gilligan and David A. J. Richards, *The Deepening Darkness: Patriarchy, Resistance, and Democracy's Future* (Cambridge: Cambridge University Press, 2009), pp. 249–53.

[82] Granville Austin, *The Indian Constitution*, p. 169.

[83] Granville Austin, *Working a Democratic Constitution*, p. 7.

[84] Granville Austin, *The Indian Constitution*, p. 47.

[85] Ibid., p. 47.

[86] See Granville Austin, *Working a Democratic Constitution*, pp. 637–45.

[87] Id., p. 638.

money does not always improve the status of members of the Scheduled Castes in the countryside, "for they are still considered polluted."[88] And the effects of caste on the psychology of family life are traumatic: "A child's break from the closest association with his mother to association primarily with his father" leads to a mistrust that sees conspiracies everywhere[89] and focuses "the individual's attention on survival for his own sake and for . . . his family," making India "a *survival society* from those at its top to those at the bottom of its vast disparity,"[90] rationalizing rampant corruption and sycophantic job performance, "derived in part from the cultural characteristic of acquiescence to the father's authority."[91] And there is "a disjunction between word and deed, or from treating them as synonymous," leading to unfulfilled government promises (as if the promise sufficed)[92] and, as Prime Minister Rajiv Gandhi observed in a 1985 speech, "whole legions [of officials] whose only concern is their private welfare at the cost of society."[93]

Despite all these problems, Austin concludes that the Constitution's "provisions setting goals for the social revolution – such as Directive Principles, the Fundamental Rights, the articles protecting minority rights, those assisting the weaker sections, and so on – somewhat have diminished the repression of hierarchy and the effects of indifference among the upper castes to conditions among the lower,"[94] pointing, in particular, to reservations in education, in legislatures, and government employment, attesting "to the paradoxical erosion of the caste system as caste allegiance facilitates upward mobility."[95] Austin concludes: "'Hindu apathy' nearly is a thing of the past. The oppressive effects of hierarchy are waning as the open society unwraps national talents. Awareness of rights is becoming unquenchable."[96]

Perhaps the best evidence of this burgeoning "awareness of rights," sponsored by an appeal to the Fundamental Rights provisions of the Indian Constitution, is the recent opinion of the Delhi High Court in *Naz Foundation v. Union of India*,[97] striking down as unconstitutional the criminalization of "sex other than heterosexual penile-vaginal,"[98] a criminal provision, paradoxically,

---

[88] Ibid., p. 639.
[89] Ibid., p. 639.
[90] Ibid., p. 640.
[91] Ibid., p. 643.
[92] Ibid., p. 644.
[93] Quoted in ibid., p. 645.
[94] Ibid., p. 640.
[95] Ibid., p. 640.
[96] Ibid., p. 667.
[97] (2009) 160 DLT 277.
[98] *Naz Foundation*, WP(C)7455/2001, p. 3.

imposed by the British colonial power. The High Court grounds its argument both in the protection of an aspect of the constitutionally guaranteed right to life and in the constitutional guarantee of equal protection, both of which the criminal law violates without meeting the high burden of justification in terms of a compelling secular purpose that is constitutionally required. The one such secular purpose that the court discusses is health risks in connection with the transmission of AIDS, but although this is the kind of secular purpose that might justify a burden on basic rights, in fact the medical facts are that criminalization defeats rather than advances this purpose because it enforces a stigma that leads men not to seek medical help. In reaching this result, the High Court discusses a number of opinions to the same effect in other jurisdictions. On the issue of the basic right in question, the High Court cites the concurring opinion of Justice Albie Sachs in the opinion of the South African Supreme Court that struck down South Africa's sodomy law:

> While recognizing the unique worth of each person, the Constitution does not presuppose that a holder of rights is as an isolated, lonely, and abstract figure possessing a disembodied and socially disconnected self. It acknowledges that people live in their bodies, their communities, their cultures, their places and their times. The expression of sexuality requires a partner, real or imagined. It is not for the state to choose or to arrange the choice of partner, but for the partners to choose themselves.[99]

On the issue of the harms to homosexuals inflicted by such laws, the High Court notes "a negative effect on the lives of these people," as the stigma of such criminal laws, even when not enforced, makes of them "'unapprehended felons,' thus entrenching stigma and encouraging discrimination in different spheres of life," analogizing the wrong as like the British imperial law criminalizing the identity of being a eunuch (*hijras*).[100]

What the High Court's use of these analogies suggests is its implicit sense that the ethical wrong inflicted by these laws, unjust dehumanization and degradation of persons, is the same wrong as one prominently condemned by the Indian Constitution's abolition of untouchability: "its practice in any form is forbidden."[101] What gives this opinion its brilliant normative edge is the way it directly connects one of the worst horrors of the caste system, clearly

---

[99] Quoted in ibid., p. 39.
[100] Ibid., p. 41.
[101] For development of this argument, see Sujit Chourdhry, "How to Do Comparative Constitutional Law in India: *Naz Foundation*, Same Sex Rights, and Dialogical Interpretation," in *Comparative Constitutionalism in South Asia*, edited by S. Khilnani, V. Raghavan, & A. Thiruvengadam (New Delhi: Oxford University Press, 2011).

recognized by both Gandhi and Nehru, with enforcing the patriarchal Love Laws. This is why the High Court finds the opinion of Justice Albie Sachs so morally cogent: "It is not for the state to choose to arrange the choice of partner, but for the partners to choose themselves."

As we have seen in Chapter 3, many in the West, including many gay men, have sought in India and Indian culture and religions alternatives to a Western sexuality cramped to the terms of Augustine's narrow procreational model of legitimate sexual relations. There are certainly remarkable forms of ravishing erotic art in India, including on Hindu temples, and both Indian literature and religion entertain themes of same-sex love.[102] But the cultural force in India of the caste system, with strict parental control of arranged marriages, family life, and employment within the terms of one's caste duties, leaves little space for the kind of freedom of choice in love, resisting the patriarchal Love Laws, that gives rise to gay rights.

It is not surprising, against this background, that a man as morally sensitive as Gandhi should, like Tolstoy, have repudiated sexual life entirely, not recognizing alternatives that were, in fact, before his eyes, in particular, the way Edward Carpenter wedded advocacy for gay rights and feminism generally to an indictment of imperialism from which Gandhi had learned so much. For Carpenter, what would ethically liberate us was not "any asceticism or inhospitality"[103] but a sexual life unburdened by the patriarchal gender binary. There can be no doubt that Gandhi's moral brilliance in part arose from the ways in which he challenged the gender binary:

> His adoption of suffragette resistance strategies, his support for certain feminist objectives, and his own self-conscious move in his public and private life towards an androgynous identity, all suggest the connections between his central thesis of non-violence and a gender politics in which he resisted British imperialism by subverting its hypermasculinity and playing on its responses to the feminine.[104]

If so, Gandhi's deep attraction to Carpenter may have rested on a common resistance to the patriarchal gender binary, which Carpenter's life and work show justify gay rights as well.

Ashis Nandy has powerfully argued that a psychology of traumatic loss leading to identification with the stereotypes of the patriarchal gender binary – a psychology akin to that used in this book's argument – clarifies the power

---

[102] See Ruth Vanita and Saleem Kidwai, eds., *Same-Sex Love in India* (New Delhi: Macmillan, 2000).
[103] Carpenter, *Civilization*, p. 41.
[104] See Robert J. C. Young, *Postcolonialism*, p. 327.

of British colonialism both in Britain and in India.[105] Both Carpenter's and Gandhi's resistance to the gender binary and thus to British colonialism show us how a psychology of resistance breaks the hold of this psychology over us – both the colonizers and colonized.

What makes the defense of gay rights in *Naz Foundation* so remarkable is that it suggests how far India has come in its social revolution, including in its understanding of the resistance to patriarchy central to Gandhi's movement, and the crucial role its constitutionalism has played, consistent with its Founders, in making this possible. The patriarchal power of the caste system still remains powerful in India, and Ratna Kapur thus worries that *Naz Foundation* extends to gays only a limited toleration, leaving intact much else that oppresses them and others.[106] But, as V.S. Naipaul observes, "the idea of freedom has gone everywhere in India . . . India was now a country of a million little mutinies."[107] The caste system, rooted in patriarchy, is loosening its hold on the psyches of Indian men and women. The constitutional recognition and vindication of gay rights in India, rooted in the resistance to patriarchy arising from the free love of equals, shows how far this development has come in India as free men and women through the love of equals release themselves and their cultures from the imperial demands of patriarchy.

---

[105] See Ashis Nandy, *The Intimate Enemy: Loss and Recovery of Self under Colonialism* (Oxford: Oxford University Press, 1983).

[106] See Ratna Kapur, "De-radicalising the Rights Claims of Sexual Subalterns though 'Tolerance,'" in *Queer Theory: Law, Culture, Empire*, edited by Robert Leckey and Kim Brooks, (New York: Routledge, 2010), pp. 37–52.

[107] V. S. Naipaul, *India: A Million Mutinies Now* (New York: Vintage, 2011; originally published, 1990), p. 517.

6

Gay Rights as Universal Human Rights

My argument is about an ethical discovery, what I call gay rights, which in turn led to new and increasingly resonant arguments about the legal recognition of such rights, often through forms of constitutional argument. There have, of course, been other ethical discoveries in our human history: democracy was one such discovery, as were human rights, the intrinsic wrongness of slavery, and the wrongness of the subjection of women. I regard these as ethical discoveries because, for long periods of human history, we lived without them, indeed regarded some of them (for example, slavery and the subjection of women) as the nature of things. Once discovered, these ethical discoveries transformed the human world, imposing ethical responsibilities and extending freedoms in ways that were once unthinkable but now are the measure of ethical seriousness and integrity.

Homosexuality has, of course, been around a long time, probably throughout our history and prehistory as a species; its presence throughout the animal and human world suggests as much.[1] I take it that sexual attraction, inclination, and desire, as well as deep-rooted emotional connection, whatever its objects, are general human properties. But the ways in which we understand and respond to them, and in turn reason normatively in relation to them, is likely to differ radically depending on the society and time period in which we live.[2] Carol Gilligan and I have argued that one of the most important factors in human history shaping our normative understanding of sexuality and gender has been patriarchy extending over time (from the agricultural

---

[1] See Clellan S. Ford and Frank A. Beach, *Patterns of Sexual Behavior* (New York: Harper & Row, 1951).
[2] On the malign consequences of failing to take seriously the different views of homosexuality in different historical periods, see William N. Eskridge, Jr., "Hardwick and Historiography," *U. Ill. L. Rev.* 199 (1999): 631.

revolution) and cultures, and has thus sometimes been naturalized as in the nature of things (see Chapter 1). The values and institutions of democracy are, however, in tension with patriarchy, and resistance to patriarchy is, we argued, rooted in our human natures and based on defensible ethical values of equal dignity and human rights. Thus, patriarchy is a cultural institution that we may and should criticize and change. Our study of resistance over time has, in turn, led us to identify the powerful psychological role in resistance of breaking the patriarchal Love Laws. If homosexuality is ancient, the right to gay love is quite recent. What I have tried to show in this book, using the perspective of resistance to patriarchy, is how it was discovered and given effect in human lives, and then I traced various stages in which it came to fuller recognition. I want here to reflect on my argument, drawing some conclusions from it – in particular, why I believe gay rights are universal human rights – as universal as basic human rights such as the right to conscience.

It was in the wake of World War II that human rights came to enjoy the normative status they are now accorded both nationally and internationally, reflected in the Universal Declaration of Human Rights, in whose design Eleanor Roosevelt played a central role.[3] In reflecting on the Universal Declaration, Mrs. Roosevelt wrote in 1958:

> Where, after all, do universal human rights begin? In small places, close to home – so close and so small that they cannot be seen on any map of the world. Yet they *are* the world of the individual person: the neighborhood he lives in; the school or college he attends; the factory; farm or office where he works. Such are the places where every man, woman, and child seeks equal justice, equal opportunity, equal dignity without discrimination. Unless these rights have meaning there, they have little meaning anywhere. Without concerted citizen action to uphold them close to home, we shall look in vain for progress in the larger world.[4]

Gay rights, consistent with Mrs. Roosevelt's brilliant analysis, indeed arise "[i]n small places, close to home," and indeed "so close and so small they indeed cannot be seen on any map of the world." Gay rights have certainly not been "seen on any map of the world," yet homosexual feeling is a deep feature of human sexuality, an enduring propensity of our human natures, and intimately personal. What her analysis suggests, consistent with her feminism,[5] is that our psyches have been so burdened by the patriarchal

---

[3] See Mary Ann Glendon, *A World Made New: Eleanor Roosevelt and the Universal Declaration of Human Rights* (New York: Random House, 2001).
[4] Eleanor Roosevelt, "In Your Hands," available at http://www.udhr.org/history/inyour.htm.
[5] On this point, see Mary Ann Glendon, *A World Made New*, pp. 90–2.

gender binary that dismisses homosexuality as unmasculine or unfeminine that we are disassociated from our most intimate moral experience of ourselves as persons. We see the issue as not a matter of public concern – trivially feminine, and thus small, too intimately private, perhaps unspeakable. What is at stake here is, however, of central ethical importance, for the patriarchal gender binary here, as elsewhere, both falsifies and denies the root of ethics in our moral personalities, the moral experience that Mrs. Roosevelt calls "equal justice, equal opportunity, equal dignity without discrimination." Our moral recovery, our ethical rebirth, here as elsewhere, arises from an experience of freedom, rooted in the dignity of each and every moral person, that resists the force that the gender binary has traditionally held over both our private and public lives. It is for this reason that feminism, understood in the way Carol Gilligan and I have come to understand it – as the freeing of ethical voice from the traumatic silencing of voice central to patriarchy – is the most important movement of democratic liberation of modernity. Such resistance requires what Mrs. Roosevelt called "citizen action" as it is only through relationship, as in the loves and friendships of the Bloomsbury Group, that we find the resonance we need to strengthen and sustain our resisting ethical voices.

I have made my argument in a certain context but one thematically consistent with Mrs. Roosevelt's analysis: the general tension between democracy and patriarchy (Chapter 1) and the particular form of that tension in the Roman Republic and Empire and tension between British constitutional democracy and the British Empire (Chapter 2). Gay rights arose in the moral experience of the men and women, American and British, who struggled to resolve the tension between democracy and patriarchy by challenging the role the gender binary played in the enforcement of patriarchy both in their love lives and in their lives as democratic citizens. The key to what was new in their moral experience, and thus to their ethical discovery, was sexual love that defied what I have called the patriarchal Love Laws, the laws that tell us who and how and how much we may love. It was through such love that they came in their lives and works to the three components of gay rights: nonreproductive sex between equals as a human and ethical good, relationships that arise from and sustain such love, and resistance to patriarchal demands both in intimate life and public life. It was the sexual love of equals across the patriarchally imposed barriers of religion, ethnicity, race, and gender that released their moral imaginations from the hierarchical gender binaries that had long confined our sense of what ethics was. Through such love and the broader and deeper moral experience it made possible, they came to question as well the patriarchal grounds of imperialism (Chapter 3).

It is an important feature of my argument that gay rights first arose in and from the experience of the sexual love of equals, which was in turn made possible by resistance to the patriarchally imposed gender binary both in love and in politics. <u>What united these men and women was their common feminist resistance to the ways in which patriarchy divided men and women from their common humanity</u>. It was the discovery that questioning the force of the gender binary in both personal life and politics led to a deeper understanding of our common humanity that leads to the claim of gays rights as universal human rights, as I now hope to show.

The ethical discovery of gay rights became central to the lived experience, as friends and lovers, of the resistance group studied in Chapter 3, and certainly shaped their work both as writers and artists, as they questioned the force the gender binary had in British imperial politics (Lytton Strachey), and explored brilliantly the connections between the traumatic force of patriarchy both in disrupting love and in rationalizing violence, including the violence of World War I and the fascist violence of Nazi Germany (Virginia Woolf). None of them, however, followed Edward Carpenter in living and writing publicly as a gay person, which imposed on them all a code of reticence about what was, in fact, central to their lives and works. Even after the Wolfenden Report and the 1967 decriminalization in England and Wales, the code of reticence continued in Britain. The reason, as I have suggested, why the later American gay rights movement had the impact in Britain and elsewhere that it had is because it was sponsored by the much more expansive conception of free speech that the Supreme Court developed after World War II in response to the ethical voices of the resistance movements that were to transform America both politically and constitutionally. Paradoxically, through the legal recognition of the claims made on behalf of gays and lesbians was more advanced in Britain and in Europe, it was the distinctively American law of free speech that made possible and credible the increasingly authentic American gay ethical voice, bridging the gap between private and public life as increasing numbers of American gays and lesbians from the 1970s onward abandoned the closet, finding in themselves the ethical responsibilities of ethical voice about the dignity of gay sexual love and resisting the homophobic practices and laws that had oppressed them for so long. It was this empowering of gay resisting ethical voice that moved protest beyond decriminalization to discrimination on grounds of sexual orientation and, finally, to recognition of same-sex partnerships and even marriage.

<u>I connect the rise of gay rights in Britain to the fall of the Empire, because its resistance, as I have shown, questioned the role patriarchal imperial masculinity had played in rationalizing the British Empire</u>. As the Empire fell

after World War II, the ethical voice of resistance to a patriarchal ethics that had not only criminalized homosexuality, but abortion and contraception, was more broadly shared in Britain, and led to the legal reforms in Britain we have studied, including abolition of the death penalty and liberalization of the divorce laws. A similar anti-patriarchal argument was sponsored as well by the American resistance movements, and explains the growing force and ultimate success of the anti-war movement over the Vietnam War as well as the Supreme Court's elaboration and protection of the constitutional right to privacy, decriminalizing contraception, abortion, and gay/lesbian sexuality (Chapter 4).

It is fair to say that the questioning of imperialism is now more politically powerful in Britain than the United States. The difference no doubt reflects in part the shadow cast by the fall of the British Empire and the rise of American power after World War II. But, many Americans, even in periods like the Spanish-American War (the Gilded Age of American greed and virulent racism) when European models of empire were still unquestioned in Europe and increasingly quite popular in the United States, also resisted such impulses, and most Americans came to regret them.[6] If such resistance is stronger in the United States today, it is because of the resistance movements that ultimately discredited the imperialistic politics that led to the Vietnam War, and that resistance is linked, as I have argued, to the rise of and increasing importance to Americans of gay rights. On the other hand, the continuing power of American patriarchy is shown by the way in which, as I have shown, American politics is polarized around social issues (including gay rights) and imperialism in a way British politics is not. President George W. Bush was thus politically successful in linking his attack on gay marriage (calling for a constitutional amendment to forbid it) to the unjustly aggressive war on Iraq. The underlying issue, as I have suggested, is a sense of American patriarchy under threat, which leads to the reactionary politics conservative Republicans have so skillfully fomented and used to serve their ends. So, if my thesis is correct, the American fundamentalist attack on gay rights should worry liberals not only because it is wrong on the merits but because it reinforces imperialistic impulses in our politics which, in light of American economic and military power, could be catastrophic.

If gay rights had emerged as an important constitutional issue in ex-colonies of Britain, it is not, I have suggested, because the officials of the British Empire were concerned with developing democratic institutions in the nations they

---

[6] On this point, see Gregg Jones, *Honor in the Dust: Theodore Roosevelt, War in the Philippines, and the Rise and Fall of America's Imperial Dream* (New York: New American Library, 2012).

colonized but did not themselves settle (Australia and New Zealand). They were not. Rather, I have examined three ex-colonies in which gay rights has importantly been constitutionally protected – Canada, South Africa, and India (Chapter 5). In each case, it has been the liberal political leadership each nation enjoyed that led to the role constitutionalism has played in protecting gay rights, sometimes quite explicitly (South Africa). There is also something else: the role democratic constitutionalism, grounded in the protection of basic human rights, plays in forging a consciousness of their rights in a democratic people, even against the enormous odds of a cultural tradition as strong as the caste system in India, grounded in the patriarchally enforced Love Laws. Once a constitutional democracy endorses, even as a long-term aim of its social revolution, the clearing of spaces where the caste hierarchies do not operate or operate with much less force, the human psyche, in which the need for loving and being loved as an equal is so central, opens its heart and mind to loving across the caste barriers that appear increasingly alien and inhuman. It is in such circumstances that gay love arises, an expression of one aspect of the universal needs of the human heart.

It is important to keep firmly in mind, in this connection, the extraordinary religious force of the repression of homosexuality in Western Christendom, vigorously enforced by the state through the death penalty, including burning at the stake. What made this so extraordinary and so psychologically deadly for homosexuals was that it was a crime so terrible it could not even be spoken. The murder of voice is the murder of the psyche, and the dominant religious tradition of the West has, in my judgment, not yet been properly accountable for the ethical enormity it thus inflicted on homosexuals. Only since the moral enormity of the Holocaust and its roots in Christian anti-Semitism have we begun to take seriously and question the role of patriarchal religion in our lives. In Britain, the Anglican Church, unlike the Catholic Church in Rome, has questioned as well the unjust role patriarchal religion played in the persecution of homosexuals as well, as we can see in the significant role it played in the Wolfenden Report and in opening the Anglican priesthood to women and homosexuals. It is a symptom of how uncritically powerful patriarchy remains in the United States that, on the issue of homosexuality, some Anglican communities would rather align themselves with homophobic African churches rather than the mother church of Great Britain.

I early set the agenda in this book in light of the worry the British gay novelist Alan Hollinghurst explores in his novel, The Stranger's Child, how – in light of massive censorship and internalized inhibition – to recover a memory that irrational prejudice, sometimes internalized, fractures, distorts, and even denies. Such denial has two dimensions.

First, there is the distortion of memory that he studies in Britain. The novel depicts a sexually active gay man and poet, who fights and dies in World War I. After his death, he is not, in view of all the homophobic pressures to make him someone he was not, remembered as he was, leading to denial, distortion, and outright misrepresentation. This is the kind of distortion of memory that has, I believe, dominated discussion of the group of artists and intellectuals whom I study in depth in Chapter 3. The facts now are certainly quite well known, but it is striking that, when Holroyd's first 1971 edition of his biography of Lytton Strachey was circulated to members of Bloomsbury still alive, some of them, like Leonard Woolf, said that homosexuality was simply "irrelevant" to relations with those of his friends who were having gay sex, which, Holroyd observes, "underrated its significance in releasing Strachey from lonely confinement to his own body."[7] Many of them or most (Duncan Grant being on exception) were keen to be publicly heterosexual (at least by the 1960s), and all resented or were embarrassed at what they saw as private matters being made public.[8] None of this is surprising in view of what we know of the tenor of public debate about homosexuality at the time of the 1967 decriminalization, including, as we have seen, the debates in Parliament, avoiding the question of and thus acquiescing in its immorality. Even Noel Annan's sympathetic account of the role of homosexuality in the Bloomsbury Group, "the cult of homosexuality,"[9] fails to take seriously the connections between their resistance to the Love Laws and their resistance to British imperialism, which is at the heart of my interpretation. What I take quite seriously, in a way others do not, is the pivotal, self-conscious importance of resistance to patriarchy in their lives and works, a tradition of ethical resistance that should be honored, not hidden or distorted or trivialized, because homosexuality was, in fact, so central to their relationships to one another.

Second, recovering the history of gay resistance in the spirit of this book has an importance beyond Britain – namely, in the lives of gay, lesbian, bisexual, and transgendered people. Gay people are still often born into families in which homosexuality cannot be discussed, and they thus cannot, as homosexuals, have any sense of having a common history on which they may draw. In such circumstances, the mind is divided into compartments, and some of one's deepest emotions are locked away, refused access to any other compartment. At the center of things, despite a conviviality mistaken for happiness, one is deeply alone because one fears to share the deepest parts of one's self

---

[7] Holroyd, *Lytton Strachey: The New Biography*, at XXXI.
[8] See ibid., at XXII–XXX.
[9] See Noel Annan, *Our Age*, pp. 98–124.

with family members one loves; one thus learns mistrust in matters of friendship and love. Such denial falsifies honest memory and one's human sense of a reliable inner truth, the basis of a secure and self-respecting sense of self, connected to friends and lovers. This book is an effort to recover or cultivate a memory that may be truer to experience and more broadly shared – namely, an experience drawn from the history of gay resistance, one in which we may find ourselves in, and advance responsibly, an honorable tradition, based on an ethical discovery important to all of us as humans. What riveted and amazed me in the resistance group I studied in my research for this book was how close their experience was to mine, connecting impulses in both feminism and gay rights that have made love possible and enduring in my own life. It should be obvious that the ire of patriarchal control of women would be aroused by their resistance to compulsory heterosexuality and the role it played in arranged marriage, but it may be less obvious why patriarchy would be aroused by male homosexuality as such, which thrived in ancient Greece and Rome, both highly patriarchal cultures. Although some forms of Greek homosexuality (for example, the resistance of the lovers, Harmodios and Aristogeiton; see the Introduction and Chapter 1) prefigure modern gay rights, other aspects of ancient patriarchy expressed a sexist contempt for the passive role in gay sex and thus was associated, as in Rome, with slave boys and, in Greece, with boys and often slaves.[10] Modern gay rights, in contrast, contests these stereotypes, and its advocates usually condemn, often vehemently, all forms of nonconsensual sex and especially sex with underage boys (pedophilia). Rather, modern forms of male homosexuality often aspire to sometimes long-term personal relationships between adult men that, when you add the adopted or natural children many contemporary gay and lesbian couples involve, are increasingly indistinguishable from marriage. Moreover, I think no gay man, and I speak from personal experience here, who has had the good fortune and experience of grace, as I have, to find enduring love for some forty years with another man, his equal in every way, has not struggled deeply (and I mean deeply) against the patriarchal assumptions that divide men competitively from one another and, if unquestioned, can make sexual love, including gay love, so darkly problematic.[11] Patriarchy is, I believe, hostile to love, and indeed thrives

---

[10] See Kenneth J. Dover, *Greek Homosexuality* (London: Duckworth, 1978); Craig A. Williams, *Roman Homosexuality*, 2nd ed. (New York: Oxford University Press, 2010).

[11] For a view of gay sexuality along these lines, see Leo Bersani, *Homos* (Cambridge, MA: Harvard University Press, 1995); Leo Bersani, *Is the Rectum a Grave? And Other Essays* (Chicago: University of Chicago Press, 2010); Leo Bersani, *The Freudian Body: Psychoanalysis and Art* (New York: Columbia University Press, 1986). For a more hopeful view, see Leo Bersani and Adam Phillips, *Intimacies* (Chicago: University of Chicago Press, 2008).

on the degree to which cultures (including patriarchal religions) endorse this hostility.[12]

What the ethical discovery comes to is an aspect of our humanity that had been not even acknowledged, let alone explored – that gays and lesbians, in loving one another as equals, resist the patriarchal Love Laws that have divided us from a sense of our common humanity, including the universal needs of the human heart. It is for this reason that I regard gay rights as universal human rights and believe that the persecution of homosexuals anywhere affronts and should affront the human conscience of people everywhere. To the extent a worldwide human rights culture has emerged and flourished since World War II,[13] gay rights should be at the cutting edge of its claims and demands.

The very idea of universal human rights arose from the confrontation of the allies after World War II with an aggressive German fascism based on the irrational, genocidal hatred of the Jews. Anyone familiar with German fascism knows of its glorification of violence against scapegoats, in particular, violence against its ostensible enemies, even when innocent and defenseless.[14] I have already discussed a form of this violence in Robert Mugabe's use of political homophobia to support a black nationalism that is as mindless as the ethnic nationalism of Hitler's Germany (Chapter 5). We see it more recently in the political homophobia in Uganda and elsewhere, in which violence against homosexuals is rampant, often fomented by newspapers and politicians, and urged on by fundamentalist religious groups from the United States.[15] What is extraordinary about these developments is that what sustains the homophobia is mindless violence, which illustrates vividly how powerful reactionary patriarchy remains in some parts of the world. It is against this background that I understand why both Prime Minister David Cameron of Great Britain and Secretary of State Hillary Clinton of the United States have invoked the protection of universal human rights as grounds for questioning and censuring such developments.[16] They are, I believe, correct in understanding the normative dimensions appropriate to criticism of this phenomenon.

---

[12] On this point, Nicholas C. Bamforth and David A. J. Richards, *Patriarchal Religion, Sexuality and Gender: A Critique of New Natural Law* (Cambridge: Cambridge University Press, 2008).

[13] See Lawrence M. Friedman, *The Human Rights Culture: A Study in History and Context* (New Orleans, LA: Quid Pro Books, 2011).

[14] For a brilliant study, see Robert O. Paxton, *The Anatomy of Fascism*.

[15] See Alexis Okeowo, "Out in Africa: A gay rights struggle with deadly stakes," *The New Yorker*, December 24&31, 2012, pp. 64–70; Josh Kron, "Resentment toward the West Bolsters Uganda's New Anti-Gay Bill," *New York Times*, Wednesday, February 29, 2012, p. A4.

[16] See ibid.

We know that courageous gay rights activists, like Frank Mugisha in Uganda, have learned that their credibility among Ugandans "means keeping a distance from well-meaning American or European politicians and human-rights groups,"[17] but we also know that such external pressures have importantly had an impact in holding homophobic Ugandan politicians more accountable to the conscience of humankind that they would otherwise be.[18] My argument shows that the sense of a dilemma faced by Munisha and other gay activists in Uganda, Zimbabwe, and elsewhere rests on a false choice between making claims to one's rights, as a gay person, in Uganda, and universal human rights, which are not in tension but are morally complementary. The assumption in Uganda and elsewhere that gay rights is a form of unjust Western imperialism is not only without rational basis, but itself uncritically reflects the imperial force of Western patriarchal religion. Once again, we see the distortion of memory about gay rights through which patriarchal psychology covers over and denies the truth of a feminist movement of ethical empowerment, only here not the memory of Britons or gays about their history but of formerly colonized peoples, who enforce on their own people an imperialism of unjust patriarchal demands that they believe they are contesting. The real choice is not between gay rights and anti-imperialism, but between a democracy founded on human rights and a fascist ethnic nationalism. What my study of the Bloomsbury Group shows us is that gay rights arise from the universal claims of the human heart, arising in the resistance of small minorities to a patriarchal imperialism that corrupts both public and private life. What we saw in Lytton Strachey in Britain in the 1920s, we see in Frank Munisha in Uganda today. The same resistance remains as well founded today across time and culture, and justifies as well a humane understanding of universal human rights that includes gay rights. All peoples should justly be held accountable to these demands. The post-World War II international rebirth of and rededication to universal human rights, as a response to the fascist nightmare of ethnic nationalism, requires of us today no less.

The idea of human rights arises from the political theory of liberalism, according to each and every person subject to political power equal respect for those aspects of human life through which we are normative agents, exercising the moral powers of rationality and reasonableness.[19] The argument for gay

---

[17] Alexis Okeowo, "Out in Africa: A gay rights struggle with dead stakes," *The New Yorker*, December 24&31, 2012, pp. 64–70, at p. 70.
[18] See, for an illuminating recent treatment of this issue, Alexis Okeowo, "Out in Africa: A gay rights struggle with dead stakes," *The New Yorker*, December 24&31, 2012, pp. 64–70.
[19] See David A. J. Richards, *A Theory of Reasons for Action* (Oxford: Clarendon Press, 1971); David A. J. Richards, *Toleration and the Constitution* (New York: Oxford University Press, 1986); James Griffin, *On Human Rights* (Oxford: Oxford University Press, 2008).

rights as universal human rights arises from the right to intimate life that, like the other liberal rights to conscience and free speech, expresses equal respect for a human dignity grounded in the needs of moral personality, including the needs of the human heart to love and be loved.[20] The idea that human rights may be limited to conscience and speech, but not extend to intimate life, itself reflects a gendered dualism of mind versus body, thought versus emotion, the gender binary that enforces patriarchy. The ethical and political importance of a feminism, like that Carol Gilligan and I have advocated,[21] is that it challenges the role that the gender binary played here and elsewhere and justifies the ethically sounder, more expansive conception of human rights (including the right to an intimate life) that has now been adopted in Britain, Europe, the United States, and many other nations.[22] It is this basic and universal human right, for example, that, having already been protected by the U.S. Supreme Court in the case of contraception and abortion services, was extended, as a matter of principle, to gays and lesbians in *Lawrence v. Texas*.[23]

What makes gay rights so important as a human rights movement, not only to gays and lesbians and bisexuals and transgendered persons but to everyone, is the way in which gay rights arises from and expresses yet another form of invaluable feminist resistance to the patriarchal gender binary. The unjust political enforcement of that binary afflicts everyone, men and women, straight and gay. It has historically afflicted gay men and lesbians in a particularly oppressive way because the forms of sexual and affectional life natural to them were condemned by the patriarchal gender binary, as ways of life and of being inconsistent with being a man or a woman – as patriarchy defined being a man or a woman. It is for this reason that gay rights arises from resistance to the gender binary, a resistance David Halperin has recently shown to be central to what he calls the gay culture of camp.[24] Halperin argues that this culture brings to bear its own criticism of the way the gender binary has afflicted them as gay men by the way it sees their own plight, as men, in the comparable plight of women, as depicted by Joan Crawford in a movie like *Mildred Pierce*. Halperin disavows any interest in psychology, but his account of the propensity to camp among gay men is related to the traumatic breaks, including breaks with their mothers, in intimate life that homophobia, as a form of patriarchy,

---

[20] See David A. J. Richards, *Women, Gays, and the Constitution*.
[21] Carol Gilligan and David A.J. Richards, *The Deepening Darkness*.
[22] On the connection between human rights and the enlarged scope of moral empathy, see Lynn Hunt, *Inventing Human Rights: A History* (New York: W.W. Norton, 2007).
[23] *Lawrence v. Texas*, 539 U.S. 558 (2003).
[24] See David M. Halperin, *How to Be Gay* (Cambridge, MA: Belknap Press of Harvard University Press, 2012).

imposes on them.[25] Camp resists the trauma by exposing and criticizing the role a patriarchal hierarchy of gender polarization has played in inflicting such painful separations on intimate relationships.[26] It calls for more honest acknowledgment of the ethically creative role relationships with women plays in gay life and resistance. Halperin thus implies a psychology of resistance – one quite similar to that advocated in this book, one that connects more explicitly than Halperin such resistance to a feminism that challenges the gender binary, whether its takes the form of patriarchal masculinity or femininity. Gay culture, whether Halperin's camp or the resistance of the Bloomsbury Group, thus understood, is an important and invaluable part of an emerging critical culture that challenges the otherwise invisible injuries patriarchy unjustly imposes on us all.

What this book's study of the resistance of the Bloomsbury Group shows is that such resistance to the patriarchal gender binary, central to the works of both Lytton Strachey and Virginia Woolf, makes possible, indeed nourishes, the love of equals. It is the knowledge arising from love and real relationship based on equality that, in turn, psychologically makes possible their remarkable ethical sensitivity to and rejection of the false relationships central to the antidemocratic hierarchies of imperialist masculinity and femininity. Relationship between and among equals becomes the ethical polestar of all our relationships, both in private and public life, calling for democracy in place of patriarchal hierarchy. This is what Leonard Woolf came to see about his role as a civil servant of British imperialism in Ceylon, and he came to see and write of it, both in his novel and his nonfiction, through the experience of loving relationship to Virginia, as she came to her comparable understanding in her astonishing novels and nonfiction through her love of him. Such real, loving relationships – when achieved through resistance to the patriarchal Love Laws that rest on lies and violence enforced by the dehumanizing gender stereotypes that polarize and divide – expose such lies and violence for what they are through the experience of love and connection across the barriers that patriarchy enforces – the barriers of religion, race, ethnicity, gender, and sexual orientation. Such resistance creatively enlarges and deepens our sense of what ethical relationships are and can and should be.

My argument in this book has been largely empirical and observational: a natural history of gay love, so to speak, showing in some detail how and why the argument for gay rights, as a human right, was implicit in the lives

---

[25] On this point, see ibid., at pp. 200, 207, 224, 289–90.
[26] In these points, see ibid., pp. 207, 317–19.

and works of the resistance group I have studied and how over time the argument came to have a larger public and political resonance. I have noted also how the argument has been embraced elsewhere, which suggests a common human experience and a common grounding in our human natures. It would be as preposterous to deny the relevance of such human experience to a democracy's understanding of the basic human rights worthy of constitutional protection as it would be to deny the relevance of experience and experiment, wherever it occurs, in any discipline, scientific or normative, conducted in the critical spirit of the inquiry for truth. U.S. Justice Antonin Scalia is as wrong as Robert Mugabe in thinking that American or Zimbabwean values must be walled off from the experience of other nations and peoples. Such insularity and chauvinism lead not to democracy but, in the end, to fascism.

What makes this difficult to see is the continuing power of patriarchy both at home and abroad. The tension between the enterprise of human rights and constitutional democracy is not seen, as it should be, in continuing tension and contradiction with our uncritically followed patriarchal heritage (for example, in still highly patriarchal religions[27]). If I am right that patriarchy has uncritically divided us (in terms of religion, race, ethnicity, and gender) from one another, it has left its marks in our ethics as well. Gay rights is the ethical discovery it is because it questions the authority of an ethics constructed by patriarchal hierarchy and sustained by violence, dehumanization, and repression of voice. It is such violence, rooted in fascism not democracy, that actuates the homophobic repression that corrupt governments, allied with patriarchal religion, fomented in the policies of George W. Bush in the United States and that antidemocratic leaders foment in Zimbabwe, Uganda, Singapore, and elsewhere. Resistance to such violence is and should be a requirement of the universal human rights that, after the nightmare of World War II, are the heritage of humankind, and gay rights are and should be among them. Homophobia is no more our natural human state than anti-Semitism, racism, or sexism; all are the products of political unreason and the unjust repressive violence that sustains such unreason. It is only under conditions of freedom from such hierarchy and violence – the ethical domain of freedom and equality – that a democratic ethics hears and gives a democratic resonance to the voice of gay rights. Its voice speaks from and to what makes us human: the universal needs of the human heart to love and be loved as an equal and to know and be known as the person we are.

---

[27] On this point, see Nicholas Bamforth and David A. J. Richards, *Patriarchal Religion, Sexuality, and Gender: A Critique of New Natural Law*.

Bibliography

Acemoglu, Daron, and James A. Robinson, *Why Nations Fail: The Origins of Power, Prosperity, and Poverty* (New York: Crown Business, 2012).
Ackerley, J.R., *Hindoo Holiday* (New York: New York Review Books, 2000; originally published, 1932).
Adam, Barry D., *The Rise of a Gay and Lesbian Movement*, rev. ed. (Farmington Hills, MI: Twayne, 1995).
Aldrich, Robert, *Colonialism and Homosexuality* (London: Routledge, 2003).
Allen, Charles, *The Buddha and the Sahibs* (London: John Murray, 2003).
Allen, Charles, *Kipling Sahib: India and the Making of Rudyard Kipling* (London: Abacus, 2009).
Altemeyer, Bob, *Right-Wing Authoritarianism Right-Wing Authoritarianism* (Winnipeg, Canada: University of Manitoba Press, 1981).
Altemeyer, Bob, *The Authoritarian Specter* (Cambridge, MA: Harvard University Press, 1996).
Altman, Dennis, *Homosexuality: Oppression and Liberation* (New York: New York University Press, 1993; first published, 1971).
Anderson, Perry, "Gandhi Centre Stage," *London Review of Books* **34**, no. 13 (July 5 2012): pp. 3–11.
Anderson, Perry, "Why Partition?" *London Review of Books* **34**, no. 14 (July 19 2012): pp. 11–19.
Annan, Noel, *Leslie Stephen: The Godless Victorian* (Chicago: University of Chicago Press, 1984).
Annan, Noel, *Our Age: English Intellectuals Between the World Wars – A Group Portrait* (New York: Random House, 1990).
AP, "Gay Man's 3-Year Sentence Upheld by Cameroon Court," *The New York Times*, Tuesday, December 18, 2012, at p. A15.
Appian, *The Civil Wars*, translated by John Carter (London: Penguin, 1996).
Arendt, Hannah, *The Life of the Mind*, one-volume edition (New York: Harcourt Brace Jovanovich, 1978).
Arendt, Hannah, *The Origins of Totalitarianism* (New York: Harcourt Brace Jovanovich, 1978).
Arnold, David, "Indo-European," *The Times Literary Supplement*, March 9, 2012, no. 5684, p. 9.

Astin, A. E., F. W. Walbank, M. W. Frederiksen, R. M. Ogilvie, *The Cambridge Ancient History*, 2nd ed., Vol. VIII. *Rome and the Mediterranean to 133 B.C.E.* (Cambridge: Cambridge University Press, 1989).

Backhouse, Roger F., and Bradley W. Bateman, *Capitalist Revolutionary John Maynard Keynes* (Cambridge, MA: Harvard University Press, 2011).

Austin, Granville, *The Indian Constitution: Cornerstone of a Nation* (Oxford: Oxford University Press, 2011; originally published, 1966).

Austin, Granville, *Working a Democratic Constitution: A History of the Indian Experience* (Oxford: Oxford University Press, 1999).

Bagnall, Roger S., *Egypt in Late Antiquity* (Princeton, NJ: Princeton University Press, 1993).

Bailey, Derrick Sherwin, *Homosexuality and the Western Christian Tradition* (Hamden, CT: Archon Books, 1975; originally published, 1955).

Baird, Robert M., and Stuart E. Rosenbaum, eds., *Morality and Law* (Buffalo, NY: Prometheus Books, 1988).

Bamforth, Nicholas, Maleiha Malik, and Colm O'Cinneide, *Discrimination Law: Theory and Context* (London: Sweet & Maxwell, 2008).

Bamforth, Nicholas C., and David A. J. Richards, *Patriarchal Religion, Sexuality, and Gender: A Critique of New Natural Law* (Cambridge: Cambridge University Press, 2008).

Banville, John, "Rebel, Hero, Martyr," in *New York Review of Books* **LIX**, no. 16 (October 25, 2012): pp. 35–7.

Barrett, Anthony A., *Agrippina: Sex, Power and Politics in the Early Empire* (New Haven, CT: Yale University Press, 1996).

Barrett, Anthony A., *Livia: First Lady of Imperial Rome* (New Haven, CT: Yale University Press, 2002).

Barton, Carlin A., *Rome Honor: The Fire in the Bones* (Berkeley: University of California Press, 2001).

Barton, Carlin A., *The Sorrows of the Ancient Romans: The Gladiator and the Monster* (Princeton, NJ: Princeton University Press, 1993).

Baum, Dan, *Smoke and Mirrors: The War on Drugs and the Politics of Failure* (Boston: Little, Brown & Company, 1997).

Bauman, Richard A., *Women and Politics in Ancient Rome* (London: Routledge, 1992).

Beard, Mary, and John North, eds., *Pagan Priests: Religion and Power in the Ancient World* (Ithaca, NY: Cornell University Press, 1990).

Beard, Mary, John North, and Simon Price, *Religions of Rome*, Vol. 1-A. *History* (Cambridge: Cambridge University Press, 2004).

Beard, Mary, John North, and Simon Price, *Religions of Rome*, Vol. 2. *A Sourcebook* (Cambridge: Cambridge University Press, 2005).

Bearak, Barr, "Some-Sex Couple Stir Fears in Malawi of a 'Gay Agenda' Promoted by the West," *The New York Times*, February 14, 2010, p. 6.

Beebe, Beatrice, and Frank Lachmann, *Infant Research and Adult Treatment: Co-Constructing Interactions* (Hillsdale, NJ: The Analytic Press, 2002).

Bersani, Leo, *Homos* (Cambridge, MA: Harvard University Press, 1995).

Bersani, Leo, and Adam Phillips, *Intimacies* (Chicago: University of Chicago Press, 2008).

Bersani, Leo, *Is the Rectum a Grave? And Other Essays* (Chicago: University of Chicago Press, 2010).
Bersani, Leo, *The Freudian Body: Psychoanalysis and Art* (New York: Columbia University Press, 1986).
Berube, Allan, *Coming Out under Fire: The History of Gay Men and Women in World War Two* (New York: Free Press, 1990).
Bloom, Paul, "The Moral Life of Babies: Can Infants and Toddlers Really Tell Right From Wrong," *The New York Times Magazine*, May 9, 2010, pp. 44–9, 56, 62–3, 65.
Boehm, Christopher, *Hierarchy in the Forest: The Evolution of Egalitarian Behavior* (Cambridge, MA: Harvard University Press, 2011).
Boehm, Christopher, *Moral Origins: The Evolution of Virtue, Altruism, and Shame* (New York: Basic Books, 2012).
Boehmer, Elleke, *Empire, the National, and the Postcolonial 1890–1920: Resistance in Interaction* (Oxford: Oxford University Press, 2002).
Bosworth, R. J. B., *Mussolini* (London: Hodder Arnold, 2002).
Bourne, H. R. Fox, *The Life of John Locke*, Volume I (New York: Harper & Brothers, 1876).
Bowles, Samuel, and Herbert Gintis, *A Cooperative Species: Human Reciprocity and Its Evolution* (Princeton, NJ: Princeton University Press, 2011).
Bowman, Alan K., Edward Champlin, and Andrew Lintott, *The Cambridge Ancient History*, 2nd ed., Vol. X. *The Augustan Empire, 43 B.C.E.–A.D. 69* (Cambridge: Cambridge University Press, 1996).
Bowman, Alan K., Peter Garnsey, and Dominic Rathbone, *The Cambridge Ancient History*, Vol. XI. *The High Empire, A.D. 70–192* (Cambridge: Cambridge University Press, 2000).
Bowman, Alan K., Peter Garnsey, and Averil Cameron, *The Cambridge Ancient History*, 2nd ed., Vol. XII. *The Crisis of Empire, A.D. 193–337* (Cambridge: Cambridge University Press, 2005).
Boyarin, Danie, *A Radical Jew: Paul and the Politics of Identity* (Berkeley: University of California Press, 1994).
Boyarin, Daniel, *Carnal Israel: Reading Sex in Talmudic Culture* (Berkeley: University of California Press, 1993).
Branch, Taylor, *Parting the Waters: Martin Luther King and the Civil Rights Movement 1954–63* (London: Papermac, 1988).
Branch, Taylor, *Pillar of Fire: America in the King Years 1963–65* (New York: Simon & Schuster, 1998).
Brooks, David, "The Moral Naturalists," *The New York Times*, July 23, 2010, A23.
Bradley, F. H., *Ethical Studies*, edited by Ralph G. Ross (New York: The Liberal Arts Press, 1959; first published, 1876).
Bradley, James, *The Imperial Cruise: A Secret History of Empire and War* (New York: Little, Brown & Company, 2009).
Brendon, Piers, *The Decline and Fall of the British Empire 1781–1997* (London: Vintage, 2008).
Brown, Judith M., and Wm. Roger Louis, eds., *The Oxford History of the British Empire*, Vol. IV. *The Twentieth Century* (Oxford: Oxford University Press, 1999).
Brown v. Board of Education, 347 U.S. 483 (1954).

Burbank, Jane, and Frederick Cooper, *Empires in World History: Power and the Politics of Difference* (Princeton, NJ: Princeton University Press, 2010).
Burkert, Walter, *Ancient Mystery Cults* (Cambridge, MA: Harvard University Press, 1987).
Burleigh, Michael, *Sacred Causes: The Clash of Religion and Politics, from the Great War to the War on Terror* (New York: HarperCollins, 2007).
Burns, Jennifer, *Goddess of the Market: Ayn Rand and the American Right* (Oxford: Oxford University Press, 2009).
Buruma, Ian, *Behind the Mask: On Sexual Demons, Sacred Mothers, Transvestites, Gangster, and Other Japanese Cultural Heroes* (Toronto, Canada: New American Library, 1984).
Buruma, Ian, *The Wages of Guilt: Memories of War in Germany and Japan* (New York: Meridian, 1995).
Bush, M. L., ed., *Serfdom and Slavery: Studies in Legal Bondage* (London: Longman, 1999).
Caesar, Julius, *The Civil War*, translated by John Carter (Oxford: Oxford University Press, 1998).
Caesar, Julius, *The Conquest of Gaul*, translated by S.A. Handford (London: Penguin, 1982).
Cahn, Naomi, and June Carbone, *Red Families v. Blue Families: Legal Polarization and the Creation of Culture* (Oxford: Oxford University Press, 2010).
Calhoun, Cheshire, "Denatrualizing and Desexualizing Lesbian and Gay Identity," *Virginia Law Review* 79 (1993): 1859.
Calhoun, Cheshire, "Sexuality Injustice," *Notre Dame Journal of Law, Ethics, and Public Policy* 9, (1995): 241.
Cameron, Averil, and Peter Garnsey, *The Cambridge Ancient History*, Vol. XIII. *The Late Empire, A.D. 337–425* (Cambridge: Cambridge University Press, 1998).
Cameron, Edwin, "Sexual Orientation and the Constitution: A Test Case for Human Rights," *South African Law Journal* 110 (1993): 450.
Cameron, Edwin, *Witness to AIDS* (London: I.B. Tauris, 2007).
Cannon, Lou, *Governor Reagan: His Rise to Power* (New York: Public Affairs, 2003).
Canny, Nicholas, *The Oxford History of the British Empire*, Volume 1. *The Origins of Empire: British Overseas Enterprise to the Close of the Seventeenth Century* (Oxford: Oxford University Press, 2001.
Cantarella, Eva, *Pandora's Daughters: The Role and Status of Women in Greek and Roman Antiquity*, translated by Maureen B. Fant (Baltimore: The Johns Hopkins University Press, 1987).
Carey, Jonathan Sinclair, "D. S. Bailey and 'the Name Forbidden among Christians,'" *Anglican Theological Review* 70, no. 2 (1988): pp. 152–73.
Carpenter, Edward, *Civilization: Its Cause and Cure and Other Essays* (London: Swan Sonnenschein, 1906).
Carroll, James, *An American Requiem: God, My Father, and the War that Came between Us* (Boston: Houghton Mifflin Company, 2001).
Carroll, James, *Constantine's Sword: The Church and the Jews: A History* (Boston: Houghton Mifflin Company, 2001).
Carson, Clayborne, and Peter Holloran, eds., *A Knock at Midnight: Inspiration from the Great Sermons of Reverend Martin Luther King, Jr.* (New York: Warner Books, 2000).

Champlin, Edward, *Nero* (Cambridge, MA: Belknapp Press of Harvard University Press, 2003).
Chan, Stephen, *Robert Mugabe: A Life of Power and Violence* (Ann Arbor: University of Michigan Press, 2003).
Chan, Stephen, *Southern Africa: Old Treacheries and New Deceits* (New Haven, CT: Yale University Press, 2011).
Chapais, Bernard, *Primeval Kinship: How Pair-Bonding Gave Birth to Human Society* (Cambridge, MA: Harvard University Press, 2008).
Chappell, David L., *A Stone of Hope: Prophetic Religion and the Death of Jim Crow* (Chapel Hill: University of North Carolina Press, 2004).
Church of England Welfare Council, *The Problem of Homosexuality: An Interim Report by a Group of Anglican Clergy and Doctors*, produced by the by the Church Information Board (for private circulation, 1954).
Cicero, *Philippics*, translated by Walter C.A. Ker (Cambridge, MA: Harvard University Press, 2001).
Cohen, I. Bernard, ed., *Puritanism and the Rise of Modern Science: The Merton Thesis* (New Brunswick, NJ: Rutgers University Press, 1990).
Committee on Homosexual Offenses and Prostitution, *The Wolfenden Report: Report of the Committee on Homosexual Offenses and Prostitution* (New York: Stein and Day, 1963).
Conquest, Robert, *Stalin: Breaker of Nations* (New York: Penguin, 1991).
Conrad, Joseph, *Youth/Heart of Darkness/The End of the Tether* (London: Penguin, 1995).
Constitution of India, available at http//lawmin.nic.in/olwing/coi/coi-english/col-indexenglish.htm
Cooper, Davina, *Sexing the City: Lesbian and Gay Politics within the Activist State* (London: Rivers Oram Press, 1994).
Cornell, Drucilla, and Nyoko Muvangua, *Ubuntu and the Law: African Ideals and Postapartheid Jurisprudence* (New York: Fordham University Press, 2012).
Crook, J. A., Andrew Lintott, and Elizabeth Rawson, *The Cambridge Ancient History*, 2nd ed., Vol. IX. *The Last Age of the Roman Republic, 146–43 B.C.E.* (Cambridge: Cambridge University Press, 1994).
Cruz-Malave, Arnaldo, and Martin F. Manalansan IV, *Queer Globalizations: Citizenship and the Afterlife of Colonialism* (New York: New York University Press, 2002).
Curley, Edwin, *Behind the Geometrical Method: A Reading of Spinoza's Ethics* (Princeton, NJ: Princeton University Press, 1988).
Damasio, Antonio R., *Descartes' Error: Emotion, Reason, and the Human Brain* (New York: Avon Books, 1994).
Damasio, Antonio R., *Looking for Spinoza: Joy, Sorrow, and the Feeling Brain* (Orlando, FL: Harcourt, 2003).
Damasio, Antonio R., *The Feeling of What Happens: Body and Emotion in the Making of Consciousness* (New York: Harcourt Brace & Company, 1999).
Davenport-Hines, Richard, *An English Affair: Sex, Class and Power in the Age of Profumo* (London: Harper Press, 2013).
Davies, Norman, *Vanished Kingdoms: The Rise and Fall of States and Nations* (New York: Viking, 2011).
Dench, Emma, *Romulus' Asylum: Roman Identities from the Age of Alexander to the Age of Hadrian* (Oxford: Oxford University Press, 2005).

Deroux, Carl, ed., *Studies in Latin Literature and Roman History II* (Bruxelles: Latomus, 1980).
Devlin, Patrick, *The Enforcement of Moral* (London: Oxford University Press, 1965).
Devlin, Patrick, "Judges and Lawmakers," 39 *Mod. L. Rev.* 1 (1976).
Diamond, Larry, *The Spirit of Democracy: The Struggle fo Build Free Societies Throughout the World* (New York: Times Books, 2008).
Dio, Cassius, *The Roman History: The Reign of Augustus*, Ian Scott-Kilvert trans. (London: Penguin, 1987).
Dixon, Suzanne, *Reading Roman Women* (London: Duckworth, 2001).
Dixon, Suzanne, *The Roman Family* (Baltimore: The Johns Hopkins University Press, 1992).
Dixon, Suzanne, *The Roman Mother* (Norman: Oklahoma University Press, 1988).
Doi, Takeo, *The Anatomy of Dependence*, translated by John Bester (Tokyo: Kodansha International, 1973).
Donaldson, Ian, *The Rapes of Lucretia: A Myth and Its Transformations* (Oxford: Clarendon Press, 1982).
Donalson, Malcolm Drew, *The Cult of Isis in the Roman Empire* (Lewiston, NY: The Edwin Mellen Press, 2003).
Doniger, Wendy, *The Hindus: An Alternative History* (New York: Penguin, 2009).
Dowling, Linda, *Hellenism and Homosexuality in Victorian Oxford* (Ithaca, NY: Cornell University Press, 1994).
Dover, Kenneth J., *Greek Homosexuality* (London: Duckworth, 1978).
Dred Scott v. Sanford, 19 Howard 393 (1857).
Dudgeon v. United Kingdom (A/45)(1982) 4 E.H.R.R. 149, ECHR.
Dudgeon, Jeffrey, *Roger Casement: The Black Diaries* (Belfast, Northern Ireland: Belfast Press, 2002).
Dugger, Celia W. "Mugabe Ally Escalates Push to Control Church: Anglican Leaders Harassed and Threatened," *The New York Times*, Monday, May 30, 2011, A6.
Earl, Donald, *The Moral and Political Tradition of Rome* (Ithaca, NY: Cornell University Press, 1967).
Edwards, Catharine, *The Politics of Immorality in Ancient Rome* (Cambridge: Cambridge University Press, 2002).
Egremont, Max, *Siegfried Sassoon: A Life* (New York: Farrar, Straus & Giroux, 2005).
Eliot, T.S., *A Choice of Kipling's Verse* (Garden City, NY: Anchor Books, 1962; first published, 1941).
Epstein, Barbara, "Anti-Communism, Homophobia, and the Construction of Masculinity in the Postwar U.S.," *Critical Sociology* 1994 20:21.
Eskridge, Jr., William N., "Hardwick and Historiography," 199 *U. Ill. L. Rev.* 631 (1999).
Evans, John K., *War, Women and Children in Ancient Rome* (London: Routledge, 1991).
Evans, Sara, *Personal Politics: The Roots of Women's Liberation in the Civil Rights Movement and the New Left* (New York: Vintage Books, 1980).
Everitt, Anthony, *Augustus: The Life of Rome's First Emperor* (New York: Random House, 2006).
Everitt, Anthony, *Cicero: The Life and Times of Rome's Greatest Politician* (New York: Random House, 2003).

Fantham, Elaine, Helene Peet Foley, Natalie Boymel Kampen, Sarah B. Pomeroy, and H. Alan Shapiro, *Women in the Classical World* (New York: Oxford University Press, 1994).
Feiling, Tom, *Cocaine Nation: How the White Trade Took Over the World* (Pegasus Books, 2010).
Ferguson, John, *The Religions of the Roman Empire* (Ithaca, New York: Cornell University Press, 1970).
Ferenczi, Sandor, "The Confusion of Tongues between Adult and Child," English translation in *International Journal of Psychoanalysis* (1949), 30, 225, German original in *Internationale Zeitschriftt fur Psychoanalyse* (1933), 19, 5. Paper read at the Twelfth International Psycho-Analytical Congress, Wiesbaden, September, 1932.
Ferguson, Niall, *Colossus: The Price of America's Empire* (New York, NY: Penguin Press, 2004).
Ferguson, Niall, *Empire: The Rise and Demise of the British World Order and the Lessons for Global Power* (New York: Basic Books, 2002).
Ferry, David, *Gilgamesh: A New Rendering in English Verse* (New York: Farrar, Straus & Giroux, 1993).
Figes, Orlando, *The Crimean War: A History* (New York: Metropolitan Books, 2010).
Flannery, Kent, and Joyce Marcus, *The Creation of Inequality: How Our Prehistoric Ancestors Set the Stage for Monarchy, Slavery, and Empire* (Cambridge, MA: Harvard University Press, 2012).
Flower, Harriet I., *The Cambridge Companion to the Roman Republic* (Cambridge: Cambridge University Press, 2004).
Fogu, Claudio, *The Historic Imaginary: Politics of History in Fascist Italy* (Toronto: University of Toronto Press, 2003).
Ford, Clellan S., and Frank A. Beach, *Patterns of Sexual Behavior* (New York: Harper & Row, 1951).
Forster, E. M., *A Passage to India* (San Diego, CA: Harvest Books, 1984; originally published, 1924).
Forster, E. M., *Goldsworthy Lowes Dickinson* (London: Edward Arnold, 1973; originally published, 1934).
Forster, E. M., *Howards End* (New York: Vintage International Edition, 1989).
Forster, E. M., *Maurice* (Toronto: Macmillan of Canada (1971; novel begun and finished, 1913–14).
Forster, E. M. *The Hill of Devi* (New York: Harcourt Brace and Company, 1953).
Forster, E. M., *Two Cheers for Democracy* (New York: Harvest Books, 1938).
Foucault, Michel, *Discipline and Punish: The Birth of the Prison*, translated Alan Sheridan (New York: Vintage Books, 1995).
Franklin, Michael J., *Orientalist Jones: Sir William, Jones, Poet, Lawyer, and Linguist, 1746–1794* (Oxford: Oxford University Press, 2011).
Freud, Sigmund, and William C. Bullitt, *Woodrow Wilson: A Psychological Study* (New Brunswick, NJ: Transaction Publishers, 1999; originally published, 1967).
Friedman, Lawrence M., *The Human Rights Culture: A Study in History and Context* (New Orleans, LA: Quid Pro Books, 2011).
Fukuyama, Francis, *The Origins of Political Order: From Prehuman Times to the French Revolution* (New York: Farrar, Straus & Giroux, 2011).
Furbank, P. N., *E.M. Forster: A Life* (San Diego, CA: Harvest Books, 1977).

Furet, Francois, *The Passing of an Illusion: The Idea of Communism in the Twentieth Century*, translated by Deborah Furet (Chicago: University of Chicago Press, 1999).
Galinsky, Karl, *Augustan Culture* (Princeton, NJ: Princeton University Press, 1996).
Gandhi, Mohandas K., *Hind Swaraj and Other Writings*, edited by Anthony J. Parel (Cambridge: Cambridge University Press, 2000).
Gardner, Jane F., *Women in Roman Law and Society* (Bloomington: Indiana University Press, 1995).
Garland, David, *The Culture of Control: Crime and Social Order in Contemporary Society* (Chicago: University of Chicago Press, 2001).
Garnett, Angelica, *Deceived with Kindness: A Bloomsbury Childhood* (London: Chatto & Windus, 1984).
Gat, Azar, *War in Human Civilization* (Oxford: Oxford University Press, 2006).
Garlick, Barbara, Barbara Garlick, Suzanne Dixon, and Pauline Allen, *Stereotypes of Women in Power: Historical Perspectives and Revisionist Views* (New York: Greenwood Press, 1992).
Gentile, Emilio, *The Sacralization of Politics in Fascist Italy*, translated by Keith Botsford (Cambridge, MA: Harvard University Press, 1996).
Gevisser, Mark and Edwin Cameron, *Defiant Desire: Gay and Lesbian Lives in South Africa* (New York: Routledge, 1995).
Gibbon, Edward, *The Decline and Fall of the Roman Empire*, Volume I, II, and III (New York: Modern Library, n.d.; originally published in six volumes between 1776 and 1788).
Gilligan, Carol, *In a Different Voice: Psychological Theory and Women's Development* (Cambridge, MA: Harvard University Press, 1982).
Gilligan, Carol, *Joining the Resistance* (Cambridge: Polity Press, 2011).
Gilligan, Carol, *The Birth of Pleasure* (Alfred A. Knopf: New York, 2002).
Gilligan, Carol, and David A. J. Richards, *The Deepening Darkness: Patriarchy, Resistance, and Democracy's Future* (Cambridge: Cambridge University Press, 2009).
Gilligan, James, *Why Some Politicians Are More Dangerous than Others* (Cambridge: Polity Press, 2011).
Gilligan, James, *Violence: Reflections on a National Epidemic* (New York: Vintage Books, 1996).
Gilmour, David, *The Ruling Caste: Imperial Lives in the Victorian Raj* (New York: Farrar, Straus & Giroux, 2005).
Glendinning, Victoria, *Leonard Woolf: A Biography* (Berkeley, CA: Counterpoint, 2008).
Glendon, Mary Ann, *A World Made New: Eleanor Roosevelt and the Universal Declaration of Human Rights* (New York: Random House, 2002).
Goldhill, Simon, *Victorian Culture and Classical Antiquity: Art, Opera, Fiction, and the Proclamation of Modernity* (Princeton, NJ: Princeton University Press, 2011).
Goldstein, Rebecca, *Betraying Spinoza: The Renegade Jew Who Gave Us Modernity* (New York: Nextbook-Schocken, 2006).
Goldsworthy, Adrian, *Caesar: Life of a Colossus* (New Haven, CT: Yale University Press, 2006).
Gopnik, Alison, *The Philosophical Baby: What Children's Minds Tell Us about Truth, Love, and the Meaning of Life* (New York: Farrar, Straus & Giroux, 2009).
Gott, Richard, *Britain's Empire: Resistance, Repression, and Revolt* (London: Verso, 2011).

Graves, Robert, *Good-Bye to All That* (New York: Anchor, 1998; originally published, 1929).
Grey, Antony, *Quest for Justice: Towards Homosexual Emancipation* (London: Sinclair-Stevenson, 1992).
Griffin, James, *On Human Rights* (Oxford: Oxford University Press, 2008).
Gullan-Whur, Margaret, *Within Reason: A Life of Spinoza* (New York: St. Martin's Press, 1998).
Gurval, Robert Alan, *Actium and Augustus: The Politics and Emotions of Civil War* (Ann Arbor: University of Michigan Press, 1995).
Hallett, Judith P., *Fathers and Daughters in Roman Society: Women and the Elite Family* (Princeton, NJ: Princeton University Press, 1984).
Hallett, Judith P., and Marilyn B. Skinner, eds., *Roman Sexualities* (Princeton, NJ: Princeton University Press, 1997).
Halley, Janet E., "The Politics of the Closet: Towards Equal Protection for Gay, Lesbian, and Bisexual Identity," University of California Law Review. 36 (1988–9): 915.
Halperin, David M., *How to Be Gay* (Cambridge, MA: Belknap Press of Harvard University Press, 2012).
Harcourt, Bernard E., *The Illusion of Free Markets: Punishment and the Myth of Natural Order* (Cambridge, MA: Harvard University Press, 2011).
Harris, William V., *War and Imperialism in Republic Rome 327–70 B.C.E.* (Oxford: Clarendon Press, 1985).
Hart, H. L. A., *Law, Liberty, and Morality* (Stanford, CA: Stanford University Press, 1963).
Hawthorne, Nathaniel, *The Scarlet Letter* (New York: Penguin, 1983; originally published, 1850).
Heath-Stubbs, John, trans., *The Poems of Sulpicia* (London: Hearing Eye, 2000).
Herman, Didi, *Rights of Passage: Struggles for Lesbian and Gay Legal Equality* (Toronto: University of Toronto Press, 1994).
Herman, Judith, *Trauma and Recovery* (New York: Basic Books, 1997).
Hetherington, Mark J., and Jonathan D. Weiler, *Authoritarianism and Polarization in American Politics* (Cambridge: Cambridge University Press, 2009).
Heyob, Sharon Kelly, *The Cult of Isis Among Women in the Graeco-Roman World* (Ann Arbor, MI: UMI Dissertation Services, 2003).
Hinds, Stephen, "The poetess and the reader: further steps towards Sulpicia," 143 *Hermathena* 29–46 (1987).
Hobson, J.A., *Imperialism: A Study* (New York: Cosmo Classics, 2005; originally published, 1902).
Hochschild, Adam, *Bury the Chains: Prophets and Rebels in the Fight to Free an Empire's Slaves* (Boston: Mariner, 2005).
Hochschild, Adam, *King Leopold's Ghost* (Boston: Houghton Mifflin, 1999).
Hochschild, Adam, *To End All Wars: A Story of Loyalty and Rebellion, 1914–1918* (Boston: Houghton Mifflin Harcourt, 2011)
Hodges, Andrew, *Alan Turing: The Enigma* (Pinceton, N.J.: Princeton University Press, 2012, first published, 1983).
Hollinghurst, Alan, *The Stranger's Child* (New York: Alfred A. Knopf, 2011).
Holroyd, Michael, ed., *Lytton Strachey by Himself: A Self Portrait* (London: Heinemann, 1971).

Holroyd, Michael, *Lytton Strachey: The New Biography* (New York: W.W. Norton, 1994).
Hopkins, Keith, *Conquerors and Slaves* (Cambridge: Cambridge University Press, 1978).
Hopkins, Keith, *Death and Renewal* (Cambridge: Cambridge University Press, 1983).
Hrdy, Sarah Blaffer, *Mothers and Others: The Evolutionary Origins of Mutual Understanding* (Cambridge, MA: Belknap Press of Harvard University Press, 2009).
Hansard, Session 1993–94, vol. 238, 21st February 1994, at Column 81. Available at http://www.parliament.uk
Hunt, Lynn, *Inventing Human Rights: A History* (New York: W.W. Norton, 2007).
Hyam, Ronald, *Empire and Sexuality: The British Experience* (Manchester, UK: Manchester University Press, 1991).
Isherwood, Christopher, *My Guru and His Disciple* (Minneapolis: University of Minnesota Press, 1980).
Israel, Jonathan I., *Radical Enlightenment: Philosophy and the Making of Modernity 1650–1750* (Oxford: Oxford University Press, 2001).
Jay, Richard, *Joseph Chamberlain: A Political Study* (Oxford: Clarendon Press, 1981).
Jeffery-Poulter, Stephen, *Peers, Queers, and Commons: The Struggle for Gay Law Reform from 1950 to the Present* (London: Routledge, 1991).
Jenkins, Roy, *Churchill: A Biography* (New York: Farrar, Straus & Giroux, 2001).
Jenkins, Roy, *Gladstone* (New York: Random House Trade Paperbacks, 1997).
Johnson, R.W., *South Africa's Brave New World: The Beloved Country since the End of Apartheid* (New York: Overlook Press, 2009).
Jones, Gregg, *Honor in the Dust: Theodore Roosevelt, War in the Philippines, and the Rise and Fall of America's Imperial Dream* (New York: New American Library, 2012).
Josephus, *The Jewish Wars Books III–IV*, translated by H. St. J. Thackeray (Cambridge, MA: Harvard University Press, 1997).
Julius, Anthony, *Trials of the Diaspora: A History of Anti-Semitism in England* (Oxford: Oxford University Press, 2010).
Kagan, Kimberly, ed., *The Imperial Moment* (Cambridge, MA: Harvard University Press, 2010).
Kalven, Harry, Jr., *The Negro and the First Amendment* (Chicago: University of Chicago Press, 1965).
Kaufman, Walter, *Nietzsche*, 4th ed. (Princeton, NJ: Princeton University Press, 1974).
Keegan, John, *The First World War* (New York: Alfred A. Knopf, 1999).
Keeley, Lawrence H., *War before Civilization: The Myth of the Peaceful Savage* (New York: Oxford University Press, 1996).
Keppie, Lawrence, *The Making of the Roman Army From Republic to Empire* (Norman: University of Oklahoma Press, 1984).
Kershaw, Ian, *Hitler: 1889–1936: Hubris* (New York: W.W. Norton, 1998).
Kershaw, Ian, *Hitler: 1936–1945: Nemesis* (New York: W.W. Norton, 2000).
Kertzer, David I., and Richard P. Saller, *The Family in Italy from Antiquity to the Present* (New Haven, CT: Yale University Press, 1991).
Keynes, John Maynard, *Essays in Persuasion* (Houndmills, UK: Palgrave Macmillan, 2010).
Keynes, John Maynard, *The Economic Consequences of the Peace* (available at ReadaClassic.com. 2010; originally published, 1919).

Keynes, John Maynard, *The General Theory of Employment, Interest, and Money* (New York: Palgrave Macmillan, 2007; originally published, 1936).
Keynes, John Maynard, *Two Memoirs* (New York: Augustus M. Kelley, 1949).
Khan, Yasmin, *The Great Partition: The Making of India and Pakistan* (New Haven, CT: Yale University Press, 2007).
Khilnani, S., V. Raghavan & A. Thiruvengadam, eds., *Comparative Constitutionalism in South Asia* (New Delhi: Oxford University Press, 2011).
Kinsman, Gary, *The Regulation of Desire: Sexuality in Canada* (Montreal: Black Rose Books, 1987).
Kipling, Rudyard, *Kim* (Oxford: Oxford University Press, 2008; first published, 1902).
Kirby, Michael, "Legal discrimination against homosexuals – a blind spot of the Commonwealth of Nations?" *European Human Rights Law Review* 2009, 1, 21–36.
Klug, Heinz, *The Constitution of South Africa: A Contextual Analysis* (Oxford: Hart Publishing, 2010).
Koestler, Arthur, *Darkness at Noon*, translated by Daphne Hardy (New York: Bantam Books, 1968; first published, 1941).
Kohler, Joachim, *Zarathustra's Secret: The Interior Life of Friedrich Nietzsche*, translated by Ronald Taylor (New Haven, CT: Yale University Press, 2002).
Konner, Melvin, *The Evolution of Childhood: Relationships, Emotion, Mind* (Cambridge, MA: Belknap Press of Harvard University Press, 2010).
Koonz, Claudia, *Mothers in the Fatherland: Women, the Family, and Nazi Politics* (New York: St. Martin's Press, 1987).
Koonz, Claudia, *The Nazi Conscience* (Cambridge, MA: Belknap Press at Harvard University Press, 2003).
Kraemer, Ross Shepard, *Her Share of the Blessings: Women's Religions among Pagans, Jews, and Christians in the Greco-Roman World* (New York: Oxford University Press, 1992).
Kraemer, Ross Shepard, ed., *Women's Religions in the Greco-Roman World: A Sourcebook* (New York: Oxford University Press, 2004).
Kron, Josh, "In Uganda, Push to Curb Gays Draws U.S. Guest," *The New York Times*, Monday, May 3, 2010, A9.
Kron, Josh, "Resentment Toward the West Bolsters Uganda's New Anti-Gay Bill," *New York Times*, Wednesday, February 29, 2012, p. A4.
Kwarteng, Kwasi, *Ghosts of Empire: Britain's Legacies in the Modern World* (New York: Public Affairs, 2011).
Labrousse, Elisabeth, *Bayle*, translated by Denys Potts (Oxford: Oxford University Press, 1983).
Lacey, Nicola, *The Life of H. L. A. Hart: The Nightmare and the Noble Dream* (Oxford: Oxford University Press, 2004).
Lakoff, George, *Moral Politics: How Liberals and Conservatives Think*, 2d ed. (Chicago: University of Chicago Press, 1996, 2002).
Langlands, Rebecca, *Sexual Morality in Ancient Rome* (Cambridge: Cambridge University Press, 2006).
Langmuir, Gavin I., *History, Religion, and Anti-Semitism* (Berkeley and Los Angeles: University of California Press, 1990).
Laplanche, J., and J.-B. Pontalis, *The Language of Psycho-Analysis*, translated by Donald Nicholson-Smith (New York: W.W. Norton, 1973).

Laqueur, Walter, *The Dream That Failed: Reflections on the Soviet Union* (New York: Oxford University Press, 1994).
Large David C., and William Weber, eds., *Wagnerism in European Culture and Politics* (Ithaca, NY: Cornell University Press, 1984).
Lawrence, T. E., *Seven Pillars of Wisdom: A Triumph* (New York: Anchor Books, 1991; originally published, 1926).
Lawrence v. Texas, 539 U.S. 558 (2003).
Leckey, Robert and Kim Brooks, eds., *Queer Theory: Law, Culture, Empire* (New York: Routledge, 2010).
Lee, Hermione, *Virginia Woolf* (London: Vintage, 1997).
Lendon, J. E., *Empire of Honour*, (Oxford: Oxford University Press, 2005).
Lenin, V. I., *Imperialism: The Highest Stage of Capitalism* (New York: International Publishers, 1939).
Lerner, Gerda, *The Creation of Patriarchy* (New York: Oxford University Press, 1986).
Levy, Paul, *Moore: G. E. Moore and the Cambridge Apostles* (Oxford: Oxford University Press, 1979).
Lintott, Andrew, *The Constitution of the Roman Republic* (Oxford: Oxford University Press, 2004).
Lintott, Andrew, *Violence in Republican Rome* (Oxford: Oxford University Press, 1999).
Livy, *Rome and the Mediterranean*, translated by Henry Bettenson (London: Penguin, 1976).
Livy, *The Early History of Rome*, translated by Aubrey De Selincourt (London: Penguin, 2002).
Livy, *The War with Hannibal*, translated by Aubrey De Selincourt (London: Penguin, 1965).
Llosa, Mario Vargas, *The Dream of the Celt*, translated by Edith Grossman (New York: Farrar, Straus & Giroux, 2012).
Losurdo, Domenico, *Liberalism: A Counter-History*, translated by Gregory Elliott (London: Verso, 2011).
Lovejoy, Arthur O., *The Great Chain of Being* (Cambridge, MA: Harvard University Press, 1964).
Loving v. Virginia, 386 U.S. 1 (1967).
Machiavelli, Niccolo, *The Prince and Discourses* Max Lerner ed. (New York: The Modern Library, 1950).
Mack, John E., *A Prince of our Disorder: The Life of T. E. Lawrence* (Cambridge, MA: Harvard University Press, 1998).
Macrobius, *Saturnalia*, translated by Percival Vaughan Davies (New York: Columbia University Press, 1969).
Madrick, Jeff, *Age of Greed: The Triumph of Finance and the Decline of America, 1970 to the Present* (New York: Alfred A. Knopf, 2011).
Magnus, Philip, *Kitchener: Portrait of an Imperialist* (New York: E.P. Dutton, 1968).
Mandela, Nelson, *Long Walk to Freedom* (Boston: Little, Brown & Company, 1995).
Marcus, Jane, *Virginia Woolf and the Languages of Patriarchy* (Bloomington: Indiana University Press, 1987).
Marsh, Peter T., *Joseph Chamberlain: Entrepreneur in Politics* (New Haven, CT: Yale University Press, 1994).

Marshall, P. J., *The Oxford History of the British Empire*, Vol. II. *The Eighteenth Century* (Oxford: Oxford University Press, 2001).
McClintock, Anne, *Imperial Leather: Race, Gender and Sexuality in the Colonial Contest* (New York: Routledge, 1995).
McCrudden, Christopher, "Institutional Discrimination," 2 *Oxford J. Legal Stud.* 303 (1982).
McDonnell, Miles, *Roman Manliness: Virtues and the Roman Republic* (Cambridge: Cambridge University Press, 2006).
McGinn, Thomas A. J., *Prostitution, Sexuality, and the Law in Ancient Rome* (New York: Oxford University Press, 1998).
Meier, Christian, *A Culture of Freedom: Ancient Greece and the Origins of Europe*, translated by Jefferson Chase (Oxford: Oxford University Press, 2012).
Meier, Christian, *Athens: A Portrait of the City in Its Golden Age*, translated by Robert and Rita Kimber (New York: Metropolitan Books, 1993).
Meier, Christian, *Caesar: A Biography*, translated by David McLintock (New York: Basic Books, 1982).
Meier, Christian, *The Greek Discovery of Politics*, translated by David McLintock (Cambridge, MA: Harvard University Press, 1990).
Miles, Barry, *Allen Ginsberg: Beat Poet* (Croydon, UK: Virgin, 1989).
Mill, John Stuart, *On Liberty* Alburey Castell, ed. (New York: Appleton-Century-Crofts, 1947).
Mill, John Stuart, *Writings on India* (Toronto: University of Toronto Press, 1990).
Minister of Home Affairs v. Fourie [2005] 2 ACC 19, 2006 (1) SA 524 (CC), 2006 (3) BCLR 355 (CC).
Mishra, Pankaj, *From the Ruins of Empire: The Intellectuals Who Remade Asia* (New York: Farrar, Straus & Giroux, 2012).
Mitchell, Leslie, *Maurice Bowra: A Life* (Oxford: Oxford University Press, 2009).
Mithen, Steven, *The Singing Neanderthals: The Origins of Music, Language, Mind, and Body* (London: Weidenfeld & Nicolson, 2005).
Moffat, Wendy, *A Great Unrecorded History: A New Life of E. M. Forster* (New York: Farrar, Straus & Giroux, 2010).
Moir, Martin I., Douglas M. Peers, and Lynn Zastoupil, eds., *J.S. Mill's Encounter with India* (Toronto: University of Toronto Press, 1999).
Montesquieu, *Considerations on the Causes of the Greatness of the Romans and Their Decline*, translated by David Lowenthal (Indianapolis: Hackett Publishing Company, 1965).
Moore, G.E., *Principia Ethica* (Mineola, NY: Dover, 2004; originally published, 1903).
Morris, Edmund, *Dutch: A Memoir of Ronald Reagan* (New York: Modern Library, 1999).
Murray, L., and C. Trevarthen, "Emotional Regulation of Interaction Between Two-Month-Olds and Their Mothers," in *Social Perception in Infants*, edited by T. M. Fields and N. A. Fox (Norwood, NJ: Ablex, 1985).
Murray, L., and C. Trevarthen "The Infant's Role in Mother-Infant Communication," *Journal of Child Language* 13 (1986): 15–29.
Mussolini, Benito, *My Autobiography with "The Political and Social Doctrine of Fascism,"* translated by Jane Soames (Mineola, NY: Dover Publications, 2006).

Mutsschler, Fritz-Heiner, and Achim Mittag, *Conceiving the Empire: China and Rome Compared* (Oxford: Oxford University Press, 2008).
M. v. H. [1999] 2 S.C.R. 3, 171 DLR (4th) 577.
Nadler, Steven, *Spinoza: A Life* (Cambridge: Cambridge University Press, 1999).
Nadler, Steven, *Spinoza's Heresy: Immortality and the Jewish Mind* (Oxford: Oxford University Press, 2001).
Nandy, Ashis, *The Intimate Enemy: Loss and Recovery of Self under Colonialism* (Oxford: Oxford University Press, 1983).
Naipaul, V.S., *India: A Million Mutinies Now* (New York: Vintage, 2011; originally published, 1990).
National Coalition for Gay and Lesbian Equality v. Minister of Justice [1998] ZACC 15, 1989 (1) SA 6, 1988 (12) BCLR 1517.
National Coalition for Gay and Lesbian Equality v. Minister of Justice (1999) 1 S.A.
National Coalition for Gay and Lesbian Equality v. Minister of Justice (2000) 2 S.A. 1.
Naz Foundation v. Union of India, (2009) 160 DLT 277.
Nehru, Jawaharlal, *An Autobiography* (New Delhi: Penguin, 2004; first published, 1936).
Nehru, Jawaharlal, *Glimpses of World History* (New Delhi: Penguin, 2004; first published, 1934–45).
Nehru, Jawaharlal, *The Discovery of India* (New Delhi: Penguin, 2004; originally published, 1946).
Neiberg, Michael S., *Dance of the Furies Europe and the Outbreak of World War I* (Cambridge, MA: Belknap Press of Harvard University Press, 2011).
Nelis, Jan, "Constructing Fascist Identity: Benito Mussolini and the Myth of *Romanita*," *Classical World* 100.4 (2007): 391–415.
Nicolson, Nigel, *Virginia Woolf* (London: Weidenfeld & Nicolson, 2000).
Nietzsche, Friedrich, *On the Genealogy of Morals*, translated by Douglas Smith (Oxford: Oxford University Press, 1996).
Nietzsche, Friedrich, *The Birth of Tragedy and On the Genealogy of Morals*, translated by Francis Golffing (New York: Doubleday & Company, 1956).
Obama, Barack, *The Audacity of Hope: Thoughts on Reclaiming the American Dream* (New York: Three Rivers Press, 2006).
Ober, Josiah, *Democracy and Knowledge: Innovation and Learning in Classical Athens* (Princeton, NJ: Princeton University Press, 2008).
Ober, Josiah, *Mass and Elite in Democratic Athens: Rhetoric, Ideology, and the Power of the People* (Princeton, NJ: Princeton University Press, 1989).
Ober, Josiah, *Political Dissent in Democratic Athens: Intellectual Critics of Popular Rule* (Princeton, NJ: Princeton University Press, 1998).
O'Brien, Tim, *The Things They Carried* (New York: Broadway Books, 1990).
Ogilvie, R.M., *A Commentary on Livy Books 1–5* (Oxford: Oxford at the Clarendon Press, 1965).
Okeowo, Alexis, "Out in Africa: A gay rights struggle with deadly stakes," *The New Yorker*, December 24&31, 2012, pp. 64–70.
Orwell, George, *A Collection of Essays* (Orlando, FL: Harvest Books, 1981).
Orwell, George, *Burmese Days* (Orlando, FL: Harvest Books, 1962; originally published, 1936).
Orwell, George, *Why I Write* (New York: Penguin, 1984).

Osgood, Josiah, *Caesar's Legacy: Civil War and the Emergence of the Roman Empire* (Cambridge: Cambridge University Press, 2006).
Osborne, John, *Look Back in Anger* (New York: Penguin, 1982).
Outrage.org.uk.
Pagden, Anthony, *Lords of all the World: Ideologies of Empire in Spain, Britain, and France c1500–c1800* (New Haven, CT: Yale University Press, 1998).
Painter, Jr., Borden W., *Mussolini's Rome: Rebuilding the Eternal City* (New York; Palgrave Macmillan, 2005).
Pakkanen, Petra, *Interpreting Early Hellenistic Religion* (Athens: E. Souvatzidakis, 1996).
Palmer, R. F. A., *The Archaic Community of the Romans* (Cambridge: Cambridge University Press, 1970).
Parker, Peter, *Ackerley: A Life of J.R. Ackerley* (New York: Farrar, Straus & Giroux, 1989).
Patel, Aniruddh D., *Music, Language, and the Brain* (Oxford: Oxford University Press, 2008).
Pateman, Carole, *The Sexual Contract* (Cambridge: Polity Press, 1988).
Paterculus, Velleius, *Res Gestae Divi Augusti* (Cambridge, MA: Harvard University Press, 2002).
Paxton, Robert O., *The Anatomy of Fascism* (New York: Vintage Books, 2004).
Perkinson, Robert, "Drug of Choice," *The New York Times Book Review*, August 1, 2010, at p. 21.
Phillips, Kathy J., *Virginia Woolf against Empire* (Knoxville: The University of Tennessee Press, 1994).
Pinker, Steven, *The Better Angels of Our Nature: Why Violence Has Declined* (New York: Viking, 2011).
Pliny the Elder, *Natural History: A Selection*, John F. Healy trans. (London: Penguin, 2004).
Plutarch, *The Lives of Noble Grecians and Romans* John Dryden trans. (New York: Modern Library, n.d.).
Poliakov, Leon, *The Aryan Myth: A History of Racist and Nationalist Ideas in Europe* translated by Edmund Howard (London: Sussex University Press, 1971).
Polybius, *The Rise of the Roman Empire*, translated by Ian Scott-Kilvert trans. (London: Penguin, 1979).
Pomeroy, Sarah B., *Goddesses, Whores, Wives, and Slaves: Women in Classical Antiquity* (New York: Schocken Books, 1995).
Pomeroy, Sarah B., *Women in Hellenistic Egypt: From Alexander to Cleopatra* (Detroit: Wayne State University Press, 1990).
Potts, Rick, *Humanity's Descent: The Consequences of Ecological Instability* (New York: Avon Books, 1996).
Power, Lisa, *No Bath but Plenty of Bubbles: An Oral History of the Gay Liberation, 1970–73* (London: Cassell, 1996).
Raditsa, Leo Ferrero, "Augustus' Legislation Concerning Marriage, Procreation, Love Affairs, and Adultery," *Aufstieg und Niedergang Der Romischen Welt* (Berlin: Walter De Gruyter, 1980), pp. 278–339.
Rather, L. J., *Reading Wagner: A Study in the History of Ideas* (Baton Rouge: Louisiana State University Press, 1990).

Rawson, ed., Beryl, *Marriage, Divorce, and Children in Ancient Rome* (Oxford: Clarendon Press, 2004).

Reagan, Ronald, *An American Life: Ronald Reagan* (New York: Simon & Schuster, 1990).

Reagan, Ronald, *Where's the Rest of Me?: The Autobiography of Ronald Reagan with Richard G. Hubler* (New York: Karz Publishers, 1965).

Reagan, Ron, *My Father at 100: A Memoir* (New York: Viking, 2011).

Reeves, Richard, *John Stuart Mill: Victorian Firebrand* (London: Atlantic Books, 2007).

Richard, Carl J., *The Founders and the Classics: Greece, Rome, and the American Enlightenment* (Cambridge, MA: Harvard University Press, 1994).

Richards, David A. J., *The Case for Gay Rights: From Bowers to Lawrence and Beyond* (Lawrence: University Press of Kansas, 2005).

Richards, David A. J., *Conscience and the Constitution: History, Theory, and Law of the Reconstruction Amendments* (Princeton, NJ: Princeton University Press, 1993).

Richards, David A. J., *Disarming Manhood: The Roots of Ethical Resistance* (Athens, OH: Swallow Press, 2005).

Richards, David A. J., *Free Speech and the Politics of Identity* (Oxford: Oxford University Press, 1999).

Richards David A. J., *Fundamentalism in American Religion and Law: Obama's Challenge to Patriarchy's Threat to Democracy* (Cambridge: Cambridge University Press, 2010).

Richards, David A. J., *Sex, Drugs, Death and the Law: An Essay on Human Rights and Overcriminalization* (Totowa, NJ: Rowman & Littlefield, 1982).

Richards, David A. J., *A Theory of Reasons for Action* (Oxford: Clarendon Press, 1971).

Richards, David A. J., *Toleration and the Constitution* (New York: Oxford University Press, 1986).

Richards, David A. J., *Women, Gays, and the Constitution: The Grounds for Feminism and Gay Rights in Culture and Law* (Chicago: University of Chicago Press, 1998).

Richards, Peter G., *Parliament and Conscience* (London: George Allen & Unwin, 1970).

Rodgers, Daniel T., *Age of Fracture* (Cambridge, MA: Belknap Press of Harvard University Press, 2011).

Roe v. Wade, 410 U.S. 113 (1973).

Roller, Matthew B., Matthew B. Roller, *Constructing Autocracy: Aristocrats and Emperors in Juliu-Claudian Rome* (Princeton, NJ: Princeton University Press, 2001).

Roosevelt, Eleanor, "In Your Hands," available at http://www.udhr.org/history/inyour.htm.

Rorabaugh, W. J., *Berkeley at War: The 1960s* (New York: Oxford University Press, 1989).

Rosenthal, Michael, *The Character Factory: Baden-Powell's Boy Scouts and the Imperatives of Empire* (New York: Pantheon, 1986).

Rotberg, Robert I., *The Founder: Cecil Rhodes and the Pursuit of Power* (New York: Oxford University Press, 1988).

Roth v. United States, 354 U.S. 476 (1957).

Rowbotham, Sheila, *Edward Carpenter: A Life of Liberty and Love* (London: Verso, 2008).

Roy, Arundhati, *The God of Small Things* (New York: HarperPerennial, 1998).

Sachs, Albie, *The Soft Vengeance of a Freedom Fighter*, new ed. (Berkeley: University of California Press, 2000).
Sachs, Albie, *The Strange Alchemy of Life and Law* (New York: Oxford University Press, 2009).
Saller, Richard P., *Patriarchy, Property and Death in the Roman Family* (Cambridge: Cambridge University Press, 1994).
Sallust, *The Jugurthine War/The Conspiracy of Catiline*, translated by S. A. Handford (London: Penguin, 1963).
Sandbrook, Dominic, *Mad as Hell: The Crisis of the 1970s and the Rise of the Populist Right* (New York: Alfred A. Knopf, 2011).
Sandmel, Samuel, *The Genius of Paul: A Study in History* (Philadelphia: Fortress Press, 1979).
Scheidel, Walter ed., Walter, *Rome and China: Comparative Perspectives on Ancient World Empires* (Oxford: Oxford University Press, 2009).
Schiller, Greta, "The Man Who Drove with Mandela" [documentary film] (Jezebel Productions, 1998).
Scott, Paul, *The Day of the Scorpion: The Raj Quartet: 2* (Chicago: University of Chicago Press, 1998; originally published, 1968).
Scott, Paul, *A Division of the Spoils: The Raj Quartet: 4* (Chicago: University of Chicago Press, 1998; originally published, 1975).
Scott, Paul, *The Jewel in the Crown: The Raj Quartet: 1* (Chicago: University of Chicago Press, 1998; originally published, 1966.
Scott, Paul, *Staying On* (Chicago: University of Chicago Press, 1998; originally published, 1977).
Scott, Paul, *The Towers of Silence: The Raj Quartet: 3* (Chicago: University of Chicago Press, 1998; originally published, 1972).
Segal, Alan F., *Paul the Convert: The Apostolate and Apostasy of Saul the Pharisee* (New Haven, CT: Yale University Press, 1990).
Seneca, Lucius Annaeus, *On Benefits* (North Sydney, Australia: Objective Systems, 2006).
Seneca, *On the Shortness of Life*, translated by C. D. N. Costa (London: Penguin, 1997).
Severy, Beth, *Augustus and the Family at the Birth of the Roman Empire* (London: Routledge, 2003).
Shaw v. Director of Public Prosecution, House of Lords [1962] A.C. 220.
Shone, Richard, *The Art of Bloomsbury: Roger Fry, Vanessa Bell and Duncan Grant* (Princeton, NJ: Princeton University Press, 1999).
Simon, Jonathan, *Governing through Crime: How the War on Crime Transformed American Democracy and Created a Culture of Fear* (Oxford: Oxford University Press, 2007).
Simpson, A. W. Brian, *Human Rights and the End of Empire: Britain and the Genesis of the European Convention* (Oxford: Oxford University Press, 2004).
Skidelsky, Robert, *John Maynard Keynes: Hopes Betrayed 1883–1920* (New York: Viking, 1986).
Skidelsky, Robert, *John Maynard Keynes: The Economist as Savior 1920–1937* (New York: Allen Lane, 1992).

Skoe, Mathile, "Sublime Poetry or Feminine Fiddling? Gender and Reception: Sulpicia through the Eyes of Two 19th Century Scholars," Nordic Symposium on Women's Lives in Antiquity, *Aspects of Women in Antiquity: Proceedings of the First Nordic Symposium on Women's Lives in Antiquity, Goteborg 12–15 June 1997*, edited by L. L. Lovén and A. Strömberg (Jonsered, Sweden: P. Astroms Forlag, 1998), pp. 169–82.

Slavitt, David R., ed. and trans., *Aeschylus I: The Oresteia* (Philadelphia: University of Pennsylvania Press, 1998).

Solmsen, Friedrich, *Isis among the Greeks and Romans* (Cambridge, MA: Harvard University Press, 1979).

Southern, Pat, *Augustus* (London: Routledge, 2001).

Spence, Jonathan, *Mao Zedong* (New York: Penguin, 2006).

Spence, Jonathan, *The Search for Modern China*, 2nd ed. (New York: W.W. Norton, 1999).

Spinoza, Benedict de, *A Theological-Political Treatise and A Political Treatise*, translated by R. H. M. Elwes (Mineola, NY: Dover Publication, 2004).

Spinoza, Benedict de, *Ethics*, translated by Edwin Curley (London: Penguin, 1996).

Spinoza, *Theological-Political Treatise*, 2nd ed., translated by Samuel Shirley (Indianapolis: Hackett, 2001).

Spurling, Hilary, *Paul Scott: A Life of the Author of The Raj Quartet* (New York: W.W. Norton, 1991).

Stambaugh, John B., *Sarapis under the Early Ptolemies* (Leiden: E.J. Brill, 1972).

Stern, Daniel N., *The Interpersonal World of the Infant* (New York: Basic Books, 1998).

Stokes, Eric, *The English Utilitarians in India* (Oxford: Oxford University Press, 1959).

Stonewall.org.uk.

Strachey, Alix, *The Unconscious Motives to War: A Psycho-Analytical Contribution* (New York: International Universities Press, 1957).

Strachey, Lytton, *Characters and Commentaries* (Westport, CT: Greenwood Press, 1961; originally published, 1933).

Strachey, Lytton, *Elizabeth and Essex: A Tragic History* (San Diego, CA: Harvest Books, 1956; originally published, 1956).

Strachey, Lytton, *Eminent Victorians* (Lexington, KY: Forgotten Books' Classic Reprint Series, 2011; originally published, 1918).

Strachey, Lytton *Queen Victoria* (Fairfield, IA: 1st World Library, 2006; originally published, 1921).

Stychin, Carl F., "Constituting Sexuality: The Struggle for Sexual Orientation in the South African Bill of Rights," 23 *J.L. & Soc'y* 455 (1966).

Suetonius, *The Twelve Caesars*, translated by Robert Graves (London: Penguin, 1979).

Syme, Ronald, *The Roman Revolution* (Oxford: Oxford University Press, 1985).

Tacitus, *Agricola, Germania, Dialogus*, translated by W. Peterson (Cambridge, MA: Harvard University Press, 1970).

Tacitus, *The Annals of Imperial Rome*, translated by Michael Grant (London: Penguin, 1998).

Taddeo, Julie Anne, *Lytton Strachey and the Search for Modern Sexual Identity: The Last Eminent Victorian* (New York: Harrington Park Press, 2002).

Tatchell, Peter, *We Don't Want to March Straight: Masculinity, Queers, and the Military* (London: Cassell, 1995).
Taubes, Jacob, *The Political Theology of Paul*, translated by Dana Hollander (Stanford, CA: Stanford University Press, 2004).
Theweleit, Klaus, *Male Fantasies*, 2 vols. (Minneapolis: University of Minnesota Press, 1987).
Thomas, Evan, *The War Lovers: Roosevelt, Lodge, Hearst, and the Rush to Empire, 1898* (New York: Little, Brown & Company, 2010).
Thucydides, *History of the Peloponnesian War*, translated by Rex Warner (Harmondsworth, England: Penguin, 1986).
Toíbín, Colm, "A Man of No Mind," in *London Review of Books* 34, no. 17 (September 13, 2012): pp. 15–16, 18–19.
Tomasello, Michael, *Why We Cooperate* (Cambridge, MA: MIT Press, 2009).
Treggiari, Susan, *Roman Marriage* (Oxford: Clarendon Press, 1991).
Treggiari, Susan, *Roman Marriage: Iusti Coniuges from the Time of Cicero to the Time of Ulpian* (Oxford: Oxford University Press, 2002).
Trivedi, Harish, *Colonial Transactions: English Literature and India* (Manchester, UK: Manchester University Press, 1995).
Tronick, E. Z., and M. K. Weinberg, "Depressed Mothers and Infants: Failure to Form Dyadic States of Consciousness," in *Postpartum Depression and Child Development*, edited by L. Murray and P. J. Cooper (New York: Guilford Press, 1997), pp. 54-81.
Tronick, Edward Z., "Emotions and Emotional Communication in Infants," *American Psychologist* 44, no. 2 (1989): 112–19.
Tronick, E. Z., and A. Gianino, "Interactive Mismatch and Repair Challenges in the Coping Infant," *Zero to Three*, 6:1–6.
Trudeau, Pierre, *Memoirs* (Toronto: McClelland & Stewart, 1995).
Trudeau, P., and T. Axworthy, eds., *Towards a Just Society: The Trudeau Years* (Markham: Viking Books, 1990).
Turcan, Rober, *The Cults of the Roman Empire* (Malden, MA: Blackwell Publishing, 2005).
Turnbaugh, Douglas Blair, *Duncan Grant and the Bloomsbury Group* (Secaucus, NJ: Lyle Stuart, 1987).
Tushnet, Mark V., "Sex, Drugs and Rock 'n' Roll: Some Conservative Reflections on Liberal Jurisprudence," *Columbia Law Review* 82, no. 7 (1982), 1531–43.
Uchitelle, Louis, "Volcker, Loud and Clear," *The New York Times*, July 11, 2010, pp. 1, 7.
van der Kolk, Bessel, Alexander C. McFarlane, and Lars Weisaeth, eds.,. *Traumatic Stress: The Effects of Overwhelming Experience on Mind, Body, and Society* (New York: The Guilford Press, 1996).
Vanita, Ruth, and Saleem Kidwai, eds., *Same-Sex Love in India* (New Delhi: Macmillan, 2000).
Veyne, Paul, *Roman Erotic Elegy: Love, Poetry, and the West*, translated by David Pellauer (Chicago: University of Chicago Press, 1988).
Visser, Romke, "Fascist Doctrine and the Cult of the Romanita," *Journal of Contemporary History* 27 (1992): 5–22.
Volkmann, Hans, *Cleopatra: A Study in Politics and Propaganda*, translated by T. J. Cadoux (London: Elek Books, 1958).

Vriend v. Alberta [1998] 1 S.C.R. 493, 156 DLR (4th) 385.
Walbank, F. W., A. E. Astin, M. W. Frederiksen, and R. M. Ogilvie, *The Cambridge Ancient History*, 2nd ed., Vol. VII, *The Rise of Rome to 220 B.C.E.* (Cambridge: Cambridge University Press, 1989).
Waldron, Jeremy, *God, Locke, and Equality: Christian Foundations in Locke's Political Thought* (Cambridge: Cambridge University Press, 2002).
Washington, James M. (ed.), *A Testament of Hope: The Essential Writings of Martin Luther King, Jr.* (San Francisco: Harper and Row, 1986).
Way, Niobe, *Deep Secrets: Boys' Friendships and the Crisis of Connection* (Cambridge, MA: Harvard University Press, 2011).
Weeks, Jeffrey, *Coming Out: Homosexual Politics in Britain, from the Nineteenth Century to the Present* (London: Quartet Books, 1977).
Whitmarsh, Tim, *Greek Literature and the Roman Empire: The Politics of Imitation* (Oxford: Oxford University Press, 2001).
Wikipedia, "Civis Romanus sum."
Wikipedia entries for Guy Burgess, Donald Maclean, Kim Philby, and Anthony Blunt.
Wikipedia, "LGBT Rights in Malaysia."
Wikipedia, "LGBT Rights in Singapore."
Wikipedia, "LGBT Rights in Zimbabwe."
Wikipedia, "Peter Tatchell."
Wikipedia, "Pierre Trudeau."
Wilkinson, Toby, *The Rise and Fall of Ancient Egypt* (New York: Random House, 2010).
Williams, Craig A., *Roman Homosexuality*, 2nd ed. (New York: Oxford University Press, 2010).
Williams, Tennessee, *A Streetcar Named Desire* (New York: New Directions, 1957).
Winks, Robin W., ed., *The Oxford History of the British Empire*, Vol. V. *Historiography* (Oxford: Oxford University Press, 1999).
Witt, R. E., *Isis in the Ancient World* (Baltimore: The Johns Hopkins University Press, 1971).
Wood, Susan E., *Imperial Women: A Study in Public Images 40 B.C.E.–AD 69* (Leiden: Brill, n.d.).
Wood, Wendy, and Alice H. Eagly, "A Cross-Cultural Analysis of the Behavior of Women and Men: Implications for the Origins of Sex Differences," *Psychological Bulletin*, 128, no. 5 (2002): 699–727.
Woolf, Leonard, *After the Deluge: A Study of Communal Psychology*, Vol. I (London: The Hogarth Press, 1953).
Woolf, Leonard, *After the Deluge: A Study of Communal Psychology*, Vol. II (London: The Hogarth Press, 1953).
Woolf, Leonard, *Barbarians at the Gate* (London: Victor Gollancz, 1939).
Woolf, Leonard, *Beginning Again: An Autobiography of the Years 1911–1918* (San Diego, CA: Harcourt Brace Jovanovich, 1964).
Woolf, Leonard, *Economic Imperialism* (London: Swarthmore Press, 1920).
Woolf, Leonard, *Empire and Commerce in Africa: A Study in Economic Imperialism* (Lexington, KY: Cornell University Library Digital Collections, 2011; originally published, 1920).
Woolf, Leonard, *Imperialism and Civilization* (London: The Hogarth Press, 1928).

Woolf, Leonard, *International Government: Two Reports* (London: Fabian Society Bookshop, 1916).
Woolf, Leonard, *After the Deluge*, Vol. 3. *Principia Politica: A Study of Communal Psychology Being* (London: The Hogarth Press, 1953).
Woolf, Leonard, *Quack! Quack!* (New York: Harcourt Brace, 1935).
Woolf, Leonard, *Socialism and Co-operation* (London: The National Labour Press, 1921).
Woolf, Leonard, *Sowing: An Autobiography of the Years 1880 to 1904* (San Diego, CA: Harcourt Brace Jovanovich, 1960).
Woolf, Leonard, *The Village in the Jungle* (London: Eland, 2005; first published, 1913).
Woolf, Leonard, *The War for Peace* (London: The Labour Book Service, 1940).
Woolf, Leonard, *The Wise Virgins* (New Haven, CT: Yale University Press, 2007; first published, 1914).
Woolf, Virginia, *A Room of One's Own* (San Diego, CA: Harvest Books, 1981; originally published, 1929).
Woolf, Virginia, *Mrs. Dalloway* (San Diego, CA: Harvest Books, 1997; first published, 1925).
Woolf, Virginia, *Three Guineas*, edited by Jane Marcus (Orlando, FL: Harvest Books, 2006; originally published, 1938).
Woolf, Virginia, *To the Lighthouse* (San Diego, CA: Harvest Books, 1981; originally published 1927).
Woolf, Virginia, *Women and Writing*, edited by Michele Barrett (Orlando, FL: Harvest Books, 1980).
Woolhouse, Roger, *Locke: A Biography* (Cambridge: Cambridge University Press, 2007).
Wyke, Maria, *The Roman Mistress* (Oxford: Oxford University Press, 2002).
Wyatt-Brown, Bertram, *Southern Honor: Ethics and Behavior in the Old South* (Oxford: Oxford University Press, 2007).
Young, Andrew, *An Easy Burden: The Civil Rights Movement and the Transformation of America* (New York: HarperCollins, 1996).
Young-Bruehl, Elisabeth, *The Anatomy of Prejudices* (Cambridge, MA: Harvard University Press, 1996).
Young-Bruehl, Elisabeth, *Where Do We Fall When We Fall in Love?* (New York: Other Press, 2003).
Young, Robert J. C., *Postcolonialism: An Historical Introduction* (Oxford: Blackwell, 2001).
Zagorin, Perez, *How the Idea of Religious Toleration Came to the West* (Princeton, NJ: Princeton University Press, 2003).
Zanker, Paul, *The Power of Images in the Age of Augustus*, translated by Alan Shapiro (Ann Arbor: University of Michigan Press, 1990).
Zastoupil, Lynn *John Stuart Mill and India* (Stanford, CA: Stanford University Press).

Index

abolitionist feminists, 178
The Aeneid (Virgil), 26, 83, 146, 176
Aeschylus, 20, 175
African National Congress (ANC), 213–214
Agrippina the Elder, 78–79
Agrippina the Younger, 79
Ainsworth, Alfred, 104
Albany Trust, 160
alloparenting, 12–13
American resistance movements
  conservative reaction, 185–202
  impact on Britain and elsewhere, 181–185
  limited impact, Britain and elsewhere, 203–207
The Anatomy of Prejudice (Young-Bruehl), 39
Anglican vs. Catholic Church, 158–159
Annan, Noel, 6
anti-Semitism, 37–38
  Christian, 29–31
  Hitler and, 33, 36–37
  political, 29–31
anti-war movement, 171, 173
Antony, Marc, 62–67
Antony (Plutarch), 65
Apostles (Cambridge University), 9, 103, 157
Apuleius, 26, 80
Arendt, Hannah, 33
arranged marriages, 50–51, 70
artists, 21
Aschylus, 22
Asiatic Society, 81
Atlas Shrugged (Rand), 190
Augustinian Christianity, 83
Augustine (St.), 29–32, 80, 82
Augustus, 67–80

Bacchus, Greek cult, 61
Bailey, Derrick, 159
Banda, Hastings, 218
Banforth, Nicholas, 158
Barbarians at the Gate (Woolf, L.), 130
Bayle, Pierre, 84–86
Bell, Julian, 158
Blair, Tony, 204
Bloomsbury Group, 5, 9, 100, 233, 242
Blunt, Anthony, 157–158
Bowra, Maurice, 164
Bradley, F. H., 150
Britain
  American resistance movements and, 181–185
  and Europe vs. U.S., gay rights, 205–206
  fall of empire, era of gay rights and, 205–206
  U.S. resistance movements vs., 181–185
British imperialism, distinctive features, 147–148
British military service, 81
British patriarchy, 80–96
  Roman vs., 82, 88–89, 91–94
Burgess, Guy, 157–158
Burmese Days (Orwell), 43, 109
Bush, George H. W., 201
Bush, George W., 201, 235

Caesar, Julius, 56, 62–67
Calhoun, John, 177–178
Cameron, David, 205
Cameron, Edwin, 215–217
Canada, 210–213
Carpenter, Edward, 43, 98–99, 166, 223, 229–230
Casement, Roger, 135–137, 208

caste system, 226–229
Catholic Christianity, 29–32
Chamberlain, Joseph, 148
China, patriarchy, 41–42
Christianity, 167–172
  anti-Semitism and, 29–31
  Augustine, 83
  Catholic, 29–32
  homosexuality repression and, 236
Church of England Welfare Committee, 158
Churchill, Winston, 153
Cicero, 63–64, 65
Civil Rights Act of 1964, 169, 183
Civilization: It's Cause and Curse (Carpenter), 223
Cleopatra, 62–67
Confessions (Augustine), 29–32, 80
Conrad, Joseph, 135
Constitution Act, 1982 (Canada), 212
cooperation, 16–17
Criminal Law Amendment Act, 1968–69 (Canada), 211
Cupid and Psyche, 26–27

Damasio, Antonio, 12
The Decline and Fall of the Roman Empire (Gibbon), 40, 44
The Deepening Darkness (Gilligan, Richards), 11, 26, 29, 175–176
democracy
  Athenian, 22–23
  patriarchy vs., 17–18, 23, 56–57, 174–176
  relationality and, 16–18
destructive forces, 4
Devlin, Patrick, 161–162
Devlin/Hart debate, 161–165
Dreadnought Hoax, 107–108
Dudgeon v. United Kingdom, 185

The Economic Consequences of Peace (Keynes), 120, 121
Eggleston, Frederic, 152
Elizabeth and Essex: A Tragic History (Strachey), 118
Eminent Victorians (Strachey), 117
Empire and Commerce in Africa (Woolf, L.), 129
Employment Equality (Sexual Orientation) Regulations 2003, 205
English Civil War, 84

Equality Act (Sexual Orientation) Regulations 2007, 205
Equal Protection Clause, Fourteenth Amendment, 169
ethics, 7
  of duty, 151
  ethical discoveries, 231
  ethical resistance, 167–171
  human relationality and, 11–13
ethnic nationalism, 220–221
European Convention on Human Rights, 184–185, 205

fall of empire
  era of gay rights, United States and Britain, 165–207
  rise of gay rights, 1967 decriminalization, 144–165
Family Law Act (Canada), 213
fascism, 34–36, 37
feminist resistance, 8, 165, 178
Ferenczi, Sandor, 90–91
The First Treatise of Government (Locke), 11
Forster, E. M., 9, 95, 99, 132–133, 138–139, 160, 208
The Fountainhead (Rand), 190
Fulvia, 59–60

Gandhi, Mohandas, 82, 223–224
Gandhi, Ragiv, 227
gay rights
  American and British, 99–100
  Britain and Europe vs. U.S., 205–206
  British patriarchy and fall of British empire, 1967 decriminalization,
  modern, 238–239
  origins, 234
  as universal human rights, 240–242
gender binary questions, feminist challenge, 165
The Ghosts of Empire (Kwarteng), 91, 147
Gibbon, Edward, 40, 44
Gide, Andre, 164
Gilgamesh, 21–22
Gilligan, Carol, 11, 26, 29, 175–176
Gilligan, James, 198
The Golden Ass (Apuleius), 26–29
Grant, Duncan, 107–108
Graves, Robert, 116
Greek cult of Bacchus, 61
Grey, Anthony, 160

Index

Hall, Radclyff, 101
Harare Declaration of Human Rights, 221
Harmodios and Aristogeiton, 2, 23, 238
Hart, H. L. A., 162–165
Hawthorne, Nathaniel, 11, 178
The Heart of Darkness (Conrad), 135
Henry VIII, 83
hieros, pater, 44–45
Himmler, Heinrich, 34
Hitler, Adolf, 33, 37
Hobson, John A., 128–129
Hollinghurst, Alan, 3, 236
Homosexual Law Reform Society, 160
honor codes, 49–50, 54–55, 57
Hortensia, 59–60
human relationality, 12–14
human rights, 10
  homophobic violence and, 239
  liberal political theory and, 240–241

Immorality and Treason (Hart), 162
imperialism
  defining features, 40
  democratic features, 42–43
  Western, 40
Imperialism: a Study (Hobson), 129
India, 222–230
  patriarchy, 41
infant research, 12–13
Isis religion, 26–28

Japan, patriarchy, 41
Johnson, Lyndon, 186
Jones, William, 81
Josephus, Titus Flavius, 47
Julia the Elder, 69–76
Julia the Younger, 76–77

Kant, Immanuel, 192
Keynes, John Maynard, 103–105, 106, 120–123, 153–154
King, Martin Luther, Jr., 167–171, 186–187
Kinnock, Neil, 204
Kipling, Rudyard, 150
Kwarteng, Kwasi, 91, 147

Ladies' Home Directory, 182
Lakoff, George, 192–193
Law, Liberty, and Morality (Hart), 163
Lawrence, T. E., 137–138
Lawrence v. Texas, 1, 100, 241

Leaves of Grass (Whitman), 97
The Letter from Birmingham Jail (King), 171
Lex Julia de adulteriis coercendis, 68–69
Lex Julia et Papia,
liberal resistance, 8–9
Llosa, Mario Vargas, 135–136
Locke, John, 11, 84–86, 89
Look Back in Anger (Osborne), 143–144, 155, 166
Love Laws, 5, 38–39, 102–103

Maclean, Donald, 157
The Man Who Drove With Mandela, 217
Mandela, Nelson, 217
Marxism-Leninism, 144–145
Maurice (Forster), 138
Meese, Edwin, 197
Memoirs (Trudeau), 212
Metamorphoses (Apuleius), 80
Mildred Pierce, 241
militarism, 45–47, 89–90
Militarism and Theology (Strachey), 115
military, gay men, lesbians, 156
Mill, John Stuart, 95–96, 162
Minister of Home Affairs v. Fourie, 216
Moore, G. E., 104, 122
moral experience, 233
Moral Order of the Strict Father model, 192–193
Moral Welfare Council, 159
mothers and sons, 53–54
Mrs. Dalloway (Woolf, V.), 123–124, 149–150
Mugabe, Robert, 1, 218–221
Mussolini, Benito, 34–36
My Early Beliefs (Keynes), 105

National Coalition for Gay and Lesbian Equality v. Minister of Justice (1999, 2000), 216
Naz Foundation v. Union of India, 227, 230
Neru, Jawaharlal, 224–226
Nietzsche, Friedrich, 32, 34, 188
Nightingale, Florence, 117–118
Nixon, Richard, 194
nonviolent protest, 167–171

Objectivism, 187–191
Octavian, 62–67
On Liberty (Mill), 95–96, 162
The Oresteia (Aschylus), 20, 22–25, 175
The Origins of Totalitarianism (Arendt), 33

Orwell, George, 43, 109, 153
Osborne, John, 143–144, 155, 166
Our Age (Annan), 6
Ovid, 76–77

Paisley, Ian, 204
Passage to India (Foster), 9, 95, 132–133
Patriarchal Religion, Sexuality, Gender: A Critique of New Natural Law (Banforth, Richards), 158
patriarchy, 146
　American, 189–192
　British, 80–96
　China, 41–42
　cultural creation of, 20
　democracy vs., 17–18, 56–57, 174–176
　India, 41
　Japan, 41
　modernist, 34
　Neolithic, 15, 18–19
　origins, cultural practice of, 15, 23–24
　patriarchal religion, 19
　reactionary politics and, 192–194, 202–203
　resistance to, 101–102, 232
　Roman, 43–80
　Roman vs. British, 82, 88–89, 91–94
　trauma at root of, 18, 24–25, 47–48
　women's sexuality and, 20–21
Pearson, Lester, 211
Plutarch, 65
political authority, patriarchal conception of, 8
political liberalism, 89
political women, 58–62
politicians, 187, 198
Polybius, 49
Pompey, 56
Principa Ethica (Moore), 104, 122
The Problem of Homosexuality (Bailey), 159
Professions of Women (Woolf, V.), 93, 150, 172
Protestant Reformation, 86

Quack! Quack! (Woolf, L.), 130
Queen Victoria (Strachey), 118–120

The Raj Quartet (Scott), 133
Rand, Ayn, 187–191
Rawls, John, 180
Reagan, Ronald, 194–198, 200–201
Reconstruction Amendments, 176, 179
religious persecution, 86
RENAMO, 218

resistance
　American resistance movements, 167–181
　Britain vs. U.S. resistance movements, 181–185
　feminist, 8
　liberal, 8–9
　movements, U.S. vs. Britain, 181–185
　to patriarchy, 101–102, 232
　Stonewall resistance, 100
Richards, David, 11, 26, 29, 158, 175–176
rituals, 49
Roe v. Wade, 172, 192
Roman patriarchy, 43–80
　British vs., 82, 88–89, 91–94
Roman Republic, 26, 45–47
Roosevelt, Eleanor, 232
Roosevelt, Theodore, 151, 179
Roy, Arundhati, 38

Sachs, Albie, 213–214, 228
Sackville-West, Vita, 6
Sasson, Siegfried, 116
Scalia, Antony, 1
The Scarlett Letter (Hawthorne), 11, 178
Scott, Paul, 133
Screen Actors Guild, 195
The Second Philippic (Cicero), 63–64, 65
The Second Treatise of Government (Locke), 11, 89
Seven Pillars of Wisdom (Lawrence), 137–138
Shaw v. Director of Public Prosecution, 182, 183
slavery, Roman vs. American, 176–178
Snow, C. P., 161
South Africa, 213–222, 228
Soviet Union, 144–145
Spinoza, Baruch, 87–88
Stanton, Elizabeth, 178
Stephens, Vanessa, 107–109
Stephens, Virginia, 107–112
Stonewall resistance, 100, 167, 181
Strachey, Lytton, 6, 103–107, 108–109, 113–115, 149, 208
The Stranger's Child (Hollinghurst), 3, 236
Street Offences Act, 160
A Streetcar Named Desire (Williams), 141–142, 166
The Subjection of Women (Mill), 95–96
The Sunday Times, 158

Tacitus, 75–76
Thatcher, Margaret, 203

Index

A Theory of Justice (Rawls), 180
A Theory of Probability (Keynes), 122
3/5 Clause, U.S. Constitution, 177
Three Guineas (Woolf, V.), 123, 125–127, 150
To the Lighthouse (Woolf, V.), 123, 124–125, 150
toleration, 86
trauma, 18, 24–25, 47–48, 55, 90–91, 147
Treaty of Amsterdam, 205
Trudeau, Pieerre, 210–212

United States (U.S.)
    American resistance movements, 167–202
    Britain *vs.* U.S. resistance movements, 181–185
    civil rights movements, 166
    conservative reaction, 185–202
    Democratic Party, 198
    gay rights *vs.* Britain and Europe, 205–206
    obscenity laws, 166
    Republican Party, 191
Universal Declaration of Human Rights, 151, 232

The Village in the Jungle (Woolf, L.), 109–110, 112, 131

Virgil, 26, 83, 146, 176
Voting Rights Act of 1965, 169, 183

war on crime, drugs, 197–200
The Well of Loneliness (Hall), 101
Where Do We Fall When We Fall in Love (Young-Bruehl), 34
Whitman, Walt, 43, 97
Why Some Politicians are More Dangerous Than Others (Gilligan, J.), 198
Wilder, Oscar, 97–98, 140
Williams, Jenifer, 164
Williams, Tennessee, 141–142, 144, 166
Wolfenden Commission, 141, 155, 158–159
Wolfenden Report, 160–162, 182, 211, 234
women's sexuality, patriarchy, 20–21
Woolf, Leonard, 6, 106–107, 109–110, 112, 129, 130, 131, 208
Woolf, Virginia, 6, 93, 123–127, 149–150, 172

Young, Andrew, 167–168
Young-Bruehl, Elisabeth, 34, 39

Zedong, Mao, 42
Zimbabwe, 218–221

Printed in Great Britain
by Amazon